Jesus

THE PREMISE OF THE PROMISE

God's Answer for Perilous Times

STEPHEN QUAYLE

Cover design and interior formatting by:

King's Custom Covers

www.KingsCustomCovers.com

Published by End Times Thunder Publishers

PO Box 10998, Bozeman, MT 59719

Phone: 1-406-586-4840

Direct inquiries and/or orders to the above address or phone number.

Neither the author nor the publisher assumes any responsibility for the use or misuse of information contained in this book.

ISBN-13: 978-1-7324012-1-1

Third Edition: January 2021

10 9 8 7 6 5 4 3 2 1

To Pastor Chuck Farina,
Whose Passion And Fire For Jesus Kept My Own Fire Burning

Foreword

I was humbled and honored when Steve asked me to write the foreword for this book. Nearly two decades ago I discovered him on my shortwave in Whitefish, Montana. He was largely unknown back then and talked about things most people were unaware of or rarely heard. I fell hard for his wonderful sense of humor and those choice phrases and words that he made up in the spur of a moment. We now call them Quaylisms, but back then I just thought they were thought provoking and humorous. He was, and is, a self-effacing man of God complete with rants and passion about the things that God has shown him. From the time I first heard him, the Lord had me continually praying for him.

I moved back to California in 2000 and it would be several years before I heard him again because I'd left my shortwave radio in storage in Missoula. I missed listening to the godly man with an edge who somehow always brought Jesus and the salvation message into almost everything that he spoke about. Then one day in 2004 my husband Steven had been looking on the relatively new medium of the internet for some Bible programs and prepping material. Somehow, he stumbled onto Steve Quayle's website! I listened to his recordings almost that whole day and as I went over to shut the computer down, I felt the Spirit reiterate to me that I should pray and intercede for Steve.

From the time I was young, the Lord called me to be an intercessor. I began to see God do the miraculous through the ministry He had given my husband, Steven, and me. We saw supernatural healings and miracles. All the while, I pursued the gift of intercession as the Lord had instructed me. And it is in that powerful intercessory relationship that I felt impressed to continually lift up Stephen Quayle.

My husband and I moved back to Whitefish in early 2006. I still had 'no idea' that Steve lived nearby, but because we were again in the local area, each day we'd drop everything to listen to his daily program. Shortly after moving back, my husband saw on Steve's website that he only lived three hours away from us! Once again, the voice of the Lord came, offering me the blessing (and the heat) of being Steve's lifelong intercessor. I was to cover his life with my own. The Lord showed me the great need in Steve's life to have a personal intercessor and that the need was immediate! I saw that hell had been unleashed upon him. He'd had a supernatural call upon his life, he'd seen the Lord Jesus Christ who told him what He would do in the future. That calling took its toll. He was attacked by demons and through demons manifesting in professing Christians, and also by so-called friends.

When we finally met in person, I was amazed at his genuine kindness, his gentle spirit and his easy laugh and smile. His heart is one of the most gracious and compassionate hearts of anyone that I've ever met.

So many things in the Lord have bound us together over the years. I've seen him grow and become more open, willing to come out of his cave. Now he appears regularly on Youtube, at conferences, speaking and giving interviews on the radio and in person, as well as conducting his own interviews. He seems to be at peace and has come to terms with the Father's calling upon his life.

I know you'll love this book about what the Lord has shown this wonderful servant of the Most High God.

Romy Zarit
Intercessor, Servant and Friend

Acknowledgments

And we beseech you, brethren, to know them which labour among you... *1 Thess 5:12*

When the Lord appeared to me and gave me a Joseph's Ministry, I was a young, brand new, baby Christian with no church background and a lot of baggage. Knowing this, Jesus promised that He would send people to help me accomplish His calling on my life and the work that He gave me. From that day until this, He has been faithful to that promise. I've been blessed to have many powerful and wonderful people help me each step of the way. Although I'm sure to forget some of them, here are a few that come to mind.

I'm grateful to Hal Lindsey who told me that Jesus loved me and led me to the Lord. Pastor John Weaver was instrumental in my understanding of what happened to me in the presence of Jesus. He explained the baptism of the Holy Spirit and the gifts and also baptized me in water. Shortly after I got saved, Bill Warwood became my best friend and prayer partner. We met daily, prayed together, and listened and learned from prominent Godly teachers and preachers of the day. We would also later go on to teach together and personally witness God do the miraculous in the lives of the college students we taught. I'm also grateful for the obedience of two nameless brothers from a west coast Bible college who tracked me down at a Bozeman Christian book store. Although they never knew me, they saw me in a vision and the Lord told them to lay hands on me so that I could fulfill the call of God on my life. They traveled all that way in obedience and supernaturally completed their assignment. I don't know who they were or what became of them, but I am so grateful for their faithfulness.

Wayne Snyder was instrumental in starting a move of God on the MSU campus, which influenced my life greatly and eventually went worldwide. Pastor Chuck Farina was my pastor for 15 years and stood with me through thick and thin. The fire of God in his heart was contagious and still burns in my own heart today. Lorne Cunningham was the Founder of Youth With A Mission (YWAM) and taught me how humility and authority go hand in hand. Campbell McAlpine taught me about the price of preaching, the place of no reputation, and hammered me about not preaching or teaching anything from the Bible unless it "burned within my heart". Dr. Donald Boyd, a professor at MSU, opened my eyes to the prophetic scriptures in his weekly Bible study that I attended.

I've been so blessed through the years to have intercessory prayer warriors lifting me up to the Lord as I was about the Father's business. There's no way I could have lasted all of these years without their continual supernatural support. Clarice Wallin and her ladies' Bible study were faithful in praying for me and were very important in my early spiritual development. I'm so thankful for Harold Bradeson who was sent to me from God in one of the darkest periods in my life. His prayers and powerful prophecies over me stay with me to this day and changed my life. I'm also grateful for Demos Shakarian, the Founder of The Full Gospel Business Men's Fellowship, who, as an answer to prayer, met me some thirty years after I was saved.

He laid hands on me and prayed and prophesied many powerful things that I still hold in my heart even today. Mary Juarez was a powerful sister who has gone to be with the Lord. Unlike any woman I've ever met in the field of deliverance, she constantly prayed for me and was even in her prayer closet interceding for me to her last dying breath. I loved her dearly. And Romy Zarit, another powerful woman of God, who was called by the Lord to cover my life with hers in prayer for all these years. Her efforts have influenced and protected me more than I know.

I am blessed to have some wonderful men of God around me who have taught me, prayed for me, stood with me and helped me to overcome some impossible odds. Although I never met him in person, Pastor Bruce York and I would spend hours on the phone. Before he died, his last words to me were, "Steve, God told me to tell you to release His warring and ministering angels to the people of God." He blessed me tremendously and I learned so much from him. Henry Gruver has taught me that a walk with God in faith is a walk in the supernatural. His friendship and fellowship is a gift from the Lord. Pastor David Lankford isn't only my pastor, he's my best friend and teacher. His life and knowledge of God's Word are unequalled in the world today. Pastor John Kyle impacted my life greatly with the timeliest word that I have ever received. His anointing in my life was extraordinary. Dr. Paul Hagstrom has gone on to be with the Lord, but while still alive was shown by the Lord how the devil has tried to kill me from my childhood. God revealed to him my calling as a Watchman and my commission to expose the secrets of the origin of evil in the universe along with Fallen Angels and Giants.

Stephen Quayle

Table of Contents

Introduction

Hast thou not known? Hast thou not heard, that the everlasting God, the LORD, the Creator of the ends of the earth, fainteth not, neither is weary? There is no searching of His understanding. He giveth power to the faint; and to them that have no might He increaseth strength. Even the youths shall faint and be weary, and the young men shall utterly fall:

But they that wait upon the LORD shall renew their strength; they shall mount up with wings as eagles; they shall run, and not be weary; and they shall walk, and not faint.

Isaiah 40:28-31

We live in an era which many people, even Christians, are calling a "Post-Christianity World".

Postchristianity is the loss of the primacy of the Christian worldview in political affairs, especially in the Global North where Christianity had previously flourished, in favor of alternative worldviews such as secularism or nationalism. It includes personal world views, ideologies, religious movements or societies that are no longer rooted in the language and assumptions of Christianity, at least explicitly, although they had previously been in an environment of ubiquitous Christianity (i.e. Christendom).[1]

In other words, people are walking away from God. As disturbing as this trend is, it's important to remember that the Bible warned us this would happen in the last days.

*Now the Spirit speaketh expressly, that in the **latter times some shall depart from the faith**, giving heed to seducing spirits, and doctrines of devils; 1 Timothy 4:1*

*This know also, that in the last days perilous times shall come. For men shall be lovers of their own selves, covetous, boasters, proud, blasphemers, disobedient to parents, unthankful, unholy, without natural affection, trucebreakers, false accusers, incontinent, fierce, despisers of those that are good, traitors, heady, highminded, lovers of pleasures more than lovers of God. **Having a form of godliness, but denying the power thereof**: from such turn away. 2 Timothy 3:1-5*

Rather than writing a book lamenting over a change that the Lord warned about, this book is designed to help you fall in love again with the real God of the Bible. It's not written from a religious or theological perspective. It's written from my own real-world experience, complete with stumbles, struggles, challenges, victories and hardheaded wisdom that the Holy Spirit has taken me through in my forty-five-plus years of walking with God. It's a manual, of sorts, on how to develop a living, thriving, and real relationship with the Everlasting God.

Believers walk away from Church and their faith for a variety of clear-cut reasons. Today churches and their leaders are more concerned about a "seeker-friendly" appearance than the genuineness of someone's relationship with the Lord and the effectual application of the Word of God in the lives of their congregants. Pickpockets in the pulpits now minimize the truth of the Bible and relegate much of its content to simple

---

[1] "Postchristianity," Wikipedia, last modified May 25, 2018, https://en.wikipedia.org/wiki/Postchristianity.

parables, allegories and life-lessons. The result is that God's promised Holy Spirit power for victorious living over the enemy, a literal devil, eludes His people. This modern day Church's message has robbed Believers of God's power and His promised victory in their lives. Not all pastors are robber barons. I have a pastor and respect him very much. I also have people in my life who are wonderful examples of mature Christians whom I've learned from and shared with.

The vast majority of Christians today have lost their fear of the Lord, that reverential awe that has historically been taught to Believers since Jesus went to be with the Father. When the fear of the Lord is gone, along with the acknowledging of Jesus as a real, vivid, existing person, then our loving desire to be accountable to our Redeemer also goes.

This waning relationship, caused by a loss of reverence, has removed Jesus from His rightful preeminent position in the life of the majority of Christians. In these seeker-friendly, lovey-dovey, me, me, me churches a watered-down message of the gospel is being presented which sometimes morphs into the degradation, avoidance and even the denial of the name of the Lord Jesus Christ.

Without Jesus being in His rightful preeminent place in the Believer's life, they are unable to see the devil's camouflage for what it is. Through the enemy's subtle (and not so subtle) attacks, the power of sin reigns in these badge-wearing-only Christians' lives, so much so that it gets difficult to tell any difference between the Church and the world.

Jesus presented a far different message to the early Church (and to us)! In Luke 4:18-19 the Lord went into the synagogue at Nazareth at the beginning of His earthly ministry and read out of Book of Isaiah. From that scheduled Torah portion, He told the people:

> *The Spirit of the Lord is upon me, because He hath anointed me to preach the gospel to the poor; He hath sent me to heal the brokenhearted, to preach deliverance to the captives, and recovering of sight to the blind, to set at liberty them that are bruised, to preach the acceptable year of the Lord.*

When we read this in our modern era, with our western mindset, from the New Testament (NT), most people don't understand that the Lord was reading from an 800-year-old book at the time! The next two verses out of Luke 4:20-21 gives a fascinating account of what happened next:

> *And He closed the book, and He gave it again to the minister, and sat down. And the eyes of all them that were in the synagogue were fastened on him. And He began to say unto them, "This day is this scripture fulfilled in your ears."*

The people around Him were stunned. "Isn't this Joseph's son?" they asked.

What they couldn't see, or understand at that time, was that in the original verse of Isaiah, Almighty God was making a promise to His people. And while it took 800 years to fulfill...

Jesus was, and is, that promise! Or say: What they could neither see, nor understand....

Jesus, The Premise of the Promise is more than just a catchy title - **It is TRUTH!**

Within Him, everything that a Believer needs to have a powerful, sustained and effectual walk has been provided.

According as his divine power hath given unto us all things that pertain unto life and godliness, through the knowledge of him that hath called us to glory and virtue, whereby are given unto us exceeding great and precious promises: that by these ye might be partakers of the divine nature, having escaped the corruption that is in the world through lust. **2 Peter 1:3-4**

Ask yourself, "Why is it that statistically the Church falls into the same kind of sin, in almost the same degree of sin, as the world?" How can this happen when we're supposed to have the "power that raised Christ from the dead" living inside of us (Romans 8:11)?

While I'll address some of those challenges within these pages, the blatant, specific reason why Christians are struggling with life's issues is two-fold:

1. Christians no longer see Jesus as a real, living and viable figure in their lives, and thus ignore the truth of His Word; *and*

2. Because they don't fully believe and trust in His Word, they fail to ask Him for biblically-based help in their time of need.

Psalm 51:17 tells us,

The sacrifices of God are a broken spirit: a broken and a contrite heart, O God, thou wilt not despise.

James 5:16 says,

…Confess your faults one to another, and pray one for another, that ye may be healed. The effectual fervent prayer of a righteous man availeth much.

The most powerful prayer that God will listen to is from someone who has a contrite heart. That doesn't mean that you have to be a "perfect" Christian to have a real, powerful and full relationship with the Lord. There's no such thing as the perfect Christian, only redeemed ones. Romans 3:22-23 addresses this:

Even the righteousness of God which is by faith of Jesus Christ unto all and upon all them that believe: for there is no difference. For all have sinned, and come short of the glory of God.

A person who has a contrite heart is someone who acknowledges Jesus' lordship over their life and seeks to walk in His ways. Crying out, "Help me Lord!" within that relationship can have powerful results in the life of a Believer, and calling upon Jesus is the key.

For thus saith the high and lofty One that inhabiteth eternity, whose name is Holy; I dwell in the high and holy place, with him also that is of a contrite and humble spirit, to revive the spirit of the humble, and to revive the heart of the contrite ones. Isaiah 57:15

When most people get into a situation that's too big for them, they'll call someone for help. They hope that someone greater than their situation will have the answer and resources to fix their problem.

The acronym H.E.L.P. perfectly describes God's promises to His children: His Everlasting Preeminence, Power, Presence, Protection, Provision, Patience, Purity, Proclamation, Peace and Promise. That's why this book is divided into ten parts, or ten H.E.L.P.s. It's designed to take the Christian through these ten promises, regardless of the season in which you may find yourself.

This book is written for people who are looking for a life-changing relationship with the Lord Jesus Christ, who may have never had a relationship with Him before, or may have never heard Him presented in a historically or biblically accurate way. Those folks will learn that when they invest in a life-changing relationship with Him, He can and will do miracles in their lives. Jesus stands alone, separate and beyond anyone who has ever lived, or will ever come into existence.

In a mind-blowing scene in heaven in Revelation 22:13, Jesus said of Himself:

I Am Alpha and Omega, the beginning and the end, the first and the last.

Do you hunger or thirst to know the real Jesus? Do you have questions like: "Who am I?" "Where am I?" "Where did it all come from?" and "Where's it all going?"

Maybe you've never known the Lord, don't have a clue of Who the real Jesus is or maybe you did follow Him at one time and through life's circumstances have let your light burn out.

This book isn't about church games or church politics. It doesn't matter what you are going through, it doesn't matter what we will face in the very near future, and it doesn't matter who in the Church has hurt or wronged you. Jesus, the real Jesus, is your promise.

If life's circumstances have broken your heart or if you're disillusioned about God, then I encourage you to read these pages carefully. Maybe you've tried the mainstream Church and have been wounded or abused. Perhaps because of this, you've blamed God for the actions of people.

People are people, regardless of whether they wear a collar or stand in a pulpit and have a title. All of us are remolded creations who came up out of a nature of sin. If you put people up on a pedestal, you're sure to be disappointed. Jesus is the only One Who has the unsoiled credentials to change and empower your life.

Psalm 46 says this:

God is our refuge and strength, a very present help in trouble.

Therefore we will not fear, though the earth be removed, and though the mountains be carried into the midst of the sea, though the waters thereof roar and be troubled, though the mountains shake with the swelling thereof. There is a river, the streams whereof shall make glad the city of God, the holy place of the tabernacles of the most High. God is in the midst of her; she shall not be moved: God shall help her, and that right early. The heathen raged, the kingdoms were moved: he uttered his voice, the earth melted. The LORD of hosts is with us; the God of Jacob is our refuge. Come, behold the works of the LORD, what desolations He hath made in the earth. He maketh wars to cease unto the end of the earth; He breaketh the bow, and cutteth the spear in sunder; He burneth the chariot in the fire. Be still, and know that I am God: I will be exalted among the heathen, I will be exalted in the earth. The LORD of Hosts is with us; the God of Jacob is our refuge. Selah.

Why isn't this book for the religious-minded or those people who consider themselves theologically astute?

First, religiousness is part of the problem. Religious people will go through the motions without heart action or an interactive pursuit of Jesus.

Second, theology is the study of a system of belief, a study of what people think. Theology is not specifically studying the Word of God to find out Who Jesus is and how to have a living, thriving, personal relationship with Jesus - the person.

In a warning to the Laodicean church in Revelation 3:15-22, Jesus Himself says this:

> *I know thy works, that thou art neither cold nor hot: I would thou wert cold or hot. So then because thou art lukewarm, and neither cold nor hot, I will spue thee out of my mouth. Because thou sayest, I am rich, and increased with goods, and have need of nothing; and knowest not that thou art wretched, and miserable, and poor, and blind, and naked: I counsel thee to buy of me gold tried in the fire, that thou mayest be rich; and white raiment, that thou mayest be clothed, and that the shame of thy nakedness do not appear; and anoint thine eyes with eyesalve, that thou mayest see. As many as I love, I rebuke and chasten: be zealous therefore, and repent. Behold, I stand at the door, and knock: if any man hear my voice, and open the door, I will come in to him, and will sup with him, and he with me. To him that overcometh will I grant to sit with me in my throne, even as I also overcame, and am set down with my Father in his throne. He that hath an ear, let him hear what the Spirit saith unto the churches.*

Most modern translations say, "I will vomit you out of my mouth"!

These flash-frozen-vomit Christians are lukewarm but think they have everything they need. They're also an exact representation of the majority of the Church today because these are the people who've gotten caught up with the programs of men, but have forgotten the person of the Savior.

While that may seem harsh, it's absolute truth. There's no more time to play religion. Superficial, in-name-only people, who call themselves Christians but do not make Jesus the absolute Lord of their lives, are in for a startling wake-up call.

We are coming into perhaps the most supernaturally revealing time, both of good and of evil, in history. The devil knows that his time is short. He's doing everything he can to thwart, discourage and even turn away Believers from the Lord. He has tried, and partially succeeded, in obscuring the person of Jesus Christ to those people who would follow Him.

Every unclean spirit is being poured forth in these days. What was once held back is being held back no longer. For such a time as this, God has provided His Holy Spirit and His gifts to help us in this cataclysmic battle. It is imperative that we walk in the truth that Jesus truly is the Lamb of God Who takes away the sin of the world. He is the King of Kings and the Lord of Lords.

At the end of time Satan and his fallen angels will be cast into the Lake of Fire, but Jesus has already visited Hell to take back the keys of Hell, death and the grave. He sits at the right hand of the Father to declare God's victory in the world of His creation and in your life.

As a testament to exactly Who He is, Psalm 40:6-9 says:

> *Sacrifice and offering thou didst not desire; mine ears hast thou opened: burnt offering and sin offering hast thou not required. Then said I, Lo, **I come: in the volume of the book it is written of me,** I delight to do thy will, O my God: yea, thy law is within my heart.*

His help is ever-present and preordained for your life even before you were born.

For you and for me, Jesus is *The Premise of the Promise.*

HELP 1

His Everlasting Preeminence

{God} Who hath delivered us from the power of darkness, and hath translated us into the kingdom of His dear Son in whom we have redemption through His blood, even the forgiveness of sins, Who is the image of the invisible God, the firstborn of every creature. For by Him were all things created, that are in heaven, and that are in earth, visible and invisible, whether they be thrones, or dominions, or principalities, or powers: all things were created by Him, and for Him. And He is before all things, and by Him all things consist. And He is the head of the body, the church: who is the beginning, the firstborn from the dead, that in all things He might have the preeminence.

Colossians 1:13-18

Preeminence

The resurrection of Jesus Christ is the manifestation of God's ability to produce victory in your life. He's able to achieve every good thing that He has provided for you in His Word and His resurrection is a declaration of Jesus' Preeminence.

The reality is that whether we acknowledge Jesus as Lord and Savior or not, He is still preeminent.

> *That at the name of Jesus every knee should bow, of things in heaven, and things in earth, and things under the earth. And that every tongue should confess that Jesus Christ is Lord, to the glory of God the Father.* **Philippians 2:10-11**

Our acknowledgement of His Preeminence in our life is required to enable us to walk in His ways and experience His promises.

It's not enough to say "I know Jesus. I know Who He is."

The devil knows Who He is too but he has no covenant with Jesus.

> *"Thou believest that there is one God; thou doest well: the devils also believe, and tremble."* **James 2:19**

As an aside, when I was meditating on this very verse one day, the Lord asked me, *"Steve, of these people that say they 'know me' how many of them do I know?"* And then He reminded me of **Matthew 7:21-23**:

> *Not every one that saith unto me, Lord, Lord, shall enter into the kingdom of heaven; but he that doeth the will of my Father which is in heaven. Many will say to me in that day, Lord, Lord, have we not prophesied in Thy name? And in Thy name have cast out devils? And in Thy name done many wonderful works? And then will I profess unto them, I never knew you: depart from me, ye that work iniquity.*

Relationship with God is a two-way street. In that relationship, we not only acknowledge His existence but also obey His Word, or at least try to. By doing so, we give Him the rightful preeminent position in our lives as King. It is also this embracing of His preeminent position and the yielding of our lives to Him that unlocks His promises.

Contrarily, today the Church is turning on the very Lord Who bought them with His blood. They neglect to acknowledge Him verbally and fail also to embrace His Preeminence in their lives, in the world, in all of creation and even over the enemy.

Make no mistake - **He is The Great I AM.**

Premise = Evidence
Preeminence = Supremency

Chapter 1

I Am

And Moses said unto God, "Behold, when I come unto the children of Israel, and shall say unto them, 'The God of your fathers hath sent me unto you;' and they shall say to me, 'What is His name?' What shall I say unto them?" And God said unto Moses, "I AM THAT I AM," and He said, "Thus shalt thou say unto the children of Israel, 'I AM hath sent me unto you.'" And God said moreover unto Moses, "Thus shalt thou say unto the children of Israel, The LORD God of your fathers, the God of Abraham, the God of Isaac, and the God of Jacob, hath sent me unto you: this is my name forever, and this is my memorial unto all generations."

Exodus 3:13-15

I AM loosely translates as "The One who is." So when God says, "…this is My name forever, and this is My memorial unto all generations," He's making a serious point.

Have you ever wondered if God really existed? Before I met Jesus, I certainly did. Understanding our human nature and our need to question those things around us and even His existence, God uses His Word to cut to the chase by calling Himself, "I AM".

It's like He's saying, "I know you're wondering about Me. Yes, I'm here. I really do exist."

For I know their works and their thoughts. It shall come, that I will gather all nations and tongues; and they shall come, and see my glory. **Isaiah 66:18**

You'll also see that you can't trust the Promisor of these H.E.L.P.s until you're convinced the Promisor is

JESUS - The Premise of the Promise

able to deliver. His very being defines Who this Promisor is, as in the Creator. He lives outside of time and space, yet He interacts with us on our earthly timeline. By His very words, everything that you can fathom, even your own life, was created when He simply spoke the universe into existence.

As mind-boggling as this concept is, understanding His Preeminence is relatively simple when you listen to Who He says He is.

> *Remember the former things of old: for I am God, and there is none else; I am God, and there is none like me, declaring the end from the beginning, and from ancient times the things that are not yet done, saying, My counsel shall stand, and I will do all my pleasure.* **Isaiah 46:9-10**

The Old Testament (OT) was originally written in Hebrew and then translated into Greek about 250 years before Jesus came to earth. This translation is called the Septuagint and with it we can compare the language of the OT to the language of the NT, which was mostly written in Greek. God's name of "I AM" is translated as *ego eimi* in the Septuagint.

Old Testament Uses of I Am (Ego Eimi)

The Almighty God referred to Himself as I AM (Ego Eimi) many more times than just at the burning bush. Here are a few examples:

- **Exodus 3:6** - Moreover he said, I Am (Ego Eimi) the God of thy father, the God of Abraham, the God of Isaac, and the God of Jacob. And Moses hid his face; for he was afraid to look upon God.

- **Deut 32:39** - See now that I, even I Am (Ego Eimi) he, and there is no god with me: I kill, and I make alive; I wound, and I heal: neither is there any that can deliver out of my hand. {"he" is italicized in the King James Version (KJV) indicating it was added by the translators and does not appear in the original text.}

- **Isaiah 41:4** - Who hath wrought and done it, calling the generations from the beginning? I the LORD, the first, and with the last; I Am (Ego Eimi) he. {Again "he" was added.}

- **Isaiah 43:10** - Ye are my witnesses, saith the LORD, and my servant whom I have chosen: that ye may know and believe me, and understand that I Am (Ego Eimi) he: before me there was no God formed, neither shall there be after me. {"he" was added.}

- **Isaiah 43:25** - I, even I Am (Ego Eimi) he that blotteth out thy transgressions for mine own sake, and will not remember thy sins. {"he" was added}

There are several more examples, but you get the gist of what is being illustrated here.

Jesus' Connection To The Father

Then answered the Jews, and said unto him, "Say we not well that thou art a Samaritan, and hast a devil?" Jesus answered, "I have not a devil; but I honour my Father, and ye do dishonour me. And I seek not mine own glory: there is one that seeketh and judgeth. Verily, verily, I say unto you, if a man keep my saying, he shall never see death." Then said the Jews unto him, "Now we know that thou hast a devil. Abraham is dead, and the prophets; and thou sayest, If a man keep my saying, he shall never taste of death. Art thou greater than our father Abraham, which is dead? And the prophets are dead. Whom makest thou thyself?" Jesus answered, "If I honour myself, my honour is nothing. It is my Father that honoureth me; of whom ye say, that he is your God. Yet ye have not known Him; but I know Him and if I should say, I know Him not, I shall be a liar like unto you. But I know Him, and keep His saying. Your father Abraham rejoiced to see my day: and he saw it, and was glad." Then said the Jews unto him, "Thou art not yet fifty years old, and hast thou seen Abraham?" Jesus said unto them, "Verily, verily, I say unto you, before Abraham was, I Am" **(Ego Eimi)**. *John 8:48-58*

I always say that the Bible tells us everything we need to know, but it doesn't tell us everything. How could it? How would God explain the vastness of Himself to His creation? How could He talk to people 4500 years ago like Abraham and Lot and still have His words, instructions and descriptions be understood by people in the 21st century? When you think about His existence outside of time and space, because He created it and doesn't live in our 3D reality, words fail to even begin to scratch the surface of Who He is. Still, somehow He's able to break down our language and communicate the basics of Himself to us.

As an example, I am father and a grandfather. I have children and grandchildren. I understand the concept of a father and a son. People throughout millennia also understood this most basic concept. God, in His infinite wisdom, chose to use this simile to explain part of Himself to His creation.

For God so loved the world, that he gave His only begotten Son, that whosoever believeth in Him should not perish, but have everlasting life. **John 3:16**

He sent His Son to be tortured on a Cross and die a gruesome death for me because somebody had to pay the price for my sin. I fully understand the idea that He cherished His Son, Jesus, above all others but it's hard to comprehend how He could send His only Son to die for a vast majority of people who couldn't give a rip about Him.

I understand the concept intellectually, but emotionally the idea of losing my son to a bunch of ingrates is an extremely hard thing to grasp. While my understanding falls short, the point is that I relate to the concept of Jesus being cherished by the Almighty - and so do you.

Although God used this illustration for us so we can understand, Jesus isn't a son in the traditional, human sense.

The Bible tells us that Jesus was born of a virgin. Obviously this means that Mary and Joseph did not have physical relations, and contrary to some sick hedonistic teachings, she especially didn't have physical relations with God.

So where and how did this Son, Jesus, come about?

The Trinity is used to describe the relationship between the Father and Jesus.

When Jesus came into the coasts of Caesarea Philippi, he asked his disciples, saying, "Whom do men say that I the Son of man am?" And they said, "Some say that thou art John the Baptist: some, Elias; and others, Jeremias, or one of the prophets." He saith unto them, "But whom say ye that I am?" And

*Simon Peter answered and said, "Thou art the Christ, the Son of the living God." And Jesus answered and said unto him, "Blessed art thou, Simon Barjona: for flesh and blood hath not revealed it unto thee, but my Father which is in heaven." **Matthew 16:13-18***

You may be familiar with the phrase "three-in-one". Think about an egg and how its shell is one part, its yoke is another and the white of an egg is another part. These are three separate parts that make up one egg. This is very much how the Bible describes God the Father, God His Son and God the Holy Spirit as being One.

The word "One" comes from the Hebrew word *echad*, which is plural and a concept that challenges our natural logic. How can something that is "one" be plural or more than one?

Hear, O Israel: The LORD our God is one LORD. **Deut 6:4**

Unto thee it was shewed, that thou mightest know that the LORD he is God; there is none else beside him. **Deut 4:35**

Wherefore thou art great, O LORD God: for there is none like thee, neither is there any God beside thee, according to all that we have heard with our ears. **2 Sam 7:22**

*And Jesus answered him, "The first of all the commandments is, Hear, O Israel; The Lord our God is one Lord." **Mark 12:29***

And this is life eternal, that they might know thee the only true God, and Jesus Christ, whom thou hast sent. **John 17:3**

Jesus was birthed out of the Almighty's heart and placed into Mary's womb.

Let that sink in for a moment.

God's action can be compared to trying to pour all the world's oceans into a single thimble, in this case, the container of a human body. There's no way that the vastness of that water supply could be contained in that tiny space. With our mortal minds, we find it impossible that all of God's vastness could be held in a human container. Yet - God did it!

In the process of being born in an earthly vessel, God found a way to walk amongst His creation in the physical 3D form of Jesus. Jesus is 100% God and 100% man at the same time, just like the water in that thimble is still the same water that filled the oceans. Another example would be how your hand is still part of your body, but is distinctly your hand. This is how the Father, the Son and the Holy Spirit could all exist at the same time, three in One.

And it came to pass about an eight days after these sayings, he took Peter and John and James, and went up into a mountain to pray. And as he prayed, the fashion of his countenance was altered, and his raiment was white and glistering. And, behold, there talked with him two men, which were Moses and Elias who appeared in glory, and spake of his decease which he should accomplish at Jerusalem. But Peter and they that were with him were heavy with sleep: and when they were awake, they saw his glory, and the two men that stood with him. And it came to pass, as they departed from him, Peter said unto Jesus, "Master, it is good for us to be here: and let us make three tabernacles; one for thee, and one for Moses, and one for Elias," not knowing what he said. While he thus spake, there came a cloud, and overshadowed them: and they feared as they entered into the cloud. And there came a voice out of the cloud, saying, "This is my beloved Son: hear him." And when the voice was past, Jesus was found alone. And they kept it close, and told no man in those days any of those things which they had seen. **Luke 9:28-36**

From the Father Himself we hear this mind-blowing admonishment to listen to Jesus, thus proving His authoritative, preeminent position. Jesus wasn't just some helper or sidekick that God sent to earth to die for you and me. God sent His Son, part of Himself.

Jesus is I AM.

Where Did Jesus Come From?

I can of mine own self do nothing: as I hear, I judge: and my judgment is just; because I seek not mine own will, but the will of the Father which hath sent me. **John 5:30**

Jesus was sent by the Father to bridge the gap between His creation and Himself. In doing so, God revealed more of Himself to that creation than ever before.

And the Father Himself, which hath sent me, hath borne witness of me. Ye have neither heard His voice at any time, nor seen His shape. **John 5:37**

Jesus saith unto him, have I been so long time with you, and yet hast thou not known me, Philip? He that hath seen me hath seen the Father; and how sayest thou then, shew us the Father? **John 14:9**

This is a stunning statement!

So does God the Father look like a physical Jesus?

The easy answer is: not exactly. Jesus, while on the earth, represented the heart of the Father. He was a mirror image of how God the Creator would act and operate. Understandably, a being that lives outside of our 3D reality would not look like us. He would be… different. But we don't have to understand that difference in order to walk in His Ways. Certainly the Father could explain that difference to us, but it's enough for Him to say that if you've seen Jesus, you've seen Me.

Deeper Into The Authority of Jesus

I am the LORD, and there is none else, there is no God beside me: I girded thee, though thou hast not known me. That they may know from the rising of the sun, and from the west, that there is none beside me. I am the LORD, and there is none else. I form the light, and create darkness: I make peace, and create evil: I the LORD do all these things. **Isaiah 45:5-8**

Far be it from me to say that I understand everything about the Father, Son and Holy Spirit and their relation to one another. If someone says that they do understand the relationship, you'd do well to run the other way.

We do, however, have the Bible to give us clues as to their relationship to one another. Those clues also help us to understand Jesus' relationship to us as individuals and the world. So for the moment, let's try to forget what other people have told us about God, either from the pulpit, from books, or from conversations, and let's look at scripture only.

> *In the beginning God created the heaven and the earth.* **Genesis 1:1**

While most people skim over this verse thinking they understand what it means, there's much more to it than just talking about creation. That's because by creating everything, and I mean everything, God sets Himself apart as the preeminent authority in all things. Originally written in Hebrew, our English translation loses some of the impact of this little ten-word verse. Specifically, the English word for "God" does not give you the full weight of what is being communicated here. In the original language, the word for God in Genesis 1:1 is *elohim,* which is plural for *eloah,* which means God. When we think about words from our English point of view, we add things to the end of words to make them plural. So you might want to add an "s" on the back of God to make it gods. To do so would be absolutely wrong.

We know this because God repeatedly says in the Bible that He is the only God.

> *Unto thee it was shewed, that thou mightest know that the LORD he is God;* ***there is none else beside him.*** *Deut 4:35*

Instead, when you look at the word *elohim,* remember that just like you and I have many facets, so does God. We are husbands or wives, but we are also brothers and sisters, dads and moms. We also have different attributes that make up our being. In my case I have graying, brown hair, but I also have hazel eyes, etc. They are, along with the rest of me, plural parts that form me.

Although it's an extremely elementary example to describe Someone as vast as God, we do get that same idea with the Holy Spirit when we look at the word "spirit" in the original Hebrew. Remember, He too is part of God, *elohim.* In the original language the word for Holy Spirit is *ruach hakodesh* and literally means the 'Breath of God'. His "breath" is a living, active part of Him and it reminds me of Jesus' appearance to the disciples after His resurrection.

> *Then the same day at evening, being the first day of the week, when the doors were shut where the disciples were assembled for fear of the Jews, came Jesus and stood in the midst, and saith unto them, "Peace be unto you." And when he had so said, he shewed unto them his hands and his side. Then were the disciples glad, when they saw the Lord. Then said Jesus to them again, "Peace be unto you. As my Father hath sent me, even so send I you." And when he had said this,* ***he breathed on them,*** *and saith unto them, "Receive ye the Holy Ghost."* **John 20:19-22**

That breath, the Holy Spirit, was what breathed life into Adam at creation.

> *Then the LORD God formed man of dust from the ground, and breathed into his nostrils the breath of life; and man became a living being.* **Genesis 2:7**

To understand how Jesus is part of God, *elohim,* you can also look at this foundational scripture from Colossians. Pay close attention to my bolded sections.

*Giving thanks unto the Father, which hath made us meet to be partakers of the inheritance of the saints in light, who hath delivered us from the power of darkness, and hath translated us into the kingdom of his dear Son, in whom we have redemption through His blood, even the forgiveness of sins, **who is the image of the invisible God, the firstborn of every creature. For by him were all things created** that are in heaven, and that are in earth, visible and invisible, whether they be thrones, or dominions, or principalities, or powers. **All things were created by Him, and for Him. And H**e **is before all things**, and **by Him all things consist**. And He is the head of the body, the church: who is the beginning, the firstborn from the dead; that **in all things He might have the preeminence**. For it pleased the Father that in Him should all fulness dwell; And, having made peace through the blood of His cross, by Him to reconcile all things unto Himself; by Him, I say, whether they be things in earth, or things in heaven. Colossians 1:12-20*

In other words, everything that exists - consists by Jesus! He was the "firstborn" of all creation. So does that mean that He too is a created being? And if He Himself were created, how could He have Preeminence?

Firstborn in a human sense isn't what God is talking about here. He was, is and always has been one with God. No one knows when God started to refer to Himself in a plural sense, but we do know that Jesus was always, always, always there with God the Father as Hebrews 13:8 points out:

*Jesus Christ the same yesterday, and today, and **forever**.*

Jesus is eternal. He was there in the beginning, part of the Father and He created all things according to Colossians. He also holds all things together. This is interesting because Job tells us the same thing about God.

*Then the LORD answered Job out of the whirlwind, and said, "Who is this that darkeneth counsel by words without knowledge? Gird up now thy loins like a man; for I will demand of thee, and answer thou me. Where wast thou **when I laid the foundations of the earth**? Declare, if thou hast understanding. Who hath laid the measures thereof, if thou knowest? Or who hath stretched the line upon it? Whereupon are the foundations thereof fastened? Or who laid the corner stone thereof when the morning stars sang together, and all the sons of God shouted for joy?" Job 38:1-7*

Further evidence of the oneness of God, and Jesus' rightful position to the title of I AM, can be found at the very beginning of the Gospel of John.

In the beginning was the Word, and the Word was with God, and the Word was God. The same was in the beginning with God. All things were made by Him; and without Him was not any thing made that was made. In Him was life; and the life was the light of men. And the light shineth in darkness; and the darkness comprehended it not. John 1:1-5

Jesus cannot be separated from the Father anymore that you could separate hydrogen from oxygen and still have water. He's part of God and therefore has God's preeminent authority. Malachi 3:6 clearly states that God is self-existent and does not change. Therefore, Jesus didn't come about later on a linear timeline. He's always been there.

Two thousand years later we still have trouble comprehending that it was God Who came to earth to be born as a man! Somehow Almighty God put Himself in the form of the person of Jesus and sent Him to earth to die for you and me. At the same time, He still remained the Father.

W.O.W. - That's the "Wonder of His Word!"

Jesus' 7 Great I AM Statements in The Gospel of John

If we look at the person of Jesus as part of the Almighty, the things that He said in the Bible about Himself take on a clearer meaning. When He told Phillip, "If you've seen me, you've seen the Father" what is it that He was really trying to communicate?

He would often paint word pictures of Himself to tell His people what He is like. There are seven wonderful I AM (Ego Eimi) statements in John that help us to understand who He is. All of these NT verses have their roots in the OT.

1. **Bread of Life** - *And Jesus said unto them, I Am the bread of life: he that cometh to me shall never hunger; and he that believeth on me shall never thirst.* **John 6:35**

In the verses leading up to referencing Himself as the Bread of Life, Jesus fed 5,000 people from 5 loaves and 2 fishes and used the example of manna to teach the people about WHO He was. The story of Moses and manna in the wilderness was something of which every Israelite was acutely aware.

> *"Our fathers did eat manna in the desert; as it is written, He gave them bread from heaven to eat." Then Jesus said unto them, "Verily, verily, I say unto you, Moses gave you not that bread from heaven; but my Father giveth you the true bread from heaven. For the bread of God is He which cometh down from heaven, and giveth life unto the world."* **John 6:31-33**

The Jews understood God to be the giver of life and thus, whether they knew it at the time or not, began to learn that the Great I AM had come down from heaven to walk in their midst.

2. **Light of the World** - *Then spake Jesus again unto them, saying, I Am the light of the world: he that followeth me shall not walk in darkness, but shall have the light of life.* **John 8:12**

This is a direct reference to David's famous Psalm 27:1. The Israelites knew that the I AM was their light.

The LORD is my light and my salvation; whom shall I fear? The LORD is the strength of my life; of whom shall I be afraid?

3. **The Door** - *Then said Jesus unto them again, "Verily, verily, I say unto you, I Am the door of the sheep."* **John 10:7**

The idea of Jesus being the door is an important one that the people of His day could relate to. It would take their minds back to the Passover where they had to put lamb's blood on their door posts so that the Death Angel would "passover" them and not harm them, Exodus 12:22.

During this time Israel was under Roman rule. The people longed for the Israelite kingdom to be restored. The Lord's reference to Himself as a door was sure to remind them about God's promise to them:

> *And I will clothe Him with thy robe, and strengthen Him with thy girdle, and I will commit thy government into His hand: and He shall be a father to the inhabitants of Jerusalem, and to the house of Judah. And the key of the house of David will I lay upon His shoulder; so He shall open, and none shall shut; and He shall shut, and none shall open.* **Isaiah 22:21-22**

4. **The Good Shepherd** - *I Am the good shepherd: the good shepherd giveth his life for the sheep.* **John 10:11**

Of course the people of that day could relate to I AM as being their shepherd. King David's wonderful Psalm 23 comes to mind:

> *The LORD is my shepherd, I shall not want. He maketh me to lie down in green pastures: He leadeth me beside the still waters. He restoreth my soul: He leadeth me in the paths of righteousness for His name's sake. Yea, though I walk through the valley of the shadow of death, I will fear no evil: for thou art with me; thy rod and thy staff they comfort me. Thou preparest a table before me in the presence of mine enemies: thou anointest my head with oil; my cup runneth over. Surely goodness and mercy shall follow me all the days of my life: and I will dwell in the house of the LORD forever.*

5. **The Resurrection and the Life** - *Jesus said unto her, I Am the resurrection, and the life: he that believeth in me, though he were dead, yet shall he live.* **John 11:25**

Resurrection from the dead was something that ancient Israel believed in and expected. Jesus saying that He was the resurrection and the life would have taken their minds right back to I AM Who was able to restore life as indicated in Isaiah 26:19:

Thy dead men shall live, together with my dead body shall they arise. Awake and sing, ye that dwell in dust: for thy dew is as the dew of herbs, and the earth shall cast out the dead.

6. **The Way, the Truth and the Life** - *Jesus saith unto him, I Am the way, the truth, and the life: no man cometh unto the Father, but by me.* **John 14:6**

This diverse title of the Lord encompasses several key thoughts from the OT showing that Jesus is part of the Great I AM.

The Way - *And thine ears shall hear a word behind thee, saying, This is the way, walk ye in it, when ye turn to the right hand, and when ye turn to the left.* **Isaiah 30:21**

The Truth - *Teach me thy way, O LORD; I will walk in thy truth: unite my heart to fear thy name.* **Psalm 86:11**

The Life - *As for me, I know that my Redeemer lives, and at the last He will take His stand on the earth. Even after my skin is destroyed, yet from my flesh I shall see God; whom I myself shall behold, and whom my eyes will see and not another. My heart faints within me!* **Job 19:25-27**

7. **The Vine** - *I Am the true vine, and my Father is the husbandman.* **John 15:1**

This particular reference to the Lord is a little different. The nation of Israel was referred to as a vine, which yielded wild grapes as a symbol of their rebellion.

> *And he fenced it, and gathered out the stones thereof, and planted it with the choicest vine, and built a tower in the midst of it, and also made a winepress therein: and he looked that it should bring forth grapes, and it brought forth wild grapes.* **Isaiah 5:2**

Because of their rebellion, Israel was judged and sent into captivity. In contrast, Jesus declares Himself to be the "True Vine" indicating that the Great I AM came down Himself to make things right.

All of these I AM statements in John are the Lord's effort to bring us back to the Rock of Ages, God Almighty, The Creator of All Things... **The Great I AM.**

Further Evidence of Jesus' Preeminence

One of the best examples of Who Jesus was, and is, comes at a very low point in His earthly ministry.

The night before His crucifixion we read in scripture that Jesus was in the Garden of Gethsemane praying to His Father. His prayer was so intense that He sweat great drops of blood. By the end of that travailing, He had His answer - He had to go to the Cross.

Jesus was resigned to His fate and unafraid when they came for Him. The Romans and Pharisees had no idea Whom they were messing with, a.k.a. the Creator of the Universe.

> *Judas then, having received a band of men and officers from the chief priests and Pharisees, cometh thither with lanterns and torches and weapons.*
>
> *Jesus therefore, knowing all things that should come upon Him, went forth, and said unto them, "Whom seek ye?"*
>
> *They answered Him, "Jesus of Nazareth."*
>
> *Jesus saith unto them, "I Am (**Ego Eimi**) he." {"he" added.}*
>
> *And Judas also, which betrayed him, stood with them.*
>
> *As soon then as He had said unto them, "I Am (**Ego Eimi**) he, they went backward, and fell to the ground.*
>
> *Then asked He them again, "Whom seek ye?"*
>
> *And they said, "Jesus of Nazareth."*
>
> *Jesus answered, "I have told you that I Am (**Ego Eimi**) he. If therefore ye seek me, let these go their way."*
>
> *That the saying might be fulfilled, which He spake, "Of them which thou gavest me have I lost none."*

Let's unpack the language here so we can understand exactly what happened. The phrase "went backward" is from the Greek word *aperchomai*. The literal translation gives an image of the soldiers and temple police staggering and stumbling backward, like they were punched by some unseen force, which knocked them off their feet!

The word "fell" from the Greek word *pipto* which means to fall, but not someone falling in the normal sense. This word is used to depict someone who fell so hard that he looks like he's dead!

The Bible says that Jesus will slay nations with the two-edged sword that comes out of His mouth (Rev 1:16). In this instance, the Lord simply saying that He was I AM literally slammed these heavily armed men off their feet and for a moment they looked like corpses! If the situation weren't so serious, it would be almost comical. As they're sprawled out on the ground, groaning and wondering what hit them, Jesus asks them again whom they're looking for. I'm guessing that they were still trying to regain their faculties, lying there trying to catch their breath. They must have answered the Lord by groaning out the response of "Jeeesuss of Nazarreth…" To which Jesus again replies, "I AM."

Since the scripture doesn't go into detail, I can only assume that His words had the same effect on them as before. So they had to be hammered again as they already were lying there dazed and confused! Ironically, the Lord had to wait for them to recover from His supernatural one-two punch before they could take Him into custody to eventually hang Him on a Cross! Amazing!

That's the preeminent power of I AM.

Ego Eimi in Revelation

There are also seven great I AM statements in the Book of Revelation. All of them use the same word - Ego Eimi.

- **Rev 1:8** - *I Am Alpha and Omega, the beginning and the ending, saith the Lord, which is, and which was, and which is to come, the Almighty.*

- **Rev 1:11** - *Saying, "I Am Alpha and Omega, the first and the last." And, "What thou seest, write in a book, and send it unto the seven churches which are in Asia; unto Ephesus, and unto Smyrna, and unto Pergamos, and unto Thyatira, and unto Sardis, and unto Philadelphia, and unto Laodicea.*

- **Rev 1:17** - *And when I saw Him, I fell at His feet as dead. And He laid his right hand upon me, saying unto me, "Fear not; I Am the first and the last."*

- **Rev 1:18** - *I Am He that liveth, and was dead; and, behold, I Am alive for evermore, Amen; and have the keys of hell and of death.*

- **Rev 21:6** - *And He said unto me, "It is done. I Am Alpha and Omega, the beginning and the end. I will give unto him that is athirst of the fountain of the water of life freely."*

- **Rev 22:13** - *I Am Alpha and Omega, the beginning and the end, the first and the last.*

- **Rev 22:16** - *I Jesus have sent mine angel to testify unto you these things in the churches. I Am the root and the offspring of David, and the bright and morning star.*

Perhaps the most intriguing entry on that list is Rev 1:8 because Jesus out-and-out tells us that He is the Almighty. A Son, yes, but words fail.

The Power to Deliver

At the beginning of this chapter, I said that you couldn't trust the Promisor of these H.E.L.P.s until you're convinced the Promisor is able to deliver.

Jesus, as the Great I AM, is preeminent and has the credentials to make good on His promises. As your Creator, He knows everything about you.

He also longs to have a real, personal relationship with you as you walk down your very own Road to Emmaus...

Chapter 2
The Road To Emmaus

And, behold, two of them went that same day to a village called Emmaus, which was from Jerusalem about threescore furlongs. And they talked together of all these things which had happened. And it came to pass, that, while they communed together and reasoned, Jesus himself drew near, and went with them. But their eyes were holden that they should not know Him. And he said unto them, "What manner of communications are these that ye have one to another, as ye walk, and are sad?" And the one of them, whose name was Cleopas, answering said unto him, "Art thou only a stranger in Jerusalem, and hast not known the things which are come to pass there in these days?" And He said unto them, "What things?" And they said unto Him, "Concerning Jesus of Nazareth, which was a prophet mighty in deed and word before God and all the people and how the chief priests and our rulers delivered Him to be condemned to death, and have crucified Him. But we trusted that it had been He which should have redeemed Israel. And beside all this, today is the third day since these things were done. Yea, and certain women also of our company made us astonished, which were early at the sepulcher and when they found not His body, they came, saying, that they had also seen a vision of angels, which said that He was alive. And certain of them which were with us went to the sepulchre, and found it even so as the women had said: but Him they saw not." Then He said unto them, "O fools, and slow of heart to believe all that the prophets have spoken. Ought not Christ to have suffered these things, and to enter into His glory?" And beginning at Moses and all the prophets, he expounded unto them in all the scriptures the things concerning Himself. And they drew nigh unto the village, whither they went: and He made as though he would have gone further. But they constrained Him, saying, "Abide with us: for it is toward evening, and the day is far spent." And He went in to tarry with them and it came to pass, as He sat at meat with them, He took bread, and blessed it, and brake, and gave to them. And their eyes were opened, and they knew Him; and He vanished out of their sight. And they said one to another,

"Did not our heart burn within us, while He talked with us by the way, and while He opened to us the scriptures?"

Luke 24:13-32

"Did not our heart burn within us, while He talked with us by the way and while He opened to us the scriptures?" For anyone who has had a life-changing introduction to Jesus, you absolutely understand how these men's hearts burned inside them while they talked to the Lord.

The story of the Road to Emmaus out of the Gospels gives us an example of the Lord Jesus, the preeminent I AM, walking directly with people and teaching truths from His Word. Just think, although it's an account from ancient history it's just as applicable today to your walk and life as it was back then. Jesus is very much alive and active in His people's lives. He's waiting for you to invite Him to have a deeper relationship.

What do I mean?

The road to Emmaus is an example of anybody's walk in life, whatever their situation may be, regardless of country, town, city or village, irrespective of your geographical location. That road represents our walk, our life's journey, while we're on Earth. It's a place in the Believer's life where God comes alongside of us to comfort, teach and fellowship, but only when we ask Him. This is contrary to the stale, dull and unconnected "religious" experience many churches teach. When He's asked to come into a heart, He just doesn't say, "Okay I'm in your heart now, I'm leaving!" No, the opposite is true:

> *Be strong and of a good courage, fear not, nor be afraid of them: for the LORD thy God, He it is that doth go with thee; He will not fail thee, nor forsake thee.* **Deut 31:6**

> *Let your conversation be without covetousness; and be content with such things as ye have: for He hath said, I will never leave thee, nor forsake thee.* **Hebrews 13:5**

He said He would never leave you or forsake you. He is here for you - *waiting.*

My Own Personal Road To Emmaus

In a recent book that I wrote, *Terminated*, I detailed my first, real encounter with the Lord. It's powerful, not because it's my testimony, but because of the panoramic vision of history that Jesus gave me. While that vision and the story was pertinent to that writing, I don't want to rehash the whole thing here. If you haven't read *Terminated*, I'd encourage you to get a copy from my website. It's an important account of what we'll face in the near future.

That being said, I think it's important for you to understand what it means to walk with Jesus down your own personal Road to Emmaus. So I'm going to recount another part of my testimony in order to help you grasp the idea.

Back in the early 1970's I was about as worldly as a worldly person could be. I was a film major at Montana State University, but honestly my major should have been classified as partying, because I did a lot of it. I had no spiritual upbringing and no knowledge of God. Let me be blunt, I wasn't raised in church and had no religious inclination whatsoever, was extremely worldly and a heathen.

One night, out of curiosity, I went to a Hal Lindsey meeting on campus because I found ancient history fascinating and he was supposed to talk about Bible prophecy. At the time, I had no idea how that experience would change my life forever.

By the end of the meeting, he told us who Jesus of Nazareth was and explained God's plan of forgiveness through the blood of Jesus. Then he pointed right at me and said, "Jesus loves you." I wasn't a very lovable guy and those words melted my heart. I asked the Lord to forgive me and to come into my life that night.

After the meeting, I went to my mom's house a few blocks away from the college to spend the night. As I walked into my room, Jesus, in physical form, stood there waiting for me. I was stunned and I fell at His feet. His presence was so thick, I couldn't get up until He reached down and stood me up.

I asked, "Who are you, Lord?"

He said, "I am Jesus, your Savior, and I'm giving you a Joseph's ministry to warn my people to prepare for what lies ahead." He also said that I would know Him in a very special way through His Word.

When I looked into Jesus' eyes, every cell, every atom, every molecule in my being exploded in sheer joy and peace. I knew that He loved me and that I was completely forgiven.

But the funny thing was that I'd never read the Bible or been to church so I had no idea who Joseph was! These words were absolutely foreign to me.

Then He showed me a panoramic view of history that illustrated what was about to transpire on earth in the near future.

After that vision He immediately baptized me in His Holy Spirit. (I say that now, but again I had no idea what the Baptism of the Holy Spirit was. I just found myself worshipping Him in some language that I'd never heard or used!)

Following that experience I tried very hard to understand exactly what had happened to me. The Bible was so foreign that I didn't even understand John 3:16!

> For God so loved the world, that He gave His only begotten Son, that whosoever believeth in Him should not perish, but have everlasting life.

I was that dense.

But one good thing about being totally ignorant of God and the Bible was that I had no preconceived ideas. I didn't have to be retaught or have any religious biases fixed.

I started hanging out at the one place that I thought could have some answers: the local Christian bookstore called House of Time in Bozeman, Montana.

I bought various books and tapes about the Bible and what it meant to be a Christian. I'd listen for hours on end to Derek Prince, Bob Mumford, Ern Baxter, Charles Simpson, Don Basham and Campbell McAlpine. I read whatever I thought would help me to grow as a Believer because I was ravenously hungry for the Word of God.

As an example of how Jesus will walk right alongside you throughout your life, one day when I was at the Christian book store two men showed up. I had no idea who they were and I'd never seen them before. They said that they'd come from a bible school on the West Coast; Portland I think. They said that they each had the same vision of a man and his name was Steve Quayle. God told them to find this man in Bozeman, Montana, lay hands on him, and pray for him that the promise that God made him about "knowing God in a very special way through His Word" would be fulfilled.

They were the same words! This is exactly what the Lord told me that night in my room! How in the world could these guys, whom I'd never met, know what Jesus told me directly?

I was floored.

They prayed for me and the very promise that God gave to me started to unfold.

I kinda feel like John and Peter when they said,

> *For we cannot but speak the things which we have seen and heard. Acts 4:20*

Jesus did all of this for me, but I'm no different than you. Acts 10:34 says that God is no respecter of persons. He loves you just as much as me and He wants to have a supernatural encounter with you too, but you have to invite Him. Your hunger is part of that invitation.

Shortly after this experience I had the opportunity to be taught in a Bible study by a wonderful man in the Lord, Dr. Don Boyd, an Assembly of God Elder and head professor at MSU. He provoked my pothead and alcoholic misfit, unreligious friends and me to learn the Word of God and in the process to be changed by that Word and the power of the Holy Spirit.

When you hunger and thirst after righteousness, when you desire to know Jesus in a real, personal and living way, God will bring you the people, the assets and the instructions that you need to grow in Him.

Wow! That's kinda like how He explained the scriptures to those two men on the Road to Emmaus.

It might be a visitation from Him personally. You might hear His audible voice. Or it could be something as simple as having His love, peace, healing and forgiveness flow through you like a warm summer breeze. It really doesn't matter. What matters is to connect with Him in a real, personal way. What He did for those men on the Road to Emmaus and what He did for me, He can do for you. If you just invite Him to walk with you.

O T Burning Hearts

People have a hard time identifying with Jesus as a person because they've been taught, or have the perception, that He's either not real or that He's some distant, detached God that has no interest in them or their life.

Nothing could be further from the truth. Jesus, the Creator of all things and the One who holds the Universe together, has a keen interest in His creation: namely, you and me. He's always had direct interaction with people, even before He came to earth to be born of a virgin.

The Lord showing up in the OT before we knew Him as Jesus is called a Christophany or Theophany by theologists. (I know what I said; I just had to borrow the word.) Far from being cold and elusive, these appearances are examples of His love and concern for those people who have a heart after Him.

It was Jesus who was the "Angel of the Lord" that's referred to fifty-six times in fifty-one verses in the OT. Throughout the Bible we see examples of how the Lord interacted with people and angels.

1. **Jesus said in John 1:18 that no one had ever seen the Father except Him:**

   *No man hath seen God at any time; the only begotten Son, which is in the bosom of the Father, He hath declared him. **John 1:18***

Therefore any appearance in the OT of God had to be Jesus.

2. **We know from scripture that only God is to be worshipped.** Here are a few examples of worshipping the Angel of the Lord and there are many more. But you'll get the gist:

   *And I John saw these things, and heard them. And when I had heard and seen, I fell down to worship before the feet of the angel which shewed me these things. Then saith he unto me, See thou do it not: for I am thy fellow servant, and of thy brethren the prophets, and of them which keep the sayings of this book: **worship God. Rev 22:8-9***

   Let no man beguile you** of your reward in a voluntary humility and **worshipping of angels**, intruding into those things which he hath not seen, vainly puffed up by his fleshly mind. **Col 2:18

   *And saith unto him, "All these things will I give thee, if thou wilt fall down and worship me." Then saith Jesus unto him, "Get thee hence, Satan: for it is written, **Thou shalt worship the Lord thy God, and him only shalt thou serve." Matt 4:9-10***

   However, we see below that the Angel of the Lord is worshipped:

   *And the **angel of the LORD** appeared unto him in a flame of fire out of the midst of a bush: and he looked, and, behold, the bush burned with fire, and the bush was not consumed. And when the LORD saw that he turned aside to see, **God called unto him** out of the midst of the bush, and said, "Moses, Moses." And he said, "Here am I." Moreover He said, "**I Am the God of thy father, the God of Abraham, the God of Isaac, and the God of Jacob.**" And Moses hid his face; for **he was afraid to look upon God. Exodus 3:2, 4, 6***

   *Joshua 5:14-15 - And He said, "Nay; but as Captain of the Host of the LORD am I now come." **And Joshua fell on his face to the earth, and did worship**, and said unto Him, "What saith my Lord unto His servant?" And the Captain of the LORD'S Host said unto Joshua, "Loose thy shoe from off thy foot; **for the place whereon thou standest is holy.**" And Joshua did so. **Joshua 5:14-15***

JESUS - The Premise of the Promise

*And the LORD appeared unto him {Abraham} in the plains of Mamre: and he sat in the tent door in the heat of the day; and he lift up his eyes and looked, and, lo, three men stood by him: and when he saw them, he ran to meet them from the tent door, **and bowed himself toward the ground**. Genesis 18:1-2*

3. **The Angel of the Lord was identified with titles or positions as well.** Many of these titles are referenced in the OT as belonging only to God. If the Angel of the Lord is using or has been given a title, then it must be God Himself!

And the angel of the LORD said unto her {Hagar}, "Behold, thou art with child, and shalt bear a son, and shalt call his name Ishmael; because the LORD hath heard thy affliction. And she called the name of the LORD that spake unto her, Thou God seest me: for she said, Have I also here looked after Him that seeth me? Genesis 16:11, 13

And he said, "Nay; but as Captain of the Host of the LORD am I now come." Joshua 5:14-15

And Manoah said unto the angel of the LORD, "What is thy name, that when thy sayings come to pass we may do thee honour?" And the angel of the LORD said unto him, "Why askest thou thus after my name, seeing it is secret?" (The KJV translates the Angel's name as "secret". In the original language it literally means incomprehensible! Sounds like God to me!) Judges 13:17-18

4. **Here are some other places in the OT where Jesus showed up to interact with man before His incarnation:**

And an angel of the LORD came up from Gilgal to Bochim, and said, "I made you to go up out of Egypt, and have brought you unto the land which I sware unto your fathers; and I said, I will never break my covenant with you." Judges 2:1

Therefore thus saith the LORD concerning the king of Assyria, "He shall not come into this city, nor shoot an arrow there, nor come before it with shield, nor cast a bank against it. By the way that he came, by the same shall he return, and shall not come into this city," saith the LORD. "For I will defend this city, to save it, for mine own sake, and for my servant David's sake." And it came to pass that night, that the angel of the LORD went out, and smote in the camp of the Assyrians an hundred fourscore and five thousand: and when they arose early in the morning, behold, they were all dead corpses. 2 Kings 19:32-35

And Jacob was left alone; and there wrestled a man with him until the breaking of the day. And when he saw that he prevailed not against him, He touched the hollow of his thigh; and the hollow of Jacob's thigh was out of joint, as he wrestled with Him. And He said, "Let me go, for the day breaketh." And he said, "I will not let thee go, except thou bless me." And He said unto him, "What is thy name"? And he said, "Jacob." And He said, "Thy name shall be called no more Jacob, but Israel, for as a prince hast thou power with God and with men, and hast prevailed." And Jacob asked Him, and said, "Tell me, I pray thee, thy name." And He said, "Wherefore is it that thou dost ask after my name?" And He blessed him there. Genesis 32:24-29

Time doesn't permit us to go into all the OT examples of Jesus showing up on people's paths back then. As you can see, He's far from being the aloof deity that the modern-Church has made Him out to be.

God wants very much to intersect with your life's path in a real and meaningful way. The question is:

Will you let Him?

More Than Just A Stroll Down The Road

If you'll recall from the story of the Road to Emmaus, those two guys were dealing with several emotions and problems at the same time.

They had come to believe that Jesus was the Messiah that was promised for hundreds of years. When He was murdered, crucified, all those Believers had to be bewildered at His death. They were sad, fearful and confused all at the same time. Then that morning they'd heard reports that He'd risen? Their world was in turmoil and they had no idea how to deal with those emotions and circumstances or what would happen next.

Sound familiar?

How many times in your life have you come across heartbreak or difficulties and had no answers? Everybody has. Most of the time people will take matters into their own hands, even if they have no clue about what to do.

Just like Jesus coming alongside those men and explaining and guiding them through the scriptures, He can come alongside you in your life as well.

There are so many benefits of a walk with the Lord that a Believer gains when we truly ask Him to come alongside, but most churches today only teach about one: salvation.

~ *For whosoever shall call upon the name of the Lord shall be saved. **Romans 10:13***

~ *And it shall come to pass, that whosoever shall call on the name of the LORD shall be delivered: for in mount Zion and in Jerusalem shall be deliverance, as the LORD hath said, and in the remnant whom the LORD shall call. **Joel 2:32***

~ *Because he hath set his love upon me, therefore will I deliver him: I will set him on high, because he hath known my name. **Psalm 91:14***

While absolutely necessary for a relationship with the Lord, salvation is only the beginning. A thriving walk with Jesus, just like any relationship, takes communication. We communicate with Him through prayer and His Word. But what exactly is prayer?

In 1 Thessalonians 5:17 the Apostle Paul said to "Pray without ceasing." How in the world can somebody do that? Everybody would need to get up off of their knees sometime or another, wouldn't they? Praying doesn't mean that you assume the position, bow your head and start moving your lips. It can, but this isn't what Paul is talking about.

Just like having a conversation with the Lord on that Road, you too can have an ongoing conversation with Him throughout your day. The great thing is that you don't have to even move your lips!

God made your brain tremendously powerful. You're able to do multiple things at once and still be thinking about something else. This is what Paul meant when he said to "pray without ceasing". Set your mind on Jesus and think to Him throughout your day. Notice I said think to Him, not necessarily about Him. Thinking to Him and listening for the Holy Spirit's reply is direct interaction and is altogether different than thinking about Him without trying to interact with Him.

> *If ye then be risen with Christ, seek those things which are above, where Christ sitteth on the right hand of God. Set your affection on things above, not on things on the earth.* **Colossians 3:1-2**

Unfortunately, what most churches teach these days is that it's okay to just think in general terms about the Lord without speaking to Him and obeying His Word. Your interaction with Him isn't only confined to conversing with Him. Setting your mind on the things above shifts your thinking pattern from focusing on yourself to focusing on Him and His kingdom.

~ *Finally, brethren, whatsoever things are true, whatsoever things are honest, whatsoever things are just, whatsoever things are pure, whatsoever things are lovely, whatsoever things are of good report; if there be any virtue, and if there be any praise, think on these things.* **Philippians 4:8**

~ *And be not conformed to this world: but be ye transformed by the renewing of your mind, that ye may prove what is that good, and acceptable, and perfect, will of God.* **Romans 12:2**

And just like any conversation on the Road, God does talk back.

~ *My sheep hear my voice, and I know them, and they follow me.* **John 10:27**

~ *Even the Spirit of truth; whom the world cannot receive, because it seeth Him not, neither knoweth Him: but ye know Him; for he dwelleth with you, and shall be in you.* **John 14:27**

~ *But the Comforter, which is the Holy Ghost, whom the Father will send in my name, He shall teach you all things, and bring all things to your remembrance, whatsoever I have said unto you.* **John 14:26**

He also speaks to us through His Word.

~ *All scripture is given by inspiration of God, and is profitable for doctrine, for reproof, for correction, for instruction in righteousness.* **2 Timothy 3:16**

~ *Thy word is a lamp unto my feet, and a light unto my path.* **Psalm 119:105**

With the Holy Spirit living inside the Believer, you are able to hear God directly as though He is whispering in your ear when you yield your heart and life to Him every day. Sometimes that voice will be still and small in your head, or it might be an overwhelming feeling in your heart, or you may get an impression of what He wants you to say or do.

Sometimes it can be like He's shaking you from the inside because of a thought that you've had and He's trying to get your attention. For myself, I'll get a burst-transmission of a concept. I'll instantly know it from Him and I'll understand what I'm supposed to do.

All of these means of communication, and more, go into an everyday walk with the Lord.

A Relationship With Him Every Day

The vast majority of Christians look at eternal resurrection through the blood of Jesus as simply "fire insurance", kind of like Martha did when Lazarus died.

Martha was Mary's sister, the Mary who anointed Jesus' feet and dried them with her hair. Lazarus died and was buried. The sisters sent for Jesus but when He finally came, their brother had been dead for four days.

> *Then Martha, as soon as she heard that Jesus was coming, went and met Him: but Mary sat still in the house. Then said Martha unto Jesus, "Lord, if thou hadst been here, my brother had not died. But I know, that even now, whatsoever thou wilt ask of God, God will give it thee."* **John 11:20-22**

Within this discourse, Martha's own religious attitude shows up in verses 23-27. Notice how Jesus responds to this religious mind-set.

> *Jesus saith unto her, "Thy brother shall rise again. Martha saith unto Him, I know that he shall rise again in the resurrection at the last day." Jesus said unto her, "I am the resurrection, and the life: he that believeth in me, though he were dead, yet shall he live: And whosoever liveth and believeth in me shall never die. Believest thou this?" She saith unto Him, "Yea, Lord: I believe that thou art the Christ, the Son of God, which should come into the world."* **John 11:23-27**

Martha gave Jesus an answer that was nonspecific, vague and generalized based upon her religious beliefs, "I know that he shall rise again in the resurrection at the last day…" It wasn't wrong, because the Hebrews knew that after we die, everyone stands before God. But Jesus stopped her and said, "No, you don't get it, Martha! It's Me. I AM the resurrection."

When you finish the story, you see that Jesus miraculously raised Lazarus from the dead and this event becomes one of Jesus' proofs that He's able to resurrect more than a body from the dead. It's about His resurrection power of our eternal souls and His ability to supernaturally affect our 3-D physical laws. He is the Resurrection, the Almighty God, the Great I AM and the preeminent Lord of all.

When we walk in relationship with Him, something happens to us in a way that our natural vision cannot see. In **2 Corinthians 5:17** it says that His resurrection power literally changes us into new creations:

> *Therefore if any man be in Christ, he is a new creature: old things are passed away; behold, all things are become new.*

If you then go to **Acts 17:28**, it says:

For in him we live, and move, and have our being…

That's super-positioning!

Think about it. How can we be on earth, struggling to pay bills, dealing with all the junk that a physical life has to offer, and yet fighting a supernatural battle?

For we wrestle not against flesh and blood, but against principalities, against powers, against the rulers of the darkness of this world, against spiritual wickedness in high places. **Ephesians 6:12**

Our walk with the Lord is more than what we can see with our eyes or feel throughout our days. We are a people held between two worlds: the physical world that we can see and feel and a supernatural one in which we will spend eternity. We serve a King who has a kingdom that isn't in this 3-D realm.

Jesus answered, "My kingdom is not of this world. If my kingdom were of this world, then would my servants fight, that I should not be delivered to the Jews, but now is my kingdom not from hence. **John 18:36**

Like I said, *super-positioning*.

In The Company of the King

This walk is a discovery of the Lord. It's a walk through the scriptures. It's a walk through history. It's a walk through human emotion. And it's a walk through the greatest event that will ever happen. If your heart is after Him, along the way you'll get to know Jesus in more than just a religious way. You will know Him as a person who has felt everything that you and I could ever feel and more.

His feelings could be best summed up as His experience on the Cross as He bore the sins of the whole world on His shoulders. Imagine every human feeling that man has ever had, his every thought or ponder, all of his heartbreak and all of his emotions. The weight of all of that and more rested on Jesus as He hung on the Cross dying.

He is despised and rejected of men; a man of sorrows, and acquainted with grief: and we hid as it were our faces from Him; He was despised, and we esteemed Him not. Surely He hath borne our griefs, and carried our sorrows: yet we did esteem Him stricken, smitten of God, and afflicted. But He was wounded for our transgressions, He was bruised for our iniquities: the chastisement of our peace was upon Him; and with his stripes we are healed. **Isaiah 53:3-5**

When I first got saved, I realized that, as I stood before God, the ultimate judge and jury, I deserved to be sentenced for a capital offense, but Jesus voluntarily took my place and was executed instead! That understanding blew my mind!

After that courtroom experience, I came to understand what would happen to any person who did not accept His free gift of eternal life made possible through His death and resurrection.

For the wages of sin is death; but the gift of God is eternal life through Jesus Christ our Lord. **Romans 6:23**

The price of rejecting Jesus and His sacrifice is death, not just physical death which happens only once, but eternal damnation in hell.

And as it is appointed unto men once to die, but after this the judgment. **Hebrews 9:27**

The Son of Man shall send forth His angels, and they shall gather out of His kingdom all things that offend, and them which do iniquity; And shall cast them into a furnace of fire: there shall be wailing and gnashing of teeth. **Matthew 13:41-42**

Imagine the wailing and gnashing of teeth as the suffering, the tears and the emotional imagery goes on forever, an eternal reminder of the cost of rejecting the Way, the Truth and the Life Who is Jesus Christ, Son of the Living God.

Contrast that with the righteous who are forgiven:

Even the righteousness of God which is by faith of Jesus Christ unto all and upon all them that believe... **Romans 3:22**

Whose sins are under the blood of the Lamb:

But if we walk in the light, as He is in the light, we have fellowship one with another, and the blood of Jesus Christ His Son cleanseth us from all sin. **1 John 1:7**

And whose tears are collected by the Lord:

Thou tellest my wanderings: put thou my tears into thy bottle: are they not in thy book? **Psalm 56:8**

Which He will eventually wipe away forever:

And I heard a great voice out of heaven saying, "Behold, the tabernacle of God is with men, and He will dwell with them, and they shall be his people, and God himself shall be with them, and be their God. And God shall wipe away all tears from their eyes; and there shall be no more death, neither sorrow, nor crying, neither shall there be any more pain: for the former things are passed away." And He that sat upon the throne said, "Behold, I make all things new." And He said unto me, "Write: for these words are true and faithful." **Rev 21:3-5**

This is He , the Great I AM, the Preeminent One Who wants to walk with you down your own Road to Emmaus.

I can't deny the manifested love of the Living God towards me and I relish the friendship of the Lord Jesus Christ above all.

Greater love hath no man than this, that a man lay down his life for his friends. Ye are my friends, if ye do whatsoever I command you. Henceforth I call you not servants; for the servant knoweth not what his lord doeth: but I have called you friends... **John 15:13-15**

Jesus is the beginning and the end of all life and in Him you'll have the life that God has designed and desired for you. That's a life which is the ultimate-best for you and one that will bring Him glory. It's a supernatural win-win scenario. It doesn't matter what you're facing or what all of us may face in the future. His answer is always the same:

Behold, I am the LORD, the God of all flesh: is there any thing too hard for me? **Jeremiah 32:27**

His interest and care of you, and for you, is always the same:

Then they cry unto the LORD in their trouble, and He saveth them out of their distresses. He sent his word, and healed them, and delivered them from their destructions. **Psalm 107:19-20**

On this road He is here to love you, guide you, help you and free you. If Jesus paid so great a price for our salvation and our road to Emmaus, are you willing to step up, put the pedal to the metal and go for what God said?

The Time That Now Is

Do you know this Jesus? Or have you been so entrenched into religion and church that you've failed to see the person of Jesus Who longs to walk with you on your life's road? Are you just going through the motions of a religion void of relationship, or are you someone who's totally cut off from the Lord because you've walked away?

In any case, it doesn't matter if you will only turn your heart toward Him and give up those games to worship Him with your whole heart.

But the hour cometh, and now is, when the true worshippers shall worship the Father in spirit and in truth: for the Father seeketh such to worship him. **John 4:23**

He is constantly thinking of you and always concerned for you.

I will praise thee; for I am fearfully and wonderfully made: marvellous are thy works; and that my soul knoweth right well. My substance was not hid from thee, when I was made in secret, and curiously wrought in the lowest parts of the earth. Thine eyes did see my substance, yet being unperfect; and in thy book all my members were written, which in continuance were fashioned, when as yet there was none of them. How precious also are thy thoughts unto me, O God! how great is the sum of them! If I should count them, they are more in number than the sand: when I awake, I am still with thee. **Psalm 139:14-18**

"*How precious also are thy thoughts unto me, O God! How great is the sum of them! If I should count them, they are more in number than the sand.*" This is exactly what I mean about how very much He cares for you.

There are approximately 700,500,000,000,000,000,000 grains of sand on earth. His thoughts of you are more than that! His thoughts to do you well are infinite, because His love for you is infinite.

This is the Person Who wants to walk beside you.

Then said Jesus unto his disciples, If any man will come after me, let him deny himself, and take up his cross, and follow me. **Matthew 16:24**

The time has come for you to put down your iPhone (denying your "self" its own pleasures), take up your cross (reading the Bible and heeding the call of God on your life) and follow Jesus on the road to Emmaus.

Colossians declares that everything was created in Him and through Him, everything that exists and is held together. Now think about the picture of you walking down the road with that Jesus, the Creator of all things.

As you journey together on your life's road, you're sharing with Him and enjoying His company. That's exactly what Jesus was doing with those two men on the Road to Emmaus.

Visualize the scene: They were walking on the very dirt that was created when God exploded the breath of life into the universe. They breathed the air that the Lord God of Heaven created. They're probably hearing the birds and seeing the flowers. And all along, God was embracing their friendship and the glory of His creation.

You are part of that creation and He longs to embrace your life as well.

The road to Emmaus is a metaphor for the walk that God has for you, which has been pre-ordained before the foundation of the world. If you will respond to the offer of His grace, provision and power, that path, His choice for your life, is already set for you. God won't force you to go down that path, but if you choose to walk it and ask God to direct you, you'll be able to walk in His righteousness and will fulfill the work that He has for you.

He is the only one Who could ask this of you. He is after all, the Great I AM and His Preeminence is everlasting.

The Blood Of Jesus

He's the only hope you will ever need.

Nothing But The Blood Of Jesus

What can wash away my sins?

Nothing but the blood of Jesus.

What can make me whole again?

Nothing but the blood of Jesus.

Oh! Precious is the flow

That makes me white as snow;

No other fount I know,

Nothing but the blood of Jesus.

HELP 2

His Everlasting Power

He spreads out the northern skies over empty space. He suspends the earth over nothing. He wraps up the waters in his clouds, yet the clouds do not burst under their weight. He covers the face of the full moon, spreading his clouds over it. He marks out the horizon on the face of the waters for a boundary between light and darkness. The pillars of the heavens quake, aghast at his rebuke. By His power he churned up the sea, by His wisdom he cut Rahab to pieces. By His breath the skies became fair, His hand pierced the gliding serpent. And these are but the outer fringe of His works, how faint the whisper we hear of Him! Who then can understand the thunder of His power?"

Job 26:7-14

Power

God in His wisdom and mercy didn't leave us, His children, powerless in a world that He told us would deteriorate before Jesus returns. In practicality that may sound religious to you or downright untrue, especially if you're struggling as a Believer, or have gone through difficult times. As someone who has been there, I'm here to tell you that His Power is ever-present for the Christian who really wants to tap into it.

This desperately needed Power is unrealized or even not sought after by today's modern-Church and many churches and Christians these days do everything they can to deny the supernatural Power of God. Many so-called theologians and pastors say that God's supernatural moving amongst His people, and the demonstration of His Power, stopped when the disciples died. They'll give excuses for their ineffectual lives by claiming, "That was just a different dispensation."

By denying the available Power of God, churches and their leaders are basically saying, "Okay, God. We can take care of this on our own."

So ask yourself, "Just how life-changing and effective have their church programs been?"

I've previously said that as we draw near to the End of the Age, we are entering into perhaps the most supernatural time in mankind's history. This is not the time for man-made programs or charts. This is the time that Christians need to be infused with supernatural Power from on high.

> *For though we walk in the flesh, we do not war after the flesh. For the weapons of our warfare are not carnal, but mighty through God to the pulling down of strong holds.* ***2 Corinthians 10:3-4***

Because of the seriousness of the hour, God has weapons for His people that He hasn't yet entrusted us with.

God's Everlasting Power is your promise for these days.

Chapter 3

The Difference Between Power and Authority

So shall they fear the name of the LORD from the west, and his glory from the rising of the sun. When the enemy shall come in like a flood, the Spirit of the LORD shall lift up a standard against him.

Isaiah 59:19

In North Hollywood, California, on February 28, 1997 the nation and the world was shocked into a new reality. Two men held up a Bank of America and got into a shoot-out with police.

In that era, police didn't carry automatic weapons or heavy firepower. Those two gunmen were not only heavily armed with military style, fully automatic AK-47s, they were also using armor-piercing rounds loaded in high-capacity drum magazines and were clad with body armor from head to toe. At that time, even the L.A.P.D. hadn't dealt with that level of violence and the ensuing gun battle forever changed how citizens in America were policed.

As a news helicopter circled overhead, the live feed carried the shoot-out all across the country. The brazen thugs took body shot after body shot and still didn't go down. In turn, they sprayed police and civilians alike with their lethal rounds. Finally, police managed to get a head shot on the first gunman, killing him. The second gunman did surrender but later succumbed to his injuries and died. Amazingly no one was killed other than the robbers, although twelve police officers and eight civilians were seriously injured after almost two thousand rounds were fired.

A reporter in a helicopter uttered the most telling statement of the whole ordeal when in the course of his reporting, he said:

These aren't people that the police are going to be able to "talk out" of this situation.

That statement reminds me of how Christians today think they can reason with, or reason away, Satan. Men can't out-think the devil, they can't out-scheme the devil and they can't bargain with him (although many of them think they can). He's one of the most powerful entities ever created, but would-be Christians think that they somehow don't need God's Power to overcome this kind of being?

Those cops definitely had the legal authority to arrest those two criminals, because after all they robbed a bank and broke the law; however, those thugs didn't recognize, or care about, the legal authority of the police. Neither does the devil care that you as a Christian have the legal authority to kick him out of your life and your family's lives.

What you need is the same thing that those cops discovered on that infamous day on the streets of Hollywood. You need more firepower.

That's where the Holy Spirit comes in.

An Outgunned Generation?

This know also, that in the last days perilous times shall come. For men shall be lovers of their own selves, covetous, boasters, proud, blasphemers, disobedient to parents, unthankful, unholy. Without natural affection, truce-breakers, false accusers, incontinent, fierce, despisers of those that are good, traitors, heady, high-minded, lovers of pleasures more than lovers of God. <u>Having a form of godliness, but denying the power thereof</u>: from such turn away. **2 Tim 3:1-6**

Getting saved is only the first step in the lifelong journey to spiritual maturity but the overwhelming majority of Christians never go beyond this first step. As a consequence, they never become "filled with the Spirit" nor do they ever manifest the mature fruit that we're told we should demonstrate. But doesn't it stand to reason that the devil would try everything he could to keep people from coming to the saving knowledge of Jesus? If they do get saved, wouldn't he also try to hinder the power of the Spirit in people's lives and keep them from growing into powerful, mature Believers? If the Church walked in the maturity and the Power that's available to them, the enemy would be devastated.

Oh… you didn't know that the devil had authority in your life and on this earth? Here's a reality check.

When Jesus was tempted by the devil in **Matthew 4:1-11**, he showed Jesus *"all the kingdoms in the world"* in verse 9 and told the Lord, *"All these things will I give thee, if thou wilt fall down and worship me."* Jesus didn't contest Satan's statement that all the kingdoms of the world had been given to him. Just the opposite, because we see an astounding statement by Paul in **2 Corinthians 4:3-4**:

*But if our gospel be hid, it is hid to them that are lost in whom **the god of this world** hath blinded the minds of them which believe not, lest the light of the glorious gospel of Christ, who is the image of God, should shine unto them.*

The god of this world?

"Wait just one second, Quayle. I thought Jesus is all-powerful and able to defeat the devil for us!"

Yes, the Lord is all-powerful, but even so, for a time and for His own reasons, God has given Satan authority over this earth. **Ephesians 2:1-2** says:

*And you hath he quickened, who were dead in trespasses and sins wherein in time past ye walked according to the course of this world, according to the **prince of the power of the air**, the spirit that now worketh in the children of disobedience.*

"Prince of the power of the air?" Sounds like kingdom talk to me.

I'm not going to pretend that I know why God has given the devil dominion on earth and one day I'll ask Him, but we need to understand the battlefield on which we're fighting.

Essentially, effective Christians should be like Special Ops dropped behind enemy lines. Like those Seal Team Six members and other elite Black Ops guys, we should be armed and ready to take out the enemy with the weapons that we've carried in with us.

In that section in Matthew 4 where Satan tried to tempt Jesus, the Lord overcame the devil through one of the weapons at His disposal, the Word of God. What isn't in the text, but is a given, is that Jesus was filled with the Holy Spirit and the Everlasting Power of God.

And you can be too.

He's made it possible for you to have access to those very same weapons.

*For though we walk in the flesh, we do not war after the flesh. For the weapons of our warfare are not carnal, but mighty through God to the pulling down of strong holds, casting down imaginations, and every high thing that exalteth itself against the knowledge of God, and bringing into captivity every thought to the obedience of Christ, and having in a readiness to revenge all disobedience, when your obedience is fulfilled. **2 Cor 10:3-6***

As Spirit-filled Believers we shouldn't be struggling in our walks, we should be deadly demon assassins, kicking butt and taking names.

That doesn't mean that throughout life we won't have struggles.

If you're on the frontline of a war and people are shooting at you, there's a chance you could be wounded.

But God has given us the firepower to overcome the enemy and contrary to most of today's pulpit teaching, you don't have to be a victim.

The Battle Rages

French philosopher Pierre Teilhard de Chardin once said;

We are not human beings having a spiritual experience. We are spiritual beings having a human experience.

Our God is a supernatural spirit being. We, as His creations, are also part spiritual beings, composed of spirit, soul, and body - whether we acknowledge His Preeminence or not. Because of this, the vast majority of the world, either intentionally or unintentionally, is looking for the supernatural in all the wrong places.

As a result, the occult is exploding. Self-proclaimed Satanists, modern day wiccans and pagans openly declare the supernatural workings of the devil. Along with that, little children are being trafficked, raped, butchered and consumed through cannibalistic ceremonies and offered up to Satan in blood sacrifices. These demonically-inspired minions certainly believe in supernatural power. People from all walks of life gravitate to Hollywood entertainment that is laced with occult beliefs and paganistic lifestyles.

For Christians, the denial of the Everlasting Power of God and the person and presence of the Holy Spirit has thrust the Church into a quagmire of sin and ineffectiveness. The majority of the Church is denying the very weapons that God has given them to defeat a real devil and his demons. Without those weapons, Christians are in a battle they cannot win even though God has given them the legal victory.

Jesus admonished His followers to wait for the promised manifestation of the in-filling of the Holy Spirit. The Church's rejection of this very real, supernatural Power is a denial of God's power-promise and a recipe for guaranteed defeat. As evidence of this self-inflicted impotence, we see that Christians statistically struggle and fail with the same sin and sickness as non-Christians.

The Barna Group researches various issues, particularly where Christianity is concerned. George Barna said back in 2008,

"We are witnessing the development and acceptance of a new moral code in America," said the researcher and author, who has been surveying national trends in faith and morality for more than a quarter-century. "Mosaics have had little exposure to traditional moral teaching and limited accountability for such behavior. The moral code began to disintegrate when the generation before them – the Baby Busters – pushed the limits that had been challenged by their parents – the Baby Boomers. The result is that without much fanfare or visible leadership, the U.S. has created a moral system based on convenience, feelings, and selfishness.

"The consistent deterioration of the Bible as the source of moral truth has led to a nation where people have become independent judges of right and wrong, basing their choices on feelings and circumstances. It is not likely that America will return to a more traditional moral code until the nation experiences significant pain from its moral choices."[2]

2 Barna, "Young Adults and Liberals Struggle with Morality". Barna.com, https://www.barna.com/research/young-adults-and-liberals-struggle-with-morality/, (August 25, 2008).

In the Sermon on the Mount, Jesus told us that we were to be a positive and powerful force on the earth for His glory:

> *Ye are the salt of the earth: but if the salt have lost his savour, wherewith shall it be salted? it is thenceforth good for nothing, but to be cast out, and to be trodden under foot of men. Ye are the light of the world. A city that is set on an hill cannot be hid. Neither do men light a candle, and put it under a bushel, but on a candlestick; and it giveth light unto all that are in the house. Let your light so shine before men, that they may see your good works, and glorify your Father which is in heaven. Matt 5:13-14*

Now in the second decade of the 21st century, the Church's positive influence in the world has seriously degraded. This goes right back to not recognizing and adhering to the power of the Holy Spirit that was promised so long ago.

The Lord gave me a word years ago and said, "I will bring situations to the forefront that will cause those who claim to know Me, versus those who do know Me, to make and take a stand."

Not only do Believers today not want to take a stand, but it's becoming harder and harder to see any difference between the Church and the world. In 2011, the Barna Group did a comprehensive study on adultery in America with particular emphasis on Christian views toward the subject. The results were shocking.

- Four out of ten Americans now believe that adultery is morally acceptable.
- What's even more shocking is that 1 out of 10 Christians find adultery acceptable!
- Over a third of husbands cheat on their wives.
- Almost a quarter of married women cheat on their husbands!
- This makes greater than 50% of all marriages marred by unfaithfulness by one spouse or the other.

Back in 2000, Christianity Today also did a study. They found that:

- 45% of Christians indicated they had done something sexually inappropriate.
- 23% admitted to having extramarital intercourse.[3]

What makes these statistics so disturbing is that these surveys were done years ago. Today the Church has less influence on society and those problems have almost certainly grown exponentially.

Across the board there is a full-blown identity crisis underway for God's people. In a more recent study, March of 2018, 51% of churchgoers had no idea what the Great Commission was![4]

> *And Jesus came and spake unto them, saying, "All power is given unto me in heaven and in earth. Go ye therefore, and teach all nations, baptizing them in the name of the Father, and of the Son, and of the Holy Ghost, teaching them to observe all things whatsoever I have commanded you. And, lo, I am with you always, even unto the end of the world." Amen. Matt 28:18-20*

---

3 Dr. Kelly Bonewell, "Adultery: Just the Statistics". Kellybonewell.com, http://www.kellybonewell.com/adultery-just-the-statistics/, (January 21, 2011). Font size?

4 Barna Group, "51% of Churchgoers Don't Know of the Great Commission". Barna.com, https://www.barna.com/research/half-churchgoers-not-heard-great-commission/, (March 27, 2018).

In a 2018 survey, the statistics for depression among Protestant Believers was startling.

Approximately three out of four pastors said they knew at least one family member, friend or congregant who had been diagnosed with bipolar disorder.

~ 74% of pastors said they knew someone diagnosed with clinical depression.

~ 57% said they knew at least three people who fell into that category.

~ Six in 10 pastors, 59%, said they had counseled at least one person who was eventually diagnosed with an acute mental illness.

~ 23% of pastors indicated that they themselves had battled a mental illness of some kind with 12% admitting that their struggle was formally diagnosed.

These findings were confirmed by the National Alliance on Mental Illness and are disturbingly similar to the general population![5] Whatever malfeasance the Bible speaks against, whether it be substance abuse, gambling, cussing, stealing, etc., either sin or ailment, both Christians and non-Christians proportionately fall into the same snares!

This ought not to be!

Yes, we are broken vessels that the Lord has made new, but that's the point. We are supposed to be new creations, delivered from those sins and sicknesses that once entrapped us. If God's Power were effectual in our lives, we wouldn't strive to be different. We would naturally be different.

I'm reminded about the demoniac in Luke 8:34-39 who was called Legion because he had a slew of demons in him. Through the Everlasting Power of God, Jesus cast those demons into swine who then killed themselves. The aftermath of that story is very telling when we read the following:

> *When they that fed them saw what was done, they fled, and went and told it in the city and in the country. Then they went out to see what was done; and came to Jesus, and found the man, out of whom the devils were departed, sitting at the feet of Jesus, clothed, and in his right mind: and they were afraid. They also which saw it told them by what means he that was possessed of the devils was healed. Then the whole multitude of the country of the Gadarenes round about besought him to depart from them; for they were taken with great fear: and he went up into the ship, and returned back again. Now the man out of whom the devils were departed besought him that he might be with him: but Jesus sent him away, saying, Return to thine own house, and shew how great things God hath done unto thee. And he went his way, and published throughout the whole city how great things Jesus had done unto him.*

It says in **John 12:32**,

> *"And I, if I be lifted up from the earth, will draw all men unto me."*

The power of God was evident in Jesus' earthly ministry and people couldn't help but talk about Him and all that God was doing.

If the Church denies the Spirit of God, then they deny the pointing unto Jesus. If they deny the pointing

---

5 Ed Stetzer, "The Church and Mental Health: What Do the Numbers Tell Us?". Christianity Today, https://www.christianitytoday.com/edstetzer/2018/april/church-and-mental-health.html, (April 20, 2018).

unto Jesus, and Jesus is not presented as the Son of God, the Lamb slain before the foundation of the world, the devil has already won a victory.

Here is what you need to take from this story: This demonstration of God's Everlasting Power can, and should, live inside of you.

> *But if the Spirit of him that raised up Jesus from the dead dwell in you, he that raised up Christ from the dead shall also quicken your mortal bodies by his Spirit that dwelleth in you.* **Romans 8:11**

As human beings we will never be perfect, but the Holy Spirit within us gives us the Power needed to overcome an enemy that seeks to steal, kill and destroy through sin and sickness.

> *Howbeit when he, the Spirit of truth, is come, he will guide you into all truth: for he shall not speak of himself; but whatsoever he shall hear, that shall he speak: and he will shew you things to come.* **John 16:13**

Like it or not, the Church has abandoned the person of the Holy Spirit and denied His gifts. We're at a place in time where going through the motions isn't enough. A supernatural war is burgeoning all around us and the Church is taking huge casualties. We will have to all walk in the purpose and Power that we have been promised or we will not survive what's coming.

The first thing you have to do is make a choice to tap into God's Everlasting Power - no more excuses, no more theology, no more doctrine which denies the power and in-filling of the Holy Spirit. Choose the truth of the Word of God and the Power of His might.

The Internal Struggle

> *For we know that the law is spiritual: but I am carnal, sold under sin. For that which I do I allow not: for what I would, that do I not; but what I hate, that do I. If then I do that which I would not, I consent unto the law that it is good. Now then it is no more I that do it, but sin that dwelleth in me. For I know that in me (that is, in my flesh,) dwelleth no good thing: for to will is present with me; but how to perform that which is good I find not. For the good that I would I do not: but the evil which I would not, that I do. Now if I do that I would not, it is no more I that do it, but sin that dwelleth in me.* **Romans 7:14-20**

Sin is not an act. Sin is a power.

That power was predetermined to enter into the human race even before the creation of Adam and Eve, as evidenced when the angels in heaven rebelled and fell. To counter these events, scripture says the following in **John 1:12**:

> *But as many as received him, to them gave he power to become the sons of God...*

Sin is the root and the acts of sin are the fruit of sin.

It says in **Romans 6:23,**

> *For the wages of sin is death; but the gift of God is eternal life through Jesus Christ our Lord.*

Sin is not just something we trip over on our walks. It is a weapon of mass destruction (WMD) to our lives.

> *Now the works of the flesh are manifest, which are these; Adultery, fornication, uncleanness, lasciviousness, idolatry, witchcraft, hatred, variance, emulations, wrath, strife, seditions, heresies, envyings, murders, drunkenness, revellings, and such like. Of the which I tell you before, as I have also told you in time past, that they which do such things shall not inherit the kingdom of God. Gal 5:19-21*

These are the things that destroy us, but these are also the things that people in the Church are now seemingly embracing. "I'm free. Anything goes so long as I know that Jesus loves me."

Give me a break. Jesus isn't some sugar daddy that rains downs His blessings on us just because He loves us. Would you, as a parent, heap more good stuff on your own kids when they were being rebellious and bad?

Of course not!

All you would end up with is spoiled, rebellious, acting-out kids. Seriously, do we really think that God, Who is way smarter than you or me, would raise us up to be children like this? On the contrary, He tells us exactly the kind of children He expects us to be in the next verses in Galatians:

> *But the fruit of the Spirit is love, joy, peace, long-suffering, gentleness, goodness, faith, meekness, temperance: against such there is no law. And they that are Christ's have crucified the flesh with the affections and lusts. If we live in the Spirit, let us also walk in the Spirit. Let us not be desirous of vain glory, provoking one another, envying one another. Gal 5:22-26*

God does love you more than you could ever know. That's why He sent His only Son to die a terrible death for you. That's also why He sent His Spirit to come along side you and infuse you with His Power. That very Holy Spirit living inside Believers gives us the Power to walk out these biblical traits. With His ever-present voice and direction, Christians do not have to strive to live out these tenets, but like a fruit tree, they grow naturally out of the Believer's life.

But to make this happen, you must be filled with the *Spirit of God.*

Power Vs. Authority

There's a huge difference between the authority granted to us as Believers and the Power that lives inside us to enforce that authority. Churches today won't acknowledge the fact that a supernatural battle is raging around us, nor our ability to use both the authority and the Power that God has given His people.

Why?

Because many churches today are afraid that they might offend people!

Excuse me?

That's right! Political correctness in the pulpits and pews across America is directly responsible for Christians getting their butts handed to them by the devil via sin and sickness. If there was ever a time when Christians needed to stand on God's authority and use His Power to overcome the enemy, it's now!

Because churches and Believers won't acknowledge this unseen, but real battle, they are ill-equipped and ill-trained to fight. Most Christians are only going through the motions of this supernatural walk and as the Word says,

> "They have a form of godliness, but deny the power thereof."

At the beginning of this chapter I recounted the North Hollywood bank heist. I pointed out that those cops had the legal authority to arrest the robbers, but that those thugs didn't acknowledge or care about the police's legal authority. What law enforcement needed was the power to stop the bad guys and not just the legal authority.

The kingdom of God and the kingdom of the devil operate in much the same way.

As a Christian, you have legal authority over the devil and his demons but, like those bank robbers, the devil doesn't care about your badge until you make him care. We've read *Matthew 28:18* in a different section. Let's break it down:

> *And Jesus came and spake unto them, saying, "All power is given unto me in heaven and in earth."*

The word for "power" here is from the Greek word *exousia* and would be better translated as "authority". That's because the word literally means "conferred power" or "delegated empowerment" like a policeman who has the authorization to operate in a designated jurisdiction - kinda like those cops in North Hollywood.

Now think about this for a moment. Earlier I mentioned 2 Cor 4:3 where Satan is called the "god of this world." I followed up with the verse out of Eph 2:2 where he is called "the prince of the power of the air."

The phrase "god of this world" is a designation, a title, an office. The word for "power" in Eph 2:2 is *exousia*. It's a designation of legal empowerment or the authority to act. What is not being given to the enemy is firepower.

The devil is not all-powerful. God has not given him AR-15's with armor-piercing rounds, or any other ordnance, which could lay waste to mankind!

What the Father has given Satan is the authority to act against, or more specifically, influence mankind.

In Matt 28:18, Jesus flat-out declares that His authority on earth is greater than the devil's. It's like He said, "Alright, I know, devil, that this world has been given to you as your playground. But I'm here to tell you that My authority trumps your authority. There's a new sheriff in town."

A good friend of mine once said, "I want to have a Job experience!"

I looked at him like he was a three-headed alien, "Are you crazy?!" I said. "In order to have a Job experience, you have to go through what Job went through!"

To which my friend replied, "No, no. I don't want the beginning and the middle part, I just want the end of the story where he gets all the blessings!"

While that does sound like the Church today, my point is that sometimes God chooses to give the enemy latitude in our lives and in this world. The story of Job is a good example.

Job was a godly man who feared and served the Lord. He had a ton of kids and great wealth. In the story in Job we see the astonishing direct conversation between God and Satan, as the devil calls into question Job's faithfulness:

And the LORD said unto Satan, "Hast thou considered my servant Job, that there is none like him in the earth, a perfect and an upright man, one that feareth God, and escheweth evil?" Then Satan answered the LORD, and said, "Doth Job fear God for nought? Hast not thou made an hedge about him, and about his house, and about all that he hath on every side? Thou hast blessed the work of his hands, and his substance is increased in the land. But put forth thine hand now, and touch all that he hath, and he will curse thee to thy face." **Job 1:8-11**

That was the gauntlet. In essence the devil said, "Of course he'll worship you! You bless and protect him. But I bet that if You took everything he has away, Job will turn his back on You." For the purpose of teaching God's people about a proper relationship with the Lord, in verse 12 the Father allowed the devil to turn Job's world upside down:

And the LORD said unto Satan, "Behold, all that he hath is in thy power; only upon himself put not forth thine hand."

In other words, God told Satan: "Give it your best shot, but don't physically harm him."

The word "power" in the verse literally means "in your hand" and is showing us how God has given Satan authority to act within certain parameters.

The story goes on to say that when Job passed all the tests, God blessed him even more. But he had to go through some very hard times before he got to those blessings. Sometimes it's like that for us.

You can see how God gave Satan the authority to act from this story about Job. So you may be thinking, "If that's an example of God only giving someone authority, what's it like when He gives someone the firepower to act?"

When the Apostle Paul wrote his letter to the Philippians, he did so from prison as he awaited extradition to plead his case before Caesar. I find that those epistles that he wrote while in custody have some of the deepest truths of the Bible. This particular verse is no exception:

That I may know him, and the power of his resurrection, and the fellowship of his sufferings, being made conformable unto his death. **Phil 3:10**

You'll notice the word "power" in the verse, but it isn't the word for "authority". Here "power" comes from the word *dunamis*, which means physical power, force, might, ability and energy. It's also the word from which we get our English word "dynamite".

That's right! *Dunamis* is firepower. **Believe me when I tell you that Jesus' power is explosive!**

🤴 For I am not ashamed of the gospel of Christ: for it is the ***power*** of God unto salvation to every one that believeth; to the Jew first, and also to the Greek. *Romans 1:16*

🤴 Jesus answered and said unto them, Ye do err, not knowing the scriptures, nor the ***power*** of God. *Matt 22:29*

🤴 And he said unto me, My grace is sufficient for thee: for my strength is made perfect in weakness. Most gladly therefore will I rather glory in my infirmities, that the ***power*** of Christ may rest upon me. *2 Cor 12:9*

🤴 And my speech and my preaching was not with enticing words of man's wisdom, but in demonstration of the Spirit and of ***power***. *1 Cor 2:4*

🤴 And it came to pass on a certain day, as he was teaching, that there were Pharisees and doctors of the law sitting by, which were come out of every town of Galilee, and Judaea, and Jerusalem: and the ***power*** of the Lord was present to heal them. *Luke 5:17*

There are many more examples, but all of these words for "power" are from *dunamis* or a form of *dunamis*.

So we see that Jesus not only has authority or jurisdiction to act, He also has firepower to act. This Power, *dunamis*, raised Christ from the grave and now lives, or should live, inside of you!

God has imparted His authority to you over the enemy and He's given you the firepower to enforce that authority. We are able to speak the Word to resist him and, via the Holy Spirit, are able to know what tactics to use against him.

As we come closer to the End of the Age, you're going to need all the firepower you can get.

Chapter 4

You Shall Receive Power

When they therefore were come together, they asked of Him, saying, "Lord, wilt thou at this time restore again the kingdom to Israel?" And He said unto them, "It is not for you to know the times or the seasons, which the Father hath put in His own power. But ye shall receive power, after that the Holy Ghost is come upon you: and ye shall be witnesses unto me both in Jerusalem, and in all Judaea, and in Samaria, and unto the uttermost part of the earth."

Acts 1:6-8

First, please understand that I do not, and am not, representing any denomination or doctrinal belief. All I am doing is laying out scripture as it is written. You haven't seen me refer to any teaching from any particular pastor or teacher and you'd be hard-pressed to say that I'm trying to sway you to believe a specific doctrinal or denominational tenet.

What I am trying to do is to point you to scripture and only scripture. Let scripture interpret itself. For the moment, put aside your preconceived ideas or doctrine that you may have learned in church or from a particular teacher. If you have no church background, all the better! Like me when I came to know the Lord, you won't have to unlearn stuff that just wasn't true.

Second, imagine the truths in this book to be like a great inheritance.

Pretend that you were dirt-poor and in a continual state of want. At the same time, what if you had a distant cousin or uncle that you didn't even know about. Let's assume for the sake of the discussion that your distant relation was rich beyond all you could imagine, but was dying and had no other blood relatives except you. What if that relative died and you were the only one in his will and would inherit all of his wealth? What if his attorneys searched for you for years and could not find you?

Let me pause in the story for a moment to ask you a question. Even though you had no idea who this man was, but your name was on his will making you his only heir, were you already rich even though you never laid eyes on that wealth?

Going on with the story, suppose the attorneys finally found you and explained what had happened. Now all you had to do to transfer those riches into your name was to act upon the promise that you'd been given by that legal document, i.e. the will. Would you choose to continue to be a pauper and stay in your current state of want, or would you choose to accept the gift of the relative even though it would forever change your life and probably your beliefs?

Silly question, right?

But this is exactly how most Christians think about the Power that has been promised to them as believers. They will acknowledge the legality of their relationship with the Lord, but they will not invoke the Power He promised to them through the Holy Spirit because it would change or go against a current belief.

My challenge to you is to lay down those church-instilled beliefs right now, at least until you finish this chapter. If you do, you may hear the Holy Spirit for the first time saying,

> *"This is the way, walk ye in it, when ye turn to the right hand, and when ye turn to the left."*
> *Isaiah 30:21.*

You are richer than you know.

What He Always Wanted To Do

In our modern-Church era, we've pretty much forgotten about Pentecost, or as the Jews call it, Shavu'ot. This is the second of three major festivals outlined in the OT also known as the Festival of First Fruits. It comes seven weeks after the second day of the Jewish Passover festival.

This is exactly the festival that the disciples were celebrating in **Acts 2:1-12** when the Holy Spirit fell on them:

> *And when the day of Pentecost was fully come, they were all with one accord in one place. And suddenly there came a sound from heaven as of a rushing mighty wind, and it filled all the house where they were sitting. And there appeared unto them cloven tongues like as of fire, and it sat upon each of them. And they were all filled with the Holy Ghost, and began to speak with other tongues, as the Spirit gave them utterance.*

> *And there were dwelling at Jerusalem Jews, devout men, out of every nation under heaven. Now when this was noised abroad, the multitude came together, and were confounded, because that every man heard them speak in his own language. And they were all amazed and marvelled, saying one to another, "Behold, are not all these which speak Galilaeans? And how hear we every man in our own tongue, wherein we were born? Parthians, and Medes, and Elamites, and the dwellers in Mesopotamia, and in Judaea, and Cappadocia, in Pontus, and Asia, Phrygia, and Pamphylia, in Egypt, and in the parts*

of Libya about Cyrene, and strangers of Rome, Jews and proselytes, Cretes and Arabians, we do hear them speak in our tongues the wonderful works of God. And they were all amazed, and were in doubt, saying one to another, What meaneth this?"

When we read this section of scripture from our Christian NT mindset, the tremendous impact of the event is lost. The NT wasn't even written when this happened. These "devout Jews" were following OT instructions when they were in the Holy City that day.

According to the scripture, Hebrews were supposed to gather in Jerusalem at the Temple for this feast. So people from all around the known world came back to the area for the celebration and observance of this Feast of the Lord, Pentecost. This is why there were so many people present who spoke different languages when the Holy Spirit fell.

As an aside, way back in **Genesis 17** we see how Abraham became the first Hebrew when he "crossed over" from his homeland of Ur and their beliefs to the land of Canaan and following God. The name "Hebrew" literally means to "cross over".

Now when Abram was ninety-nine years old, the LORD appeared to Abram and said to him, "I am God Almighty. Walk before Me, and be blameless. I will establish My covenant between Me and you, and I will multiply you exceedingly." Abram fell on his face, and God talked with him, saying, "As for Me, behold, My covenant is with you. And you will be the father of a multitude of nations. No longer shall your name be called Abram, but your name shall be Abraham. For I have made you the father of a multitude of nations. I will make you exceedingly fruitful, and I will make nations of you, and kings will come forth from you. I will establish My covenant between Me and you and your descendants after you throughout their generations for an everlasting covenant, to be God to you and to your descendants after you. I will give to you and to your descendants after you, the land of your sojournings, all the land of Canaan, for an everlasting possession; and I will be their God."

This multitude of various nationalities found in Jerusalem on the Day of Pentecost was the fulfillment of God's promise to Abraham. People from all over the known world had come to believe in the God of Israel and crossed over to follow Him. They were Hebrews. This gathering in Jerusalem at the time was not unique. Every year Pentecost was celebrated, and still is, in Israel and other parts of the world. Those who saw and experienced the falling of the Spirit had to be stunned because nothing like that had ever happened before... or had it? Is there any indication in scripture that this falling of the Holy Spirit had happened before in the OT?

The answer may surprise you.

Leviticus 23 gives instructions and a time-line for how and when the Hebrews are supposed to celebrate the Feast of Pentecost:

*And ye shall count unto you from the morrow after the sabbath, from the day that ye brought the sheaf of the wave offering; seven sabbaths shall be complete, even unto the morrow after the seventh sabbath shall ye number fifty days; and ye shall offer a new meat offering unto the LORD. **Leviticus 23:15-16***

So we see seven Sabbaths here, counted from the second day of Passover (Lev 23:9-14).

In Exodus 19, we see Moses and the Israelites have left Egypt and are at Mt. Sinai "in the third month". Since we know that they left Egypt the second day after the death angel killed the Egyptians' first born and "passed over" the Hebrews, they are at Mt. Sinai seven weeks after the first Passover. We now know the time period as Pentecost.

Before Moses went up to the mountain to talk to God, Exodus 20:18-21 says the following:

> *And all the people saw the thunderings, and the lightnings, and the noise of the trumpet, and the mountain smoking: and when the people saw it, they removed, and stood afar off. And they said unto Moses, "Speak thou with us, and we will hear: but let not God speak with us, lest we die." And Moses said unto the people, "Fear not: for God is come to prove you, and that his fear may be before your faces, that ye sin not." And the people stood afar off, and Moses drew near unto the thick darkness where God was."*

There are so many nuggets of truth here and in a moment you'll understand why this section links back to Acts 2.

Verse 18 says that

> *"...all the people saw the thunderings, and the lightnings, and the noise of the trumpet, and the mountain smoking..."*

How do people "see" thunder? You can't see thunder. Nor can you "see" trumpet sounds. A closer look at the original Hebrew yields some interesting finds.

The word for "thunderings" is *hakkovlot* and literally means a sound or voice. The word "lightnings" comes from the word *hallappidim* and means "a torch" or "fire". The words "noise of the trumpet" comes from two words, *kovl hashofar*, which means "voice like a horn or trumpet".

So literally they saw fire that was making a sound like a horn or a trumpet. Have you ever heard someone use the expression, "The flames were licking..." Fire has been compared to tongues for centuries. I don't know where the phrase comes from but given the Pentecost history in the NT, and this analogous reference about sound, I would not be surprised if what they saw on Mt. Sinai were tongues of fire!

One more thing before I tie all of this together.

If you've ever seen the classic Cecil B. Demille movie, The Ten Commandments, you'll remember that after God gave Moses, Charlton Heston, the tablets containing the Law, Moses started walking back down the mountain toward the camp. While much of that movie isn't accurate, this event is. The Bible tells us that as Moses is coming down, he hears a ruckus in the camp (Exodus 32:17-18). When he gets there, he finds that because he'd been gone so long the people thought that he was dead and decided to make a graven image to the Lord.

Needless to say, God was flat-out angry and so was Moses. We read in Exodus 32:26-28 the following:

> *Then Moses stood in the gate of the camp, and said, "Who is on the LORD'S side? Let him come unto me." And all the sons of Levi gathered themselves together unto him. And he said unto them, "Thus saith the LORD God of Israel, 'Put every man his sword by his side, and go in and out from gate to gate throughout the camp, and slay every man his brother, and every man his companion, and every man his neighbour.' And the children of Levi did according to the word of Moses: and there fell of the people that day about three thousand men."*

Three thousand?

Let's do a comparison.

~ Moses went up to get God's Word, the Ten Commandments, on the first ever Day of Pentecost.

~ The Israelites were terrified because they saw fire and heard voices and trumpet sounds at the same time.

~ Because they were so scared, they told Moses that they didn't want to talk with God directly, or fellowship with Him face-to-face, but that only Moses should talk to God.

~ When Moses was gone so long, they lost faith, built an idol, and fell.

~ God was so angry with them that He killed three-thousand people. He probably would have killed more, but Moses interceded on their behalf and talked God out of killing all of them.

Fast forward about 1478 years, give or take, after Jesus came, was crucified and then rose. On that Day of Pentecost in Acts we see:

~ Hebrews from all over the world were gathered in Jerusalem.

~ This time 120 of them were inside and waited for God to show up.

~ They saw tongues of fire and heard a sound.

~ God filled His people with His Holy Spirit - His breath! (Remember at Mt. Sinai they were too scared to deal with Him face-to-face. He reversed that relationship in Acts 2.)

~ They spoke in other tongues.

~ 3,000 of them were saved that day and they were baptized and filled with His Holy Spirit. (The same number that God killed in Exodus 32).

God has always wanted to personally interact with us, His creation, even as far back as the OT. We were the ones who were not ready because of our fear, inadequacies and sin.

It took Jesus to bridge that divide and to fill us with His Spirit.

If you want your walk to be powerful, you have to have the generator of that Power, the Holy Spirit, living inside you. You might be saved because you believe and walk, but you will only find true victory on this path by moving down it with the Holy Spirit leading you and generating that Power.

Somebody should tell the Church that.

A Fractured Church

It's estimated that there are somewhere between 34,000 to 40,000 denominations worldwide. This weakened state of church unity is diluted even more when you add all the "non-denominational" congregations to that list. There are also more than 40,000 church organizations.

I'm an equal opportunity offender, so please forgive me if you find your particular church flavor here.

Within the Baptist camp alone, the list is endless. You have the American Baptist Association, American Baptist Churches, Association of Reformed Baptist Churches of America, Baptist Bible Fellowship International, Baptist General Conference, Central Baptist Association, Christian Unity Baptist Association, Free Will Baptist, etc. etc. And this list doesn't even take into consideration Southern Baptist denominations, which in and of themselves have about seven categories with tons of other denominations!

Then, of course, you also have an extensive list of Pentecostal or Charismatic denominations. We have denominations that play with snakes, we have denominations that won't allow instruments, and we have denominations where women can't cut their hair or wear makeup and have to wear long dresses. There are those denominations where everyone pretty much wears the same color, like black; we have denominations where men can't cut their facial hair and denominations where women are not allowed to teach. We have liberal denominations where almost everything is allowed, including things that the Bible specifically forbids, like homosexuality. We have conservative denominations which won't even allow a woman to speak in church (and that's not biblical). We have middle-of-the-road denominations where some things are allowed, but not everything. These groups remind me of James 1:8 where it talks about not being a "double-minded man".

What really baffles me are the denominations with "Unity" or "United" in titles. We are anything but united!

We have creeds, statements of faith, bylaws and rules. But do you know what we don't have?

Power from on high! *Dunamis!*

When was the last time you saw someone raised from the dead, miraculously healed or someone delivered from demons during your local Sunday morning service? Of course miracles do happen from time to time, but these kinds of demonstrations of God's Everlasting Power are the exception, not the rule!

> *And he said unto them, "Go ye into all the world, and preach the gospel to every creature. He that believeth and is baptized shall be saved; but he that believeth not shall be damned. And these signs shall follow them that believe: In my name shall they cast out devils; they shall speak with new tongues; they shall take up serpents; and if they drink any deadly thing, it shall not hurt them; they shall lay hands on the sick, and they shall recover. Mark 16:15-18*

Our failure in battle is our failure alone. Jesus has kept His promises. He wants to arm us with *dunamis*, but we have to be willing to take it. We seem to be stuck in our own doctrines, theologies and fears, refusing to lay down our lives for our King. We're not willing to die to ourselves in order to be the best we can be for Him. Along the way, we just keep making excuses as to why His promised Power doesn't follow His people.

Well, enough of the excuses. The hour is too late. The End of the Age is upon us and if you thought that those statistics about sin and sickness in the Church were bad, buckle up because it's about to get a lot worse.

We cannot afford to play the church, denomination or religion card anymore and expect our faith to survive.

Relationship Not Religion

What happens when you're going through life the best you can, but you know that there's something more? You know this can't be all. You may be frustrated because you've got thoughts a good Christians shouldn't have. You stumble and fall. There's no power in your walk and Jesus isn't as real as He should be.

People tend to take themselves out of the game because they're not a good Christian or they don't think they're "spiritual" enough to walk as He wants them to walk. But like I said in the very first chapter, there is no such thing as a good Christian, only forgiven ones saved through the blood of Jesus.

> *And a certain ruler asked him, saying, "Good Master, what shall I do to inherit eternal life?" And Jesus said unto him, "Why callest thou me good? None is good, save one, that is, God."* **Luke 18:18-19**

Not to belabor this point, but it's critical. I can't tell you how many times I've had people come to me and say that they just weren't "good" enough or that they couldn't be the "perfect Christian". One last time - there isn't any such thing! You can't be the perfect Christian, but even if you were the very best Christian that walked the earth, keep this in mind:

> *But we are all as an unclean thing, and all our righteousness are as filthy rags; and we all do fade as a leaf; and our iniquities, like the wind, have taken us away.* **Isaiah 64:6**

It is only by the Lord's shedding of His blood that your and my sin is taken away.

> *In whom we have redemption through his blood, the forgiveness of sins, according to the riches of his grace.* **Ephesians 1:7**

And it's only by the Holy Spirit that you can walk for Jesus as you're supposed to walk:

> *For they that are after the flesh do mind the things of the flesh; but they that are after the Spirit the things of the Spirit.* **Romans 8:5**

The only way, and I mean the only way, that the Spirit can truly guide us is for us to yield our hearts to Him continually. We're all supposed to work out our own salvation with fear and trembling.

> *Wherefore, my beloved, as ye have always obeyed, not as in my presence only, but now much more in my absence, work out your own salvation with fear and trembling.* **Philippians 2:12**

We need to stick our noses in His Word and study and meditate on it so it can wash through us. We need to seek His will in every part of our lives and confess our sin, thoughts and actions, to Him every day. When we fall, and we will, we have to be quick to repent and get up.

In the end this is a relationship between you and the Lord. This is not religion! Relationships cost us. They take time, effort, patience and yielding to the other person. There are expectations and requirements placed on us when we enter into a relationship.

When you get married, your husband or wife expects you to not sleep around. In a friendship relationship we respect one another and in a professional relationship, you do what an employer or client requires. Our relationship with the Lord is no different.

It is the Lord's unconditional love that saved us, but once we understand that love, and we truly want to grow in our relationship, we have to walk in obedience.

Changed

People are fearful of Jesus - the Person, His Preeminence, and His Power - because within that relationship there's a cost to us. Our salvation is a free gift:

> *For by grace are ye saved through faith; and that not of yourselves: it is the gift of God, not of works, lest any man should boast.* **Ephesians 2:9**

But it's not free in the sense that we don't have any responsibilities.

> *And he said to them all, "If any man will come after me, let him deny himself, and take up his cross daily, and follow me."* **Luke 9:23**

The power of the Holy Spirit living inside of us makes us walk as we should when we yield our will to Him. I've already quoted **2 Corinthians 5:17**, but it's worth repeating:

> *Therefore if any man be in Christ, he is a new creature: old things are passed away; behold, all things are become new.*

What does being a "new creation" mean in practicality?

The word "new" in this verse comes from the Greek word *kainós,* which literally means "new in quality or innovation". It can mean "fresh", as in a "fresh start" or it also can mean "not found exactly like this before."

"Creation" comes from the Greek word *ktísis,* which definitively means a creation "founded from nothing".

So let's break this down.

When we absolutely surrender our lives to Jesus, He - the I AM Who created all things - totally remakes you from scratch, fresh, from the thin air and as His new creation, you are unique. You are His new masterpiece.

> *For we are his workmanship, created in Christ Jesus unto good works, which God hath before ordained that we should walk in them.* **Ephesians 2:10**

At that point of our new creation we're a blank slate. That doesn't mean that as brand new Christians we're perfect. The opposite is true. Usually the new Christian has a ton of junk to work through. I know I did. I stumbled a lot and fell sometimes, but I kept repenting, kept sticking my nose in His Word and learning, and I kept yielding my will and my life on a daily basis to His Spirit.

The devil or our own flesh won't just roll over and die because Jesus has made us a New Creation. Every Christian has to recognize the carnal man inside, the flesh, and put it under the subjection of the Word of God.

~ *Watch and pray, that ye enter not into temptation: the spirit indeed is willing, but the flesh is weak.* **Matt 26:41**

~ *For the flesh lusteth against the Spirit, and the Spirit against the flesh: and these are contrary the one to the other: so that ye cannot do the things that ye would.* **Galatians 5:17**

~ *For when ye were the servants of sin, ye were free from righteousness.* **Romans 6:20**

~ *Among whom also we all had our conversation in times past in the lusts of our flesh, fulfilling the desires of the flesh and of the mind; and were by nature the children of wrath, even as others.* **Ephesians 2:3**

When we do subdue our flesh and fully submit our lives to God, He is able to shape us into His image. It is then that He can do miracles to, through and around us.

~ *I am crucified with Christ: nevertheless I live; yet not I, but Christ liveth in me: and the life which I now live in the flesh I live by the faith of the Son of God, who loved me, and gave himself for me.* **Galatians 2:20**

~ *If there be therefore any consolation in Christ, if any comfort of love, if any fellowship of the Spirit, if any bowels and mercies, fulfil ye my joy, that ye be likeminded, having the same love, being of one accord, of one mind. Let nothing be done through strife or vainglory; but in lowliness of mind let each esteem other better than themselves. Look not every man on his own things, but every man also on the things of others. Let this mind be in you, which was also in Christ Jesus.* **Philippians 2:1-5**

~ *I beseech you therefore, brethren, by the mercies of God, that ye present your bodies a living sacrifice, holy, acceptable unto God, which is your reasonable service. And be not conformed to this world: but be ye transformed by the renewing of your mind, that ye may prove what is that good, and acceptable, and perfect, will of God.* **Romans 12:1-2**

~ *To speak evil of no man, to be no brawlers, but gentle, shewing all meekness unto all men. For we ourselves also were sometimes foolish, disobedient, deceived, serving divers lusts and pleasures, living in malice and envy, hateful, and hating one another. But after that the kindness and love of God our Saviour toward man appeared, not by works of righteousness which we have done, but according to his mercy he saved us, by the washing of regeneration, and renewing of the Holy Ghost; which he shed on us abundantly through Jesus Christ our Saviour.* **Titus 3:2-6**

~ *For we are his workmanship, created in Christ Jesus unto good works, which God hath before ordained that we should walk in them.* **Ephesians 2:10**

This is not change as a result of striving to be a good Christian. As I said earlier, these attributes are a natural result of God's Holy Spirit growing them out of our lives when we lay down our will before Him. **Galatians 5:22-26** talks about the "fruit of the Spirit" being self-evident.

> *But the fruit of the Spirit is love, joy, peace, long-suffering, gentleness, goodness, faith, meekness, temperance: against such there is no law. And they that are Christ's have crucified the flesh with the affections and lusts. If we live in the Spirit, let us also walk in the Spirit. Let us not be desirous of vain glory, provoking one another, envying one another.*

There are many Believers who are trying to walk this Christian path the best they know how. In the other extreme, it seems like everybody wants to be faith-charged, to get out of the boat and "Walk with Jesus". When we take our eyes off Him is when we sink.

The mainstream-corporate-Church which professes faith in Jesus Christ has taken its eyes off the only One Who can keep them from sinking. That which used to represent the lordship of Jesus Christ has now become a capsized, sinking ship.

But there is hope. In this hour, Jesus has shown up along your path and desires to open your eyes to the revelation of His person and His Power. Set aside your preconceived ideas, your doctrine, what people have told you, your fears of the supernatural realm and go straight to the Word. Look at His promises there for you to live a powerful and effectual life. Don't make excuses for the text, but embrace the truth of the message of His Holy Spirit power.

The Shaking

I believe that God wants to shake some paradigms. The disciples were specifically told to stay and wait for the promise of the Father. This is not a religious or theological statement. It is a biblical fact.

Here's another fact that's going to get some of you mad at me again. In the scriptures the only indication that people had received the Holy Spirit was that they began to speak in other tongues as the Spirit gave them utterance.

> *And when the day of Pentecost was fully come, they were all with one accord in one place. And suddenly there came a sound from heaven as of a rushing mighty wind, and it filled all the house where they were sitting and there appeared unto them cloven tongues like as of fire, and it sat upon each of them. And they were all filled with the Holy Ghost, and began to speak with other tongues, as the Spirit gave them utterance. Acts 2:1-4*

> *And it came to pass, that, while Apollos was at Corinth, Paul having passed through the upper coasts came to Ephesus: and finding certain disciples. He said unto them, "Have ye received the Holy Ghost since ye believed?" And they said unto him, "We have not so much as heard whether there be any Holy Ghost." And he said unto them, "Unto what then were ye baptized?" And they said, "Unto John's baptism." Then said Paul, "John verily baptized with the baptism of repentance, saying unto the people, that they should believe on him which should come after him, that is, on Christ Jesus. When they heard this, they were baptized in the name of the Lord Jesus. And when Paul had laid his hands upon them, the Holy Ghost came on them; and they spake with tongues, and prophesied. Acts 19:1-6*

I know that as some of you read these scriptures you're already trying to reason them away with doctrine, but you do so at your own peril. I'm not speaking to you from the standpoint of a denomination or church. I'm simply recounting what is in the Word.

And besides, if you are right that tongues isn't for today, where is the evidence of your being baptized with the Spirit? Where is the Power that God has promised you?

Speaking in tongues isn't the only evidence, but it is the first evidence. If you've raised someone from the dead, laid your hands on them and healed them or even operated in one of the other gifts that we are promised, then you are certainly showing the evidence of being filled with the Spirit.

However, if all you have is doctrine and you're sitting there arguing with the words on this page because you need to justify the lack of supernatural Power in your walk, then it sounds like more of the same excuses.

My advice to you is to stop making excuses this very minute and repent. Then, get on your face before God and earnestly ask Him to give you what He promised, the in-filling of the Holy Spirit. Don't stop asking until He does. While you're at it, surrender your life to Him anew. Ask Him to search your heart and show you those things in your life that you've held back or taken back from Him. Ask Him to forgive you and change you. Ask Him to fill you with *dunamis*.

> *And I say unto you, Ask, and it shall be given you; seek, and ye shall find; knock, and it shall be opened unto you. For every one that asketh receiveth; and he that seeketh findeth; and to him that knocketh it shall be opened. If a son shall ask bread of any of you that is a father, will he give him a stone? Or if he ask a fish, will he for a fish give him a serpent? Or if he shall ask an egg, will he offer him a scorpion? If ye then, being evil, know how to give good gifts unto your children: how much more shall your heavenly Father give the Holy Spirit to them that ask him?* **Luke 11:9-13**

One of the most important things that Christians need to understand about God's Everlasting Power is what Jesus Himself said.

> *But ye shall receive power, after that the Holy Ghost is come upon you: and ye shall be witnesses unto me both in Jerusalem, and in all Judaea, and in Samaria, and unto the uttermost part of the earth.* **Acts 1:18**

If you want His Power, His *dunamis*, do whatever it takes to be filled with His Spirit.

The Word of Power

Today, there's very little preaching under the anointing.

Here's what I mean: Henry Gruver is a personal friend of mine. As many of you may know, he's a powerful man of God who has a well-known, prayer-walking ministry. I have fellowshipped with and learned much from this man over the years.

If I have a question, or thought, I can get on the phone right now and call him. He'll not only take my call, but will probably ask me how my family and I are doing. He knows them too. We are friends and brothers.

Contrast that with the President of the United States. I know who the President is and I can tell you about many things that he's done in his time in office via the news reports that I've read or the stories I've heard. I probably could even dig up the phone number to the Whitehouse switchboard and call him, but he certainly wouldn't take my call or enter into a conversation with me. That's because I only know him based upon articles, pictures and his title. I have no direct connection to him.

Today most pastors and teachers talk about the Word of God in general terms but they never invoke the Word from the pulpit, thus enabling it as the sword it is designed to be.

> *For the word of God is quick, and powerful, and sharper than any two-edged sword, piercing even to the dividing asunder of soul and spirit, and of the joints and marrow, and is a discerner of the thoughts and intents of the heart.* **Hebrews 4:12**

The KJV version doesn't really do this verse justice, so let's take a look at it in the original Greek. By the way, I use the KJV of scripture for copyright reasons, but I always suggest that you take the time to study the Word out for yourself and get down to the original language with a lexicon. There are several free ones available online.

A closer look at this verse allows us to understand the difference between using the Word as a simple reference, or using it effectively under the anointing of the Holy Spirit.

The word "Word" is a title and comes from the Greek word *logos*. It means a word that embodies an idea. When this word is found in the NT, it usually refers to the written Word of God, or is used as a title.

The word for "quick" is *zōn* which means "to live" or living.

The word for "powerful" is *energēs* which means "to work" or active. It's also the word from which we get our word "energy".

"Sharp" comes from *tomōteros* and pretty much means "sharp - like a sword."

So the first part of the verse would be better translated, "The written Word of God is a living, active and full-of-energy sharp sword."

That should cause you to ask the question, "How can a sword, or an inanimate object, be alive?"

Because that sword, the Word of God, or the Bible, is not inanimate! Although you only see it as ink on paper, there's something supernatural about those words that transcend our 3D universe to make it a living, breathing entity! Crazy? There's textual proof and we've already seen it:

> *In the beginning was the Word, and the Word was with God, and the Word was God. The same was in the beginning with God. All things were made by him; and without him was not any thing made that was made.* **John 1:1-2**

Again, the word for "Word" here is *logos* and it's a title, the title for Jesus: we know this because we've already seen a direct correlation to this verse in *Colossians 1:13-17*:

> *Who hath delivered us from the power of darkness, and hath translated us into the kingdom of his dear Son in whom we have redemption through his blood, even the forgiveness of sins, who is the image of*

the invisible God, the firstborn of every creature. For by him were all things created, that are in heaven, and that are in earth, visible and invisible, whether they be thrones, or dominions, or principalities, or powers: all things were created by him, and for him. And he is before all things, and by him all things consist.

Jesus is the Word of God that is sharper than a two-edged sword and is able to pierce between soul and spirit, and physically divide flesh, bone and marrow. He's also the One Who can discern or judge the thoughts and intentions of the heart.

The Bible is a 2-D representation of Who Jesus is and with the Holy Spirit, the *ruach hakodesh,* the very breath of God, it is somehow able to have a physical and a supernatural effect on our 3-D universe!

But what pastors and teachers fail to do today is to activate that living, breathing, discerning power from the pulpit. Instead, these seeker-friendly, church-growth-minded leaders tell stories, scripture-laced motivational speeches or even talk about things that have nothing to do with God or the Bible! And we wonder why Believers are drowning in sin and sickness?

There's also another word for "word" used in the NT. It's the Greek word *rhéma.* This word gives a fuller understanding of God's Word as we see in *John 6:63:*

It is the spirit that quickeneth; the flesh profiteth nothing: the words that I speak unto you, they are spirit, and they are life.

Breaking this scripture down to the original Greek, we see the Spirit here is pneuma, which literally means "wind". This goes along with the idea of the Holy Spirit being God's very breath. Jesus uses the phrase "the words", a plural form of the word rhema, meaning "the spoken words". So in essence, it is God's voice carried on His wind or breath.

The rest of the verse pulls all of these thoughts together in a cohesive idea when Jesus says, "the words (*rhéma*) that I speak unto you, they are spirit (*pneuma*), and they are life."

Rhéma is used some seventy times in the NT, far less than logos, but the concept is very powerful. These rhéma words of the Bible carry life in and of themselves. So this word, logos, that is itself alive, when spoken in faith, imparts God's life to the Believer. It's like God giving His son or daughter supernatural CPR!

God uses His logos Word to speak His rhéma word to us. The more we read the written Word, storing it up inside us like a battery containing electricity, the more God can speak instant rhéma words to us.

Something important to remember is that God's rhéma words always correspond with His written logos Word. They will never contradict one another because they are in essence the same communication from the Master, just in different ways. For instance, a Christian walking with and hearing from the Lord can never say, "The Holy Spirit told me that it was okay to sleep with that person that wasn't my husband or wife because they're really my 'soul mate' and I didn't get it right when I got married." The Bible expressly forbids adultery and thus, God will never say that it's okay with Him.

How God handles our disobedience is another issue, but my point is that the Holy Spirit speaking to our hearts through the rhéma Word will never contradict the written Word. When used properly, these instant rhéma words guide us when we listen and act on them.

There's a huge difference between logos and rhéma. In church circles, the end-time outpouring of the Holy Spirit is often referred to as the "latter rain". But you need to understand that hearing God's voice is so important that you won't get the latter rain until you get the real rhéma.

Henry Gruver and I can personally talk, but I'll probably never get a phone call from the President. Yet, you and I are able to have a direct conversation with the Creator of the universe via the Holy Spirit using the rhéma Word. Who needs the President anyway?

The effective use of the Word of God through preaching and teaching can powerfully change people's lives forever.

Everything else is just noise.

Chapter 5

A Prevailing Kingdom

Now when John had heard in the prison the works of Christ, he sent two of his disciples, and said unto him, "Art thou he that should come, or do we look for another?" Jesus answered and said unto them, "Go and shew John again those things which ye do hear and see: The blind receive their sight, and the lame walk, the lepers are cleansed, and the deaf hear, the dead are raised up, and the poor have the gospel preached to them. And blessed is he, whosoever shall not be offended in me."

And as they departed, Jesus began to say unto the multitudes concerning John, "What went ye out into the wilderness to see? A reed shaken with the wind? But what went ye out for to see? A man clothed in soft raiment? Behold, they that wear soft clothing are in kings' houses. But what went ye out for to see? A prophet? Yea, I say unto you, and more than a prophet. For this is he, of whom it is written, 'Behold, I send my messenger before thy face, which shall prepare thy way before thee.' Verily I say unto you: Among them that are born of women there hath not risen a greater than John the Baptist. Notwithstanding he that is least in the kingdom of heaven is greater than he. And from the days of John the Baptist until now the kingdom of heaven suffereth violence, and the violent take it by force.

Matthew 11:9-12

At the Cross everybody expected, and wanted, Jesus to do what religion would say to do. What they lost track of was the sinful nature of man. They wanted Him to restore the physical kingdom of Israel in our 3D realm. They were carnal men and women expecting a carnal solution.

I suggest that today we're no different.

The Power of the Cross

In reality, what those bystanders really saw that day at Jesus' crucifixion was something beyond their expectations. They witnessed the supernatural pervading our physical 3D reality.

Remember the scene:

 Jesus was placed on the Cross at 9 a.m. - *And it was the third hour, and they crucified him.* **Mark 15:25**

 It became dark from noon until 3 a.m. - *Now from the sixth hour there was darkness over all the land unto the ninth hour.* **Matthew 27:45**

 In the OT, darkness was associated with judgment and the people of that day would know this very well (remember, the NT hadn't been written yet).

 As an example, the ninth plague of the exodus event saw darkness over Egypt for a period of three days. The darkness was so thick that it could be felt (*Ex. 10:21-22*). At the end of that plague of darkness, all the firstborn sons of Egypt died (*Ex. 11:4-5*). Darkness preceded death.

 While Jesus hung from that Cross, God poured out His judgment on His own firstborn son, Jesus, for you and me - *For he hath made him to be sin for us, who knew no sin; that we might be made the righteousness of God in him.* **2 Cor 5:21**; *Who his own self bare our sins in his own body on the tree, that we, being dead to sins, should live unto righteousness: by whose stripes ye were healed.* **1 Peter 2:24**

I believe that every power of Hell, every demon and every principality had all gathered around the Cross in that darkness to mock, scorn and ridicule Jesus. How shocked they must have been when Jesus died and then went into hell to preach to the souls that were held captive by the enemy. It's like He said, "I'm here!"

The angels must have also been shocked by the unfolding of these events. Recently I had a friend say to me, "The angels absolutely knew who Jesus was and they had to be spitting mad because they could only sit there and watch how people treated Him." As I told my friend, we have to understand that as the angels observed the crucifixion, they didn't understand salvation's plan. Only God the Father knew what He'd planned to do all along because there's certain "secret things of the Lord" that only He knows.

The secret things belong unto the LORD our God: but those things which are revealed belong unto us and to our children for ever, that we may do all the words of this law. **Deut 29:29**

Jesus had to die and take upon Himself the sin of the world, past, present and future and He did it willingly.

No man taketh it from me, but I lay it down of myself. I have power to lay it down, and I have power to take it again. **John 10:18**

Thinkest thou that I cannot now pray to my Father, and he shall presently give me more than twelve legions of angels? But how then shall the scriptures be fulfilled, that thus it must be? **Matt 26:53-54**

And every priest standeth daily ministering and offering oftentimes the same sacrifices, which can never take away sins: But this man, after he had offered one sacrifice for sins for ever, sat down on the right hand of God; From henceforth expecting till his enemies be made his footstool. For by one offering he hath perfected for ever them that are sanctified. Whereof the Holy Ghost also is a witness to us: for after that he had said before, "This is the covenant that I will make with them after those days, saith the Lord, I will put my laws into their hearts, and in their minds will I write them, and their sins and iniquities will I remember no more." Now where remission of these is, there is no more offering for sin. **Hebrews 10:11-18**

Jesus didn't have to die. **He chose to die.**

Jesus knew what it was going to take to bridge the gap between God and us. He's already paid that price and made provision for us to live a powerful and effectual life. The vision of you walking in that Power is absolutely yours if you ask.

This vision, this understanding, this relationship with Jesus is available to all who will seek God with a repentant heart and simply cry out and say, "Help me, Lord! Reveal Yourself to me!"

Crossing the Kingdom's Threshold

When we come to know Jesus He immediately makes us a new creation and places us in a new kingdom. Quantum Physics calls this "superpositioning", the ability to be in two states or two places at one time.

When we become new creations, the redemptive Power of God suddenly begins to motivate and empower our lives. Essentially, it's that same resurrection power that pulled Jesus out of the grave!

Jesus said, "My kingdom is not of this earth," but at the same time we're told to pray for the kingdom to come.

After this manner therefore pray ye: Our Father which art in heaven, Hallowed be thy name. Thy kingdom come. Thy will be done in earth, as it is in heaven. **Matt 6:9-10**

So we have a kingdom that is "now," but also "not yet". We are citizens of this kingdom with all the rights and advantages of that citizenship. We are also to pray for the full fruition of that kingdom to manifest according to the will of the Father. That's mind-bending.

So if we can't see this kingdom, how do we know it even exists?

We see the evidence of this invisible kingdom in the regenerating power of God working in people's lives and we also see evidence of a real enemy to that kingdom.

The Word makes it clear that we are opposed by demonic forces who seek to destroy us and the kingdom of our King.

> *Be sober, be vigilant; because your adversary the devil, as a roaring lion, walketh about, seeking whom he may devour.* ***1 Peter 5:8***

> *For we wrestle not against flesh and blood, but against principalities, against powers, against the rulers of the darkness of this world, against spiritual wickedness in high places.* ***Eph 6:12***

Jesus told us that there's a power of the enemy that can hurt you, but the Lord also promised to give us Power that's greater than that of the enemy.

In the end, the devil can only go as far as the people of God let him.

The devil is compared to a lion, seeking whom he "may" devour, but Jesus IS the Lion of the Tribe of Judah with a two-edged sword that comes out of his mouth. This is our King and He can lay waste to nations.

> *And one of the elders saith unto me, Weep not: behold, the Lion of the tribe of Judah, the Root of David, hath prevailed to open the book, and to loose the seven seals thereof.* ***Rev 5:5***

> *And out of his mouth goeth a sharp sword, that with it he should smite the nations: and he shall rule them with a rod of iron: and he treadeth the winepress of the fierceness and wrath of Almighty God.* ***Rev 19:15***

> *And he had in his right hand seven stars: and out of his mouth went a sharp twoedged sword: and his countenance was as the sun shineth in his strength.* ***Rev 1:16***

Jesus doesn't put on boxing gloves and step into the ring with the devil like it's some competition. The devil is a created being. Jesus has total dominion over him and the Lord has given us His dominion to fight the adversary here on earth by using the Power (dunamis) that's available to us via the Holy Spirit.

A supernatural war, carried out on this physical plane, is being waged against the Christian. Satan knows that his time is short so he is throwing everything he can at the believer.

Remember that these demonic entities are powers and principalities (Eph 6:12). These powers have the ability to affect our physical life, but our King has not left us powerless against them. He's armed us with everything we need, but we have to want to take up those arms.

> *Finally, my brethren, be strong in the Lord, and in the power of his might. Put on the whole armour of God, that ye may be able to stand against the wiles of the devil. For we wrestle not against flesh and blood, but against principalities, against powers, against the rulers of the darkness of this world, against spiritual wickedness in high places. Wherefore take unto you the whole armour of God, that ye may be able to withstand in the evil day, and having done all, to stand. Stand therefore, having your loins girt about with truth, and having on the breastplate of righteousness and your feet shod with the preparation of the gospel of peace. Above all, taking the shield of faith, wherewith ye shall be able to quench all the fiery darts of the wicked and take the helmet of salvation, and the sword of the Spirit, which is the word of God, praying always with all prayer and supplication in the Spirit, and watching thereunto with all perseverance and supplication for all saints.* ***Eph 6:10-18***

That's the Power of His might, not our own, not our programs, not our churches. In this hand-to-hand combat, you have to be able to stand in the battle and trade blows with the enemy. Paul tells us to pray always in the Spirit, but how do you pray in the Spirit unless you are filled with the Spirit?

God has made His living, breathing and powerful Holy Spirit available to us to infill us so we can defeat the enemy. But are you willing to receive this gift of God? Or will you continue to make doctrinal excuses or lackadaisically walk through this supernatural relationship?

Your spiritual life depends on your answer.

Nothing in ourselves, apart from Jesus and the promise of the Spirit of God, will give us true victory in our lives. When we accept the Word of the Lord in faith, and see His Power and strength manifested in our lives, we are able to walk in His promise of Power.

The choice is yours.

> *God is our refuge and strength, a very present help in trouble. Therefore will not we fear, though the earth be removed, and though the mountains be carried into the midst of the sea.* **Psalm 46:1-2.**

Power in the Blood

Would you be free from the burden of sin?

There's pow'r in the blood, pow'r in the blood;

Would you o'er evil a victory win?

There's wonderful pow'r in the blood.

There is pow'r, pow'r, wonder-working pow'r

In the blood of the Lamb;

There is pow'r, pow'r, wonder-working pow'r

In the precious blood of the Lamb.

Would you be free from your passion and pride?

There's pow'r in the blood, pow'r in the blood;

Come for a cleansing to Calvary's tide;

There's wonderful pow'r in the blood.

There is pow'r, pow'r, wonder-working pow'r

In the blood of the Lamb;

There is pow'r, pow'r, wonder-working pow'r

In the precious blood of the Lamb.

Would you be whiter, much whiter than snow?

There's pow'r in the blood, pow'r in the blood...

Sin-stains are lost in its life-giving flow;

There's wonderful pow'r in the blood.

There is pow'r, pow'r, wonder-working pow'r

In the blood of the Lamb;

There is pow'r, pow'r, wonder-working pow'r

In the precious blood of the Lamb.

Would you do service for Jesus your King?

There's pow'r in the blood, pow'r in the blood;

Would you live daily His praises to sing?

There's wonderful pow'r in the blood.

HELP 3

His Everlasting Presence

Thou wilt shew me the path of life.

In thy presence is fullness of joy.

At thy right hand there are pleasures for evermore.

Psalm 16:11

Presence

As we begin this H.E.L.P. on God's Everlasting Presence, there's a fallacy, a misunderstanding that the Lord has prompted me to clear up right away. This misunderstanding is at the root of those false doctrines that are being spread from many pulpits throughout the world. It's contained in statements from Believers and non-believers alike, which start with, "If God loves me, why does He allow _____". Fill in the blank.

It's true that God loves us and 1 John 4:8 says, *"God is love,"* but God being love is only one aspect of who He is.

God is also righteous,

> *O righteous Father, the world hath not known thee: but I have known thee, and these have known that thou hast sent me.* **John 17:25**

God is Holy,

> *Because it is written, Be ye holy; for I am holy.* **1 Peter 1:16**

Just like there are many facets to your personality and life as a human being, because we are made in the image of God (Genesis 1:27), there are many facets to God that are independent from one another.

This is why it drives me crazy when I hear someone say, "God has set me free!" and then they live however they want, even if it's in direct opposition to the Word of God.

The freedom that Jesus bought for us by His own blood is freedom from us having to sin!

> *For the law of the Spirit of life in Christ Jesus hath made me free from the law of sin and death.* **Romans 8:2**

That freedom is not to do whatever we want and still expect Him to bless us regardless of our actions. The depth of our relationship with Him is contingent upon the effort that we put into that relationship. The byproduct of our relationship with the Lord is our being able to enter into His Presence.

God's Presence is a separate facet from His love. It's also a separate facet from His forgiveness… and His mercy, and His righteousness and the other aspects of His character.

Our recognizing and accepting one part of God does not necessarily guarantee us that we will experience another part of God. You can receive God's forgiveness and be saved because Romans 10:13 says,

> *For whosoever shall call upon the name of the Lord shall be saved.*

But your salvation by the Lord is separate from you being able to dwell in His Presence where Psalm 16:11 says, *"In His presence there is fullness of joy."*

It should be our desire to enter into and dwell in God's Presence, but that entering and dwelling is not a guarantee.

And believe me when I tell you that you need to be in His Presence on a regular basis. That's because the world has gone nuts!

No longer can we use the future tense to describe the End Times canvas because, as I said earlier, everything that the enemy can unleash upon mankind is being unleashed in this day and age. If there was ever a time when the children of the Most High needed His Presence to lead and guide them, to protect and provide for them, and to fill them with His joy and peace, it's right now!

As things become even darker in the physical realm, if people won't fall to their knees and accept God's forgiveness through the Lord Jesus Christ, they'll be driven to their knees by the most perilous circumstances that have ever been seen in the history of the world.

It is in the midst of the earth's enveloping darkness, that the promise of God's Everlasting Presence is very real and constant. Everyone has a built-in hunger to know His Presence, which cannot be found in buildings or philosophies of men. It can only be found in the company of the King.

Churches are filled with people who say they know the Lord, but are clueless about what His Presence is. In 2 Cor 3:17, Paul tells us:

Now the Lord is that Spirit: and where the Spirit of the Lord is, there is liberty.

Believers today are bound by the same problems and trials as people who don't know the Lord. Obviously there's something that God's people are missing here when it comes to His Everlasting Presence. This H.E.L.P., while it may sound at times religious or formal, is intended to give you a real pathway to that Presence. This is not about stroking you on the back and telling you everything is going to be alright. If you want that kind of message, just sit in any mega-church sermon this coming Sunday. You'll hear plenty of platitudes but very little, if any, practical advice about how to get into the Lord's Everlasting Presence.

One caution before we begin: Do not mistake my words for legalism. I'm just being real. If you've ever been in His Presence, there's nothing else in the world like it. You'll want to go back again and again. His Presence will give you peace. It will give you strength. It will give you true joy. And it will give you hope. If all who call themselves a Believer or go to church knew what it was like, we as a people would be much more effective in the world and lead more satisfied lives than we do. The fact is, we are not. In these days, we're under attack and need His continual Presence more than ever.

God's supernatural indwelling of the Believer is the tangible manifestation of His promise to never leave us or forsake us. I maintain that anybody who has a life encounter with Jesus will be able to walk through life with Jesus. I believe anyone who simply has head-knowledge of Jesus will be persuaded by argument or by coercion against a real relationship with Him.

That indwelling of His Presence is not as complicated as you may think. First, through the simple act of repenting of our sin, telling God what He already knows, and accepting God's forgiveness through the Lord Jesus Christ and turning away from our sin, we start down the road. From that point, like any relationship, coming into and remaining in His Presence takes effort. We have to continually speak to Him, continually seek Him and continually seek to do His will in our lives.

For I know the thoughts that I think toward you, saith the LORD, thoughts of peace, and not of evil, to give you an expected end. Then shall ye call upon me, and ye shall go and pray unto me, and I will hearken unto you. And ye shall seek me, and find me, when ye shall search for me with all your heart.
Jeremiah 29:11-13

In this section you'll begin to see what it really means to have God's Everlasting Presence in your life throughout your days, your months and your years. In doing so, you'll also begin to glean the difference between the ways of God and the heart of God. When you understand the heart of God, why God does what He does, you come right back to justice and mercy. You also come right back to the Holiness of God that is not present in mankind outside of that which is imparted to him through Jesus Christ and the Holy Spirit.

When we allow God to shape us and to conform us into His image, only then do we become a fitting home for His Everlasting Presence.

Chapter 6
A Biblical Assembly

And let us consider one another to provoke unto love and to good works, not forsaking the assembling of ourselves together, as the manner of some is; but exhorting one another. And so much the more, as ye see the day approaching.

Hebrews 10:24-25

Earlier in this book, I said that I hoped to shake some people's paradigms and here is one of those moments. Please consider this section very carefully. If you're a Christian who loves God but is stuck in the modern church paradigm, the truths contained within this chapter could change your life.

From the time that most of us get saved, we're taught to "find a good church" to fellowship in and be taught from, but even though this may appear to be sound advice, it's a trap! Here's why.

Nowhere in the NT and beyond is "church" equated with the Presence of the Lord. I specifically say 'beyond' the NT because the advent of Jesus and His crucifixion and resurrection changed how the Believer should worship forever.

People who go to church religiously, go for three reasons:

1. **Guilt** - They know they messed up and know that they are unworthy. They go to meet the One Who they instinctively know can forgive them and change them. Instead of finding a real personal connection with the God of forgiveness, most of the time they're presented with only ritual and rules, be it modern or traditional.

2. **Hunger** - They want to know more about God and go there to be taught. The problem is that, instead of finding His Presence, they're often presented with liturgy, traditions, habits, rules and dogma and other nonsense that has nothing to do with finding the Presence of God, generally speaking. That's because any church that doesn't preach the word of God in its fullness, totality and in its power might as well call themselves The Country Club.

3. **Habit** - For these people, finding God's Presence may not even be in the equation. They have become entrenched in the religious system of this world and as a consequence, they're only going through the motions of a walk with the Lord. Because there's no power in their lives to combat the enemy, outside of church it's hard to see any difference between these badge-wearing Christians and the world. The Presence of God is nowhere in their lives nor do many of them even care to enter into His Presence. They're happy with things just the way they are.

So are there people who go to church who really want to find the Presence of God?

Absolutely!

And please don't misunderstand. I'm not saying don't go to church. I am saying don't go to a dead church that doesn't preach the Word. I'm also saying that church should be a supplement to your efforts to find the Lord's Presence and not the mainstay of your walk.

Going to church isn't the way to find His Everlasting Presence.

Important Definitions

But while he thought on these things, behold, the angel of the Lord appeared unto him in a dream, saying, "Joseph, thou son of David, fear not to take unto thee Mary thy wife: for that which is conceived in her is of the Holy Ghost. And she shall bring forth a son, and thou shalt call His name JESUS: for He shall save his people from their sins. Now all this was done, that it might be fulfilled which was spoken of the Lord by the prophet, saying, 'Behold, a virgin shall be with child, and shall bring forth a son, and they shall call His name Emmanuel, which being interpreted is, God with us.'" Matthew 1:20-23

The word Emmanuel means "God With Us", not "the Building for Us".

And yet, in the two-thousand years since Jesus physically came to earth and ascended to the right hand of the Father, we continue to hear religion tell us that we need to build the next monumental edifice in order for the people to come and worship. It doesn't matter what denomination that you belong to, most of the time the building in which you're meeting has become synonymous with the Presence of the Lord.

Not only is this factually wrong, it's just not biblical.

There are two important words that will help you understand exactly how we should meet together in fellowship.

The first word from the Greek is *ekklésia* or *ecclesia* and it literally means, "called out" or "called forth". It comes from another Greek word, *ekklésian*, which means "a gathering of citizens called out from their homes into some public place" or an assembly.

Used some 115 times in the NT, it originates from the Greek understanding of a government assembly in ancient Athens where important official decisions were made.[6]

Jesus says the following out of Matthew 16:18:

> And I say also unto thee, that thou art Peter, and upon this rock I will build my church; and the gates of hell shall not prevail against it.

The word for Peter is *petros*, which literally in Greek means "pebble". He then referred to Himself as the "rock" from the Greek word *petra* which means "a mass of connected rock".

So from that point, was He saying "I'm this huge, unmovable, unstoppable, unbreakable mass of connected rock and I want you to build monumental edifices all over the earth on that foundation?"

Absolutely not, because when we complete the sentence, He says, "On this rock I will build my *ekklésia*".

Drilling down to the original language does two things. First, it pretty much shoots a hole in the Catholic Church's doctrine of Peter being the first Pope. With such a terrible doctrinal foundation, it puts into question all of their other teaching given the fact that they are so completely wrong on this fundamental point.

Second, Jesus is telling us that His people will be gathered together on Himself as the foundation of their lives. That has nothing to do with buildings! In fact, translators in the KJV and most other versions have substituted the word "church" for "gathering". More on the word "church" in a moment.

The other word that we need to understand when it comes to the Everlasting Presence of the Lord in our gatherings is the Greek word *koinonia*. This word is particularly interesting because it has multiple meanings.

It can mean to share something that you have with other people, i.e. food, thoughts, efforts, etc.

It can also mean to have contact with people, to interact with them on a personal basis and most commonly it means fellowship.

Lastly, another meaning is to contribute financially to something like a tithe or offering.

Here is the use of the word in a couple of different places in scripture:

> That which we have seen and heard declare we unto you, that ye also may have fellowship with us: and truly our fellowship is with the Father, and with his Son Jesus Christ. *1 John 1:3*

> If we say that we have fellowship with him, and walk in darkness, we lie, and do not the truth: But if we walk in the light, as he is in the light, we have fellowship one with another, and the blood of Jesus Christ his Son cleanseth us from all sin. *1 John 1:6-7*

> And they continued stedfastly in the apostles' doctrine and fellowship, and in breaking of bread, and in prayers. *Acts 2:42*

There is no singular word equivalent in the English language to describe the broadness of the meaning of *koinonia*. The word in the original language gives the Christian a depiction of someone who has an interactive, vibrant and well-rounded relationship between God and fellow Believers who are all sharing

---

6 Wikipedia, "Ecclesia (ancient Athens)", last updated July 1, 2018, https://en.wikipedia.org/wiki/Ecclesia_(ancient_Athens).

a new life through Jesus. The idea of *koinonia* captures the entirety of that relationship with the Believer's active participation in Christian community in sharing spiritual blessings as well as physical and material blessings.

What neither *ecclesia* nor *koinonia* is talking about is a church building, or organized religion for that matter!

These words are centered squarely on the idea of relationship, however over the past two millennia, since the Lord ascended to the Father, the meaning and use of these words have become skewed. Christians today have substituted these acts of relationship and interaction with going to a building on Sunday and expecting God to show up.

How could this happen?

Can God Be Contained?

For whatever reason, men seem to think that we have to memorialize and compartmentalize God. This isn't only a modern day Church problem, it's been going on for millennia.

David wanted to build the Temple, a house, for the Lord. God didn't let him build it, but promised that his seed, Solomon, would build it.

> *And it came to pass that night, that the word of the LORD came unto Nathan, saying, "Go and tell my servant David, 'Thus saith the LORD, Shalt thou build me an house for me to dwell in? Whereas I have not dwelt in any house since the time that I brought up the children of Israel out of Egypt, even to this day, but have walked in a tent and in a tabernacle. In all the places wherein I have walked with all the children of Israel spake I a word with any of the tribes of Israel, whom I commanded to feed my people Israel, saying, Why build ye not me an house of cedar?' "Now therefore so shalt thou say unto my servant David, 'Thus saith the LORD of hosts, I took thee from the sheepcote, from following the sheep, to be ruler over my people, over Israel: And I was with thee whithersoever thou wentest, and have cut off all thine enemies out of thy sight, and have made thee a great name, like unto the name of the great men that are in the earth. Moreover I will appoint a place for my people Israel, and will plant them, that they may dwell in a place of their own, and move no more; neither shall the children of wickedness afflict them any more, as beforetime, And as since the time that I commanded judges to be over my people Israel, and have caused thee to rest from all thine enemies. Also the LORD telleth thee that he will make thee an house. And when thy days be fulfilled, and thou shalt sleep with thy fathers, I will set up thy seed after thee, which shall proceed out of thy bowels, and I will establish his kingdom. He shall build an house for my name, and I will stablish the throne of his kingdom for ever. 14I will be his father, and he shall be my son. If he commit iniquity, I will chasten him with the rod of men, and with the stripes of the children of men: But my mercy shall not depart away from him, as I took it from Saul, whom I put away before thee. And thine house and thy kingdom shall be established for ever before thee: thy throne shall be established for ever. 2 Samuel 7:4-16*

It was like God said, "Seriously, David? I've been moving around with you all this whole time and I've done all this stuff and now you want to put Me in a box?" Remember that He loved David and in the end He said, "However, because it's you I'll make sure that your kingdom is set up and that you go down in history. And I'll also make sure, because you want it, that your son builds the house."

God didn't allow David to build the Temple, but let Solomon build it. Why? Was God in some desperate need for an edifice to call His home?

Of course not.

He allowed Solomon to build it because they, Israel, wanted to build it, but it wasn't God's ideal. As parents, often times we'll acquiesce to our children's gifts even though we may not have wanted them in the first place.

I definitely remember a meal or two fixed for me by my kids that I would have rather skipped. But because it was from them, I ate it and smiled no matter how bad it might have tasted.

The fact is, God He doesn't need a building.

> *Thus saith the LORD, The heaven is my throne, and the earth is my footstool: where is the house that ye build unto me? and where is the place of my rest?* **Isaiah 66:1**

He always, always, always wanted to personally dwell with us.

> *Now therefore ye are no more strangers and foreigners, but fellow citizens with the saints, and of the household of God; And are built upon the foundation of the apostles and prophets, Jesus Christ Himself being the chief corner stone in whom all the building fitly framed together groweth unto an holy temple in the Lord in whom ye also are builded together for an habitation of God through the Spirit.* **Eph 2:19-22**

> *Know ye not that ye are the temple of God, and that the Spirit of God dwelleth in you?* **1 Cor 3:16**

> *And I will walk among you, and will be your God, and ye shall be my people.* **Leviticus 26:12**

Think about it: God is a supernatural being Who is not confined to our physical laws and even our physicality. Why in the world would we think that we could contain His Presence in a building?

> *Howbeit the most High dwelleth not in temples made with hands…* **Acts 7:48**

Consider for a moment that He is the creator of the whole universe. How big of a building would you need to fit His expanse? I'd submit that there's not enough room on the whole earth that could contain Him.

Next, think about His majesty and His regality. There's not enough gold, diamonds and jewels on the planet that could rightly adorn His throne room.

Lastly, contemplate His holiness for a second. How could anything that we make be pristine enough to entertain such a Holy God, especially since our righteousness is as filthy rags?

In fact, when Solomon (the wisest man to ever live) started to build the first Temple, he understood how absurd the idea was to try to put God's Presence in a building.

But who is able to build him an house, seeing the heaven and heaven of heavens cannot contain him? who am I then, that I should build him an house, save only to burn sacrifice before him?
2 Chronicles 2:6

He built the temple anyway and today men still build churches thinking that they can box in God.

The Truth About The "Church"

The word "church" comes from the Old English and German word "kirche." In Scotland, it was "kirk." Here's what the English Oxford Living Dictionary has to say about this word:

Old English cir(i)ce, cyr(i)ce, related to Dutch kerk and German Kirche, based on medieval Greek kurikon, from Greek kuriakon (dōma) 'Lord's (house)', from kurios 'master or lord'. Compare with kirk.[7]

In the earlier Greek it was pronounced "ku-ri-a-kos" or "ku-ri-a-kon."

So here's the problem: Church, *kuriakos,* means master or lord, or it's understood to mean "the Lord's house". But it's not anywhere close to the words *ecclesia* (gathering) or *koinonia* (fellowship)!

I always say that when you really want to understand the Bible, you need to go down to the original language, be it Hebrew in the OT or Greek and Aramaic for the NT. This example is exactly why we have to take personal responsibility before the Lord to:

Study to shew thyself approved unto God, a workman that needeth not to be ashamed, rightly dividing the word of truth. **2 Timothy 2:15**

This book's translation of choice is the King James Version. As I said earlier, I use it because there's no copyright on it and I'm able to include scriptures freely within these pages without having to spend a small fortune in teaching these Everlasting H.E.L.P.s. But the KJV was first published in 1611 for the British people, which means that it didn't come into being until more than 1600 years after Jesus ascended back to the Father.

How much of the understanding of the original language was lost in those 1600 years? How many of you who are reading these pages are fully comfortable in your understanding and reading of Shakespeare? Most of us would say "not very" because that stuff is just hard to read. Surprise! Shakespeare was a contemporary of the time that the KJV was written and therefore written in the same type of English.

Also, original biblical texts like the Dead Sea Scrolls and others hadn't been found at the time that the KJV was written.

Lastly, not only did Jesus and the disciples not talk in old English, but also many of the cultural nuances of the languages are lost on modern day Bible readers. These nuances are extremely important in understanding the meaning behind words like *ecclesia* as an example. That's because if we lived back then we would naturally understand that this word meant, "to gather together in a group of like-minded people to partake in our King's business" and not necessarily go to a building to practice a religion.

So you may be wondering if you can trust the Bible that you are reading. I can tell you that you can absolutely trust it, because as I've already pointed out, the Bible just isn't ink on paper. The Bible is Jesus

---

7 English Oxford Living Dictionaries, "church," https://en.oxforddictionaries.com/definition/church.

written out for us in text and it is "living and active". So we have a powerful combination of teaching and guidance between the Bible and the Holy Spirit, which should dwell in you. You need His Holy Spirit to teach, clarify and direct you as you read. The Holy Spirit in you is the whole point of being in His Everlasting Presence.

> *But the anointing which ye have received of Him abideth in you, and ye need not that any man teach you: but as the same anointing teacheth you of all things, and is truth, and is no lie, and even as it hath taught you, ye shall abide in Him.* ***1 John 2:27***

This substitution of *kuriakos*, "church," for *ecclesia*, "assembly," 112 times in the KJV for just one form of the word has skewed our understanding of how and why Christians gather to fellowship, learn and worship. This lack of understanding has institutionalized church building and religion and has, at the same time, distanced the people seeking to stay in His Presence from a direct relationship with God.

Further, if "church" isn't what people think it is, how can they find true fellowship with Him and one another, or the Presence of God? The whole basis of relationship is fellowship, fellowship with each other and fellowship with the Lord.

This misunderstanding of what *ecclesia* and *koinonia* are has confused today's modern church-goer into thinking that the Presence of God can be found in church where we conduct ceremony and liturgy in order to get into God's Presence. Thus, people go to "church" seeking His Presence but will not find it there because all along, He is supposed to dwell in them!

Mankind has always thought that they could worship God on their own terms, in their own understanding and in their own ways. Those efforts have always been for the selfish celebration of their own pomp, splendor and religious ceremony. With that structured religious edifice, they sought to control and, in essence, dominate the people.

Look at the contrast between man's organized religious structure and how the Lord viewed a relationship between Himself and those who chose to follow Him.

Jesus comes along and He takes the shepherd. Jesus comes along and takes the king. Jesus comes along and takes anybody and everybody who wants to walk with Him, free of the heart mask of religious ceremony.

That's what *koinonia* is - sharing our lives together, with the King and with one another.

A Better Model - A Biblical Model

Don't get me wrong.

I love going to a place where other Believers meet, worshiping God with them and learning from His Word. Just because Believers gather and worship Him in something we've mislabeled as "church", doesn't mean that God's Presence doesn't show up.

On the contrary, I've been in numerous services where His Presence was as thick as the first time that I met Him in person.

I would submit to you that His Presence isn't in that place of gathering because of the building.

Seriously, can you imagine God hanging out in a building waiting for us to show up? His Presence visits individual Christians gathered as a group in that building, making the experience a corporate one because each individual is enveloped in His Presence, thereby making His Presence thick throughout that place.

In other words, His Presence is not in the building because of the building, His Presence is in the people, and it's in the building in spite of the building.

> *Whither shall I go from thy spirit or whither shall I flee from thy presence? If I ascend up into heaven, thou art there: if I make my bed in hell, behold, thou art there. If I take the wings of the morning, and dwell in the uttermost parts of the sea even there shall thy hand lead me, and thy right hand shall hold me. If I say, "Surely the darkness shall cover me; even the night shall be light about me." Yea, the darkness hideth not from thee; but the night shineth as the day: the darkness and the light are both alike to thee.*
> *Psalm 139:7-12*

Within mankind, God's creation, there's a common hunger, a yearning, to have a relationship with their Creator. That's what spiritual hunger is. It doesn't matter if you're on fire for the Lord or if you're a devil-worshipping Satanist who sacrifices babies. Both of these individuals are trying to fill that hunger in some way. The difference between the person who serves the Lord and the one who serves the devil is what choices they make in order to quench that yearning.

In one way or another, that hunger leads us to the place where we begin to understand that life is bigger than ourselves. For Christians, our wants, our desires, our thoughts and our own stuff pales in comparison to a Holy God when viewed with our new creation mindset. This understanding then opens the door to a larger universe in which we begin to see God in His rightful glory as the Creator of all things. Contrarily, the Satanist seeks to satisfy those wants and desires while entertaining the thoughts that the devil has twisted with his lies.

The other thing that Christians who yearn for God's Presence recognize is that we've been placed here for only a short period of time, whether it be for ten years or a hundred years.

> *Whereas ye know not what shall be on the morrow. For what is your life? It is even a vapour, that appeareth for a little time, and then vanisheth away. James 4:14*

And this limited linear, 3D existence on earth is only but a proving ground for an eternity that we are to spend with the Lord. That recognition should cause us to pursue the overriding purpose that God has for our lives. That purpose is to first seek Him daily and worship Him and then to set about the Father's business that He's laid before us. The Believer should desire to run this race to the best of his ability because He knows us better than we know ourselves and He always seeks to do what's best for our good and His glory.

> *Know ye not that they which run in a race run all, but one receiveth the prize? So run, that ye may obtain. And every man that striveth for the mastery is temperate in all things. Now they do it to obtain a corruptible crown; but we an incorruptible. I therefore so run, not as uncertainly; so fight I, not as one that beateth the air: But I keep under my body, and bring it into subjection: lest that by any means, when I have preached to others, I myself should be a castaway.*
> *1 Cor 9:24-27*

This desire to walk as the Lord would have me walk was not born out of a church. It was instilled in me by the Presence of the Everlasting God who placed His Holy Spirit in me. While accurate and anointed pulpit teaching is important, ultimately it is the Presence of the Lord within the Believer that challenges the Christian to grow into maturity and gives the strength to persevere even in the most difficult times.

In fact, not only does this growth into maturity not happen outside of a personal relationship with the Lord, I've said on more than one occasion that churches are an aberration and they're not the ideal in any way, shape or form. To illustrate this point, you can't show me in the Bible where any of the mighty men and women of God had an encounter with the Living God in a religious building, outside of their personal fellowshipping with God.

The Lord God Almighty is bigger than any building that could be made by man, yet your spirit is a suitable habitation for His Holy Spirit when you yield your life to Him. If you can find your way around the Church paradigm and invest in this personal relationship with Jesus, then God, the Creator of all the stars in the sky, will make His Everlasting Presence known in you.

Does The Devil Use Church?

At the risk of sounding juvenile - Duh!

Of course the enemy uses church and religion to undermine God. He also uses twisted theology to seed lies into congregations' hearts and puts men as barriers between God, the Creator, and man, His creation.

And because we are mortal, most people would rather have that go-between as a buffer between them and God. They do this for at least three reasons:

1. They don't want to lay down their lives in order to reach the place where God's Presence dwells,

2. They're afraid of Him, or

3. They don't know that they can do an end-run around church and go straight to the Father through Jesus.

> *Seeing then that we have a great high priest, that is passed into the heavens, Jesus the Son of God, let us hold fast our profession. For we have not an high priest which cannot be touched with the feeling of our infirmities; but was in all points tempted like as we are, yet without sin. Let us therefore come boldly unto the throne of grace, that we may obtain mercy, and find grace to help in time of need.* **Hebrews 4:14-16**

> *To the intent that now unto the principalities and powers in heavenly places might be known by the church the manifold wisdom of God, according to the eternal purpose which he purposed in Christ Jesus our Lord: In whom we have boldness and access with confidence by the faith of him.* **Eph 3:10-12**

As evidence of this mindset, I will remind you of how the people wanted Moses to be the one to talk directly to God because they were afraid of what they saw on the mountain from the distance! It's human nature.

The problem is that when you set people between you and God, you surrender your direct connection with God and become susceptible to man's thoughts and whims. Much of the nonsense coming from pulpits all around the world is serving the purposes of Satan and not deepening Christians' relationships with God.

That's because the right teachers build up Believers. The wrong teachers tear down Believers. Someone who's never walked with Jesus can't teach you how to walk with Jesus. Many of the people in churches today who call themselves pastors or ministers went to cemetery - uh, I mean - seminary, and learned doctrines of men to teach their flocks. Much of that theology is laced with humanism, relativism, social justice, and modern political correctness! This is the kind of junk that is being taught by those Pickpockets in the Pulpits that I mentioned at the very beginning of this book.

> *But there were false prophets also among the people, even as there shall be false teachers among you, who privily shall bring in damnable heresies, even denying the Lord that bought them, and bring upon themselves swift destruction. And many shall follow their pernicious* [destructive] *ways; by reason of whom the way of truth shall be evil spoken of. And through covetousness shall they with feigned words make merchandise of you: whose judgment now of a long time lingereth not, and their damnation slumbereth not.*
> *2 Peter 2:1-3*

All the while, God longs for you to enter, to really enter, into His Everlasting Presence and His Holy Spirit is standing by to teach you in all things. Nonetheless, the enemy has convinced Christians that we need churches and organized religion to find God. Nothing could be further from the truth!

This is why it was so critical to Jesus that His disciples wait for the promise of the Holy Spirit. That's why this unity that we addressed in the last chapter will never happen! You cannot have unity in the spirit without the Holy Spirit. Men will continue to do what men do and in the meantime, God waits for you to recognize that you can plug directly into Him.

Church was not, and never is, supposed to be a substitute for a direct relationship between you and God. He not only longs for you to talk with Him on a regular basis, to worship Him in private and to yield your life to Him throughout the day, He expects it!

The Consequences of Distancing Ourselves

By now you probably get the feeling that the devil's out to get you and fool you into thinking that getting into God's Presence is almost impossible. And you would be absolutely right. But the truth is even worse than that. People will fail to go directly to God, and instead go to the priest, pastor or elder at church. They will do this when Satan's attack is already inflicting serious damage to their lives.

Like on a modern day battlefield, the enemy already has a strategy that he thinks will defeat you. If you're depending on church, or religion, to come to your rescue and somehow shield you, you've already lost the battle.

Don't get me wrong. Having strong prayer warriors do battle on your behalf in the heavenlies is a powerful counter to the devil's fiery darts. In fact, as I was writing this very important chapter, my family and I came under direct, constant and serious demonic attacks that were a distraction and hindrance from getting this chapter done. The Presence of God's Holy Spirit in me prompted me to call my prayer warrior brothers and sisters in the Lord, to pray on my behalf for this important work that I'm now undertaking. The attacks subsided and I was able to finish the chapter and the book.

This battle, for you and for me, is real. When you enter into God's Presence and listen, really listen, you'll begin to hear the figurative sound of a battle cry. It is then, that the Holy Spirit will flip you from defensive mode, to offensive mode. As you grow in the Lord, you'll begin to understand that we are not just supposed to sit back and take shots from the devil. On the contrary, we have all been enlisted into God's army to destroy the works of the evil one through Jesus.

> *Little children, let no man deceive you: he that doeth righteousness is righteous, even as he is righteous. He that committeth sin is of the devil; for the devil sinneth from the beginning. For this purpose the Son of God was manifested, that he might destroy the works of the devil.* **1 John 3:7-8**

> *Finally, my brethren, be strong in the Lord, and in the power of his might. Put on the whole armour of God, that ye may be able to stand against the wiles of the devil. For we wrestle not against flesh and blood, but against principalities, against powers, against the rulers of the darkness of this world, against spiritual wickedness in high places. Wherefore take unto you the whole armour of God, that ye may be able to withstand in the evil day, and having done all, to stand. Stand therefore, having your loins girt about with truth, and having on the breastplate of righteousness; And your feet shod with the preparation of the gospel of peace; Above all, taking the shield of faith, wherewith ye shall be able to quench all the fiery darts of the wicked. And take the helmet of salvation, and the sword of the Spirit, which is the word of God.* **Eph 6:10-17**

And there's really something to taking every thought captive.

> *For though we walk in the flesh, we do not war after the flesh, for the weapons of our warfare are not carnal, but mighty through God to the pulling down of strong holds, casting down imaginations, and every high thing that exalteth itself against the knowledge of God, and bringing into captivity every thought to the obedience of Christ.* **2 Cor 10:3-5**

None of these things can wait to be done in church if you are in the midst of a battle. All of these weapons have to be secured first in the Presence of the Most High and then implemented by us individually against an angry demonic opponent.

There is a war raging!

Think about it like this: Lucifer was an anointed cherub. He was the number one or two being in heaven. Because He didn't want robots serving Him, God gave the angels free will.

With that free will, Lucifer led one-third of the angels to rebel.

> *And there appeared another wonder in heaven; and behold a great red dragon, having seven heads and ten horns, and seven crowns upon his heads. And his tail drew the third part of the stars of heaven, and*

did cast them to the earth: and the dragon stood before the woman which was ready to be delivered, for to devour her child as soon as it was born. **Revelation 12:3-4**

We are so caught up in our lives, our church routines and ceremonies that most Christians have no clue that they should be loaded for bear and on the frontline.

The pseudepigraphal Book of Enoch is not in the biblical canon but many of the authors of the NT were very familiar with its content. Both the Lord and apostles quoted from portions of it and it is specifically referenced in the Book of Jude. Several copies of the earlier sections of Enoch were also preserved among the Dead Sea Scrolls.

A pow-wow of sorts was called by some 200 Fallen Angels on the top of Mt. Hermon and is recounted in Enoch 6:1-6:

And it came to pass when the children of men had multiplied that in those days were born unto them beautiful and comely daughters. And the angels, the children of the heaven, saw and lusted after them, and said to one another: 'Come, let us choose us wives from among the children of men and beget us children.' And Semjâzâ, who was their leader, said unto them: 'I fear ye will not indeed agree to do this deed, and I alone shall have to pay the penalty of a great sin.' And they all answered him and said: 'Let us all swear an oath, and all bind ourselves by mutual imprecations not to abandon this plan but to do this thing.' Then sware they all together and bound themselves by mutual imprecations upon it. And they were in all two hundred; who descended [in the days] of Jared on the summit of Mount Hermon, and they called it Mount Hermon, because they had sworn and bound themselves by mutual imprecations upon it.

Those 200 angels on Mt. Hermon that came to earth to have a good time are only a fraction of a third of the innumerable angels. If something's non-number-able, and there's a third of them, that's a lot of angels that fell!

But ye are come unto mount Sion, and unto the city of the living God, the heavenly Jerusalem, and to an innumerable company of angels. **Hebrews 12:22**

Add to that third of fallen angels all the evil presences of entities that were hybrids throughout the ages and then add those evil spirits that walk the earth. There's a lot of stuff to come camp out on your doorstep. And they are extremely motivated!

They hate mankind because we are created in the image and likeness of God and we are redeemable and they're not.

For verily He took not on Him the nature of angels; but He took on Him the seed of Abraham. **Hebrews 2:16**

Those fallen angels and evil entities have nothing but contempt that God would give to us the chance to be redeemed. In addition, the devil and his minions are still livid over this statement out of Genesis 1:26:

And God said, Let us make man in our image, after our likeness: and let them have dominion over the fish of the sea, and over the fowl of the air, and over the cattle, and over all the earth, and over every creeping thing that creepeth upon the earth.

I suppose you could say that one good thing that evil helps us with is our understanding of God's holiness and the goodness of His Presence. It's evil that enables us to see the contrast between light and darkness. As a photographer you can't have a good picture without contrast. Contrast is how you separate the light from the darkness, the blacks and whites, the shades of grey and the different hues of color. It's only by contrast that the picture becomes clear.

So let me ask you, "What part in your Sunday morning visit to that building can prepare you in any way for the daily and continuous attacks by an angry devil?"

Only being in the Everlasting Presence of the Most High can truly prepare you for battle.

Chapter 7
Breaking Down Barriers

The heavens declare the glory of God; and the firmament sheweth his handywork.

Psalm 19:1

Radio show host Alex Jones has a website called Prison Planet. *I love that.* I don't always agree with Alex, but on this point, he's absolutely right. The globe became a prison planet right after Adam and Eve sinned and fell. Sin, and God's subsequent judgment of Adam and Eve, changed the earth spiritually and also changed our planet's physical laws.

Before the fall, Adam and Eve had child-like innocence and were unafraid.

And they were both naked, the man and his wife, and were not ashamed. **Genesis 2:25**

They freely walked with God in the garden, but when they willingly sinned, they lost that innocence and their eyes were opened.

And the eyes of them both were opened, and they knew that they were naked; and they sewed fig leaves together, and made themselves aprons. **Genesis 3:7**

That first act of sin began a snowball effect for mankind. From that point on, all of mankind has been deemed guilty of sin with a punishment of death before God.

For as in Adam all die... **1 Corinthians 15:22**

That loss of innocence and a death sentence separated us from the Presence of God even though it was always His desire for us to stay in His Presence. This is why He sent His Son, to bridge the gap of our separation from His Everlasting Presence.

Accompanying these spiritual consequences of Adam and Eve's sin were also the physical consequences. I believe it was then that mankind was physically locked into the 3D reality of this earth, hence a prison planet.

> *Unto the woman he said, I will greatly multiply thy sorrow and thy conception; in sorrow thou shalt bring forth children; and thy desire shall be to thy husband, and he shall rule over thee. And unto Adam he said, Because thou hast hearkened unto the voice of thy wife, and hast eaten of the tree, of which I commanded thee, saying, Thou shalt not eat of it: cursed is the ground for thy sake; in sorrow shalt thou eat of it all the days of thy life; Thorns also and thistles shall it bring forth to thee; and thou shalt eat the herb of the field; In the sweat of thy face shalt thou eat bread, till thou return unto the ground; for out of it wast thou taken: for dust thou art, and unto dust shalt thou return.* **Genesis 3:16-19**

From that point on, the world changed. Life became difficult. Death followed every man from Adam on. The physics of our planet changed and we were separated by our sin from God's Everlasting Presence.

Jesus is the ultimate jailkeeper who sets us free and takes us from the guttermost to the uttermost.

> *For I reckon that the sufferings of this present time are not worthy to be compared with the glory which shall be revealed in us. For the earnest expectation of the creature waiteth for the manifestation of the sons of God. For the creature was made subject to vanity, not willingly, but by reason of him who hath subjected the same in hope, Because the creature itself also shall be delivered from the bondage of corruption into the glorious liberty of the children of God. For we know that the whole creation groaneth and travaileth in pain together until now. And not only they, but ourselves also, which have the firstfruits of the Spirit, even we ourselves groan within ourselves, waiting for the adoption, to wit, the redemption of our body.* **Romans 8:18-23**

I've said it before, and I'll say it again, "We are in the world but not of the world."

> *{God} Who hath delivered us from the power of darkness, and hath translated us into the kingdom of his dear Son: In whom we have redemption through his blood, even the forgiveness of sins.* **Col 1:13-14**

Sin may have physically separated us from God's Presence, but He would do whatever He had to do in order to be reunited with us.

> *Who shall separate us from the love of Christ? shall tribulation, or distress, or persecution, or famine, or nakedness, or peril, or sword? As it is written, For thy sake we are killed all the day long; we are accounted as sheep for the slaughter. Nay, in all these things we are more than conquerors through him that loved us. For I am persuaded, that neither death, nor life, nor angels, nor principalities, nor powers, nor things present, nor things to come, Nor height, nor depth, nor any other creature, shall be able to separate us from the love of God, which is in Christ Jesus our Lord.* **Rom 8:35-39**

God was so serious about enabling you to enter into His Everlasting Presence that He would literally tear down anything that stood in the way between you and Him.

Putting God in a Box

The glory of God is like a beautiful golden stream of translucent water. I've seen it and I can tell you without a doubt that it's literally gold and translucent and it bathes you and submerges you in His Presence.

Some people have also seen the "glory cloud" of God, which represents His Presence. In these eyewitness accounts it looks like a heavy mist, fog or literal cloud. This observation is collaborated in the OT where there are scriptural accounts of this glory cloud.

> *And it came to pass, when the priests were come out of the holy place: (for all the priests that were present were sanctified, and did not then wait by course: Also the Levites which were the singers, all of them of Asaph, of Heman, of Jeduthun, with their sons and their brethren, being arrayed in white linen, having cymbals and psalteries and harps, stood at the east end of the altar, and with them an hundred and twenty priests sounding with trumpets:) It came even to pass, as the trumpeters and singers were as one, to make one sound to be heard in praising and thanking the LORD; and when they lifted up their voice with the trumpets and cymbals and instruments of musick, and praised the LORD, saying, For he is good; for his mercy endureth for ever: that then the house was filled with a cloud, even the house of the LORD; So that the priests could not stand to minister by reason of the cloud: for the glory of the LORD had filled the house of God.* **2 Chron 5:11-14**

The glory of God is synonymous with His Everlasting Presence.

In the previous section, I discussed how there was no way to contain God's glory in a building. And yet, He allowed the Israelites to build a temple dedicated to Him where they could worship Him. What is more mind-blowing than that is the fact that He allowed His Presence to be contained in a box!

I'm referring to the Ark of the Covenant. Initially the Ark only contained the stone tablets with the Ten Commandments on them.

> *There was nothing in the ark save the two tables of stone, which Moses put there at Horeb, when the LORD made a covenant with the children of Israel, when they came out of the land of Egypt.* **1 Kings 8:9**

And then God had Moses add a gold jar of manna, the food the Israelites ate in the wilderness, and Aaron's staff that had budded.

> *And the house of Israel called the name thereof Manna: and it was like coriander seed, white; and the taste of it was like wafers made with honey. And Moses said, This is the thing which the LORD commandeth, Fill an omer of it to be kept for your generations; that they may see the bread wherewith I have fed you in the wilderness, when I brought you forth from the land of Egypt. And Moses said unto Aaron, Take a pot, and put an omer full of manna therein, and lay it up before the LORD, to be kept for your generations.* **Exodus 16:31-34**

> *And the LORD said unto Moses, Bring Aaron's rod again before the testimony, to be kept for a token against the rebels; and thou shalt quite take away their murmurings from me, that they die not.* **Numbers 17:10**

What else did it contain?

God's Glory.

*And there I will meet with thee, and I will commune with thee from above the mercy seat, from between the two cherubims which are upon the ark of the testimony, of all things which I will give thee in commandment unto the children of Israel. **Exodus 25:22***

So consider this for a moment: The Everlasting God Who lives outside of time, the infinite and abounding God unconstrained by space, the transcendent God Who is beyond all that we mortals can consider or imagine, and the pervasive God which is in everything that He has created - allowed His Presence to be captured within a container made with human hands. All because He understood the weakness of His people in needing one location for them to come and meet with Him.

Like I said, mind-blowing.

The Ark of the Covenant eventually was placed into the Holy of Holies in the first Temple, or as many people call it, Solomon's Temple.

*And the oracle he prepared in the house within, to set there the ark of the covenant of the LORD. And the oracle in the forepart was twenty cubits in length, and twenty cubits in breadth, and twenty cubits in the height thereof: and he overlaid it with pure gold; and so covered the altar which was of cedar. So Solomon overlaid the house within with pure gold: and he made a partition by the chains of gold before the oracle; and he overlaid it with gold. And the whole house he overlaid with gold, until he had finished all the house: also the whole altar that was by the oracle he overlaid with gold. **1 Kings 6:19-22***

The oracle in the above verse would be better translated as "the inner sanctum". That's because we know from scripture that the Temple had three locations: The Outer Court, The Holy Place and The Holy of Holies, the inner sanctum.

But before the Outer Court was the outermost area of the temple, called the Court of the Gentiles. That's because it could be entered by all people and was, by far, the largest of all the courts. The Court of the Gentiles, and an outer adjoining area called Solomon's Porch, was frequently visited by the sick and the poor seeking God's Presence. But it was as close as they could get to that Presence held in the Ark, in the Holy of Holies.

*And as the lame man which was healed held Peter and John, all the people ran together unto them in the porch that is called Solomon's, greatly wondering. **Acts 3:11***

*And by the hands of the apostles were many signs and wonders wrought among the people; and they were all with one accord in Solomon's porch. **Acts 5:12***

A fence called the *soreg* separated the court of the Gentiles from the rest of the temple mount complex. Gentiles (non-Israelites) and ritually unclean Israelites were forbidden, under the threat of death, from passing through its gates into the interior areas of the Temple. To highlight this threat, stones were placed along the *soreg* with a warning written on them that any Gentile or unclean person entering into the complex could be killed. In Ephesians, Paul referred to this fence.

Wherefore remember, that ye being in time past Gentiles in the flesh, who are called Uncircumcision by that which is called the Circumcision in the flesh made by hands; That at that time ye were without Christ, being aliens from the commonwealth of Israel, and strangers from the covenants of promise, *having no hope, and without God in the world: But now in Christ Jesus ye who sometimes were far off are made nigh by the blood of Christ. **Ephesians 2:11-13***

There was a place beyond the *soreg* where women and ceremonially clean Israelites could go, called the Outer Court, or Women's Hall. In order to get there, one needed to enter through the Beautiful Gate. It's important to note that the doors of the gate were so massive; the strength of twenty men was needed to open and close them!

*And a certain man lame from his mother's womb was carried, whom they laid daily at the gate of the temple which is called Beautiful, to ask alms of them that entered into the temple. **Acts 3:2***

It was in the Outer Court that Israelite women could worship God, but they could not go beyond that point into the Court of Israel unless they were bringing a sacrifice. This was also the place that, at the time of Jesus, a market was set up and foreign currency was exchanged and where animals were sold for sacrifices. It was at this market where on two separate occasions, once at the beginning of His ministry and once just before He was crucified, Jesus rebuked the people.

*And the Jews' passover was at hand, and Jesus went up to Jerusalem, And found in the temple those that sold oxen and sheep and doves, and the changers of money sitting: And when he had made a scourge of small cords, he drove them all out of the temple, and the sheep, and the oxen; and poured out the changers' money, and overthrew the tables; And said unto them that sold doves, Take these things hence; make not my Father's house an house of merchandise. And his disciples remembered that it was written, The zeal of thine house hath eaten me up. Then answered the Jews and said unto him, What sign shewest thou unto us, seeing that thou doest these things? **John 2:13-18***

*And Jesus went into the temple of God, and cast out all them that sold and bought in the temple, and overthrew the tables of the moneychangers, and the seats of them that sold doves, And said unto them, It is written, My house shall be called the house of prayer; but ye have made it a den of thieves. **Matt 21:12-13***

Beyond this court was the Holy Place where only the priests who were ceremonially clean could enter. On the other side of the Holy Place lay the Holy of Holies where God's Presence dwelled.

A veil separated the Holy Place from the Holy of Holies, which could only be entered by the High Priest on the Day of Atonement, once a year.

*Now when these things were thus ordained, the priests went always into the first tabernacle, accomplishing the service of God. But into the second went the high priest alone once every year, not without blood, which he offered for himself, and for the errors of the people: The Holy Ghost this signifying, that the way into the holiest of all was not yet made manifest, while as the first tabernacle was yet standing. **Heb 9:6-8***

This veil was huge. It was reported to be four inches thick, twenty-two yards long and eleven yards wide and it was also laced with gold.

The reason that there was a veil between the Holy Place and the Holy of Holies is because it separated God from the people's sin. In fact, if anyone went into the Holy of Holies except for the High Priest on the appointed day, they would die. Even on that day, if the High Priest's sin wasn't ceremonially cleansed, he would be killed.

The Holy of Holies, where God's Everlasting Presence dwelt, was a serious place and not one that the people would think about casually.

With this foundation, it's also important to note that the placement of the Temple, and specifically the Holy of Holies, put it directly across from Calvary where Jesus was crucified.

The first Temple, Solomon's Temple, was destroyed in 587 BCE by King Nebuchadnezzar II. Just before the king came to sack the city and destroy the temple, the Ark with God's Presence was reportedly whisked away and placed in hiding.

When the Temple was rebuilt in 516 BCE, the Ark of the Covenant was never brought back and did not occupy the second rendition of the Holy of Holies. Although the second temple's dimensions were the same as the first, it had the most important part of the edifice missing, the Everlasting Presence of God held within the Ark of the Covenant as specified by scripture.

This means that in the thirty-three years that Jesus walked amongst the people, He knew that the Holy of Holies was devoid of the Ark and therefore, God's Presence. He longed for the day when the people's hearts would be turned back to His Father, not on a religious basis but in a genuine, heartfelt way.

> *Jesus saith unto her, Woman, believe me, the hour cometh, when ye shall neither in this mountain, nor yet at Jerusalem, worship the Father. Ye worship ye know not what: we know what we worship: for salvation is of the Jews. But the hour cometh, and now is, when the true worshippers shall worship the Father in spirit and in truth: for the Father seeketh such to worship him. God is a Spirit: and they that worship him must worship him in spirit and in truth.* **John 4:21-24**

Jesus came to take the Everlasting Presence of God from behind man-made walls and put it in the hearts of men.

A Veil Torn

I went through that lengthy discussion above to illustrate one very important point. There were insurmountable hurdles placed between God and man because of our sin.

Think about this, God can't even *look* on our sin.

> *Thou art of purer eyes than to behold evil, and canst not look on iniquity: wherefore lookest thou upon them that deal treacherously, and holdest thy tongue when the wicked devoureth the man that is more righteous than he?* **Habakkuk 1:13**

He allowed the barriers to be placed between Himself and the people so that they would recognize how very short they fell in their own righteousness.

First, you have Gentiles and sick people who couldn't even step foot toward His Presence in the Holy of Holies.

 Then there was a huge gate that stood between the outside of the Temple complex and everyone else. It even took twenty men to open and close it!

 Next, if you were an Israelite or a woman, you could get a little closer, but only if you were ceremonially clean.

 Beyond that, if you were a priest, you could get closer than anyone else by going into the Holy Place, but you still could only look at the curtain that His glory resided behind.

 Finally, if you were the High Priest you had the opportunity to go in and see His glory, but you were probably scared to death that you were going to die!

And still, God waited for His creation to be in a heart-place where He could fellowship with us and looked forward to the time when we could live in His Everlasting Presence.

The word "presence" in the Bible is the Greek word *parousia* which comes from another word, *parōn*, which means "to be present", "arrive", or "to enter into a situation". Specifically that word speaks of someone important coming, like an owner who alone can deal with a situation. However, *parousía*, the specific word in scripture that is used for "presence", is even more descriptive. *Parousía* is a technical term used in reference to a royal visit by a king, or emperor. The word literally means "the being beside" as in the "personal presence" of the king.

All I can say is Hallelujah! This personal audience with our King is what He wants to have with you and me every day.

He's so serious about this direct connection that He sent His own Son to earth to die on a Cross for us. At that execution, something phenomenal happened to this sin barrier that existed between us and our King.

As He hung there on the Cross on Calvary, Jesus had a direct view of the temple and, because of its height, probably saw the top of the Veil that separated man from God's Presence.

*Now from the sixth hour there was darkness over all the land unto the ninth hour. And about the ninth hour Jesus cried with a loud voice, saying, Eli, Eli, lama sabachthani? that is to say, My God, my God, why hast thou forsaken me? Some of them that stood there, when they heard that, said, This man calleth for Elias. And straightway one of them ran, and took a spunge, and filled it with vinegar, and put it on a reed, and gave him to drink. The rest said, Let be, let us see whether Elias will come to save him. Jesus, when he had cried again with a loud voice, yielded up the ghost. And, behold, the veil of the temple was rent in twain from the top to the bottom; and the earth did quake, and the rocks rent; And the graves were opened; and many bodies of the saints which slept arose, And came out of the graves after his resurrection, and went into the holy city, and appeared unto many. Now when the centurion, and they that were with him, watching Jesus, saw the earthquake, and those things that were done, they feared greatly, saying, Truly this was the Son of God. **Matthew 27:45-54**

This huge, four-inch-thick veil that was laced with gold was torn from the top to the bottom. With the death of Jesus our Messiah, the final atonement for mankind's sin was made and God Himself tore down the barrier that mankind had erected.

> *Having therefore, brethren, boldness to enter into the holiest by the blood of Jesus, By a new and living way, which he hath consecrated for us, through the veil, that is to say, his flesh; And having an high priest over the house of God; Let us draw near with a true heart in full assurance of faith, having our hearts sprinkled from an evil conscience, and our bodies washed with pure water.* **Hebrews 10:19-22.**

The tearing of the Veil was God's pronouncement to the world that the King had arrived and anyone and everyone could come into His Everlasting Presence, His *parousía,* through the final atoning sacrifice of His own Son.

Chapter 8

Abide

I am the true vine, and my Father is the husbandman. Every branch in me that beareth not fruit he taketh away: and every branch that beareth fruit, he purgeth it, that it may bring forth more fruit. Now ye are clean through the word which I have spoken unto you. Abide in me, and I in you. As the branch cannot bear fruit of itself, except it abide in the vine; no more can ye, except ye abide in me. I am the vine, ye are the branches: He that abideth in me, and I in him, the same bringeth forth much fruit: for without me ye can do nothing. If a man abide not in me, he is cast forth as a branch, and is withered; and men gather them, and cast them into the fire, and they are burned. If ye abide in me, and my words abide in you, ye shall ask what ye will, and it shall be done unto you. Herein is my Father glorified, that ye bear much fruit; so shall ye be my disciples. As the Father hath loved me, so have I loved you: continue ye in my love. If ye keep my commandments, ye shall abide in my love; even as I have kept my Father's commandments, and abide in his love. These things have I spoken unto you, that my joy might remain in you, and that your joy might be full.

John 15:1-11

So what does it mean to abide in God's Everlasting Presence?

"Abide" comes from the Greek word *menó*, which means to "stay", "wait" or "remain". So what Jesus is telling us here is to stay in Him. How does someone stay in someone else?

Again we see this same kind of idea in the OT.

He that dwelleth in the secret place of the most High shall abide under the shadow of the Almighty. I will say of the LORD, He is my refuge and my fortress: my God; in him will I trust. Surely he shall deliver thee from the snare of the fowler, and from the noisome pestilence. He shall cover thee with his feathers, and under his wings shalt thou trust: his truth shall be thy shield and buckler. Thou shalt not be afraid for the terror by night; nor for the arrow that flieth by day; Nor for the pestilence that walketh in darkness; nor for the destruction that wasteth at noonday. A thousand shall fall at thy side, and ten thousand at thy right hand; but it shall not come nigh thee. Psalm 91:1-7

In this instance, "abide" comes from the Hebrew word *lun*, which literally means "to lodge" or "to pass the night". It is the same concept as presented in the NT and tells us that the Creator of the Universe wants us to stay with Him.

So how is it that the modern-Church thinks that once a week, Sunday, they can go to a building and hang out for a while, go to Cracker Barrel after church to eat, and somehow they've stayed with the King? How in any stretch of the imagination can this be related to what God is trying to communicate to His people in both the OT and NT when He tells us to abide with Him?

It can't! And I would further submit to you that the Church today is doing the very same thing that the Israelites did with the Temple. They are the ones putting up barriers between them and God. Their motivations have previously been discussed so I won't go back there, but the current way we worship God and seek His face is not what He wants us to do.

He wants us to abide in his Everlasting Presence, but how do we do that?

The Physics of His Presence

The revelation or witness that gives you and me the immediate understanding of the Presence of God is the Spirit of God.

For what man knoweth the things of a man, save the spirit of man which is in him? Even so the things of God knoweth no man, but the Spirit of God. 1 Cor 2:11

If you've ever been around thriving, growing, maturing, worshiping and praying Christians, you really do get a sense that there's something different about them. Many times I think they kind of glow. This may well be my imagination, but I've heard other people say that as well. All I can attribute this to is the Spirit of God that lives inside of them.

Earlier I asked how a person could stay in God and God in them. The answer is, via His Holy Spirit. John 4:24 said that *"God is a Spirit: and they that worship him must worship him in spirit and in truth."*

Our time on earth is only for a moment when compared to the expanse of eternity, because our spirits live on perpetually. Although it feels sometimes like this physical life is all there is, I can assure you that it is not.

Also when they shall be afraid of that which is high, and fears shall be in the way, and the almond tree shall flourish, and the grasshopper shall be a burden, and desire shall fail: because man goeth to his long home, and the mourners go about the streets: Or ever the silver cord be loosed, or the golden bowl be broken, or the pitcher be broken at the fountain, or the wheel broken at the cistern. Then shall the dust return to the earth as it was: and the spirit shall return unto God who gave it. Ecclesiastes 12:5-7

And although we forget that we are spirit beings residing inside a physical body, the physical reality is that we often times see that spiritual realm invade our physical realm. That glow on mature Believer's faces is just one example. But it is an example that we can also see in scripture when it comes to the residual effects of someone being in the Presence of God.

God met Moses on Mount Sinai and revealed to him that He, God, was the Great I AM. When Moses came down from the mountain, they had to veil his face because it radiated God's glory and glowed.

> *And it came to pass, when Moses came down from mount Sinai with the two tables of testimony in Moses' hand, when he came down from the mount, that Moses wist not that the skin of his face shone while he talked with Him. And when Aaron and all the children of Israel saw Moses, behold, the skin of his face shone; and they were afraid to come nigh him. And Moses called unto them; and Aaron and all the rulers of the congregation returned unto him: and Moses talked with them. And afterward all the children of Israel came nigh: and he gave them in commandment all that the LORD had spoken with him in mount Sinai. And till Moses had done speaking with them, he put a vail on his face. But when Moses went in before the LORD to speak with Him, he took the vail off, until he came out. And he came out, and spake unto the children of Israel that which He was commanded. And the children of Israel saw the face of Moses, that the skin of Moses' face shone: and Moses put the vail upon his face again, until he went in to speak with Him.* **Exodus 34:29-35**

Remember my earlier comment about people's faces shining because of being in the Presence of God? When Moses was in the Presence of God, he became a reflection of God's glory. But the thing to remember is that he didn't get it on his own. He didn't get it until it was imparted to him.

He spent a great deal of time with God and I dare say that Moses didn't see his life as his own. He had surrendered all of his self-will to the Almighty and pledged to serve Him above all else. The result? The Presence of God's glory rested on him in such a way that it was visible for all to see.

There's an interesting physics lesson associated with the fading light of Moses' face after he came down from the mountain. Before Jesus' death and resurrection, the Spirit of God would rest on people, but then He would leave. Moses' glowing face was a perfect example. When Moses was in the Presence of God, he was in the Presence of the creator of life and the author of life. When he went down off the mountain, he came out of that glorious dimension into the physical dimension. The problem is that this life in the fallen state has a way of literally sucking the light and life right out of us, and the same was true with Moses.

> *But if the ministration of death, written and engraven in stones, was glorious, so that the children of Israel could not stedfastly behold the face of Moses for the glory of his countenance; which glory was to be done away (fading).* **1 Cor 3:7**

When Moses met with God up on that mountain, God's supernatural realm permeated Moses' physical realm and the combination of the physical and the supernatural put Moses in a different quantum state. Whether it was by design or circumstance, Moses walked away from that long meeting, forty days according to Exodus 24:18, with the remnant of God's Presence all over Him in the form of that shininess. Could it be that God wanted the people to see that Moses' authority was not self-generated, but God-generated so He allowed his face to glow? I think so.

The Quantum Connection

There's a direct quantum connection between what happened to Moses on Mt. Sinai and the transfiguration of Jesus in the garden in the NT.

> *And it came to pass about an eight days after these sayings, He took Peter and John and James, and went up into a mountain to pray. And as He prayed, the fashion of his countenance was altered, and his raiment was white and glistering. And, behold, th ere talked with Him two men, which were Moses and Elias: Who appeared in glory, and spake of his decease which He should accomplish at Jerusalem. But Peter and they that were with Him were heavy with sleep: and when they were awake, they saw his glory, and the two men that stood with Him. And it came to pass, as they departed from Him, Peter said unto Jesus, Master, it is good for us to be here: and let us make three tabernacles; one for thee, and one for Moses, and one for Elias: not knowing what he said. While he thus spake, there came a cloud, and overshadowed them: and they feared as they entered into the cloud. And there came a voice out of the cloud, saying, This is my beloved Son: hear Him. And when the voice was past, Jesus was found alone. And they kept it close, and told no man in those days any of those things which they had seen.*
> *Luke 9:28-36*

I believe that something physical happened in both the Mt. Sinai and the garden examples. Within these two stories we see Heaven invading earth for the briefest of moments. The results are astonishing.

In Moses' case, because he was camped out with God for so long, the changed atmosphere pervaded his own body with this shining residue. I believe that it was probably more than just his face that shown, although scripture doesn't specify. In Peter's case, he was only briefly exposed to this glory and therefore it didn't stick.

And Jesus Himself gave an indication in Matthew 13:43 our connection to Him would cause us to shine:

> *Then shall the righteous shine forth as the sun in the kingdom of their Father. Who hath ears to hear, let him hear.*

If a glimpse of this other-dimensional realm could make Moses' face shine, think about what really happens to us when the Holy Spirit, God's Everlasting Presence, comes to live inside of us. The thought is staggering because when we crossover to the kingdom of God, the Bible says that we become new creations.

What then should the inside of our spirits look like when we become a habitat for the Holy Spirit?

~ *John 1:9 - That was the true Light, which lighteth every man that cometh into the world.*

~ *Matt 5:6 - Let your light so shine before men, that they may see your good works, and glorify your Father which is in heaven.*

~ *John 8:12 - Then spake Jesus again unto them, saying, I am the light of the world: he that followeth me shall not walk in darkness, but shall have the light of life.*

~ *Luke 11:33-36 - No one lights a lamp and puts it in a place where it will be hidden, or under a bowl. Instead they put it on its stand, so that those who come in may see the light. Your eye is the lamp of your body. When your eyes are healthy, your whole body also is full of light. But when they are unhealthy, your body also is full of darkness. See to it, then, that the light within you is not darkness. Therefore, if your whole body is full of light, and no part of it dark, it will be just as full of light as when a lamp shines its light on you."*

~ ***1 John 1:5-7*** *- This then is the message which we have heard of Him, and declare unto you, that God is light, and in Him is no darkness at all. If we say that we have fellowship with Him, and walk in darkness, we lie, and do not the truth: But if we walk in the light, as He is in the light, we have fellowship one with another, and the blood of Jesus Christ his Son cleanseth us from all sin.*

This light, this power, this universe-creating, creation-changing newness that raised Christ from the dead should live inside the Christian.

But if the Spirit of Him that raised up Jesus from the dead dwell in you, He that raised up Christ from the dead shall also quicken your mortal bodies by his Spirit that dwelleth in you. ***Romans 8:11***

Let There Be Light

You cannot separate light and power. So by the Church not embracing the power of the Holy Ghost, and routinely abiding in God's Everlasting Presence, many who sought to walk with Him have had their lights go out.

Jesus talks about the results of His disciples hiding their lights under a bushel. That bushel can be sin, it can be all the cares of this world, it can be all of the stuff in the world that seeks to drag you away from the truth of His Presence.

Ye are the light of the world. A city that is set on an hill cannot be hid. Neither do men light a candle, and put it under a bushel, but on a candlestick; and it giveth light unto all that are in the house. Let your light so shine before men, that they may see your good works, and glorify your Father which is in heaven. Matt 5:14-16

So why is it that more people are walking away from God than there are new people seeking God?

Since most people will try to go to church to "find" God, the answer has to be that there just aren't enough people in those churches who are living with the power of the Holy Ghost in their lives. There's not enough light being presented, not in the individuals and not through them corporately as they meet at church. It boils down to men and women not dwelling in the powerful, recharging Presence of the Most High. Instead, they go to church where they are content to listen to word games and participate in institutionalized church programs.

I've got news for them. God doesn't need or want their programs!

What He needs and wants is a people who are sold out for Him. These are the kind of people who will lay at His feet and empty themselves of their sin, their wants and their fears. These are the kind of people who will count everything else as loss.

But what things were gain to me, those I counted loss for Christ. Yea doubtless, and I count all things but loss for the excellency of the knowledge of Christ Jesus my Lord: for whom I have suffered the loss of all things, and do count them but dung, that I may win Christ, And be found in him, not having mine own righteousness, which is of the law, but that which is through the faith of Christ, the righteousness which is of God by faith: That I may know him, and the power of his resurrection... **Phil 3:7-10**

The experience of dwelling in His Everlasting Presence for even one minute will cause you to be changed and be drawn back to Him continually. All we have to do is to get over ourselves, our wants, our desires and our preconceived ideas and lay down our lives before Him. That's a lot easier said than done.

So how can we remind ourselves what His Presence is like when we're not in the mindset to seek Him?

Get alone with God.

The Transformational Power of His Presence

I know people who had their greatest transformational moments by looking at God's handiwork - like a baby's hand, or walking in a forest, or taking in the sight of a beautiful lake. The night sky is a glorious example of His majesty and shows a light-filled tapestry where darkness cannot prevail because even in spite of its great darkness you naturally look at the stars. That's the power of His light. As you behold the glory of His creation and earnestly talk with Him in prayer, the cares of this world melt away.

Job saw God's Presence in the whirlwind. Job is also the oldest book of the Bible and gives the first example of how to talk directly to God. In that conversation with Job, we see God ask Job celestial questions. God puts Job into the context of the cosmos, showing him that His ways and thoughts are not Job's ways and thoughts.

For my thoughts are not your thoughts, neither are your ways my ways, saith the LORD. For as the heavens are higher than the earth, so are my ways higher than your ways, and my thoughts than your thoughts. **Isaiah 55:8-9**

God created mankind to have fellowship with Himself. When we have fellowship with God, we carry His Presence into the world and unbelievers see and sense that Presence within us and are drawn to Him. They want to know how He comforts us, what our joy is, how He intervenes in our lives and how they can have the same kind of peace as we do .

At the end of the day it's His Presence.

They don't want to hear a debate on evolution; they want the truth and the power of the Word. They want to know what's in it for them. They want to know why He makes a difference and how they can feel that difference themselves.

The answer is to get alone with God and let His Holy Spirit blow across your heart.

But God hath revealed them unto us by his Spirit: for the Spirit searcheth all things, yea, the deep things of God. For what man knoweth the things of a man, save the spirit of man which is in him? even so the things of God knoweth no man, but the Spirit of God. **1 Cor 2:10-11**

The Reality of His Presence

In an earlier chapter I shared about my personal, face-to-face encounter with Jesus. Although I described the factual specifics of that visitation, I'm compelled to share with you what it "felt like" in His Presence.

His holiness, His majesty and His power made the very air in my room feel heavy. I fell down at His feet as though dead and the weight of His Presence tried to force me prone. When He reached down to pick me up, I was able to stand. I was enveloped by the cocoon of His Presence which distorted time and space and I understood that I wasn't exactly in the physical realm, but I was physically there.

More than any other feeling, it was like that Presence permeated me, going in and through every cell of my body and I was completely enveloped in the love of God and His love surrounded me.

I've seen Him other times since then, but this first experience stands out in my mind. Unfortunately, even after being in His very Presence, I too sometimes struggle to get my mindset right to enter into the Presence of God.

So how can we as people, stuck on a prison planet, with all the cares of it, enter into His Presence on a regular basis?

We can become like trees planted near a river or lake. Their roots go deep into the ground and drink up as much water and nutrition as they can. When a tree is cut off from its water source, it dies. When Christians are cut off from the source of Living Water - Jesus through His Presence and His Word - we too can dry up and even die spiritually.

There cometh a woman of Samaria to draw water: Jesus saith unto her, Give me to drink. (For his disciples were gone away unto the city to buy meat.) Then saith the woman of Samaria unto Him, How is it that thou, being a Jew, askest drink of me, which am a woman of Samaria? for the Jews have no dealings with the Samaritans. Jesus answered and said unto her, If thou knewest the gift of God, and who it is that saith to thee, Give me to drink; thou wouldest have asked of Him, and He would have given thee living water. The woman saith unto Him, Sir, thou hast nothing to draw with, and the well is deep: from whence then hast thou that living water? Art thou greater than our father Jacob, which gave us the well, and drank thereof himself, and his children, and his cattle? Jesus answered and said unto her, Whosoever drinketh of this water shall thirst again: But whosoever drinketh of the water that I shall give him shall never thirst; but the water that I shall give him shall be in him a well of water springing up into everlasting life. **John 4:7-14**

So if you have walked with the Lord, but now find yourself disillusioned with church and even God, how can that life changing power that you once knew just disappear? Luke 8:4-15 addresses this directly:

And when much people were gathered together, and were come to Him out of every city, He spake by a parable: "A sower went out to sow his seed: and as he sowed, some fell by the way side; and it was trodden down, and the fowls of the air devoured it. And some fell upon a rock; and as soon as it was sprung up, it withered away, because it lacked moisture. And some fell among thorns; and the thorns sprang up with it, and choked it. And other fell on good ground, and sprang up, and bare fruit an hundredfold." And when He had said these things, He cried, "He that hath ears to hear, let him hear." And His disciples asked Him, saying, "What might this parable be?" And He said, "Unto you it is given to know the mysteries of the kingdom of God: but to others in parables; that seeing they might not see, and hearing they might not understand. Now the parable is this: The seed is the Word of God. Those by the way side are they that hear; then cometh the devil, and taketh away the word out of their hearts, lest they should believe and be saved. They on the rock are they, which, when they hear, receive the word with joy; and these have no root, which for a while believe, and in time of temptation fall away. And that which fell among thorns are they, which, when they have heard, go forth, and are choked with cares and riches and pleasures of this life, and bring no fruit to perfection. But that on the good ground are they, which in an honest and good heart, having heard the word, keep it, and bring forth fruit with patience."

Believers, whether new or old, will face the cares of this world. Often times when they're not as strong as they should be, the devil seizes on the opportunity and attacks them. Because their roots in the Word are superficial, not deep enough, they dry up.

God's Presence is our living water and we need to continually drink of the nutrition of that relationship.

The Way Back

This is a very important point for you to understand if you're a new Believer. If you've once walked with God, but walked away, get back to His river of life where He can once again feed you and make you strong.

If it's sin that cut you off from God's Presence, take a lesson from David.

David delighted in the Presence of the Lord. Initially he spent a lot of his life alone with God as he took care of the sheep. He always had a song in his heart because he had a heart of worship. He didn't sing just to sing. He didn't play his instruments just to play. As he sang and as he played, his goal was always to enter into the Presence of God.

~ *Psalm 42:8 - Blessed is the man whom thou choosest, and causest to approach unto thee, that he may dwell in thy courts: we shall be satisfied with the goodness of thy house, even of thy holy temple.*

~ *Psalm 91:1 - He that dwelleth in the secret place of the most High shall abide under the shadow of the Almighty.*

This sense of God's Presence and David's understanding of the Father's power and glory made him fearless. He took on the lion and the bear as a youth and because of that sense of God's power living in Him and guiding him, he would also be the guy who would ultimately take on the Giant, Goliath.

David was only a scrawny kid when he went to the front line to visit his brothers who were supposed to be fighting with the army of Israel against the Philistines. What he saw surprised him. Both Israel's mighty army and King Saul were hiding behind shelter as the Giant, Goliath, blasphemed the God of Israel and taunted the Israelite army.

David was furious. The fact that he was a young teenager didn't matter to him. He told Saul and the army that he would take on the giant. After they tried to suit him up with armor that didn't fit, he told the king in **1 Samuel 17:37,**

> *…The LORD that delivered me out of the paw of the lion, and out of the paw of the bear, he will deliver me out of the hand of this Philistine…*

David chose five smooth stones from a brook, took his sling and his staff and went out to meet the giant. When Goliath saw the boy David, he was insulted. He expected that Israel would send a warrior to fight and die, not a scrawny youth.

> *And the Philistine said unto David, Am I a dog, that thou comest to me with staves? And the Philistine cursed David by his gods. And the Philistine said to David, Come to me, and I will give thy flesh unto the fowls of the air, and to the beasts of the field.* **1 Samuel 17:43-44**

But the Philistine had no idea who it was that he was threatening that day. This ruddy boy was the same one that fellowshipped at the Master's feet. Despite his small stature, God had placed in him a power that only comes from spending time in the Everlasting Presence of the Most High.

David's response says it all. He yelled at the giant:

> *Thou comest to me with a sword, and with a spear, and with a shield: but I come to thee in the name of the LORD of hosts, the God of the armies of Israel, whom thou hast defied. This day will the LORD deliver thee into mine hand; and I will smite thee, and take thine head from thee; and I will give the carcases of the host of the Philistines this day unto the fowls of the air, and to the wild beasts of the earth; that all the earth may know that there is a God in Israel. And all this assembly shall know that the LORD saveth not with sword and spear: for the battle is the LORD'S, and he will give you into our hands.* **1 Samuel 17:45-47**

With the first shot of his sling, David's stone was sure and hammered into the Philistine's forehead. David then took Goliath's own sword and chopped off the giant's head where he fell. From that point on, it was a rout for the army of Israel.

To be fair to King Saul and the armies of Israel, Believers today are no different.

They were looking at the size of the giant and not the size of our God. This is a pattern with mankind. We get overwhelmed with the size of the enemy and the powers coming against us and forget Who it is that fights for us, or the One that we fight for. Remember, no matter what circumstances caused you to walk away from Him, no matter what you may be going through now, God is bigger than your disappointments and failures.

A true, unreligious, unguarded moment in His Everlasting Presence will remind you that no giant is too big.

David never forgot what it was like to be in the Presence of the Almighty. Later after he became king and found great success, he sinned with Bathsheba. Since he above all people knew better, although his sin was great, the price he paid was huge and justifiably so. He sent a man to die so that he as King could take his wife.

What can we learn from David?

Once we fall into sin, how do we get back to the place of God's Presence? How did David find his way back into God's Presence?

First of all, he prayed that God wouldn't take His Holy Spirit away. So David repented. Repentance brings restoration. David also yielded to God's judgment on his sin and he didn't fight it.

Someone reading this book might feel like objecting and say, "But Jesus died for our sins. David didn't have Jesus!"

It's true that Jesus died for the forgiveness of our sins, but sin is sin and you have to lay it down at the Master's feet to be forgiven.

> *For when we were yet without strength, in due time Christ died for the ungodly. For scarcely for a righteous man will one die: yet peradventure for a good man some would even dare to die. But God commendeth his love toward us, in that, while we were yet sinners, Christ died for us. Much more then, being now justified by his blood, we shall be saved from wrath through Him. For if, when we were enemies, we were reconciled to God by the death of his Son, much more, being reconciled, we shall be saved by his life. And not only so, but we also joy in God through our Lord Jesus Christ, by whom we have now received the atonement.* **Romans 5:6-11**

The consequences of sin in our own lives is something that we often have to walk out. That journey can be extremely painful. Going back to David, after he sinned with Bathsheba and Uriah, in addition to losing the son that he fathered with Bathsheba, his consequence was that his own son Absalom turned against him. David returned, recommitted himself to the Lord, repented and left the judgment for his sin up to God. This formula still works for Believers today.

If you're reading this book and walked away from God because of something that happened, or didn't happen, at church, or you fell into sin and haven't got back up, the King of the Universe wants you back. Not back at church, but back in His Presence where you first met Him.

Take the first step. Remember your first love. Remember that first change in you when something deep inside said, "You know, there's a real God!"

Peter's also a good example of someone who understood what it was like to be in the Presence of the Lord. After all, he was with Jesus before He ascended. He was also the first one to verbally confess this stunning statement:

> *When Jesus came into the coasts of Caesarea Philippi, He asked his disciples, saying, Whom do men say that I the Son of man am? And they said, Some say that thou art John the Baptist: some, Elias; and others, Jeremias, or one of the prophets. He saith unto them, But whom say ye that I am? And Simon Peter answered and said, Thou art the Christ, the Son of the living God. And Jesus answered and said unto him, Blessed art thou, Simon Barjona: for flesh and blood hath not revealed it unto thee, but my Father which is in heaven.* **Matthew 16:13-17**

It was the same Peter who denied the Lord three times when the pressure was on. But even in that sin, the Lord showed Peter His mercy and forgiveness after He rose.

> *And when they looked, they saw that the stone was rolled away: for it was very great. And entering into the sepulchre, they saw a young man sitting on the right side, clothed in a long white garment; and they were affrighted. And He saith unto them, Be not affrighted: Ye seek Jesus of Nazareth, which was crucified: He is risen; He is not here: behold the place where they laid Him. But go your way, tell his disciples and Peter that He goeth before you into Galilee: there shall ye see Him, as He said unto you.*
> *Mark 16:4-7*

"And make sure you tell Peter!" Wow, what a demonstration of God's love for this man who loved the Lord.

More to the point, God loves you the same way. Yes, He does want you back.

His Presence - Our Goal

Until people have the anointing and presence of the Holy Spirit in their lives, what they can do for God is limited. That's because human effort doesn't have the same outcome as God's calling and implementation of His power.

People ask me, "How can Believers, new or rededicated Christians, find the Presence of God?" The first thing that I tell them to do is to turn off the devil vision, or television. Devil vision produces double vision, which produces a double-minded man.

> *A double minded man is unstable in all his ways. James 1:8*

The other thing to do is get alone with God. Get away from so many voices and so many choices. Go someplace that is serene and pray the simplest prayer, "Lord, I'm a mess. Help!" Or simply say "Lord, help. Reveal yourself to me, Jesus. I really want to know you."

Now comes the hard part.

You wait for Him. If you're not feeling His Presence, and you will know when you do, ask Him again... and again... and again... and again. Purpose not to leave until He has touched you with His Presence.

Reveal your heart to Him. Talk to Him. Tell Him those things that you wouldn't dare tell anyone else. After all, He already knows them. But He wants you to come to Him and talk with Him. Repent, because in contrast to His holiness, everyone needs to repent of something. Be real with Him.

So maybe you've picked up this book and you've never really met Jesus. Maybe you've had a religious experience at some church, but have never felt His Presence. Maybe you don't have any experience with Him at all, but now you too think there's something to this Jesus stuff. Maybe you did once walk with Him, but think that your particular sin is so dark that God wouldn't forgive you. Here is His promise to you:

> *Come now, and let us reason together, saith the LORD: though your sins be as scarlet, they shall be as white as snow; though they be red like crimson, they shall be as wool. Isaiah 1:18*

There is no longer a veil between Him and you. If you sincerely come to Him in repentance and seeking His face, I promise you He will not turn you away.

Some of you may be stuck on the church hamster wheel and you're thinking that by just going through the motions, you'll get the desired results. Or maybe you could read a hundred books on a subject of finding His Presence and that alone will get you there.

The fact is that neither ceremony nor head-knowledge can bring you into the King's Presence. Finding God's Presence takes effort because you have to surrender everything to Him: Your time, your secrets, and your will.

No matter who you are, no matter what you've done, and no matter where you're coming from, my suggestions of the following steps are all the same. But be warned, they take serious, soul-searching effort. I've already mentioned a couple of them, but here's the list in a nutshell.

1. **Repent and believe on the Lord Jesus!** There's no other way to begin this process. Repentance shows God that you're serious about fellowshipping with Him. In addition, it is this process of repentance that opens the door of fellowship by allowing Him to wash away your sin.

   If we confess our sins, He is faithful and just to forgive us our sins, and to cleanse us from all unrighteousness. **1 John 1:9**

2. **After repentance, whether you're a new Believer or have come back to the Lord, earnestly ask God to reveal His Son Jesus to you.** In this process, cry out to Him to fill you with His Holy Spirit. Don't be afraid of this. It's your power receptacle to plug into. And believe me, you need that power desperately.

   If ye then, being evil, know how to give good gifts unto your children: how much more shall your heavenly Father give the Holy Spirit to them that ask Him? **Luke 11:13**

3. **Pray without ceasing.** In other words, make it a point to go through your day thinking to the Lord and listening to His small quiet voice in return. I pray continually throughout the day. I talk to the Lord throughout the day conversationally, not that He responds conversationally. But that interaction with Him, even in the small things, is powerful.

   Rejoice evermore. Pray without ceasing. In every thing give thanks: for this is the will of God in Christ Jesus concerning you. **1 Thess 5:16-18**

4. **Ask God to lead you to the resources or the people that He wants in your life.** After walking with Jesus for forty-six years, the most powerful advice I can give someone is to bring the right people in your life and take out the wrong people in your life

   This then is the message which we have heard of Him, and declare unto you, that God is light, and in Him is no darkness at all. If we say that we have fellowship with Him, and walk in darkness, we lie, and do not the truth: But if we walk in the light, as He is in the light, we have fellowship one with another, and the blood of Jesus Christ his Son cleanseth us from all sin. **1 John 1:5-7**

5. **Share.** People want to hear your faith and the power of God working in your life. As Derek Prince once said, "You can't have a testimony without a test!" Finding His Presence, especially for the first time, is a life-changing event. We're called to do that very thing.

*Let the redeemed of the LORD say so... **Psalm 107:2***

And in the future, when you blow it, sin, and you will, my admonishment is to confess your sin to the Lord quickly, then claim the blood of Jesus over it and then go on. Don't let the enemy beat you up with guilt or allow him to keep bringing you back to the same areas where you've failed. And believe me, he will try.

Because we are free-willed creations, for most of us this living sacrifice of ourselves is extremely difficult. If it were not so, then everybody who called themselves a Christian these days would be on fire for Jesus, but there is no other way to enter into His Presence.

> *I beseech you therefore, brethren, by the mercies of God, that ye present your bodies a living sacrifice, holy, acceptable unto God, which is your reasonable service. And be not conformed to this world: but be ye transformed by the renewing of your mind, that ye may prove what is that good, and acceptable, and perfect, will of God. **Romans 12:1-2***

Surrendering our wants, our desires, and our will to Him on a regular basis is the only way to continually enjoy the benefits of His Presence.

His Everlasting Presence can change your life forever and it is yours if you will seek Him.

In The Garden

I come to the garden alone,
While the dew is still on the roses,
And the voice I hear falling on my ear
The Son of God discloses.

And He walks with me, and He talks with me,
And He tells me I am His own;
And the joy we share as we tarry there,
None other has ever known.

He speaks, and the sound of His voice
Is so sweet the birds hush their singing,
And the melody that He gave to me
Within my heart is ringing.

I'd stay in the garden with Him,
Though the night around me be falling,
But He bids me go; through the voice of woe
His voice to me is calling.

HELP 4

His Everlasting Protection

The angel of the LORD encampeth

round about them that fear him,

and delivereth them.

Psalm 34:7

Protection

We live in a time when Satan doesn't even bother to hide anymore and people still don't see him.

A supernatural bloodbath is unfolding all around us and if there was ever a time when we need God's Everlasting Protection, it's now.

Within this H.E.L.P. you'll find answers to many questions you may be asking, but I have to warn you that you may not like what you hear. When it comes to the Almighty's Protection, people naturally assume that God will remove us from trouble. Nothing could be further from the truth.

I'm reminded of a section from the story of the road to Emmaus when the two men were trying to convince Jesus to stay with them.

> *And they drew nigh unto the village, whither they went: and he made as though he would have gone further. But they constrained him, saying, Abide with us: for it is toward evening, and the day is far spent.* *Luke 24:28-29*

"The day is far spent." This is where we are right now and night is coming when no one can work.

> *I must work the works of him that sent me, while it is day: the night cometh, when no man can work.* *John 9:4*

As Christians we are called to work, or fight, on behalf of our King. Within that arena, God provides protection to His people. This is what the Bible says about these days:

> *This know also, that in the last days perilous times shall come.* *2 Tim 3:1*

Those perilous times have now begun. We see clear evidence of them in the civil division that the devil has sown in our society.

> *And because iniquity shall abound, the love of many shall wax cold.* *Matt 24:12*

We see it in the falling away of Believers.

> *Let no man deceive you by any means: for that day shall not come, except there come a falling away first, and that man of sin be revealed, the son of perdition.* *2 Thess 2:3*

We see it in the exponential growth of knowledge. Travel around the world is easier and faster than ever and that smart phone in your hand makes you a Google genius.

> *But thou, O Daniel, shut up the words, and seal the book, even to the time of the end: many shall run to and fro, and knowledge shall be increased.* *Daniel 12:4*

We see it in the rise of "spiritualism".

> *Now the Spirit speaketh expressly, that in the latter times some shall depart from the faith, giving heed to seducing spirits, and doctrines of devils.* *1 Tim 4:1*

We also see it with other End Time prophecies coming true about the environment, sexual immorality, homosexuality, an increase in violence, an increase of earthquakes and natural disasters, mass animal deaths and war.

All around us we see the accelerating of events that will lead us to the culmination of history, but none of these signs is as disconcerting as the real-life danger that Christians all around the world are facing. That danger comes in both physical and supernatural forms.

Like it or not - We are at war.

The supernatural war impacts the earthly war. Victory in the supernatural impacts victory in the natural. Because Christians don't accurately understand spiritual warfare, they are prey to Satan and his demonic powers. All of us are guilty of this at one time or another.

As an example, I can talk about spiritual warfare until I'm blue in the face, but have at times failed to recognize that I was under extreme demonic or Fallen Angel attack. Like most people, I'd chalk it up to discomfort due to circumstance or just having a bad day.

While things do go wrong in our lives, it's important to always remember that our enemy is real and his attacks can be effective, more so when we're not paying attention. These attacks are becoming more intense and numerous as we move forward toward the End of the Age. It is in this environment that we need God's Everlasting Protection now more than ever.

Chapter 9
Battle Cry

For we wrestle not against flesh and blood, but against principalities, against powers, against the rulers of the darkness of this world, against spiritual wickedness in high places.

Ephesians 6:12

As we have seen in the previous sections, drilling down to the original language of the text helps us to better understand what the Lord is trying to communicate through His Word. This excerpt out of Ephesians is no exception. In fact, when you understand what it's saying, you'll view this supernatural war in a whole new light.

The word for "rulers" is *arché* and is plural. Its meaning indicates more than one ruler and more likely a group of rulers. Now keep that in the back of your mind for a moment. It literally means "one who was in the beginning" or the "preeminent one". But because it is plural, it means those "entities who were there from the beginning, who came first".

Huh… interesting.

The word for "powers" is *exousia* and is the same word that we saw in the last H.E.L.P., which means "to have the authority to act".

"Darkness of this world" is better translated "world forces of darkness" and is from the word *kosmokratór*. It quite literally means "ruler of this world" but again since we are dealing with a plural it means a group of evil, dark, rulers - kind of like a demonic cabal.

So let's pull this all together in a way that makes sense.

The Apostle Paul, the author, is basically telling us here that there is a literal Fallen Angel, shadow, cabal who has been granted the authority to act on earth against God's creation. In essence, mankind is on center stage and evil is being orchestrated against us by Fallen Angel Overlords who rule this planet.

That ancient evil is rising at the End of the Age, as the Bible said it would. Because of this, God's Everlasting Protection is an absolute necessity.

Recently I received an email from a listener and reader who asked a very incisive question on the issue of spiritual warfare. I can't think of a better way to start this discussion off than by sharing it with you here.

Steve,

Thank you sooo much for all you do. Believe me, a lot more people than you know (those with ears to hear) are with you in Spirit!

Here is a big problem I see, and this is parked squarely on me as well, you have mentioned it too but it remains. I am writing you because I think you both know and live out the answer. But I don't seem to get it - I do not know.

Spiritual warfare and how to use Luke 10:19: "Behold, I give unto you power to tread on serpents and scorpions, and over all the power of the enemy: and nothing shall by any means hurt you."

The body of Christ seems to be standing like a wide eyed deer at night before a Screaming Peterbilt! Can there be a more important problem to solve right now?

I really hope you and Tom Horn hook up and do a CD set because you two are so good together.

There are so many of us. What? Do we think we are just to witness the end time events?

Yes, I have read the whole armor of God scripture but it never seems to sink in. During these highly charged times what is a Christian to do? Enough said.

Steve, thank you.

Michael

First, thank you so much, Mike, for bringing this very important issue front and center. From the outset I can tell you that you are absolutely correct: There is no more important issue we face. This issue is life and death for the Believer.

We've entered into a new season, a new time, the End Times, where everything has changed. The spiritual battle that has been unseen for centuries is becoming seen in our 3D reality. Evil is becoming bolder because Satan knows that his time is short.

This H.E.L.P. should address many of your issues and show Believers how to activate God's Everlasting Protection in their lives.

Perilous Times

God's people cannot survive these days without God's Protection. As the supernatural war becomes more real and in our face, our need for God's Protection will become more apparent. That's because it will take the power of God to even keep us alive. This is exactly what the Word says: If God didn't move on our behalf, there would be no flesh left alive.

> For then shall be great tribulation, such as was not since the beginning of the world to this time, no, nor ever shall be. And except those days should be shortened, there should no flesh be saved: but for the elect's sake those days shall be shortened. *Matt 24:21-22*

The threats against humanity are bigger on a global scale than at any time since the creation of man. We're faced with biological warfare that can cause the entire planet to become extinct. We're faced with genetic and mutagenic alterations to the human genome that will make it impossible for mankind, as God created us, to survive or thrive. There are wars and rumors of wars, including the potential of a nuclear war, and earthquakes and natural disasters spreading throughout the globe in unprecedented numbers.

Yet, just as God protected Noah and his family from the corruption of their DNA and also rescued them from the flood, God will protect us.

One of the ways that God protects us is by His Holy Spirit. It is that same Spirit that helps us to understand Who it is we are fighting for and Who is fighting for us. Along with that, we must also understand that God has not left us defenseless. In providing His people defensive and offensive weapons, He's basically telling us that we must also fight in this battle and not expect Him to do all the work when it comes to our protection.

Because of this, Christians need to be trained in spiritual warfare, so pay attention. The ancient enemies that we are fighting, the Fallen Angels, have literally had thousands of years to hone their war skills against the people of God.

Not Protection From The Battle, Protection In The Battle

> For though we walk in the flesh, we do not war after the flesh, for the weapons of our warfare are not carnal, but mighty through God to the pulling down of strong holds. *2 Cor 10:3-4*

How can you have weapons that are mighty through God if you don't realize that you're in the midst of a battle?

Consider the statement in Ephesians 6:12 when it says *"we wrestle not against flesh and blood."* Everything in that statement is talking about a supernatural, or a higher dimensional order of being. And when you couple that with 2 Corinthians 10, which goes into that in great detail about this supernatural battle, you begin to understand that, like it or not, you are in the fight already. Will you simply be target practice for the enemy's fiery darts (Eph 6:6) or will you inflict pain right back at the devil and his hordes ? I don't know about you, but I want to give at least as much as I get.

Specifically **2 Corinthians 10:4** says:

> *For the weapons of our warfare are not carnal, but mighty through God to the pulling down of strong holds.*

What strongholds? The answer can be found in verse 5 where it says, *"and every high thing that exalteth itself against the knowledge of God."*

What is meant by every "high thing"?

Looking at the original language we see that the word for "high thing" in Greek is *hupsóma* which means "that which is lifted up" and can mean a physical barrier, or even a presumption. The word for "exalteth" literally means "to lift up" from the Greek word *epairó*.

When you look at the rest of verse 5, it specifically references *"casting down imaginations"* and *"bringing into captivity every thought to the obedience of Christ"*.

Why?

Why go from talking about a physical world that is falling apart to talking about stuff that's going on in your head?

Remember, demons and other entities are not only confined to our physical plain. They also exist in the supernatural realm, which we cannot see without the help of the Holy Spirit. They can interact with us without people ever knowing that they did so. Literally they can whisper in your ear and you'll think that the thought you just had was your own.

How's that for military grade PSYOPs (Psychological Operations)? Still think this isn't a war? This is why it is so important to base our lives on the Word of God. It is the anchor for the Believer's life even when we can't see the enemy.

Getting back to verse 5, we understand that someone, or something, is continually trying to raise up a barrier, mental or otherwise, between the knowledge of God and His creation. Since this is obviously not talking about humans, one has to come to the conclusion that it's talking about spiritual entities trying to lay encumbrances on God's elect: you and me, to thwart us.

Talk about a worldwide conspiracy! The devil and his minions continually assault the mind of Believers and try to block the truth of God and His Word from being activated and used in our lives. We're told in verse 6 to take revenge on the devil for those acts of spiritual sabotage.

This isn't the namby-pamby doctrine of a "love, love, love," or "do whatever I want because I am free" that you hear from many church pulpits today.

This is the language of war.

If we're going to make war on the enemy and we intend to pull down strongholds, the key components of our weapons are the gifts of the Holy Spirit. These gifts are categorically what it takes for Believers to wage war effectively.

Our Weapons

The Lord has provided for us a supernatural armory chock-full of high-explosive weapons to use in this spiritual war. But like any weapons, you had better know how to use them or you could shoot off your foot, or worse.

> ~ *1 Cor 4:7-8 - But unto every one of us is given grace according to the measure of the gift of Christ. Wherefore he saith, "When he ascended up on high, he led captivity captive, and gave gifts unto men."*

> ~ *1 Cor 12:7-11 - But the manifestation of the Spirit is given to every man to profit withal. For to one is given by the Spirit the word of wisdom; to another the word of knowledge by the same Spirit; to another faith by the same Spirit; to another the gifts of healing by the same Spirit; to another the working of miracles; to another prophecy; to another discerning of spirits; to another divers kinds of tongues; to another the interpretation of tongues. But all these worketh that one and the selfsame Spirit, dividing to every man severally as He will.*

Here's what I mean by knowing how to use those weapons against the enemy. One of the weapons that Christians have at our disposal is the "discerning of spirits". Let me be clear. Contrary to the nonsense that goes on in some churches or with televangelists today, discernment is not guessing, it's not getting a hunch and it's definitely not pulling out the Psychology Today Magazine and evaluating someone's "state of mind".

It is the Holy Spirit showing you the spirit, or entity, behind a man, and with that understanding is not based upon just his words or actions. It is a supernatural knowing of things you could not know. All the Gifts of the Spirit are important, but this one is crucial when it comes to knowing and understanding the spiritual forces that engage us. Paul in Galatians 6:7 said, *"Be ye not deceived"* so it stands to reason that we could be deceived if we're not diligent.

The only thing that's going to keep us from being deceived is that we have a love for the truth and we pour our request unto the Lord. Then we need to listen to His response through the Holy Spirit and sometimes through other brothers and sisters who operate in the Gifts of the Spirit.

Think of the Gifts of the Spirit as light bulbs designed to light up when God wants us to pay attention. The power behind those light bulbs is our faith.

> *But without faith it is impossible to please Him, for he that cometh to God must believe that He is, and that He is a rewarder of them that diligently seek Him.* **Hebrews 11:6**

So what is faith?

> *Now faith is the substance of things hoped for, the evidence of things not seen.* **Hebrews 11:1**

In your Sunday morning service, when was the last time you saw anybody operate in the gift of discerning of spirits? While there are some churches that operate, or at least say they operate, in some of the other gifts, the vast majority of mainstream churches will not touch this discerning gift with a ten-foot pole. Why?

It may be because they don't think they need it. Or it may be that those churches are less inclined to operate in the gifts. Or they say that the gifts have passed away when Jesus ascended to be with the Father. But God gave us those gifts to defend ourselves against ruthless, demonic entities. By denying the gifts, those churches have automatically disarmed themselves of these promised defensive measures, making them target fodder for the enemy.

In the thick of the battle, we must stand for Jesus or we'll fall for anything that the devil plays out before us. Our weapons are designed to help us not only survive this war but also make us victorious in it through the Lord's promised power.

> *And Jesus came and spake unto them, saying, "All power is given unto me in heaven and in earth."*
> *Matthew 28:18*

> *Behold, I give unto you power to tread on serpents and scorpions, and over all the power of the enemy: and nothing shall by any means hurt you.* ***Luke 10:19***

Deliverance is directly related to the gift of discerning of spirits and is one of the most overlooked spiritual gifts. It is a ministry that focuses on demonic confrontation through the power of the Holy Spirit by mature, called, Christians who also operate in the gift of discerning of spirits. Their confrontation is directly with the powers of evil and wicked spirits who have inhabited, i.e. demon-possessed, spiritually imprisoned and routinely afflicted people. These afflicted people are under direct and indirect influence of demonic and satanic spirits and are victims of these evil powers of darkness.

Those who are called to this ministry cannot go up against the enemy until they are certain of their authority in Jesus Christ. Jesus Himself and His disciples routinely interacted with demons.

> *And they arrived at the country of the Gadarenes, which is over against Galilee. And when he went forth to land, there met him out of the city a certain man, which had devils long time, and ware no clothes, neither abode in any house, but in the tombs. When he saw Jesus, he cried out, and fell down before him, and with a loud voice said, What have I to do with thee, Jesus, thou Son of God most high? I beseech thee, torment me not. (For he had commanded the unclean spirit to come out of the man. For oftentimes it had caught him: and he was kept bound with chains and in fetters; and he brake the bands, and was driven of the devil into the wilderness.) And Jesus asked him, saying, What is thy name? And he said, Legion: because many devils were entered into him. And they besought him that he would not command them to go out into the deep. And there was there an herd of many swine feeding on the mountain: and they besought him that he would suffer them to enter into them. And he suffered them. Then went the devils out of the man, and entered into the swine: and the herd ran violently down a steep place into the lake, and were choked.* ***Luke 8:26-33***

> *And when they were come to the multitude, there came to him a certain man, kneeling down to him, and saying, Lord, have mercy on my son: for he is lunatick, and sore vexed: for ofttimes he falleth into the fire, and oft into the water. And I brought him to thy disciples, and they could not cure him. Then Jesus answered and said, O faithless and perverse generation, how long shall I be with you? how long shall I suffer you? bring him hither to me. And Jesus rebuked the devil; and he departed out of him: and the child was cured from that very hour. Then came the disciples to Jesus apart, and said, Why could not we cast him out? And Jesus said unto them, Because of your unbelief: for verily I say unto you, If ye have faith as a grain of mustard seed, ye shall say unto this mountain, Remove hence to yonder place; and it shall remove; and nothing shall be impossible unto you. Howbeit this kind goeth not out but by prayer and fasting.*
> *Matt 17:14-21*

Deliverance involves hand-to-hand spiritual combat in close quarters where the fighting can get messy. Within these prayer sessions, the underbelly of evil is exposed. It can get dark and messy but Jesus is the Light and the Holy Spirit leads those Christians who are ministering.

Deliverance is serious business and should only be done by people who are called to this ministry. It must be done in the absolute faith of knowing Jesus, who He is, and knowing that the power and authority delegated by God does not belong to the minister but to Him. I've seen people lose track of the fact that they are fallible human beings and claim this authority and power as their own, with ugly results. It's God's delegated authority and it is very powerful.

One time the Lord specifically told me that people don't want to deal with the deliverance ministry because they don't want the responsibility.

In a separate instance, the Lord told me years ago, *"The invisible will become visible. That which terrified men in their dreams will take on a physical manifestation. Men's hearts will fail them for fear of looking after those things coming upon the earth."*

The gates of Hell are opening now! And these are not the evangelical nursery school gates that are designed to keep the little kiddies from being run over in the street. The Bible says:

> *Be sober, be vigilant; because your adversary the devil, as a roaring lion, walketh about, seeking whom he may devour.* **1 Peter 5:8**

These Fallen Angels and entities have been warring against mankind for millennia. Do you think mankind is really that tough to figure out?

In order to have God's Everlasting Protection, you have to understand the nature of the battle; you have to understand the weapons of the enemy; you have to understand the wiles of the enemy and the fact that you cannot deal with those wiles or the enemy's weapons in your own strength.

You cannot out-guess, out-fight, out-think, out-smart or out-maneuver the devil. It cannot be done! Our victory comes from standing in faith, trusting and knowing that it's God Who is the Lord of Hosts and Who fights for us. I am not aware of any OT or NT incident of warfare where anyone got a victory apart from God or His anointing.

Their Weapons

Like in any physical conflict, our enemy is also loaded for bear. But we don't understand the nature of battle because we think of sin as separate types of acts: i.e. adultery, fornication, murder and so on. All of that's bad, but the very nature of sin is the power of rebellion transmitted from the fallen angels and genetically introduced into fallen man's genome.

Sin is a power, not just an act.

However, with every weapon or assault of the enemy, God gives His people the ability to counterpunch.

The biggest counter punch is the act of redemption when we say "God, forgive me". The next counterpunch is telling God, "Please help me not to do what I know is wrong". The third and most lethal counterpunch to the devil is the fact that if we do sin, we have an advocate with the Father.

My little children, these things write I unto you, that ye sin not. And if any man sin, we have an advocate with the Father, Jesus Christ the righteous. And He is the propitiation for our sins, and not for ours only, but also for the sins of the whole world. 1 John 2:1-2

And:

If we confess our sins, He is faithful and just to forgive us our sins, and to cleanse us from all unrighteousness. 1 John 1:9

Can you imagine how frustrating that must be for the devil? He hits us with what he thinks will be a devastating blow, be it sin, or pain or whatever. Then God turns it right around and helps us to escape, or to grow even stronger from the experience.

And we know that all things work together for good to them that love God, to them who are the called according to his purpose. Romans 8:28

So what does the enemy do? He tries to convolute that message of deliverance and victory into something other than what the Bible says it is. One of the devil's greatest weapons is to manipulate man into thinking that God didn't say what He said. Gee, I seem to remember him pulling that stunt in the Garden with Eve.

Satan will take God's truth and make it into the religion of man to water it down and make it ineffective. In the Bible, Paul taught freedom in the Holy Ghost. Men, under Satan's bondage, teach bondage and call it religion.

Stand fast therefore in the liberty wherewith Christ hath made us free, and be not entangled again with the yoke of bondage. Galatians 5:1

The devil also knows how to use a special guilt on God's people to keep them forever under his thumb. But it's like the Lord says, *"What are you doing under the thumb?"* It's not just a Rolling Stone song, it's a tactic that Satan uses again and again.

Facing our Giants

Pastors, preachers and teachers will quote **Joshua 1:6-7** as a proof text on how people can be courageous in the face of danger, but those same pastors, preachers and teachers won't address the more salient points.

Be strong and of a good courage, for unto this people shalt thou divide for an inheritance the land, which I sware unto their fathers to give them. Only be thou strong and very courageous, that thou mayest observe to do according to all the law, which Moses my servant commanded thee. Turn not from it to the right hand or to the left, that thou mayest prosper whithersoever thou goest.

Forty years before, the Israelites had traveled from Egypt for forty days to this very same spot. They had sent twelve spies into the land to investigate. Here is the first report that they brought back:

*And they returned from searching of the land after forty days. And they went and came to Moses, and to Aaron, and to all the congregation of the children of Israel, unto the wilderness of Paran, to Kadesh; and brought back word unto them, and unto all the congregation, and shewed them the fruit of the land. And they told him, and said, "We came unto the land whither thou sentest us, and surely it floweth with milk and honey; and this is the fruit of it. Nevertheless the people be strong that dwell in the land, and the cities are walled, and very great: and moreover we saw the children of Anak there. The Amalekites dwell in the land of the south: and the Hittites, and the Jebusites, and the Amorites, dwell in the mountains: and the Canaanites dwell by the sea, and by the coast of Jordan." And Caleb stilled the people before Moses, and said, "Let us go up at once, and possess it; for we are well able to overcome it." But the men that went up with him said, "We be not able to go up against the people; for they are stronger than we." And they brought up an evil report of the land which they had searched unto the children of Israel, saying, "The land, through which we have gone to search it, is a land that eateth up the inhabitants thereof; and all the people that we saw in it are men of a great stature. And there we saw the giants, the sons of Anak, which come of the giants: and we were in our own sight as grasshoppers, and so we were in their sight." **Numbers 13:25-33**

Only Joshua and Caleb said that the Israelites could go in and defeat the giants and the "strong" inhabitants of the land. The rest of the people didn't trust that God could deliver them and so they chickened out. The result was that God punished their unbelief by causing them to wander the desert for forty years until everyone of that generation, except Joshua and Caleb, died off!

So while there's certainly a solid lesson here about trusting God in the face of danger, let's try to be a little more sympathetic to the doubting Israelites. After all, there were giants! And I'm not talking just tall people; these giants were at least thirty-six foot tall! They ate giant grapes and they ate people, for crying out loud. Who could blame the Israelites for being concerned about what lay in front of them? But this is where real courage comes in.

In spite of the overwhelming odds, Joshua and Caleb, like David would do more than 350 years later, didn't look at the giants. They looked at God!

Wandering in the wilderness for forty years gave the Israelites plenty of time to remember the sight of those massive giants. The sight must have haunted them in their dreams. When they finally returned to the Jordan and got ready to cross over, God knew their hearts and reminded them exactly who He was and who they were in Him.

So why am I telling you all of this in this book on the Everlasting H.E.L.P.s of God? Yes, I know a lot about giants, but there's a wonderful lesson here that applies directly to you and me in these days.

Remember, Joshua and Caleb had to fight physical giants. They had to deal with superior forces, superior intellect, superior size and superior strength, but God basically told them, "Go in and take them. I'm on your side!"

So my question to you is: **Do we really believe that God is on our side?**

As outlined in the previous section, we're in the midst of a war and the enemy is dead serious. Do not be dissuaded because like Joshua and Caleb, we too can say, "Yup, we can take 'em."

What shall we then say to these things? If God be for us, who can be against us? **Romans 8:31**

The good news is that God is on our side. The bad news is that if we struggle and don't trust God, we can't expect Him to provide for and protect us. Remember the double-minded man James described?

But let him ask in faith, nothing wavering. For he that wavereth is like a wave of the sea driven with the wind and tossed. For let not that man think that he shall receive any thing of the Lord. A double minded man is unstable in all his ways. **James 1:6-8**

Coming into these days, all of us will face our giants. How will you respond? Will you recognize who you are in Him, or will you look like a grasshopper in your own sight when compared to the demonic hordes that are now beginning to swarm?

The Battle Belongs to the Lord

God created man to have dominion, to rule and reign, over His creation. Joshua knew that it would only be by God's supernatural provision that he and the Israelites could occupy the Promised Land and slay those giants.

Joshua and Caleb were intimately aware of Who God was and how strong His power was. They were always with Moses when he interacted with God, except on Mt. Sinai, and they were there to see the mountain quake; they heard the horns; and they witnessed first-hand the plagues of Egypt along with God's miraculous deliverance. In doing so, they developed a supernatural framework from which to view the task of going into the Promised Land and defeating the giants.

In some respects Believers today have it tougher than they did. Due to the lack of the miraculous moving of the Holy Spirit, the vast majority of modern-day Christians have no practical working basis from which to view God's might. That first witness of His power enables us to trust Him.

As we discussed in the H.E.L.P. on God's Power, Jesus said that His disciples were to receive Power when the Holy Spirit came. That Power, both what Joshua saw and ours, is essential in defeating physical or spiritual giants.

God's Everlasting Protection is a byproduct of that power. It's ours when we seek Him but we also have to do our part by having courage, the kind of courage that comes from knowing God and His character and understanding that He can be trusted even in the face of our own doubts, unbelief, insecurities and battles.

In this way ordinary people, serving an extraordinary personal God, can perform selfless acts of bravery. Throughout history, ordinary people became heroes by conquering impossible odds because of their faith. Faith in God, and His Word, makes all the difference when it comes to taking down giants.

Ephesians 6:10
"Be strong in the Lord and in the power of His might" is more than just a Sunday school verse. It needs to be our battle cry. With that kind of faith, His Everlasting Protection will follow.

I went to visit a friend of mine in San Diego, California a little more than a decade after I'd gotten saved in the mid 1980's. It was during a time that was one of the darkest periods in my walk. His name was

Harold Bradeson and he was a mighty man of God. He showed God's Protection in a powerful illustration and it is one of the hallmarks of my life!

Harold took me to a high spot that overlooked the vast city below and walked me right to the edge of the steep cliff. I thought, "Oh, no! He's going to test my faith and ask me to jump!" Instead, what he said next would forever ring in my spirit.

Below us the sprawl of civilization stretched as far as the eyes could see. Roads were like a distant grid and I could barely make out vehicles, which looked no bigger than ants scurrying around the vast city. Harold turned to me and began to prophecy as if the Lord Himself were speaking to me. He said,

> *"Steve, do you see those people down in the valley? They think they are safer without Me than you are here, standing on the edge of a cliff. You will always be at the precipice, (of what's going to happen), but I will always be there standing with you."*

At the same time, I sensed the presence of angels all around me as if God's bodyguards surrounded me. The Lord's presence was thick in that place and I knew that God renewed His calling on my life regardless of my difficult circumstances.

People always say that I'm edgy, so now you know why!

God's Everlasting Protection offers you and me the safest haven that we will ever need.

Chapter 10
The God of War

The LORD is a man of war: the LORD is his name.

Exodus 15:3

The entire OT as well as the NT is set in the arena of conflict. One of God's titles is the Lord of Hosts, which means "the lord of the armies", or the "Commander-in-Chief".

God's not surprised by the level of spiritual warfare we are seeing in these days. This spiritual conflict has been taking place since before the creation of earth and man. We're only just now getting to the battlefield. God has been here all along.

A war on pre-adamic earth was fought by Michael and his angels against the devil and his angels. Judgment followed when Satan and his angels lost and were cast down to earth.

And there was war in heaven. Michael and his angels fought against the dragon and the dragon fought and his angels, and prevailed not. Neither was their place found any more in heaven. And the great dragon was cast out, that old serpent, called the Devil, and Satan, which deceiveth the whole world. He was cast out into the earth, and his angels were cast out with him. And I heard a loud voice saying in heaven, "Now is come salvation, and strength, and the kingdom of our God, and the power of his Christ, for the accuser of our brethren is cast down, which accused them before our God day and night. And they overcame him by the blood of the Lamb, and by the word of their testimony; and they loved not their lives unto the death. Therefore rejoice, ye heavens, and ye that dwell in them. Woe to the *inhabiters of the earth and of the sea for the devil is come down unto you, having great wrath, because he knoweth that he hath but a short time!" **Revelation 12:7-12***

When the devil and his angels rebelled, Jesus said that He saw Lucifer fall like lightning. The earth has become the battlefield and we need God's Everlasting Protection in the midst of the fight.

Running To The Fight

*Proclaim ye this among the Gentiles, "Prepare war, wake up the mighty men, let all the men of war draw near; let them come up. Beat your plowshares into swords, and your pruninghooks into spears. Let the weak say, I am strong. Assemble yourselves, and come, all ye heathen, and gather yourselves together round about, thither cause thy mighty ones to come down, O LORD. Let the heathen be wakened, and come up to the valley of Jehoshaphat. For there will I sit to judge all the heathen round about. Put ye in the sickle, for the harvest is ripe. Come, get you down; for the press is full, the fats overflow; for their wickedness is great. Multitudes, multitudes in the valley of decision: for the day of the LORD is near in the valley of decision. The sun and the moon shall be darkened, and the stars shall withdraw their shining. The LORD also shall roar out of Zion, and utter His voice from Jerusalem; and the heavens and the earth shall shake: but the LORD will be the hope of His people, and the strength of the children of Israel. **Joel 3:9-16***

Most people run away from a battle, but you and I are called to run to the fight. The idea that God would allow his creation to be helpless against vastly superior intellect, strength and weaponry is not consistent with the character and nature of God. We don't fight alone; the Lord of Hosts, our Commander, leads the way.

God, as the "Lord of War", automatically thrusts Believers into the supernatural context of war. Spiritual warfare and deliverance are not optional. They are mandatory. We are on the battlefield, this 3D reality that we call earth. All around us interdimensional supernatural beings want to steal from us, kill us, and destroy us (John 10:10).

We have two choices. We can sit back and get maimed or we can turn the tables on the devil and his hordes and take the fight to them. These are your only two options, especially in these days when demonic activity has increased so dramatically. Making no choice is making the choice to become prey.

God's supernatural Protection is afforded to those Believers who will join Him in this fight. The degree to which we obey God in our calling and our walks, as revealed to us by the Holy Spirit, is the degree to which we can count on God's Protection.

So what does this direction to protection look like in practicality? It depends on the depth of your relationship with the Lord. If you're a Spirit-filled Christian, then all of the weapons that we've already discussed are at your disposal. If you're a Christian but not Spirit-filled, I have no idea how this interaction will take place. I'm not saying that the Lord can't let His will be known to non-spirit-filled Believers. He's God. He can do anything He wants, but this example is based on my experience and those of other Spirit-filled Believers.

The Holy Spirit starts this process by giving me a thought or a feeling, a dream or a vision, about my circumstances, situation, or location. Or, as I'm reading the Word, something that I've been thinking about or feeling could jump off the page at me. The Holy Spirit inside of me is waving a figurative red flag and saying, "Pay attention!" It could even be from something in the Bible that's talking about a whole different subject, but the Holy Spirit has used it to give me guidance.

IMPORTANT CAVEAT - The Holy Spirit will NEVER contradict God's Word. For example, someone might be toying with the idea of having an affair and they read something out of the Word and latch onto it, saying, "See! The Holy Spirit's saying it's okay to sleep with so and so." No, that's never going to happen because the Word specifically says not to be adulterous, so the Holy Spirit will never say it's OK. I'm sure there are other examples but you get the idea.

To continue my illustration: I've had a thought or feeling that's been verified by the Word. God could then make His will known to me through a "Word" from another Believer, most likely someone who operates in the gift of knowledge, wisdom, faith or prophecy. Hearing this Word brings an instant witness to my spirit, and corresponds with the thoughts I had in my own head, and the previous scripture(s) that the Holy Spirit used to speak to my heart.

ANOTHER CAVEAT - God will always speak to you first before He sends someone to you with a Word. I am always suspecting of people saying that they have a Word from the Lord for me when God has never told me any such thing. A real word will be witnessed to by the Holy Spirit living inside of you, because He's already been talking to you about the subject. There are countless real life examples of people being ambushed by sidewalk or parking lot prophets saying that "God told me to tell you..." God will never violate that first-person witness between yourself and the Holy Spirit. If someone says that they have a Word from the Lord for you, and you haven't heard it yourself, or it isn't in sync with the Holy Spirit in you - run the other way.

As you develop this spiritual antenna to hear and know the Lord's voice in your walk, and you've experienced these supernatural confirmations, your faith will grow and you'll find His Everlasting Protection. If everything that He's said to you has come true, or has been established by two or three other witnesses (2 Cor 13:1), can't you also trust Him to lead you in this war and for the Protection that He's promised?

The Bible is full of examples of people who had to trust God to lead them in this fight and to protect them in the midst of it. David was a man of war. David knew that in order to protect those things that God had entrusted to him, he would have to do what was necessary. God gave David victory over Goliath. But before David could use his sling to defeat Goliath, David had to first be able to use that same sling to take out the lion and the bear.

Like David, our skill and trust in spiritual warfare is honed in the small things. Only then will be able to go out and slay giants for God.

> *Trust in the LORD with all thine heart; and lean not unto thine own understanding. In all thy ways acknowledge Him, and He shall direct thy paths.* **Proverbs 3:5-6**

But even in slaying those giants, we must always remember that there's indication in the OT that God's people never had a victory apart from Him - none. You can't go out and help God defeat the enemy; God has to defeat your enemies for you and uses you in that process.

And all this assembly shall know that the LORD saveth not with sword and spear: for the battle is the LORD'S, and He will give you into our hands. **1 Samuel 17:47**

You and I are called, are expected, to be in this fight. In fact, Jesus Himself said of John the Baptist:

And from the days of John the Baptist until now the kingdom of heaven suffereth violence, and the violent take it by force. **Matt 11:12**

This is the fight to which we must run.

The Shadow War

In the last chapter I spoke about various weapons that the enemy uses against us. It was by no means an exhaustive list, but only some things for you to think about. When we read the Bible, often we fail to see the practical implications of these supernatural actions. It's extremely important for you to see how these demonic entities implement their strategies and weapons.

As I write these words, the United States is a philosophically and emotionally divided country. The division hasn't been this great since the Civil War. We see hard lines being drawn in the proverbial sand between the Left and the Right. To add to this environment, President Trump is trying to fill a vacant seat on the U.S. Supreme Court with a man by the name of Brett Kavanaugh who, by all accounts prior to these confirmation hearings, has had an excellent reputation.

Please don't misunderstand my words here. They are not political, nor am I trying to make a political point. My goal is to simply show you the spirit behind people's actions. And believe me when I tell you, Satan will use people whenever and however he can in order to thwart God's kingdom.

The President has also let it be known of his desire to upend the Deep State. Whether you believe that the Deep State exists or what it is, is a subject for a different time. You may also believe that Trump is a wolf in sheep's clothing and is part of the apparatus that he vehemently opposes publicly. Again, neither of these points is important to this discussion because we are really talking about spirits and entities that are behind people's action.

The word that is omitted from Mr. Trump's diatribe on the Deep State is the word "Luciferian".

Behind both the Left and the Right paradigms is a supernatural wickedness that is orchestrating division and evil in our society. These demonically influenced people are more than evil men and women. They are sold-out to Satan himself and are known as Luciferians.

In this supernatural battlefield, we know that Satan is the god of this world and that his time is short. He's now wielding all of his weapons in order to do as much damage as possible.

The evil that is being fomented (in this case, by the Left) could actually be driven by the manifestation of the Fallen Angels in physical form. Since these beings can masquerade in any form that they want, you and I see them, and have seen them for years, as people. In other words, some of the people that you see with business suits are not human men and women, but evil entities who have morphed their true identities into human form.

You think this analysis is farfetched? Then I will remind you of the fact that the Apostle Paul said that we "could entertain angels unaware". If that were true, why would we not expect that some of those angels could be of the Fallen kind? The devil inserts himself into the country's political process through the evil spouting from their lips, and negatively influences our society with those beings.

What has the Left so upset about Judge Kavanaugh is that he's reportedly a Christian and Pro-Life. As such, he could well be the swing vote to overthrow Roe vs. Wade and put a stop to the shedding of innocent blood in our country through abortion, at least federally.

Again, these are just the facts and I'm not trying to lift up one party over the other, although I'm sure you can guess my preference. I believe abortion is evil, it's demonic and I make no bones about that. But as far as the political parties go, earlier in the book I called myself an equal opportunity offender. I believe both parties have sold out, as evidenced by how they've voted and lined their pockets over the years, although certainly one more than the other. I don't trust any of them, but I do know what the Lord has told me.

> He said, "Steve, the reason why the Left and the satanists want the blood of the innocents through abortion is because it is that blood that fuels the ritual magic used against my people. Because of this, they will fight to their end to maintain this ritual sacrifice through abortion of the innocents."

"Ritual magic", that's what He said. Ritual magic demands innocent blood to be effective. No wonder God is so opposed to the shedding of innocent blood - as well as the murder of innocent babies.

The Lord also showed me that ritual magic will be the fuel for the war against Christians in the very near future. The vast majority of these Believers would not speak-up, stand-up or even pray-up against the slaughter of the innocents or the shedding of their innocent blood. They don't understand that ritual magic will be like rocket fuel in a steamroller, mowing everybody down in its path. These Believers are ignorant or not smart enough to pull the plug on the machine before it ultimately consumes them.

The devil will also soon use more numerous weapons than he's deploying now. Although they are just trickling out, soon there will be a torrent of torture and murder that Believers won't be able to stand up against without God's Everlasting Protection.

If you are not absolutely dependent on the Lord, you'll be in for a rude awakening. In our lifetimes we will see the Antichrist conduct counterfeit signs and wonders. Lukewarm, flash-frozen-vomit Christians, who have basically denied God, will accept those signs and embrace the Son of Perdition.

But my larger point is that this is a supernatural war against unseen forces and at times we have seen, and we will see, those entities and weapons deployed in our physical realm. This is why I speak about Ephesians 6 with such passion. People are clueless to the reality of this battle. They think that this is the Tooth-Fairy and the Grinch making war against them.

What they fail to recognize is that these are the most powerful entities in the world that have previously tried to overthrow God's kingdom. And guess what: If they tried to overthrow God's kingdom, and the Bible says that there is war in the heavens, how do people think they're going to escape this without God's Everlasting Protection?

The Future Is Now

Ye stiffnecked and uncircumcised in heart and ears, ye do always resist the Holy Ghost. As your fathers did, so do ye. Which of the prophets have not your fathers persecuted? And they have slain them which shewed before of the coming of the Just One; of whom ye have been now the betrayers and murderers. **Acts 7:51-52**

Prophecy is always acknowledged as something that's coming on the scene but never acknowledged when it arrives on the scene. This explains how the vast majority of Israel missed the Messiah's coming even though they'd been told about it, sometimes in great detail, for centuries.

The Church today is no different.

Surely the Lord GOD will do nothing, but He revealeth His secret unto His servants the prophets. **Amos 3:7**

We have been told about what to expect at the End of the Age, yet the vast majority of Christians remain unrepentant and disconnected from a direct relationship with God and His Holy Spirit. But God always warns His people and even goes so far as to send out His angels to warn and protect. I've had people contact me over the years to tell me how someone strange came to warn them to leave. They would relate how, after the fact, that they thought it was an angel disguised as a man.

Be not forgetful to entertain strangers, for thereby some have entertained angels unawares. **Hebrews 13:2**

We saw this kind of thing happen in the OT with Lot and Sodom:

For we will destroy this place, because the cry of them is waxen great before the face of the LORD; and the LORD hath sent us to destroy it. **Genesis 19:13**

Or people have had dreams and visions about leaving the place they that were in and they listened. That listening, and more importantly obeying, saved their lives. We will need this kind of heart if we want to walk in His Everlasting Protection.

Disobedience always brings death but obedience always brings life.

The Fullness of Time

I'm constantly bombarded with the question, "Steve, how much longer do you think we have?"

All I can say is that I'm not a soothsayer and I don't read tealeaves or chicken bones. I have no idea. Like you, I watch the events unfold in the news and put them up against the Word of God to glean understanding about where we are in time.

If Jesus told His disciples that He didn't know when things at the end were going to transpire, but only His Father in heaven did, who am I? Nor did Jesus show me when things would transpire, only some of the things that would happen.

We're facing a building super-storm of events all racing to a head: genetic breakthroughs that will ultimately corrupt man's genome; the destruction of our eco-system by persistent geo-engineering; hot spots all around the world and particularly in the middle east that could launch us into the next world war, a war that we will not be able to step back from. The gates of Hell are opening to release giants and entities that have been imprisoned or dormant for millennia. These events all point to the End of the Age being close, so if I have to guess, I'd say - not very long.

The Bible discusses such things. The book of Daniel indicates a general time line of events. The idea of "time" is broken down into general times, the End Times, and then specific times when events take place. The phrase "In that day," in the OT is often used by the prophets to proclaim the coming of the Messiah, Jesus.

God declared what was going to happen in Israel's future but the people who should have been paying attention would dismiss the event, i.e. Israel rejected the Messiah. Even in our lives, how many times has God made promises to us but when those promises were fulfilled, we didn't even recognize it as an answer to prayer.

Many Christians today even doubt that we're in the End Times. Call it doubt, call it unbelief or whatever, but I think there may be other psychological or scientific reasons as to why we don't see time for what it is.

The way the brain relates to timing is the way it relates to motion. We don't see motion, per se. What we see are a bunch of images, and our brain puts those images together, one right after another in quick succession, to create the illusion of motion for us.

This is a lot like the first movie camera called the Strip Kinetograph built by Thomas Edison and his team. Movies today are put together in the same way as individual images running one right after another. The brain puts the images together in one fluid stream of motion.

Albert Einstein didn't believe that time was really linear, meaning that each minute passes one after another forever. Rather, he believed in a circular concept of time and that the past, the present and the future all existed at the same time. His idea of dynamically curved space-time in general relativity speaks to this concept.

The Bible alludes to this idea in Isaiah 46:9-10 when God says, *"Remember the former things of old: for I am God, and there is none else; I am God, and there is none like me, declaring the end from the beginning, and from ancient times the things that are not yet done..."*

Our stream of consciousness where time is concerned is a lot like this stream of pictures strung one right after the other.

> *People who specialize in such things argue that acceleration is more than just a nagging feeling that life is speeding by. The impressive sounding International Geosphere-Biosphere Programme (IGBP), an organization that studied global change, found in its research that the "human enterprise" did indeed experience "dramatic acceleration" along social, economic, and environmental lines over the past two centuries. Things really picked up in the 1950s, according to the IGBP, with some even making the case that Earth entered a new epoch that decade. Production and consumption, as well their environmental impact, rapidly escalated during what the organization called the "Great Acceleration," a period of time in which we are still living.[8]*

8 Lawrence Samuel, "Is Time Speeding Up?" Psychology Today, https://www.psychologytoday.com/us/blog/future-trends/201808/is-time-speeding (August 20, 2018)

I should clarify for some of you who just did a double-take. I didn't fall off some New Age cliff where this stream of consciousness is concerned. It pertains to the flow of events from a reader's perspective. That's what I'm talking about here: the flow of accelerating events in our 3D world.

So you can see by the above article excerpt, this acceleration of time is not just in your head. When it comes to prophecy, we see technology and world events rushing by, frame after frame, faster and faster until, before we know it, we will be at the end. But it is in the distance between then and now that we will need God's Everlasting Protection because rest assured, those are dangerous times indeed.

Because of that danger, the Bible says that God will "shorten the days". But what does that mean in practicality?

There are 365 days in a year, 52 weeks in a year, 7 days in a week, 24 hours in a day, 1440 minutes in a day and 86400 seconds in a day. These seem to be hard facts and yet God is perfectly capable of manipulating time as demonstrated in Joshua 10:12-13:

> Then spake Joshua to the LORD in the day when the LORD delivered up the Amorites before the children of Israel, and he said, "In the sight of Israel, Sun, stand thou still upon Gibeon; and thou, Moon, in the valley of Ajalon." And the sun stood still, and the moon stayed, until the people had avenged themselves upon their enemies. Is not this written in the book of Jasher? So the sun stood still in the midst of heaven, and hasted not to go down about a whole day.

We see this manipulation of time by God a second time in Isaiah 38: 4-8:

> Then came the word of the LORD to Isaiah, saying, "Go, and say to Hezekiah, 'Thus saith the LORD, the God of David thy father, I have heard thy prayer, I have seen thy tears: behold, I will add unto thy days fifteen years. And I will deliver thee and this city out of the hand of the king of Assyria: and I will defend this city. And this shall be a sign unto thee from the LORD, that the LORD will do this thing that he hath spoken. Behold, I will bring again the shadow of the degrees, which is gone down in the sun dial of Ahaz, ten degrees backward.'" So the sun returned ten degrees, by which degrees it was gone down.

Here's a different thought: Consider for a moment that, rather than removing some of those 86,400 seconds in the day, God may well change our brain's perception of time, or specifically our stream of consciousness. What if He's already started doing this? We look at events in our lives that are forthcoming, but suddenly we find them in the past, here and gone.

I maintain that there's really no such thing as time, as shown by the fact that Jesus died once for all men, at all times. Rather, what we perceive as linear time is really like the curved surface of a basketball with the lettering written across it. Time is not linear, as we perceive it, it is circular. Certainly this idea fits with what Einstein believed.

So when it comes to God shortening the days, which is our perception, could it be that God is compressing time and events like we do with computer data on zip files? In other words, the events still take place in the time allotted, but God is condensing the time together, "shortening the days", in order to get us to the end faster.

Regardless of whether He is compressing the time or not, even within that period, God has appointed specific times.

> *Now learn a parable of the fig tree, when his branch is yet tender, and putteth forth leaves, ye know that summer is nigh. So likewise ye, when ye shall see all these things, know that it is near, even at the doors. Verily I say unto you, this generation shall not pass, till all these things be fulfilled. Heaven and earth shall pass away, but my words shall not pass away. But of that day and hour knoweth no man, no, not the angels of heaven, but my Father only.* **Matt 24:32-36**

Another example of God's timing is the fact that Jesus was born at the specific place, at the specific time that God ordained. And He told mankind that it was going to happen through the prophet Micah.

> *But thou, Bethlehem Ephratah, though thou be little among the thousands of Judah, yet out of thee shall he come forth unto me that is to be ruler in Israel; whose goings forth have been from of old, from everlasting.* **Micah 5:2**

Paul points out that it was in the fullness of time that Jesus was born.

> *But when the fullness of the time was come, God sent forth His Son, made of a woman, made under the law, to redeem them that were under the law, that we might receive the adoption of sons. And because ye are sons, God hath sent forth the Spirit of His Son into your hearts, crying, Abba, Father. Wherefore thou art no more a servant, but a son; and if a son, then an heir of God through Christ.* **Gal 4:4-7**

God created time and space and exists outside of it, and He is more than capable to give you what you need during these days including His Everlasting Protection, regardless of how much time we have.

Chapter 11
Perspective

And thine house and thy kingdom shall be established for ever before thee: thy throne shall be established for ever.

2 Sam 7:13

There is no question; we will see horrific times in the not-too-distant future. In that difficult period, when things seem to be at their worst, God will raise up a standard and you will see His true Church arise. If you stay close to Him, purpose to serve Him and continually seek His presence, you will also experience His Everlasting Protection like never before.

Pitching Your Tent

In the last chapter I talked about David. In his life, David had been through some harrowing events. Because he appears often in the OT and he wrote many of the psalms, including Psalm 91, we have direct insight into those events. Although he met danger on a regular basis, David's protection came from living under the shadow of the Almighty.

He that dwelleth in the secret place of the most High shall abide under the shadow of the Almighty. **Psalm 91:1**

The word translated here as "dwelleth" is from the Hebrew word *yashab*, which means to "sit", "remain" or "dwell". It gives the understanding of someone who is staying where they are and not leaving.

The phrase "secret place" comes from the word *sether* and literally means "a covering" like a pavilion or a hiding place, or a secret place. As we saw in the H.E.L.P. of Presence, the word "abide" is the word *lun*, which means to "lodge", "stay the night" or "to pitch your tent". The word "shadow" is from the word *tsel*, which means "shadow" or "protection".

If we put all of this together in our modern-day vernacular we read, "The person that stays and camps out under the covering of God to hide from the world will be protected under His shadow."

God is inviting us to camp out with Him just like He did with the children of Israel during their forty years in the wilderness. That place is where the shadow of His Protection can rest on us. But God's people also have to claim His Protection and not just assume, or presume, that they get it automatically.

 When you claim His Protection, you're acknowledging that there is an ongoing battle.

 You're also acknowledging that your strength alone is not enough to defeat the enemy. This acknowledgment puts God in His rightful place as your Deliverer.

 This acknowledgment enables God, as He did with Israel's marvelous victories, to give you the victory over the enemy.

As you may recall from the word *exousia*, you can have a legal claim to His Protection, but no functional ability to utilize it. By claiming that Protection, you give yourself both the legal and functional ability to enact His Protection.

David sought the presence of the Lord above everything else. Then he sought the protection of his sheep because his father Jessie had tasked him to tend the flock. The boldness in David was a byproduct of the love he had for God. That love and the worship in his heart for the Father fueled the courage that he needed in his exploits. It was also that love and worship that God would see as the two most qualifying attributes to make him a shepherd over Israel.

Psalm 91 makes it obvious that God has determined to protect His people. The root of this supernatural war is spiritual rebellion, led by the Fallen Angels. We, His children, exist in the physical realm and cannot fight that supernatural war without His help. The Holy Spirit, who is our Comforter and our Protection, was sent to live inside of us and empower us to win this fight.

> *And I will pray the Father, and He shall give you another Comforter, that He may abide with you for ever, even the Spirit of truth, whom the world cannot receive, because it seeth Him not, neither knoweth Him. But ye know Him, for He dwelleth with you, and shall be in you. I will not leave you comfortless: I will come to you.* **John 14:16-18**

The Worship/Presence Connection

God's Protection is directly related to our praise and worship. That's because the Lord inhabits the praise and worship of the saints.

> *But thou art holy, O thou that inhabitest the praises of Israel.* **Psalm 22:3**

So if we want God's Protection, doesn't it stand to reason that if we remain in His presence, His Protection is automatically given to us?

The protection of all the mighty men of God, whether it be Paul, David, Jehoshaphat, Moses, Joshua or Caleb was a result of God's people remaining in His presence. As Psalm 91 points out, God is telling us to stay close enough to Him so as to have His shadow fall on us (that's pretty close). Considering all that will be occurring in the months and years to come, and given the evil that is befalling the earth and the hazards of that evil, staying by His side is excellent advice.

If we want to be protected during these days, we have to be in His presence. One of the ways that you can get into His presence is by having a heart of worship like David.

As you walk with God, remember that nothing can happen to you that He doesn't already know about or has allowed. Regardless of the situation, He can give you "peace that surpasses all understanding" in the midst of difficult times. His peace can envelop us even when the devil dishes out his worst. In the meantime, if we set our hearts to be about the Father's business, we will not look at the circumstances. Instead, we will focus on His goals and His purposes.

If you know Him and He knows you, if you seek Him and spend time in His presence, if you live your life for Him instead of your own purposes, He can surround you with His angels in protection and even if you die, you will be protected in eternity. It's truly a win-win proposition. Live your life without fear and with purpose, seeking His presence and He will direct your path.

The Power of Praise

Did you know that our praise and worship drives the demons absolutely crazy?

That's because every time a Christian gives glory to God in genuine thanksgiving and praise, it reminds the devil, the demons and the Fallen Ones of their fatal choice. Although they beheld God with their own eyes and heard Him with their own ears, they chose to separate themselves forever by making war against the King of Glory.

It's important to remember that true praise and worship, in the Spirit, is not the same as jumping around on stage with a Christian rock band. It's not about the music, it's about your heart.

I see a very dangerous trend in our modern-Church era. People are substituting the harmonics of rebellion in song and music for true praise and worship; they are not the same. Because most Christians don't understand the difference, or in some cases they don't even care, they're falling into the devil's snare.

David knew how to worship God and he enjoyed being in His presence. And even while Saul, the king of Israel at the time, couldn't get into the presence of the Lord, David was called in to soothe Saul's mood (1 Sam 16:14-23).

How did David know how to worship God at such a young age? It was because he'd spent a great deal of time alone with God and worshipping Him while tending the sheep. True worship will always produce concern for the state of the sheep.

You also can't go into the presence of the King and try to hide your sin, whatever it may be, without confessing it. The Bible says:

> *If I regard iniquity in my heart, the Lord will not hear me.* **Psalm 66:18**

The worship that we offer God in heartfelt repentance superimposes us into God's eternal Kingdom where we share in Jesus' victory over death, Hell and the grave. But contrary to some modern Christian entertainers (and I mean to call them entertainers, not worship leaders) you cannot regard iniquity in your heart and be openly sinning. There's nowhere in the Word that supports the belief that praise and worship gets you off the hook for sin or allows you freedom from repentance. Remember, to repent means to say you're sorry and turn the other way.

When His people worship Him in spirit and in truth, amazing things can happen. In the OT the Glory of God was present when His people began to worship Him. We saw the glory cloud of God came down when Solomon dedicated the Temple with worship, but at the same time, as I said, our worship should not be constrained to a building or places of worship. Worship can happen wherever you are and whenever you are led.

> But the hour cometh, and now is, when the true worshippers shall worship the Father in spirit and in truth: for the Father seeketh such to worship Him. God is a Spirit: and they that worship Him must worship Him in spirit and in truth. John 4:23-24

The key here is that we who worship Him must worship Him in spirit and in truth.

As an aside, I can tell you from personal experience that when He shows up in your worship, His power is evident. In fact, there's no time that I can remember where Jesus physically showed up and people stayed vertical. Even in the Garden of Gethsemane when Jesus said, "I AM," they all fell backwards. That's because gravity changes in the presence of eternity. I can say firsthand that when He appeared to me, I didn't intentionally fall.

The other thing that happens when you are in His presence is that any sin that you may be holding in your heart has to go. You'll feel the burden to empty it because of His power and Purity. His very presence delivers us.

Jehoshaphat understood the direct connection between worshipping God and receiving His Everlasting Protection. When he faced a superior enemy, he knew that he was toast if God didn't show up. He realized that the only thing he could do was to worship God and totally trust Him to deliver.

> And he said, "Hearken ye, all Judah, and ye inhabitants of Jerusalem, and thou king Jehoshaphat, Thus saith the LORD unto you, 'Be not afraid nor dismayed by reason of this great multitude; for the battle is not yours, but God's. To morrow go ye down against them. Behold, they come up by the cliff of Ziz; and ye shall find them at the end of the brook, before the wilderness of Jeruel. Ye shall not need to fight in this battle, set yourselves, stand ye still, and see the salvation of the LORD with you, O Judah and Jerusalem. Fear not, nor be dismayed, to morrow go out against them, for the LORD will be with you.'"
> 2 Chronicles 20:15-17

> And they rose early in the morning, and went forth into the wilderness of Teko: and as they went forth, Jehoshaphat stood and said, "Hear me, O Judah, and ye inhabitants of Jerusalem. Believe in the LORD your God, so shall ye be established, believe His prophets, so shall ye prosper." And when he had consulted with the people, he appointed singers unto the LORD, and that should praise the beauty of holiness, as they went out before the army, and to say, "Praise the LORD; for his mercy endureth for ever." And when they began to sing and to praise, the LORD set ambushments against the

children of Ammon, Moab, and mount Seir, which were come against Judah, and they were smitten. For the children of Ammon and Moab stood up against the inhabitants of mount Seir, utterly to slay and destroy them and when they had made an end of the inhabitants of Seir, every one helped to destroy another. And when Judah came toward the watch tower in the wilderness, they looked unto the multitude, and, behold, they were dead bodies fallen to the earth, and none escaped. And when Jehoshaphat and his people came to take away the spoil of them, they found among them in abundance both riches with the dead bodies, and precious jewels, which they stripped off for themselves, more than they could carry away: and they were three days in gathering of the spoil, it was so much.
2 Chronicles 20:20-25

Before these Endtimes days are over, you too will be faced with a choice to worship God like Jehoshaphat and ask Him to deliver you, or be subject to the enemy.

As for me and my house, we will serve the Lord. Joshua 24:15

Power Praying

Here's something to remember: God will never hurt us, God will never betray us, God will never abandon us. When it comes to protection, and everything else we need, for that matter, this relationship that we have with the Creator of the Universe is always based upon looking to Jesus, the Author and Finisher of our Faith.

As we walk into these days, in the physical realm people can have everything they need: all the food, all the water, all the ammo, they can have a bug-out location or shelter set aside. They can have all of that and still get killed if they're trying to survive on their own strength and not looking to God for His Protection.

As a human, I can't fight against what I can't see. In fact, a highly placed source once told me in a coded message that very thing. He warned me about plans to shoot a Hellfire Missile up my backside. You can't fight against a predator drone a hundred feet over your head but the Holy Spirit can, and did for me, through the work of intercessory prayer.

When we intercede for others for their provision and protection, we're sowing good seed. That very act of intercession on our part enables God to raise up prayer warriors to intervene on our behalf. Prayer really does change things and prayer really does keep people alive. I'm living proof.

In addition, prayer is also a primary tool in receiving God's Everlasting Protection. Here are some key verses when it comes to God's Protection:

~ **Eph 6:8** - Praying always with all prayer and supplication in the Spirit, and watching thereunto with all perseverance and supplication for all saints.

~ **James 5:13-16** - Is any among you afflicted? Let him pray. Is any merry? Let him sing psalms. Is any sick among you? Let him call for the elders of the church; and let them pray over him, anointing him with oil in the name of the Lord. And the prayer of faith shall save the sick, and the Lord shall raise him up, and if he have committed sins, they shall be forgiven him. Confess your faults one to another, and pray one for another, that ye may be healed. The effectual fervent prayer of a righteous man availeth much.

- **Matt 26:41** - Watch and pray, that ye enter not into temptation. The spirit indeed is willing, but the flesh is weak.
- **Phil 4:6** - Be careful for nothing; but in every thing by prayer and supplication with thanksgiving let your requests be made known unto God.
- **Col 4:2** - Continue in prayer, and watch in the same with thanksgiving.

How many Christians really believe that God will answer their prayers? Prayer is a two-way conversation and interaction with God. By developing our relationship with Him, by speaking to Him on a regular basis and by reading His Word often, your trust in and understanding of Him grows. We call this faith.

How many people really take the Lord's Prayer seriously? *"Lead me not into temptation and deliver me from"* the Evil One.

Here's what Jesus didn't say, "I'm gonna teach you how to pray but just take what I said and kind of mix and match it. Do whatever's good in your own sight so long as it makes you feel good."

No! This is the Son of God we're talking about, giving us instructions on how to approach His Heavenly Father! I'd say that we should pay attention.

Specifically He said, "Lead Me not into temptation."

Lead me not into temptation?

He is the only one in this flesh suit who never sinned but He was still careful to pray against temptation! If Jesus prayed that He wouldn't be tempted, do you think we should too? What He is essentially praying here is, "Protect me from temptation." As I said before, we cannot simply assume God's Protection. We have to activate it in our lives and our walks, through prayer, through worship and through repentance.

Before He ascended to be with the Father, the Lord also gave His disciples some very telling instructions about prayer.

> *And, behold, I send the promise of my Father upon you, but tarry ye in the city of Jerusalem, until ye be endued with power from on high.* **Luke 24:49**

Jesus made it clear, by basically saying, "Hey! You guys can't go out and do anything until the promise the Father has been given to you. You need to be plugged into His power! Now go and wait in Jerusalem until you get it." He was serious about the Holy Spirit and we should be just as serious.

Something else the Lord taught us about prayer can be found in Matthew 6:5-8:

> *And when thou prayest, thou shalt not be as the hypocrites are: for they love to pray standing in the synagogues and in the corners of the streets, that they may be seen of men. Verily I say unto you, they have their reward. But thou, when thou prayest, enter into thy closet, and when thou hast shut thy door, pray to thy Father which is in secret; and thy Father which seeth in secret shall reward thee openly. But when ye pray, use not vain repetitions, as the heathen do, for they think that they shall be heard for their much speaking. Be not ye therefore like unto them: for your Father knoweth what things ye have need of, before ye ask Him.*

Prayer is serious business and we need to approach it seriously if we want to survive and thrive during these days.

End Time Attitude Adjustment

The Lord's Prayer is also an instruction in attitude and it reminds me of two important aspects of how an airplane can fly.

Altitude is a plane's distance from the earth, how high the plane is from the ground. Attitude is how the plane is positioned in the air, i.e. nose down, nose level, nose up.

You can't gain altitude if your attitude, your plane's nose, isn't pointed up. This is what the Lord's Prayer does for us. It points us in the right direction. "Thy kingdom come, Thy will be done." With an understanding of God's heavenly rule in your life, your attitude will change and you'll be able to gain altitude.

As an example, Moses was drawn by the Lord to go up the mountain toward God's presence, thereby setting his attitude. He gets to the top, altitude, and is changed by the Glory of God that surrounded him.

We should purpose our hearts to seek the things of God and to do God's will. This could be called our attitude, or the direction in which our nose is pointed. Attitude directs us toward God's Presence, and we gain altitude in our walk which puts us into His presence. In His presence, we begin to understand more of the Bible and of Him and our lives are transformed by His glory.

Attitude = Altitude.

I mentioned Moses. I think the most tragic event in the history of Israel was when they told Moses that they didn't want to talk directly to God. Think about what they had just gone through. They'd been miraculously delivered out of the Egyptians' hands, provided for along their journey to Mt. Sinai, saw what they saw and heard what they heard on top of that mountain. It was an open invitation to enter into direct relationship with God.

Instead they basically said, "Moses, you go talk to Him, we can't stand to hear Him."

I believe the modern-Church is there also. Churches hire men and women to represent them before God. When the idea is put in this framework, does that sound right to you?

I don't believe in a professional clergy.

I do believe that shepherds are real and in the administrative positions as outlined in the Bible. But I don't believe in a professional clergy caring for the sheep because the vast majority of them are simply filling a position with no clue about the nature of this supernatural war. Our war is against unseen forces. How are we supposed to fight a battle when the officers in charge of the army don't even know who the enemy is or what tactics are being deployed against them?

Don't misunderstand me, I said "professional clergy" where people are paid a salary to shepherd. This is different from men and women of God receiving gifts and offerings from the saints. The Bible is very clear about the leaders that God has appointed over the Body:

> *And he gave some, apostles; and some, prophets; and some, evangelists; and some, pastors and teachers. For the perfecting of the saints, for the work of the ministry, for the edifying of the body of Christ, till we all come in the unity of the faith, and of the knowledge of the Son of God, unto a perfect man, unto the measure of the stature of the fullness of Christ.* **Eph 4:11-13**

As an aside, I also believe that the people who function in these offices are evident by their actions and their anointing. If someone has to tell me that he's a prophet, or an apostle, or a bishop, or whatever, I'm always suspect. The Holy Spirit in me and you will be a witness to the work of God through those people. They don't need pomp and circumstance to elevate themselves above the rest of the sheep. God does this by using them to serve and nurture the sheep. If it worked for David, it can work for them.

Most of us who have been saved and baptized in the Holy Spirit believe in God. But honestly, do we really believe that our lives should be based all on His terms? Or do we believe that we can live life on our own terms, seasoning it with His truth rather than being immersed in an obedient relationship with Him as King? The psalmist said it best:

> If I regard iniquity in my heart, the Lord will not hear me. **Psalm 66:18**

So how do we get inequity out of our heart?

We pray the same kind of prayer that David did:

> Purge me with hyssop, and I shall be clean: wash me, and I shall be whiter than snow. **Psalm 51:7**

And in answer to that prayer, Isaiah 1:18 says:

> "Come now, and let us reason together", saith the LORD. "Though your sins be as scarlet, they shall be as white as snow; though they be red like crimson, they shall be as wool."

Red as crimson means as deeply stained as they could be, but through His Son God has made it possible for our sin to be totally washed away. In Revelation 3:8 Jesus Himself counseled the church at Laodicea to get their new white garments from Him:

> I counsel thee to buy of me gold tried in the fire, that thou mayest be rich and white raiment, that thou mayest be clothed, and that the shame of thy nakedness do not appear; and anoint thine eyes with eyesalve, that thou mayest see.

If you will recall, the church at Laodicea was the same one that was neither hot nor cold so Jesus said He would spit them out of His mouth.

> I know thy works, that thou art neither cold nor hot: I would thou wert cold or hot. So then because thou art lukewarm, and neither cold nor hot, I will spue thee out of my mouth. Because thou sayest, I am rich, and increased with goods, and have need of nothing; and knowest not that thou art wretched, and miserable, and poor, and blind, and naked. **Revelation 3:15-17**

This sounds so much like the Church today. How can we expect God to cover us with His Protection when we think that we already have everything that we need? The Church believes that they are self-sufficient and act like they don't need Jesus' help, but all the while they refuse to recognize that they are "wretched, and miserable, and poor, and blind, and naked."

Lord, may we refocus our eyes and lives on You so that You can cleanse our hearts and place us under the shadow of Your wings in these days.

Reality

I've been called a fear monger more than once. However, early in my walk the Lord gave me the courage to see this world as it really is, not as I wish it to be. There's a word for this; it's called reality. The reality is that people will die during these days, people you know and people you love. You may not even make it through the Great Tribulation. But people die all the time. What's the difference between somebody being killed in a car wreck, or some guy being killed on the battlefield if they're both Christians?

The truth is that it's not about whether we live or die. It is about how we live our life before the Lord. Are we serving Him? Are we doing His will? Are we effective in the purpose that He's given us, especially in these days?

So without getting into a long discussion about why His people suffer, I'll cut to the chase and refer you to the Word. Its author is way smarter than I am anyway.

That ye may be the children of your Father which is in heaven, for He maketh His sun to rise on the evil and on the good, and sendeth rain on the just and on the unjust. **Matt 5:45**

And fear not them which kill the body, but are not able to kill the soul: but rather fear Him which is able to destroy both soul and body in hell. Are not two sparrows sold for a farthing? and one of them shall not fall on the ground without your Father. But the very hairs of your head are all numbered. Fear ye not therefore, ye are of more value than many sparrows. **Matt 10:28-31**

God's Everlasting Protection is about more than your physical life, hence the word "everlasting". Our God is an eternal being Who has designed us to be with Him in eternity. Yes, we desire and need His Protection in this life, in these days, but the larger picture is that with this earth walk, He's preparing us to rule and reign with Him (Rev 20:4-6).

So, do we hold onto this life with a death grip like people in the world, partying, getting all we can get, living life however we want, pretending to have morals but not serving the King? Or do we truly believe that this life is but a vapor compared to the forever life we will have after we leave this place? Are we mindful of the One whom we serve?

There is no question, we are walking into some extremely difficult days. People are going to die, including Christians. But even in those difficult times, God's Everlasting Protection surrounds His people. His Protection is always for our good and His glory. Ultimately He will determine who lives and dies, not the devil. He will warn and guide those people whose lives He wants to extend.

No man of God in the Bible was ever killed by an accident. When it was time for them to go home, they knew when their time was up. Purpose to be a man or woman of God and you'll not worry about when your time in this 3D existence is up. That is the ultimate protection.

Consider Job and all he went through. You think you might have it bad? He lost everything and everyone that he ever loved. In spite of that, he said I will walk with God.

Though He slay me, yet will I trust in him: but I will maintain mine own ways before Him. **Job 13:15**

The battles that rage all around us, whether physical or spiritual, are frightening but in spite of the bombs and fiery arrows, we can always lean on God.

"What time I am afraid, I will trust in thee." **Psalm 56:3**

Speaking of men of God, I think about the Apostle Paul and all the things he went through and how God protected Him. To say that his life and walk wasn't easy would be an understatement.

Of the Jews five times received I forty stripes save one. Thrice was I beaten with rods, once was I stoned, thrice I suffered shipwreck, a night and a day I have been in the deep. In journeyings often, in perils of waters, in perils of robbers, in perils by mine own countrymen, in perils by the heathen, in perils in the city, in perils in the wilderness, in perils in the sea, in perils among false brethren, in weariness and painfulness, in watchings often, in hunger and thirst, in fastings often, in cold and nakedness. **2 Cor 11:24-27**

The crazy thing is that we know that this is only a partial list. That's because in Acts 28:3 we see that even though a poisonous snake bit him, he didn't die. Through all of this, God protected him because He had a plan for His life. In the end, Paul said that he was being, "Poured out as a drink offering" (2 Tim 4:6). Historically Paul knew that he must be taken to Rome and had to testify to Caesar and proclaim the gospel. To do this, God put him in a prison and he was eventually killed. Nonetheless, Paul served God wholeheartedly and willingly right up until the end. Would you?

My brethren, count it all joy when ye fall into divers temptations. **James 1:2**

That word "temptations" would be better rendered trials. So yes, during these days we will have trials, big ones, but your ultimate protection is always pitching your tent under God's shadow and never leaving His side, in this life or the next.

God Protects

Whatever we have gone through or will go through, God has already made provision to protect us. As an example, in spite of the Great Falling Away which is already happening, God can protect you in your walk if you let Him.

Trust in the LORD with all thine heart; and lean not unto thine own understanding. In all thy ways acknowledge Him, and He shall direct thy paths. **Proverbs 3:5-6**

And He's already protected us from the power of sin. This is especially important in these days because the demonic influence in the world is increasing exponentially. God gives you a choice to sin or not sin and always, always, always makes a way of escape.

There hath no temptation taken you but such as is common to man, but God is faithful, who will not suffer you to be tempted above that ye are able, but will with the temptation also make a way to escape, that ye may be able to bear it. **1 Corinthians 10:13**

Ultimately His greatest protection for His people was accomplished at Calvary when He conquered sin for us. The greatest part of that Protection is that He invites us to participate in that victory with Him.

To him that overcometh will I grant to sit with me in my throne, even as I also overcame, and am set down with my Father in His throne. **Rev 3:21**

Something I always say is that God often uses His people in naturally supernatural ways. In this I mean that we just purpose to walk with Him, one step at a time, and are obedient. Then one day we will look back at our lives and see miracles. Those miracles are a result of our being obedient when we hear Him say go to the left or go to the right. It's a matter of obedience and it's in our obedience that we find His Protection.

Keep in mind that God will always provide a ram in the bush as He did with Abraham. When Abraham was expecting something, God came through. Too many people are looking to sacrifice for God, but they don't realize that man's efforts and our flesh will not get the job done. You do your part and God will do His.

Abraham was willing to sacrifice his own son, but God provided a substitute in the ram. So we go from the ram in the bush and its sacrifice, to the God of Heaven putting the Lamb on the tree in Jesus Christ. From the Lamb on the tree, we go to the empty tomb because Jesus died and ascended to the Father to assume His rightful place as King of Kings on the throne of glory.

For me and for you, God's Everlasting Protection is ultimately Jesus. *Amen and amen.*

The Battle Hymn Of The Republic

Mine eyes have seen the glory of the coming of the Lord
He is trampling out the vintage where the grapes of wrath are stored,
He has loosed the fateful lightening of His terrible swift sword
His truth is marching on.
Glory! Glory! Hallelujah! His truth is marching on.
I have seen Him in the watch-fires of a hundred circling camps
They have builded Him an altar in the evening dews and damps
I can read His righteous sentence by the dim and flaring lamps
His day is marching on.
Glory! Glory! Hallelujah! His truth is marching on.
I have read a fiery gospel writ in burnish`d rows of steel,
"As ye deal with my contemners, So with you my grace shall deal;"
Let the Hero, born of woman, crush the serpent with his heel
Since God is marching on.
Glory! Glory! Hallelujah! His truth is marching on.
He has sounded forth the trumpet that shall never call retreat
He is sifting out the hearts of men before His judgment-seat
Oh, be swift, my soul, to answer Him! be jubilant, my feet!
Our God is marching on.
Glory! Glory! Hallelujah! His truth is marching on.
In the beauty of the lilies Christ was born across the sea,
With a glory in His bosom that transfigures you and me:
As He died to make men holy, let us die to make men free,
While God is marching on.
Glory! Glory! Hallelujah! His truth is marching on.

HELP 5

His Everlasting Provision

But my God shall supply all your need

according to His riches in glory

by Christ Jesus.

Philippians 4:19

Provision

If you've been walking with the Lord for a while, you probably have been in that place of desperation where you were crying out to God for His supernatural Provision. In this very moment, if you have surrendered your life to our King, repented and walk with Him closely, I can wholeheartedly tell you that He's heard your cries and seen your tears.

I know this because in a scene from the future we read in Revelation 21:4:

> *And God shall wipe away all tears from their eyes; and there shall be no more death, neither sorrow, nor crying, neither shall there be any more pain: for the former things are passed away.*

God is, has been, and will always be concerned about your needs. There are times when He miraculously meets those needs like He did with Elijah.

> *And Elijah the Tishbite, who was of the inhabitants of Gilead, said unto Ahab, "As the LORD God of Israel liveth, before whom I stand, there shall not be dew nor rain these years, but according to my word." And the word of the LORD came unto him, saying, "Get thee hence, and turn thee eastward, and hide thyself by the brook Cherith, that is before Jordan. And it shall be, that thou shalt drink of the brook; and I have commanded the ravens to feed thee there." So he went and did according unto the word of the LORD: for he went and dwelt by the brook Cherith, that is before Jordan. And the ravens brought him bread and flesh in the morning, and bread and flesh in the evening; and he drank of the brook.* 1 Kings 17:1-6

Now you could be thinking, "Yes, Steve. That's what I need. I need God to send food, or money, or companionship from the thin air and bless me! If God could do it for Elijah, I'm sure He could do it for me!"

Not so fast. Do you know what Elijah had to endure and why God sent the ravens to feed him by the brook?

This man of God just pronounced drought and famine on the land at God's direction. That really didn't make him a popular guy. He was also the same guy who went up against the prophets of Baal, and the same man Jezebel wanted to kill.

God used the birds to feed him because he was faithful to first do what God had told him. God continued to use him and to provide for him because he was obedient.

Most Christians struggle when God doesn't meet our needs in the way we've asked Him to. His Provision for us is often provided in His warnings to us to take action before something happens.

When we've not heeded His warnings, we might wonder where He is in our current situation. He can and often does provide for us in the moment like Elijah, but we, as His growing and obedient servants, need to learn how to listen to those warnings and heed the call to preemptive action. Your obedience to those calls and adherence to those warnings may very well save your life.

You may question, "Can I trust God for His Provision?" With unequivocal certainty, you can absolutely trust Him. In the course of my walk these last forty-something years I've seen Him do the miraculous on my behalf. I know that you can trust Him because He's been faithful to me. I'm no different than you. If He's been faithful to me, He will be faithful to you. Here's one amazing example of that faithfulness.

The first book that I read after my encounter with Jesus was, *The Happiest People on Earth*. It was written by Demos Shakarian, who also happened to be the Founder of The Full Gospel Business Men's Fellowship. I was so impacted by the book that just as soon as I finished it, I asked the Lord, *"God, please let me meet this man before he dies."*

What does this have to do with God's Everlasting Provision?

Your dependence on God's Provision is directly tied to your belief in His faithfulness. And true to His faithfulness, God answered my prayer thirty years later. It doesn't matter how long God takes to do something on our behalf because His timing is always perfect. My divine appointment with Demos became another mainstay of my life.

When I met him, Demos grabbed my hand and immediately started prophesying over me. He didn't know me, he didn't know how I met the Lord and he didn't know what God's call on my life was. But the Word that He gave me through the Holy Spirit reconfirmed what Jesus had told me the first time I met Him in my room thirty years before.

He specifically said something that I hold in my heart until today and, like Nehemiah, I won't disclose it. I can tell you that it had to do with many of the things that will occur in the years leading up to the return of the Lord.

God is faithful. He answers prayer and God's Everlasting Provision will be there when you need it the most.

Chapter 12

Faithfulness in the Small Things

For the kingdom of heaven is as a man travelling into a far country, who called his own servants, and delivered unto them his goods. And unto one he gave five talents, to another two, and to another one; to every man according to his several ability; and straightway took his journey. Then he that had received the five talents went and traded with the same, and made them other five talents. And likewise he that had received two, he also gained other two. But he that had received one went and digged in the earth, and hid his lord's money. After a long time the lord of those servants cometh, and reckoneth with them. And so he that had received five talents came and brought other five talents, saying, "Lord, thou deliveredst unto me five talents: behold, I have gained beside them five talents more." His lord said unto him, "Well done, thou good and faithful servant: thou hast been faithful over a few things, I will make thee ruler over many things: enter thou into the joy of thy lord." He also that had received two talents came and said, "Lord, thou deliveredst unto me two talents: behold, I have gained two other talents beside them." His lord said unto him, "Well done, good and faithful servant; thou hast been faithful over a few things, I will make thee ruler over many things: enter thou into the joy of thy lord." Then he which had received the one talent came and said, "Lord, I knew thee that thou art an hard man, reaping where thou hast not sown, and gathering where thou hast not strawed and I was afraid, and went and hid thy talent in the earth: lo, there thou hast that is thine." His lord answered and said unto him, "Thou wicked and slothful servant, thou knewest that I reap where I sowed not, and gather where I have not strawed. Thou oughtest therefore to have put my money to the exchangers, and then at my coming I should have received mine *own with usury. Take therefore the talent from him, and give it unto him which hath ten talents. For unto every one that hath shall be given, and he shall have abundance: but from him that hath not shall be taken away even that which he hath. And cast ye the unprofitable servant into outer darkness: there shall be weeping and gnashing of teeth."*

Matthew 25:14-30

In my life, I've had too much horsepower and too little common sense at times. That's because I've always had a penchant for speed. Unfortunately that need for speed has caused me more than one injury over the years and I'm also prone to clumsiness to the detriment of my well-being. Because of these two tendencies, I've had several serious injuries, with some head injuries, over the years. Some of them were not my own doing. Some of them were also demonically induced.

One of the first accidents happened when I was a little kid. I'd gotten out of our car and stepped into the path of oncoming traffic, only to be hit by another car traveling approximately 40 mph. The impact sent me flying through the air for a good long way. Amazingly, as a testament to God's Protection on my life, and His Provision for you, I'm here to tell you the story.

I also remember pulling a wheelie on my Sting-Ray bicycle when I was a kid, but I came back down, I lurched to the right and suddenly found myself flying over my handle bars. The result was a perfect face-plant on the hard pavement. My front teeth were knocked out and I sustained a concussion. But since I was already in braces the dentist was able to put the teeth back and reset them.

When I was older I had pleurisy and passed out at the top of the stairs and gravity took over. I tumbled all the way down the stairs, hitting my head. While it may have knocked some sense into me, I was no worse for the wear.

The most deadly accident that I ever had was when I rolled my dune buggy. I should have been killed but God was obviously not done with me yet. Later I found out about His supernatural intervention on my behalf from two people with Youth With A Mission (YWAM) who were in Kona, Hawaii, at the time. Kona was four hours behind me, but at the exact moment of the accident, they clearly heard the Lord say, *"Pray for Steve right now or he's dead!"* When they heard His voice, right before they started to pray they were compelled to check the time. Later they told me what that time was. They had no idea that my watch had stopped at that exact moment, the moment they had started to pray.

I believe that many of these incidents, and more, were directly induced demonic attacks. Dr. Paul Hegstrom was one of the founders of Life Skills International and a very intuitive and gifted Spirit-filled Believer. He'd heard me on Coast to Coast one night talking about Fallen Angels. He sent me an email and we started corresponding and became friends. He's since gone to be with the Lord, but while he was alive he shared with me that one night he'd been sick with an intestinal disorder that required him not to wander far from the bathroom. The Lord prompted him to use the time wisely and read one of my books, Genesis 6 Giants. He read it all that night in one sitting. When he was finished, the Lord told him something very interesting.

The Lord said, "*Steve, from the time he was born, has been called and...*" his words, "*the Fallen Angels have been trying to destroy him since.*"

That's what I mean about demonically inspired attacks.

But why me?

Look, I know me and I can tell you that I'm nobody special. Back when I was a little kid, I certainly didn't talk about Giants. I hadn't been on the radio or written a book that would have made those Fallen Angels mad enough to kill me. What could be so concerning to them that as a child I would raise their ire?

Something else that I need to bring out for your benefit, to help you understand why I'm so passionate about God's Provision, is because of how my name is found in the Ancient Bible Code.

Little did I know that a mathematics professor who understood the Bible Code would take it upon himself to run my name in the Code. Interestingly, not only does my name appear in the code but the Equal Distance Letter Sequencing (EDLS) put my name smack dab in the middle of Genesis 6, in the exact place where scripture talks about fighting Giants and slaying the enemies of God!

Please understand that I'm very uncomfortable talking about myself because I never want to take away any of the attention or glory from Jesus. He is the One who has preserved me all these years and made me who I am. But I tell you all these things to echo what Paul said in 1 Thess 5:12:

> And we beseech you, brethren, to know them which labour among you...

You've probably read, or heard me talk about, how Jesus first appeared to me right after I got saved. I'm the first to say that Jesus didn't appear to me because I was better than anybody else or because I was special. In fact, the opposite was true. The first night I ever saw Him was the night I got saved and it would take years for me to become a mature Believer. I was a mess and the Holy Spirit had a lot of cleaning up to do in my life. God saved me and called me - IN SPITE OF ME.

I can honestly say that all I am, or will be, is because of Jesus. Who am I that He should use me? But He does use me for whatever reason. I'm far from perfect. At times I'm probably not the best example of a Believer but I try to serve Him and to walk the best that I can despite my flaws. When I sin, I learned long ago to repent quickly. That's really all He wants from any of us.

Here's the bottom-line: At that first meeting, He told me that He was giving me a Joseph's ministry and that He wanted me to get his people prepared for the End of the Age.

As I've shared, the crazy thing was that I was a brand-spanking new Christian with no previous Bible teaching or upbringing. I had no clue about what the End of the Age was, or even who Joseph was!

I share this story now because of one of the things I later found out about Joseph.

Joseph warned God's people before a deadly seven year famine came and he prepared them during the good years. Through God's warning to the Hebrews and that preparation, even all of Egypt was saved because of the faithfulness of a man.

Let me be clear - I am no Joseph. But I do purpose to be faithful to God's warnings and to do what He told me to do even in the small things and so should you.

Jesus told me to prepare you for the End of the Age. I've tried to do the best that I've learned how.

With the burden and calling that God put on my life, I tell you that God's provision for you in the future is based on you being faithful in preparation NOW.

We have very clear evidence that we've entered into the End of the Age, despite the assertions to the contrary by many Christian leaders and their congregations. Right now we find ourselves in the midst of the "Great Falling Away" and world events are lining up to make for a very uncomfortable future, biblically and socially. It's against this backdrop that God told me to prepare His people. Just as in Joseph's day, if there was ever a time when we needed God's Everlasting Provision, it's now.

In The Worst of Times

It would be some 430 years of Hebrew residency in Egypt before God would rescue the children of Israel out of slavery. As He did, God whisked them out to the wilderness to become their sole source of provision.

Today, God does the same for us as Christians, but rather than taking us out of physical bondage, we are stolen away from spiritual bondage.

> Know ye not, that to whom ye yield yourselves servants to obey, his servants ye are to whom ye obey; whether of sin unto death, or of obedience unto righteousness? But God be thanked, that ye were the servants of sin, but ye have obeyed from the heart that form of doctrine which was delivered you. Being then made free from sin, ye became the servants of righteousness. **Romans 6:16-18**

In the context of this slave comparison, when God calls us out of the world unto Himself, He then makes sure that we are fed spiritually and, at times, physically. I say "at times" because Christians have a bad habit of taking back their lives from Him. When we do, we tend to stop depending on Him and we do things for ourselves without ever consulting Him.

Yes, we are supposed to work and provide for our families. At the same time, we should take great care to consult the Master about the decisions in our lives, if we are indeed His.

Instead, we too often take things into our own hands. Then, when we get in a jam, we cry out for God to deliver us. It seems to me that it would be a better use of our time and energy to check with Him first, and wait for Him to guide us via His Holy Spirit. Wow, that sounds kind of biblical, doesn't it?

> Therefore I say unto you, take no thought for your life, what ye shall eat, or what ye shall drink; nor yet for your body, what ye shall put on. Is not the life more than meat, and the body than raiment? Behold the fowls of the air: for they sow not, neither do they reap, nor gather into barns; yet your heavenly Father feedeth them. Are ye not much better than they? Which of you by taking thought can add one cubit unto his stature? And why take ye thought for raiment? Consider the lilies of the field, how they grow; they toil not, neither do they spin: And yet I say unto you, that even Solomon in all his glory was not arrayed like one of these. Wherefore, if God so clothe the grass of the field, which to day is, and to morrow is cast into the oven, shall he not much more clothe you, O ye of little faith? Therefore take no thought, saying, "What shall we eat?" or, "What shall we drink?" or, "Wherewithal shall we be clothed?" For after all these things do the Gentiles seek, for your heavenly Father knoweth that ye have

need of all these things. But seek ye first the kingdom of God, and His righteousness; and all these things shall be added unto you. **Matt 6:25-33**

When we wholeheartedly trust in the Lord and walk with Him, our needs are met. King David said it best.

I have been young, and now am old; yet have I not seen the righteous forsaken, nor his seed begging bread. **Psalm 37:25**

This may sound fine and dandy if you're in your own comfortable life without a care in the world, but we live in a day when the analogy will become reality, as God may soon lead us out of the world into the wilderness.

It's one thing to read about how God supernaturally delivered His people. It's an entirely different thing for us to be thrust into a life-and-death struggle where we absolutely need God to show up. That's what I call having skin in the game.

Sometimes we're a little tough on the children of Israel because of our perception of their attitudes during their wanderings. But let's face it, it couldn't have been easy roaming the desert for 40 years and wondering if you were going to get what you needed to survive. Still, I would hope that my attitude toward God's Provision would be a positive one after seeing what He had done.

That firsthand account of His miraculous Provision should create the basis for how we view our circumstances. Do you honestly think that God can stretch your dollars to meet your household budget, fix your marriage or make sure your kids don't grow up to be psychopaths? Has He intervened in any of these areas, or others, in the past and you saw His positive influence? If so… why do you doubt His provision now?

Likewise, those Israelites got to see God do the miraculous, from the astonishing act of splitting a body of water called the Red Sea, to the everyday, mundane, but necessary provision for His people by having their shoes and clothes not wear out.

And I have led you forty years in the wilderness: your clothes are not waxen old upon you, and thy shoe is not waxen old upon thy foot. **Deuteronomy 29:5**

These two examples, both the big and the little, were at the hand of an omnipotent God whose primary goal was to make sure that His people, His children, were provided for.

And the Hebrews still grumbled and so do we!

But soon your mettle may also be tested, as you and I will be led into a physical wilderness and will have to lean on His Everlasting Provision just as the Israelites did.

Will your response be any different than theirs?

It's one thing to read about God's Provision from the vantage point of peace and safety, but it's an entirely different thing to consider that that peace and safety will soon be snatched out from under you like a rug.

We have been warned about what's coming, and coming soon.

Supernatural Warnings

The word preparation means to take action ahead of time, before an event occurs, so that you're not taken by surprise. Preparation is preemptive in its nature and in biblical times was often a response by the people who obeyed God's warning.

From the word preparation we get the title of "Prepper". A Prepper is simply someone who is taking preemptive steps to safeguard against a food, water or shelter shortage or even to protect themselves and their loved ones from anticipated violence.

You may think it strange to speak about prepping in the context of God's Everlasting Provision but as you will see, God often warns His people in advance of events to give them time to prepare. In doing so, He shows them how they should participate in their own deliverance.

Off the top of my head, I can think of three Prepper examples that stand out from the Bible.

The first is Noah who was warned by God to prepare an ark for the salvation of his family. What's curious is that he had no idea how much of an impact he would have on mankind and the animal kingdom. He was just being obedient.

> And God said unto Noah, "The end of all flesh is come before me; for the earth is filled with violence through them; and, behold, I will destroy them with the earth. Make thee an ark of gopher wood; rooms shalt thou make in the ark, and shalt pitch it within and without with pitch." **Genesis 6:13-14**

Many times God will use dreams to warn His people of impending danger, but it's up to the Believer to be obedient to what God has shown him . It says in Job:

> In a dream, in a vision of the night, when deep sleep falleth upon men, in slumberings upon the bed. Then he openeth the ears of men, and sealeth their instruction. **Job 33:15-16**

The second example of a biblical Prepper that comes to mind is Joseph who interpreted Pharaoh's dream of a great famine coming.

> And Joseph said unto Pharaoh, The dream of Pharaoh is one: God hath shewed Pharaoh what he is about to do. The seven good kine are seven years; and the seven good ears are seven years: the dream is one. And the seven thin and ill favoured kine that came up after them are seven years; and the seven empty ears blasted with the east wind shall be seven years of famine. This is the thing which I have spoken unto Pharaoh: What God is about to do he sheweth unto Pharaoh. Behold, there come seven years of great plenty throughout all the land of Egypt: And there shall arise after them seven years of famine; and all the plenty shall be forgotten in the land of Egypt; and the famine shall consume the land; And the plenty shall not be known in the land by reason of that famine following; for it shall be very grievous. And for that the dream was doubled unto Pharaoh twice; it is because the thing is established by God, and God will shortly bring it to pass. Now therefore let Pharaoh look out a man discreet and wise, and set him over the land of Egypt. Let Pharaoh do this, and let him appoint officers over the land, and take up the fifth part of the land of Egypt in the seven plenteous years. And let them gather all the food of those good years that come, and lay up corn under the hand of Pharaoh, and let them keep food in the cities. And that food shall be for store to the land against the seven years of famine, which shall be in the land of Egypt; that the land perish not through the famine. **Genesis 41:25-36**

The third example of people having a part in their own deliverance and provision is the first Prepper found in the NT.

It's the woman who sent a lunch of five loaves of bread and two fishes with her son as he went to hear Jesus. She sent him with more than he needed because she didn't know when he would return home. She obviously wanted to make sure that he had enough to eat while he was away.

> *After these things Jesus went over the sea of Galilee, which is the sea of Tiberias. And a great multitude followed Him, because they saw His miracles which He did on them that were diseased. And Jesus went up into a mountain, and there He sat with His disciples. And the Passover, a feast of the Jews, was nigh. When Jesus then lifted up His eyes, and saw a great company come unto Him, He saith unto Philip, "Whence shall we buy bread, that these may eat?" And this He said to prove Him: for He Himself knew what He would do. Philip answered Him, "Two hundred pennyworth of bread is not sufficient for them, that every one of them may take a little." One of His disciples, Andrew, Simon Peter's brother, saith unto Him, "There is a lad here, which hath five barley loaves, and two small fishes: but what are they among so many?" And Jesus said, "Make the men sit down." Now there was much grass in the place. So the men sat down, in number about five thousand. And Jesus took the loaves; and when He had given thanks, He distributed to the disciples, and the disciples to them that were set down; and likewise of the fishes as much as they would. When they were filled, He said unto His disciples, "Gather up the fragments that remain, that nothing be lost." Therefore they gathered them together, and filled twelve baskets with the fragments of the five barley loaves, which remained over and above unto them that had eaten.* **John 6:1-13**

I guarantee you that the boy's mother had no idea that her faithfulness in providing for her son would be used to feed more than 5,000 people that day. Nor do we know how God will multiply our preps and whom they will bless when the time comes.

It isn't about what we don't have; it's about what we do have that God can use.

God Uses What You Have

Moses was looking for something outside of himself to deliver God's people. Little did he know that he had all he needed in his hand:

> *And Moses answered and said, "But, behold, they will not believe me, nor hearken unto my voice: for they will say, 'The LORD hath not appeared unto thee.'" And the LORD said unto him, "What is that in thine hand?" And he said, "A rod." And He said, "Cast it on the ground." And he cast it on the ground, and it became a serpent; and Moses fled from before it. And the LORD said unto Moses, "Put forth thine hand, and take it by the tail." And he put forth his hand, and caught it, and it became a rod in his hand. "That they may believe that the LORD God of their fathers, the God of Abraham, the God of Isaac, and the God of Jacob, hath appeared unto thee."* **Exodus 4:1-5**

> *"And thou shalt take this rod in thine hand, wherewith thou shalt do signs."* **Exodus 4:17**

As a testament to how God can use and multiply our preps, take a look at the example of Elijah and the widow of Zarephath.

> And the word of the LORD came unto him, saying, "Arise, get thee to Zarephath, which belongeth to Zidon, and dwell there: behold, I have commanded a widow woman there to sustain thee." So he arose and went to Zarephath. And when he came to the gate of the city, behold, the widow woman was there gathering of sticks: and he called to her, and said, "Fetch me, I pray thee, a little water in a vessel, that I may drink." And as she was going to fetch it, he called to her, and said, "Bring me, I pray thee, a morsel of bread in thine hand." And she said, "As the LORD thy God liveth, I have not a cake, but an handful of meal in a barrel, and a little oil in a cruse: and, behold, I am gathering two sticks, that I may go in and dress it for me and my son, that we may eat it, and die." And Elijah said unto her, "Fear not; go and do as thou hast said: but make me thereof a little cake first, and bring it unto me, and after make for thee and for thy son. For thus saith the LORD God of Israel, 'The barrel of meal shall not waste, neither shall the cruse of oil fail, until the day that the LORD sendeth rain upon the earth.'" And she went and did according to the saying of Elijah: and she, and he, and her house, did eat many days. And the barrel of meal wasted not, neither did the cruse of oil fail, according to the word of the LORD, which he spake by Elijah. *1 Kings 17:8-16*

One of the most important points of this illustration is that the woman obeyed the Word of the Lord.

It'll be the same for us when food, water and shelter become scarce in the days to come. Like that woman, those of us who have prepared may want to keep our preps just for our loved ones and us. I would suggest to you that the judgment and tribulation that is befalling the earth is not only a physical judgment, but a spiritual one and ultimately, it's the Holy Spirit who will provide for you and your family during these days.

You may have done well in your prepping, but I will be the first to tell you that no matter how much you've stored up, it's not enough without God's Everlasting Provision.

In order to activate that Provision, you must, must, must lean on Him during these days. You have to be intimately familiar with the voice of the Holy Spirit. There may be a time when He tells you to share the preps and you know, because you've done the math, that you don't have enough. With some prayer and faith added to your supplies, you could very well experience a widow of Zarephath moment first-hand.

We as Believers are not called to simply survive during the days to come. We are told that we will see miracles and are called to be salt and light to a dying world.

Shattering The Left/Right Paradigm

At the risk of sounding political, I have to delve into the Left/Right paradigm for a moment and dredge out the despicable topic of socialism.

So here's a question for you: If Jesus were here right now, would He be a registered Democrat or Republican?

He would be neither!

God's kingdom is not a democracy; it's a theocracy with Jesus calling the shots. But as long as I've been saved, we've had both sides of the political aisle trying to claim the moral high ground based upon their party's platform.

That's not to say that we shouldn't take a stand on certain moral practices that God Himself finds abhorrent, i.e. the killing of innocents through the ritualistic blood sacrifice of abortion. But the idea that the Bible gives one party or the other cart blanche because we wear a button with a donkey or elephant on it is ridiculous!

This next story is a perfect example.

There's a different kind of preparation and provision that occurred in the Book of Acts with the prophet Agabus. He was the guy who prophesied that a Great Famine was coming to Jews in Jerusalem.

> *And in these days came prophets from Jerusalem unto Antioch. And there stood up one of them named Agabus, and signified by the spirit that there should be great dearth throughout all the world: which came to pass in the days of Claudius Caesar. Then the disciples, every man according to his ability, determined to send relief unto the brethren which dwelt in Judaea.* **Acts 11:27-29**

Concerning Agabus, although previously cited, these scriptures are worth repeating:

> *Surely the Lord GOD will do nothing, but he revealeth his secret unto his servants the prophets.* **Amos 3:7**

> *...for the testimony of Jesus is the spirit of prophecy.* **Revelation 19:10**

Remember, we're talking about God's Everlasting Provision here. It would certainly stand to reason that during a famine, people need God's Provision. While we hear a lot about the more sensational famines of the OT, we don't really hear about this NT famine, which Agabus foretold via the Holy Spirit. Would it surprise you that many of Paul's Epistles touch on this famine in one way or another? There are four excerpts that have a direct connection to this famine.

> *And the multitude of them that believed were of one heart and of one soul: neither said any of them that ought of the things which he possessed was his own; but they had all things common. And with great power gave the apostles witness of the resurrection of the Lord Jesus: and great grace was upon them all. Neither was there any among them that lacked: for as many as were possessors of lands or houses sold them, and brought the prices of the things that were sold, And laid them down at the apostles' feet: and distribution was made unto every man according as he had need.* **Acts 4:32-35**

Notice that the implication here is that they took it upon themselves to sell everything and combine their resources. And while it does say that power and grace was on them "all" and that they did not lack, we see later in various entries from Paul's letters that he had collected offerings for the Jews in Jerusalem because many of them lacked.

> *Now concerning the collection for the saints, as I have given order to the churches of Galatia, even so do ye. Upon the first day of the week let every one of you lay by him in store, as God hath prospered him, that there be no gatherings when I come. And when I come, whomsoever ye shall approve by your letters, them will I send to bring your liberality unto Jerusalem.* **1 Corinthians 16:1-3**

Moreover, brethren, we do you to wit of the grace of God bestowed on the churches of Macedonia. How that in a great trial of affliction the abundance of their joy and their deep poverty abounded unto the riches of their liberality. For to their power, I bear record, yea, and beyond their power they were willing of themselves; Praying us with much intreaty that we would receive the gift, and take upon us the fellowship of the ministering to the saints. **2 Corinthians 8:1-4**

But now I go unto Jerusalem to minister unto the saints. For it hath pleased them of Macedonia and Achaia to make a certain contribution for the poor saints which are at Jerusalem. **Romans 15:25-26**

So we have a prophet of God telling Christians that there was going to be a famine in the land in Jerusalem. Then we have new Believers, freshly filled with the Spirit and excited about the things that God told them, taking it upon themselves to sell everything they have and combining it all together.

I'll pause here to point out that liberals will often cite this event out of Acts as supporting evidence for socialism. Nothing could be further from the truth!

There are four very important points that need to be brought out regarding these scriptures.

1. I maintain that the Believers of Acts did not have a mandate from God to sell everything and combine their resources. There's nowhere in scripture where this idea is required or even suggested.

2. Obviously their experiment in socialism failed because we see in letters after Acts that there were quite a few people that were poor and needed help.

3. If it hadn't been for the generosity of offerings from the Gentiles responding to the gospel across the known world, a lot of people in Jerusalem would have died.

4. I believe that the devil used the Believers' zeal in Jerusalem against them because he wanted to wipe them out. When they sold everything, they in turn hurt themselves in the end and it was the Gentiles' generosity, through God's direction and provision that saved them.

They were warned by God of a great famine that was coming. The Gentile saints participated in the deliverance of the Jews in Jerusalem from that famine. God used people in His work of deliverance and Provision.

And He still does today.

Doing Our Part

God's commandment is always, "You do what's possible, and I will do the impossible." If a brother or sister be naked, and destitute of daily food, and one of you say unto them, "Depart in peace, be ye warmed and filled"; notwithstanding ye give them not those things which are needful to the body; what doth it profit? **James 2:15-16**

The stark reality is that we should not assume or presume that manna will fall from heaven in our hour of need - if we don't live in that realm of faith already. Manna may fall from heaven, but it's not assured.

A better way forward is that each man seek the Lord beforehand and purpose in his heart to acquire what God has shown him that he needs. Their provision should be their own Ark. They should be considering their provisions carefully, buying canned food, canned fruit, growing vegetables and everything they can do while they have time to do it.

That's the principle.

Inevitably, I'll have someone tell me that they don't have to prep for anything and that they're just going to trust God.

My first question would be, *"Do you trust God for everything you have now and even with your very life?"*

To which they might answer in the affirmative.

Then my next question will be, *"Really? But you have a job where you make money. You use that money to pay your mortgage that you borrowed, so you could buy your house. So now you're in debt and your employer is the one who is paying you to eat? So... how can you say that you trust God for everything?"*

I'm not saying that this common lifestyle is wrong. All of us have had a mortgage or bills at one time or another.

But my point is that if someone's going to challenge the idea of prepping because they're *"just going to trust God to take care of them,"* what evidence in their life is there to substantiate such a claim? Based upon their lifestyle, will they be capable of living on strictly a faith basis when things get really tough? Such a lackadaisical attitude toward preparing in the wake of God's warnings is the equivalency of slothfulness.

Goodnight! Even animals and insects instinctively know when tough times are coming, i.e. the winter or famine, and they will gather and store food so they can survive. A person who doesn't want to at least do the same should take a lesson from the ant.

> Go to the ant, thou sluggard; consider her ways, and be wise, which having no guide, overseer, or ruler, provideth her meat in the summer, and gathereth her food in the harvest. **Proverbs 6:6-8**

I would much rather people tell me that they don't think they will need to prep because they don't think anything is going to happen. Those people would be wrong, but at least they're intellectually honest.

Those people who refuse to do their part but have received warning will still have to give an account for their actions, or lack thereof, before the Lord. Bottom line? That attitude's a cop-out.

If you do your part, God will do His part.

Chapter 13
The Future That Is Now

Be careful for nothing; but in every thing by prayer and supplication with thanksgiving let your requests be made known unto God.

Phil 4:6

There've been countless pages written and scores of sermons preached about what the End of the Age would look like but even when it's staring us in the face, very few Christians recognize it for what it is. Perhaps that's because most of those aforementioned lessons have skewed the Believer's thought process so they won't look at the signs of the times or are just too afraid of the truth to grasp the seriousness of this moment. Whatever the reason, we are all equals in the experience that awaits us in our immediate future, but we are not alone. God is here, at this juncture, at this moment, waiting to direct and provide for us.

We must learn to lean on His Spirit during these days. If we don't, we'll go without and maybe even perish. God's direction can come through direct revelation, or sometimes the Spirit speaks to us through people, God's prophets, just as He did in the OT.

But before we bend an ear to those prophets, we must understand how the prophetic gift is used in God's Kingdom, especially when it comes to His Provision.

There's a difference between the Spirit of prophecy, which is part of the manifestation of the gifts of the Spirit, and someone who operates in the office of a prophet.

> *But the manifestation of the Spirit is given to every man to profit withal. For to one is given by the Spirit the word of wisdom; to another the word of knowledge by the same Spirit; To another faith by*

the same Spirit; to another the gifts of healing by the same Spirit; To another the working of miracles; to another prophecy; to another discerning of spirits; to another divers kinds of tongues; to another the interpretation of tongues: But all these worketh that one and the selfsame Spirit, dividing to every man severally as he will. **1 Cor 12:7-11**

And God hath set some in the church, first apostles, secondarily prophets, thirdly teachers, after that miracles, then gifts of healings, helps, governments, diversities of tongues. **1 Cor 12:28**

A person operating in the gift of prophecy may not normally operate in that gifting on a continual basis. In fact, any Spirit-filled Believer can be given a prophecy and not necessarily be a "prophet". The person whom God has appointed as a prophet continually operates in the power of the Holy Spirit in this arena. That power is evident in their lives and the hand of God is clearly on them.

Regardless of whether it is someone operating in the gift of prophecy or an actual prophet of God, my suggestion is to always weigh what is said against the Word of God to ensure that it is corroborated in scripture. Many times you'll hear the prophecy repeated by two or three other independent sources.

Because the scope of this section, or even this book, is not necessarily on the gifts and offices of the Holy Spirit, I won't go beyond these comments. I only mention it because just as the Lord sent men of God to Israel to warn them what was coming, so will He do with us. Indeed, He already has. Are we listening?

Those warnings can be imperative for our survival even though they may be hard for us to fathom, or accept. Most of the time such warnings depict an America that will be changed forever. But you must be strong and courageous and your faith has to outweigh your flesh. In light of the truth, biblical faith must be the footing from where we operate.

Biblical faith has nothing to do with the traditions of men, but rather the power of God acting in and on behalf of His people. It takes more faith to be obedient to what God shows you is going to happen in the future, before it happens, than to react to it once it happens.

It was too late for Noah to start building the Ark after the flood. It was too late for Joseph to store up wheat in the midst of famine. It was too late for those Christians in Acts to prepare after that famine started.

Listen now. Prepare now.

Over-Spiritualizing God's Provision

As we move deeper into the twenty-first century, our very existence in the near future will be placed in this End Time framework. Jesus talked about this period as shown in Matthew 24:21 when He said that there's never been a time like this, nor will be again. It will be a time of great wrath.

Therefore rejoice, ye heavens, and ye that dwell in them. Woe to the inhabiters of the earth and of the sea! for the devil is come down unto you, having great wrath, because he knoweth that he hath but a short time. **Rev 12:12**

In that environment, we are called to survive, having prepared beforehand. Since we know what's coming, I suggest that we have enough oil for our lamps.

Then shall the kingdom of heaven be likened unto ten virgins, which took their lamps, and went forth to meet the bridegroom. And five of them were wise, and five were foolish. They that were foolish took their lamps, and took no oil with them, but the wise took oil in their vessels with their lamps. While the bridegroom tarried, they all slumbered and slept. And at midnight there was a cry made, Behold, the bridegroom cometh; go ye out to meet him. Then all those virgins arose, and trimmed their lamps. And the foolish said unto the wise, Give us of your oil; for our lamps are gone out. But the wise answered, saying, Not so; lest there be not enough for us and you: but go ye rather to them that sell, and buy for yourselves. And while they went to buy, the bridegroom came; and they that were ready went in with him to the marriage: and the door was shut. Afterward came also the other virgins, saying, Lord, Lord, open to us. But he answered and said, Verily I say unto you, I know you not. Watch therefore, for ye know neither the day nor the hour wherein the Son of man cometh. **Matt 25:1-13**

Over the years I've heard dozens of sermons and lessons on this parable and have heard it often said that the oil of the lamps represents the Holy Spirit. That might be true but I think this parable in particular is another excellent example on doing our part in God's Everlasting Provision.

View the story from a more pragmatic approach. If you look at the parable from a future, reality-based standpoint, instead of just being a story about spirituality, it takes on a deeper meaning.

Consider for a moment that the Lord told this parable about a time toward the end of the Great Tribulation, just before the Bridegroom makes His appearance. We know this because the virgins are waiting for the Bridegroom and the Bridegroom doesn't show up until the end, a time when the Great Falling Away is nearly complete because the Bridegroom will soon come to put an end to it.

About the time this was originally written, oil was one of the most precious commodities in the Mideast. It gave them light and light is what gave them the ability to see and work in the dark.

Because half of the virgins were lazy, they didn't maintain their supply of oil, they didn't prepare, and their supply ran out. We too will face a time when we need physical supplies to live. My question is, "Have you done your share of preparation for the coming darkness?"

When that darkness comes, you won't be able to go out and get more oil.

Lights Out

Right now we're living/working at the beginning of the worst onslaught of spiritual darkness, biblically, that mankind has ever seen. "The night comes when no man can work."

When that onslaught hits us in full-force, both physical and spiritual prepping should be completed. **Proverbs 22:3** is sound advice:

A prudent man foreseeth the evil, and hideth himself: but the simple pass on, and are punished.

This scripture is very applicable as well as **Isaiah 26:20-21** which says:

Come, my people, enter thou into thy chambers, and shut thy doors about thee: hide thyself as it were for a little moment, until the indignation be overpast. For, behold, the LORD cometh out of his place to punish the inhabitants of the earth for their iniquity: the earth also shall disclose her blood, and shall no more cover her slain.

His Provision in these days also includes the wisdom, via His Holy Spirit, to know when it's time to retreat and hunker-down so He can hide us. We will soon face those days so we must be about the Father's business while it is still light.

Keeping Your Powder Dry

Obviously our safety and security are part of God's Everlasting Provision. In scripture we see God miraculously intervene on Israel's behalf and wipe out her enemies. But how many times in the Bible do we see Israel having to take an active part in their security while God is leading them?

Tons.

Over the years, many Christians have challenged me on my stand on self-defense. I remind people that in the Bible, God's people just didn't rollover and die for their enemies. When Nehemiah and the Israelites were rebuilding the wall of the Temple, they worked with a trowel in one hand and a spear in the other.

> *And it came to pass, when our enemies heard that it was known unto us, and God had brought their counsel to nought, that we returned all of us to the wall, every one unto his work. And it came to pass from that time forth, that the half of my servants wrought in the work, and the other half of them held both the spears, the shields, and the bows, and the habergeons; and the rulers were behind all the house of Judah. They which builded on the wall, and they that bare burdens, with those that laded, every one with one of his hands wrought in the work, and with the other hand held a weapon. For the builders, every one had his sword girded by his side, and so builded. And he that sounded the trumpet was by me. And I said unto the nobles, and to the rulers, and to the rest of the people, "The work is great and large, and we are separated upon the wall, one far from another. In what place therefore ye hear the sound of the trumpet, resort ye thither unto us: our God shall fight for us."*
> *Nehemiah 4:15-20*

For the pacifist Christians amongst us, I challenge you to show me anywhere in scripture where it says that self-defense is wrong. It isn't there. The God of the Bible never changes; that's what we are told. The same God that led the Israelites into battle is the same God that sent Jesus. He didn't suddenly become a pacifist-love-god. He's a God of war. He always has been and always will be.

Even Peter had a sword in the Garden of Gethsemane. Do you know how he got it?

Jesus told him to carry it.

> *And He said unto them, "When I sent you without purse, and scrip, and shoes, lacked ye any thing?" And they said, "Nothing." Then said He unto them, "But now, he that hath a purse, let him take it, and likewise his scrip: and he that hath no sword, let him sell his garment, and buy one. For I say unto you, that this that is written must yet be accomplished in me, And he was reckoned among the transgressors: for the things concerning me have an end." And they said, "Lord, behold, here are two swords." And He said unto them, "It is enough."* Luke 22:35-38

Some people will say that Jesus only told Peter to carry a sword so that Isaiah 53:12 could be fulfilled.

Therefore will I divide him a portion with the great, and he shall divide the spoil with the strong; because he hath poured out his soul unto death: and he was numbered with the transgressors; and he bare the sin of many, and made intercession for the transgressors.

When Jesus was arrested in the Garden of Gethsemane, His words seemingly allude to this.

In that same hour said Jesus to the multitudes, "Are ye come out as against a thief with swords and staves for to take me? I sat daily with you teaching in the temple, and ye laid no hold on me. But all this was done, that the scriptures of the prophets might be fulfilled." Then all the disciples forsook Him, and fled. **Matt 26:55**

What is Jesus really saying in Luke 22:35-38? If you read the scripture in its context, the Lord is telling His disciples that things were changing. This is why He tells them, "*he that hath a purse, let him take it, and likewise his scrip: and he that hath no sword, let him sell his garment, and buy one.*" Surely the same people that say we shouldn't defend ourselves, carry wallets with money to pay for things, don't they?

Pacifists will also use the following scripture about Peter's sword experience in the Garden as a proof text.

And, behold, one of them which were with Jesus stretched out his hand, and drew his sword, and struck a servant of the high priest's, and smote off his ear. Then said Jesus unto him, "Put up again thy sword into his place: for all they that take the sword shall perish with the sword. Thinkest thou that I cannot now pray to my Father, and he shall presently give me more than twelve legions of angels? But how then shall the scriptures be fulfilled, that thus it must be?" ~~Luke 26:51-54~~ Matthew 26: 51-54

But that phrase "...they that take the sword shall perish with the sword" is an idiom of the day for a mercenary, or Merc as we would call him. It pertains to someone who makes his living by killing and would be used regarding a professional soldier, mercenary or in some cases just a flat-out killer. Peter was none of those things.

And in Hebrews 12:4 it says:

Ye have not yet resisted unto blood, striving against sin.

This scripture alludes to violence, but isn't necessarily talking about shedding other people's blood. It indicates that violence can come to us. Our God who is a God of War didn't shy away from defending His People during OT times so why would He shy away from defending us now? And we shouldn't shy away either.

Jesus never wasted words and always meant what He said. So when He follows His statement in ~~Luke~~ Matthew 26:53 26 with the fact that He commands legions of angels, we should take notice. Some people might want to apply this verse literally. They say that people shouldn't take up arms to defend themselves. If that were true, please tell me when Jesus called down 10,000 angels to defend Him. While I'm certain He could, the point is that He didn't. He went to the Cross, died and rose again.

We can't apply part of the passage literally and not all of the passage. Jesus always taught using examples from the people's environment. Luke 26 *Matthew* is no different. He used this experience in the Garden with the sword to fulfill prophecy, that much is true. But using this scripture to make a debate in favor of pacifism misses the whole point. His disciples had to understand that He did not HAVE to be killed; He CHOSE to die on the Cross out of His deep love for us.

We are told to occupy this place until He comes again. We are in the world, but not of it. We are already in His kingdom, but we have to live and exist here with all the pressures of the world.

> *I pray not that thou shouldest take them out of the world, but that thou shouldest keep them from the evil. They are not of the world, even as I am not of the world. Sanctify them through thy truth: thy word is truth. As thou hast sent me into the world, even so have I also sent them into the world. And for their sakes I sanctify myself, that they also might be sanctified through the truth. Neither pray I for these alone, but for them also which shall believe on me through their word; That they all may be one; as thou, Father, art in me, and I in thee, that they also may be one in us: that the world may believe that thou hast sent me.* **John 17:15-21**

In this End Times world, we'll have to deal with feeding and protecting ourselves and our families. If we don't, there's a warning for us in **1 Timothy 5:8**:

> *But if any provide not for his own, and specially for those of his own house, he hath denied the faith, and is worse than an infidel.*

God loves you and your family and He wants you all to have provision and to be safe in the days to come. Don't you have a responsibility to God, and to your family, to be obedient to work with God to keep them safe?

We've been created in God's image and likeness. So then we're just supposed to turn around and say, "God's a God of war, but He really wants us to be a bunch of pacifists"?

This is not consistent with God's nature. It's one thing to turn the other cheek at an insult. Allowing people to harm you or your family by not defending yourself is tantamount to saying that God sanctions suicide. Clearly He does not. He trains us to be like Him with the same fierce fighting heart that He put in us. If you're a believer, you're going to have to admit that you are also a warrior after God's own heart, not a pacifist.

> *He teacheth my hands to war, so that a bow of steel is broken by mine arms.* **Psalm 18:34**

In fact, those who would shrink from the battle would do well to reread **Revelation 21:8**:

> *But the fearful, and unbelieving, and the abominable, and murderers, and whoremongers, and sorcerers, and idolaters, and all liars, shall have their part in the lake which burneth with fire and brimstone: which is the second death.*

Notice that the "fearful (cowards) and unbelieving" are thrown in the lake of fire with people who have offended God with their lifestyle choices and rebellion.

More evil has been stopped by non-passive Believers, than by pacifist Christians. If God has given us a gift of life, and we were created in His image and likeness, we have every right to defend that image and likeness even unto death.

Dumb Unto Death?

If people want to lie down and die, I certainly can't stop them. But it reminds me of the verse out of **Isaiah 53:6:**

> All we like sheep have gone astray; we have turned every one to his own way; and the LORD hath laid on him the iniquity of us all.

God comparing us to sheep isn't an accident. Sheep are some dumb animals. Don't believe me? Take a look at what this real-life shepherd has to say about sheep after spending so much time with them:

He (the pastor) went on to describe how sheep were so dumb that they were prone to putting themselves in danger and doing stuff that was harmful to their health because they were not smart enough to know better. This caused a lot more work and worry for the shepherd, who had to go out of his way to make sure they did not wander off, eat the wrong plant or do something else stupid.

Boy was the pastor talking about something that was in my wheelhouse. Just that morning, I had opened the gate to the pasture, turning the ewes out on some of the best, most lush brome pasture ever. You know the whole, "He leads me to green pastures" part. Only to have them turn around and charge back to me as I carried a bucket of grain to the steers. Acres of lush green grass and they only wanted the steer feed that probably had things in it that were not good for sheep. Stupid animals, the pastor sure had it right. Sheep are mindless creatures only worried about themselves, even to the point of being harmful and causing me more worry and work.

Then my pastor made his point, we humans are a lot like sheep. Wow was that a low blow. Sheep are dumb animals who cannot take care of themselves or make good decisions...[9]

"*Sheep are dumb animals who cannot take care of themselves or make good decisions*"? Yup, I'd say that the Lord hit the nail right on the head. Sometimes we're not so bright. Not in Moses' time and not in the 21st century.

Another verse that comes to mind is **Rev 13:7:**

> And it was given unto him to make war with the saints, and to overcome them: and power was given him over all kindreds, and tongues, and nations.

As it pertains to this verse, I think that the reason the Beast overcomes the saints is because they act like sheep! Dumb sheep!

It all goes back to the fact that biblical faith is not presumption nor is it assumption.

---

9 Glen Brunkow, "Now, About Those Dumb Sheep..." Midwest Messenger, https://www.agupdate.com/midwestmessenger/opinion/columnists/glenn_brunkow/now-about-those-dumb-sheep/article_648ae549-7e53-58e2-b82f-b35465a6476f.html, (May 24, 2017).

Provision in Battle

The Father gave Jesus a twofold mission. The Son was first sent to die on a Cross, thereby destroying the works of the evil one.

> *He that committeth sin is of the devil; for the devil sinneth from the beginning. For this purpose the Son of God was manifested, that he might destroy the works of the devil.* **1 John 3:8**

His sacrifice as the Lamb of God washed away our sins and bridged our relationship with the Father, which had been broken in the Garden of Eden when Adam and Eve sinned.

The second part of Messiah's mission is yet to happen.

When He comes back, it will be to rule and reign. In doing so, He absolutely destroys Satan, the Antichrist and his armies. Talk about overwhelming force, upon His appearance Jesus brings with Him the armies of heaven and a two-edged sword in His mouth - not a pacifier.

> *And I saw heaven opened, and behold a white horse; and He that sat upon Him was called Faithful and True, and in righteousness He doth judge and make war. His eyes were as a flame of fire, and on His head were many crowns; and He had a name written, that no man knew, but He himself. And He was clothed with a vesture dipped in blood: and His name is called The Word of God. And the armies which were in heaven followed Him upon white horses, clothed in fine linen, white and clean. And out of His mouth goeth a sharp sword, that with it He should smite the nations: and He shall rule them with a rod of iron: and He treadeth the winepress of the fierceness and wrath of Almighty God. And He hath on His vesture and on His thigh a name written, KING OF KINGS, AND LORD OF LORDS.* **Rev 19:11-16**

> *And then shall that Wicked be revealed, whom the Lord shall consume with the spirit of his mouth, and shall destroy with the brightness of his coming.* **2 Thess 2:8**

> *And I saw the beast, and the kings of the earth, and their armies, gathered together to make war against him that sat on the horse, and against his army. And the beast was taken, and with him the false prophet that wrought miracles before him, with which he deceived them that had received the mark of the beast, and them that worshipped his image. These both were cast alive into a lake of fire burning with brimstone.* **Rev 19:19-20**

We're part of those armies, even though you may not feel like a soldier. Our Commander-in-Chief is the **Lion of the Tribe of Judah.**

> *And one of the elders saith unto me, Weep not: behold, the Lion of the tribe of Judah, the Root of David, hath prevailed to open the book, and to loose the seven seals thereof.* **Rev 5:5**

Satan is no comparison to Jesus and he's certainly not the lion he pretends to be:

> *Be sober, be vigilant; because your adversary the devil, as a roaring lion, walketh about, seeking whom he may devour.* **1 Peter 5:8**

The battle for your survival will be fought in the environment of where you live and work but you don't have to go through life walking in your own strength. Jesus walks alongside you as your Provider and Defender. He is your Strength and your Victory. While it may be true that the devil can hurt you, we'll also see God provide for us like never before.

Of all the times in which God could have chosen for you to be born and live, He chose you to participate in the greatest final act in history. My prayer is that you and I will rise to the challenge and see God do the miraculous.

Chapter 14
Manna From Heaven

And the children of Israel said unto them, "Would to God we had died by the hand of the LORD in the land of Egypt, when we sat by the flesh pots, and when we did eat bread to the full; for ye have brought us forth into this wilderness, to kill this whole assembly with hunger." Then said the LORD unto Moses, "Behold, I will rain bread from heaven for you; and the people shall go out and gather a certain rate every day, that I may prove them, whether they will walk in my law, or no."

Exodus 16:3-4

The word *manna* literally means: "What is it?"

God fed the children of Israel with something that they'd never seen before. This time around, I have no idea how God's going to provide and deliver His people in 21st century style. I know Him by His character, and if He says He will do it, He will do it. And with history as our example, we know that He will do something great.

No doubt someone will say, "See! It was God that supplied the manna to the children of Israel. They didn't have to prepare. It just fell from heaven!"

Are you kidding me?

The Israelites didn't just wander off into the desert just because they felt like it. God judged Egypt with different plagues (ten in fact) to convince the pharaoh to let the Hebrews go. At the last plague, God specifically told Moses to make sure that the people had everything packed, were fully dressed, had their staff in their hands and they had to make sure their sandals were on! **That was preparation.**

And thus shall ye eat it; with your loins girded, your shoes on your feet, and your staff in your hand; and ye shall eat it in haste: it is the LORD'S passover. **Exodus 12:11**

In addition, the Hebrews had to journey a long way before they would see God rain manna down from heaven. Why would you expect it to be any different with us?

God is God, He could have fed Joseph and His people without them storing up food for seven years. Why didn't He? Because He wanted people to have an active hand in their own provision by preparing for what was coming. Then, and only then, He took care of the rest. This is consistent with His character.

After all, Joshua and Caleb had to go in and physically slay the Giants of the Promised Land. God didn't do it for them, but when they participated in the plan of God, He delivered the Giants into their hands.

Almost without exception, He always wants us to display our faith in action and then He provides.

Faith in Action

Now faith is the substance of things hoped for, the evidence of things not seen. **Hebrews 11:1**

When you believe God for Provision, or for deliverance in the face of danger, you're using His Word like the deed of a property or title of a car that says you trust that you own His positive outcome in that need.

Notice I said "His positive outcome" and not your positive outcome.

For Christians who desire His highest for their lives, you'll understand this statement. If you're someone who wants God to do it your way, all the time, you'll struggle with the idea. God doesn't think like you.

For my thoughts are not your thoughts, neither are your ways my ways, saith the LORD. **Isaiah 55:8**

This desire to have it "our way" goes right back to faith, or lack thereof.

Trying to get God to answer our prayers with a predetermined outcome in mind is like having a spiritual arm wrestling match with the Most High. How do you think that'll turn out?

Rather, when we fully surrender our lives to God, we're basically saying, *"God, I know You know better than I do. I know that You can see into the future, and the end from the beginning. I don't want what I want, I want what You want."*

Sometimes God protects us from ourselves when it comes to faith. In fact, James 4:3 says:

Ye ask, and receive not, because ye ask amiss, that ye may consume it upon your lusts.

The mindset of surrendering to God gives us the right framework to see Him move on our behalf. This mindset will keep you from asking Him for that Mercedes or Porsche. This mindset will keep you from marrying that person who will ultimately make you miserable. This mindset will keep you from walking into harm's way even before you get there. And it is the kind of mindset that says:

And we know that all things work together for good to them that love God, to them who are the called according to his purpose. **Romans 8:28**

In other words, that mindset says, *"I trust You, God, even though I can't see a way forward."* It's that kind of faith that caused the Israelites to leave Egypt. It's that kind of faith that caused Joshua and Caleb to take on Giants.

It's that kind of faith that you and I will need for the End of the Age.

Making Mountains Out of Mustard Seeds

And Jesus said unto them, Because of your unbelief: for verily I say unto you, If ye have faith as a grain of mustard seed, ye shall say unto this mountain, Remove hence to yonder place; and it shall remove; and nothing shall be impossible unto you. **Matt 17:20**

Out of curiosity I did a quick Google search on this verse and found numerous hits. I was surprised that many selections were fixated on the size and weight of the mustard seed. In doing that, the teachers were trying to quantify faith instead of qualify their faith.

Faith is simply believing that God is Who He said He is, and that He will do what He said He will do. Through the parable, Jesus is showing that it's not the size, or having great faith, that will move a mountain. It's having faith that it's God Who will be the One to move the mountain.

Everyone who has been redeemed by the blood of Jesus has been given the faith they need so they can walk this walk:

For I say, through the grace given unto me, to every man that is among you, not to think of himself more highly than he ought to think; but to think soberly, according as God hath dealt to every man the measure of faith. **Romans 12:3**

In our time of need for God's Provision, the point is to activate the faith that we've already been given. That boy surrendered his lunch of loaves and fishes to the disciples. Jesus took that lunch, or prep if you will, and multiplied it.

God always looks to people who have obeyed the warnings and prepared. That's what He multiplies.

Warning Sirens

All of the prophets were heralders of preparation, warning sirens if you will.

Their messages were always twofold: First, they warned about the people needing heart preparation, getting right with the Living God. Second, they warned the people on how God would lead them. And as I always say, *"Where He leads, He feeds."*

Those warnings from the great men of faith in the Bible always caused them to battle ridicule, contempt, doubt and scorn from their peers.

I am as one mocked of his neighbour, who calleth upon God, and he answereth him: the just upright man is laughed to scorn. **Job 12:4**

People who couldn't see what God was going to do, or were too preoccupied with their own lives and sin, often hurled insults to the men and woman of God who heard from the Lord. And it's the same way today.

In fact, most people don't have a predisposition to hear what God is saying. This is why so many dreams and Words of the Lord that Christians have received by the Spirit have come to naught. That's because instead of Believers letting the dream or Word rest in their heart, or nurturing it with prayer and also seasoning it with the Word, they go right out and tell someone what they saw or dreamed. They'll tell non-Christians about the dream/word and ask them what they think. When they don't receive a positive response, or doubt is seeded in their heart by this trusted source, they abort the seed that God planted.

The result is that the dream, vision or Word, and purposes of God, fail because they don't allow that seed to grow into fruition.

Make sure, as God shows you what you need to do for your provision, that you nurture that seed properly and that you only release it when the Lord tells you to release it.

Smoke and Mirrors

Considering those things that the Lord has shown me about the future, I asked Him, *"God when will You provide for Your people?"* His very clear reply was, *"Steve, when My people have no choice but to look to Me."*

In the near future God's people will only have Him to provide for them. I don't know exactly how this will come about, or the chain of events that will prompt this desperate plight, although, like you, I can certainly venture a guess based upon the news, Words, dreams and visions that men and women of God have received over the years.

One of those triggering events will be the failure of the money system.

When it will fail, I don't know, but right now we're approaching a $250 trillion dollar deficit. Let that simmer in your mind for a second.

The United States' GDP (gross domestic product) or the total amount of money our whole economy makes in a year, is only $19.39 trillion dollars. If we didn't spend money on anything else, not defense, not healthcare, not infrastructure, not support of any kind, and we did this for at least 12 ½ years, we could pay the money back.

Oh, but wait. If we didn't spend money on anything else, we couldn't make money and therefore couldn't raise money to pay the debt back anyway! Besides, with no defenses, we'd be overrun by our enemies and would cease to exist as a country.

So you get the point: We can never pay back this debt!

Let that sink in for a second.

If you're a foreign power like China, Russia, Saudi Arabia, etc. and you've bought our debt, U.S. Treasury Bonds, thereby lending us money, and one day we go to you and say, *"Gosh, we're sorry, China, but we can't pay you back all those trillions of dollars that we owe you."*

What do you think IS GOING TO HAPPEN?

They will come to take what's theirs. We certainly would.

One day this game of musical chairs is going to stop. And when we can't pay back that debt, the money will fail. I promise you, the outcome to our money failing will be war.

But here's the kicker. If you understand how the financial system works, then you already know that everything is based upon smoke and mirrors, lies and Madison Avenue anyway! It's air. It's not real.

Just Weights and Measures

There are always those Christians who get mad at me when I talk about gold and silver. But unlike the Monopoly money that I mentioned, gold and silver are tangible assets. In fact, think about it: God created gold and silver. Precious metals also are not debt instruments like fiat currency. They are, from biblical times until now, considered just weights and measures.

> *Thou shalt not have in thy bag divers weights, a great and a small. Thou shalt not have in thine house divers measures, a great and a small. But thou shalt have a perfect and just weight, a perfect and just measure shalt thou have: that thy days may be lengthened in the land which the LORD thy God giveth thee. For all that do such things, and all that do unrighteously, are an abomination unto the LORD thy God.* **Deut 25:13-16**

In biblical times, commodities and precious metals were traded and sold and were used as money. Goods and these metals were required to be measured and weighed according to established standards that no one was allowed to deviate from.

Today the paper, fiat currency, that we use has no intrinsic value whatsoever. It's only considered valuable because the U.S. government says that they will back it and make good on it. As I just illustrated in the last section, the U.S. government is at least 12 years behind making good on the debt that we owe to foreign countries. Some of those countries even have nuclear missiles pointed at us. How exactly are they going to make good on that dollar in your hand if they have nothing of value to pay back the debt?

You see my point?

There's nothing of worth that is backing that paper. It's a total fraud. That's why I'm so passionate about gold and silver: It's tangible, it's worth something.

Hey, but who am I? Don't believe me. Instead, check out what God thinks of unjust weights and measures.

> *A false balance is abomination to the LORD: but a just weight is his delight.* **Proverbs 11:1**

> *Divers weights, and divers measures, both of them are alike abomination to the LORD.* **Proverbs 20:10**

Since God never changes, it's a pretty safe assumption that He still hates unjust weights and measures. And I'm even willing to take this one step farther.

How do you think He feels about a worldwide system that is based upon fraud and lies, resulting in the vast majority of people being stolen from, because the system is fraudulent? I will tell you…

God is angry. He's not only angry, He's seething.

He put the economies of the world into motion, but fallen, rebellious men decided that they didn't want the just system that God made. Instead those same men, inspired by the Fallen Angels, I would venture, invented the Fractional Reserve Banking system in its place.

Fractional Reserve Banking is a whole topic in and of itself and one you should be familiar with. I don't want to take the time to go into it, but there are plenty of books on the subject. One book in particular comes to mind, which is called *The Creature From Jekyll Island* by G. Edward Griffin. Although I don't believe him to be a professing Christian, he's done an excellent job of breaking down the lie behind our monetary system and it's well worth the read.

But back to my point: Why would anyone want to settle for a fiat currency that man took upon himself to create?

In addition, in the Bible, we're also warned against borrowing and lending:

> *Owe no man any thing, but to love one another: for he that loveth another hath fulfilled the law.* **Rom 13:8**

> *The rich ruleth over the poor, and the borrower is servant to the lender.* **Prov 22:7**

We're talking about God's Everlasting Provision, but so many Christians are wrapped up in the cares and system of this fallen world. We have loans, we have banks, we have stuff. And for some reason, our idea of God's Provision is that He should help us keep our stuff. By the way, it's that same stuff that we bought through a system that He finds abhorrent!

So here's a reality check: The money system of the world is a Ponzi Scheme, legalized, but a Ponzi Scheme nonetheless. Like all Ponzi Schemes, it's destined to fall apart and because it's so pervasive, it will fall hard.

That's when the money will fail.

When the Money Fails

There are examples from scripture of what it looks like when the money fails. Those examples show that people become desperate. We need look no further then one of the original Prepper himself - Joseph.

And there was no bread in all the land; for the famine was very sore, so that the land of Egypt and all the land of Canaan fainted by reason of the famine. And Joseph gathered up all the money that was found in the land of Egypt, and in the land of Canaan, for the corn which they bought: and Joseph brought the money into Pharaoh's house. And when money failed in the land of Egypt, and in the land of Canaan, all the Egyptians came unto Joseph, and said, Give us bread: for why should we die in thy presence? for the money faileth. Genesis 47:13-15

Because he'd prepared at the Lord's direction, Joseph saved his people from starvation and at the same time, rescued all of Egypt as well. Much like that scenario, in our day when the money fails people will get desperate when they get hungry. My advice is don't wait until disaster strikes to learn to depend on God. Learn to depend on God now, when you have food, water, shelter and transportation and you will not be subject to the Powers-That-Be during a time when the rest of the world is looking for answers.

Those very same Powers will try to force Christians to compromise their beliefs and even to turn their backs on the Living God. If you have not prepared and have not learned to depend on God for His Provision, you'll be subject to the will of those satanically-influenced Powers.

Being under someone else's influence is not something you want. This leads me to the other part of that story with Joseph.

On behalf of the Pharaoh, Joseph gained ownership of everything that the Egyptians had as they traded their belongings for food and seed, year by year.

You don't want to be subject to the government and go to the FEMA camps, thereby trading your freedom and your life, for the sake of food, water and shelter. Instead, make sure that you're listening to the prompting of the Holy Spirit now as He leads you to safety and provision.

Hunger can be a powerful motivator. Don't be suckered by your empty belly.

Into the Wilderness

Most of you reading these words have undoubtedly heard the phrase, "cities of refuge" when it comes to End Times provision. First, this label is not entirely accurate because they won't be cities of refuge, but more specifically they'll be outposts for refugees. These will be places across the world where people have been led by God for decades to prepare food, water, clothes and a variety of things for this very time. It's to these outposts that God will lead His people.

I get asked all the time, "Where will these places be located?"

My blunt answer is, "I have no idea." I'm just a guy and God hasn't revealed such things to me. But He has made it clear that there will be such places. God's prophets will know where to go. God will send those men and women of faith to His people to show them where to go.

People have also asked me what "the wilderness" means or what it will look like.

Again, my honest answer is, "I don't know." At this point, who really knows what the wilderness will look like, but I certainly don't think it means that everybody should move to the woods in Montana, Kentucky or the Smoky Mountains.

The wilderness is an illustration of where God meets His people, either in captivity or leading them to safety. The wilderness has to do with being in the position of where God wants you, versus where you want to be. It's also an environment that lacks the comforts of home.

For instance, I promise you that in the wilderness you're not going find HDTVs and you won't be able to dial 1-800 Wilderness Pizza! There'll come a time in the not too distant future when the homes we live in now will not be the place that we stay, as God leads us into that wilderness.

Soon everything that Christians own will be tied to the Mark of the Beast. You can say, "No, Steve, not me. I won't take the mark!"

The problem is that I'm not necessarily talking about the mark. I'm talking about things that are tied to the mark, or the system, i.e. your cell phone, your computer, your bank account, your social security number, your car, your employer and even your friends and family. This system is systemic and becoming more so every day. Soon you'll not be able to own anything that's not part of that system.

We will have to make a choice of yielding to the Antichrist and his world system, or not. This transition to the Mark of the Beast will not be optional. It will be an absolute decision that has to be made by each individual. No one will be able to shove it down your throat. God has even prohibited the devil from doing this, but you will need to choose. I should also point out that convincing people to take the mark doesn't preclude Satan from trying to destroy everybody in the meantime.

We're already seeing these lines being drawn. For example, we will live to see the day when Christians will deny Jesus and embrace Transhumanism, thereby exchanging their spiritual birthright for the promise of eternal life apart from God. That too is part of the system that we are told to come out of.

> *And I heard another voice from heaven, saying, Come out of her, my people, that ye be not partakers of her sins, and that ye receive not of her plagues.* **Rev 18:4**

For those of us who refuse to participate in that Antichrist system or to accept the mark, we will automatically be placed in a figurative wilderness. That refusal will cause us to be forced by the Powers-That-Be, the devils that are, to vacate our lives. Believers will have everything they own confiscated and they'll be forced to endure very difficult circumstances. You need only look at old news footage of what the Jews endured at the hand of the Nazis to understand how difficult it will be. But that's just the beginning because it will be even worse.

I believe that those Christians who are praying and seeking the Father's voice beforehand will be able to hear God's direction as He leads us out to safety before they come for us.

In the first wilderness, He was with the Hebrews and He led them out from Egypt to Himself. That's really the key here: He's bringing us to Himself. He's going to strip away the trappings and distractions of the world.

> *Watch ye therefore, and pray always, that ye may be accounted worthy to escape all these things that shall come to pass, and to stand before the Son of man.* **Luke 21:36**

As far as how God will provide, I can't tell you what heaven's menu will look like for those End Times saints. Will there be more manna? Will we have quail or fish or meat? Who knows?

The real question is: Will you be content with manna at the hand of God? Or, because of your lack of faith, will you be lured by the GMOs, or the Soylent Green, Gray or Blue that will be offered at the FEMA camps?

We can read Revelation to get an idea of what John saw, but we really have no idea what the landscape will look like after… the judgments of God.

Leveling the Playing Field

When we think about modern technology and weapons, a good chunk of it is already dedicated to real-time surveillance of the populace, with more coming online in the next few years. We know from scripture that the Antichrist's end-goal is to number, or mark, every person on the planet. And, without that number or mark, you won't be able to buy food.

> *And he causeth all, both small and great, rich and poor, free and bond, to receive a mark in their right hand, or in their foreheads. And that no man might buy or sell, save he that had the mark, or the name of the beast, or the number of his name.* **Rev 13:16-17**

But another way that God is going to provide is by leveling the playing field in those days in order to preserve His people. There are several ways He can do this and some of them we have already been told about by people who have had dreams and visions.

Consider the effect of an EMP (Electro Magnetic Pulse) on satellites and the surveillance systems stretched out across the planet. A global EMP event is not unprecedented. The Carrington Event was the result of a massive solar storm in 1859 in which a huge CME (coronal mass ejection) was slung off the sun and bombarded earth. At the time, there was no rating for solar storms so it's unknown just how powerful the event was, but it's thought to have been the largest event of this kind that man had ever experienced.

Keep in mind that our electrical infrastructure and technology was not very advanced back then. The pulse knocked out the rudimentary electrical grid at the time and even caused telegraph stations to operate without being connected.

An earth-directed CME of that size and strength in our modern day would send mankind back to the Stone Age. The electrical grid would go down, never to be the same, if it ever came back up again. Cars and electronics would stop. Because of our dependence on technology, it's estimated that millions would be killed within the first few weeks.

This event is not unique.

In July of 2012, a massive solar eruption hurled a plasma death spear into space in the form of a CME. It was thought to be as large, if not larger, than the one that caused the Carrington Event. The scary part is that it only missed the earth by a mere three weeks. Had our planet's orbit been advanced by just three weeks, we would have taken a direct hit.

There's also a significant threat of an instantaneous pole shift.

When it comes to pole shifts, there are two basic varieties. One would make life uncomfortable because it is a magnetic pole reversal in which the North Pole becomes the South Pole, or anywhere in between, but there's not a physical change of the earth's crust.

I say that this would make life uncomfortable because everyone and everything that depends on knowing where true north is, like navigation equipment, is set up for that particular vantage point.

Magnetic pole reversals normally take months, if not years, to migrate to where they will finally be before they stabilize. In fact, our north pole has already started to shift over the last few years and is not where you might think it is. At the penning of this book, it's reported to be in northern Canada, after already migrating to and from Siberia, Russia.

Far more destructive than a simple migrating magnetic pole would be something called Earth Crustal Displacement. Crustal displacement is the physical relocation of the earth's top layer, the crust, in a sudden and violent manner.

Try to wrap your head around this idea for a moment.

Every inch of dirt that you're standing on could be ripped from under your feet and relocated to someplace thousands of miles away. One can only guess what would happen to the buildings and people who were on the surface of the earth at the time that such a shifting took place.

You might think it sounds far-fetched, but there is precedence in the Bible for such an event.

And the channels of the sea appeared, the foundations of the world were discovered, at the rebuking of the LORD, at the blast of the breath of his nostrils. **2 Sam 22:16**

"And it shall come to pass at the same time when Gog shall come against the land of Israel," saith the Lord GOD, "that my fury shall come up in my face. For in my jealousy and in the fire of my wrath have I spoken, Surely in that day there shall be a great shaking in the land of Israel; So that the fishes of the sea, and the fowls of the heaven, and the beasts of the field, and all creeping things that creep upon the earth, and all the men that are upon the face of the earth, shall shake at my presence, and the mountains shall be thrown down, and the steep places shall fall, and every wall shall fall to the ground." **Ezekiel 38:18-20**

I don't know exactly how such an event would occur, only that the Bible says it will occur. "Planet X" or "Nibiru" would have the mass and gravity to pull the earth over on its axis, thereby displacing the crust. This would cause an instantaneous pole reversal.

Ancient history points to planetary events that changed the face of earth and planets' orbits within our solar systems and is exactly what caused the ancients to set up observatories worldwide. Archaeological evidence points to the fact that those same ancients were terrified about the potential of planetary catastrophes.

While we don't know when Nibiru will make its appearance, we are seeing an uptick in volcanic eruptions and massive earthquakes all over the world. Although Nibiru is not mentioned by name in the Bible, Jesus spoke about great earthquakes in diverse places.

Stresses on our planet are already being felt and I believe that we could well be feeling the beginning effects of that approaching body. As to how long it will take to fully make its appearance, I have no idea. But the point is that such a passing body would cause Earth Crustal Displacement.

We are beginning to see the travailing of our planet.

For we know that the whole creation groaneth and travaileth in pain together until now. **Rom 8:22**

Speaking of heavenly bodies affecting the earth, there are other types of astral-catastrophism that could negatively affect the earth. Along with solar eruptions you have to consider gamma-ray bursts from distant stars and even errant meteor impacts or showers.

Any of these instances would have the same kind of impact on our lives and we will absolutely need God's Provision and direction.

But nature isn't the only thing that God would allow to level the playing field. As you may know, electronics and the electrical grid will be the first to go down from the EMP of a nuclear detonation, or in a nuclear war.

When it comes to God's interdiction on our behalf, those previously-mentioned surveillance satellites, as well as the rest the world's satellites, would be the first things to go down after an EMP. What makes this potential interesting is that in a war you want to blind the eyes and ears of your enemy, that's called C3, command, communication, and control. So could it be that God will blind our enemies as a way of making provision for us?

Once the satellites go down and the power goes down, the Antichrist and his flunkies will be grossly limited in what they can and can't do to God's people.

Another thing that we've been warned about are the volcanoes going off all over the world. Henry Gruver had the vision of planes dropping out of the sky due to the volcanic emissions on the West Coast. This is entirely believable because jet engines don't do well when it comes to severe volcanic ash. There've been several examples of this over the years as airliners were rerouted away from volcanic ash plumes in Iceland, Chile and other places.

Speaking about Henry's vision of the volcanoes, he also saw Chinese invasion troops landing all the way up and down the west coast of America. At the same time, he saw volcanoes going off all over the Cascade region. The Lord showed him that as the Chinese tried to move inland, the molten lava from those volcanoes literally dissolved them.

But there is a burning question that I have to present to you (no pun intended): If God's given the ultimate storm warning, the hurricane from Hell warning, how many Christians even believe it's going to happen?

The presentation of God's prophetic warnings are a provision for His people to prepare for the times that are coming upon the earth.

The Ultimate Provision

Hebrews 1:3 says that Jesus upholds all things by the word of His power, even down to the smallest part of an atom. That's our God.

He is also the same God Who sent His only Son to die on a Cross to provide you and me a way back to Him. This is the greatest promise of His Provision: Knowing that he who has the Son, has eternal life.

> *The LORD is my light and my salvation; whom shall I fear? the LORD is the strength of my life; of whom shall I be afraid?* **Psalm 27:1**

The closer we get to Jesus, the more we fall in love with Him. The more that we fall in love with Him, the less we worry about. That walk of peace makes heaven become more real than the physical reality around us.

> *While we look not at the things which are seen, but at the things which are not seen: for the things which are seen are temporal; but the things which are not seen are eternal.* **2 Cor 4:18**

Learning to depend on God's Everlasting Provision in both the good times and the hard times helps us to walk ever closer to God. In the end, that's all that really matters.

> *But as it is written, Eye hath not seen, nor ear heard, neither have entered into the heart of man, the things which God hath prepared for them that love him.* **1 Cor 2:9**

Nearer, my God, to Thee

Nearer, my God, to Thee,
Nearer to Thee;
E'en though it be a cross
That raiseth me,
Still all my song shall be
Nearer, my God, to Thee
Nearer to Thee.

Though, like a wanderer,
The sun gone down,
Darkness comes over me,
My rest a stone;
Yet in my dreams I'd be
Nearer, my God, to Thee
Nearer to Thee.

There let me see the sight,
An open heaven;
All that Thou sendest me,
In mercy given;
Angels to beckon me
Nearer, my God, to Thee
Nearer to Thee.

Then, with my waking thoughts
Bright with Thy praise,
Out of my stony griefs
Bethel I'll raise,
So by my woes to be
Nearer, my God, to Thee
Nearer to Thee.

HELP 6

His Everlasting Patience

Commit thy way unto the LORD; trust also in Him; and He shall bring it to pass. And He shall bring forth thy righteousness as the light, and thy judgment as the noonday. Rest in the LORD, and wait patiently for Him: fret not thyself because of him who prospereth in his way, because of the man who bringeth wicked devices to pass.

Psalm 37:5-7

Patience

I have to admit that sometimes I really don't understand why God does what He does. This particular H.E.L.P., His Everlasting Patience, in this particular book is a good example.

That's because as I've already shared, when the Lord gave me the premise for this book I saw the 10 H.E.L.P.s all at one time. His Everlasting Patience was on that list. I have no choice but to include the H.E.L.P. in the book. Don't get me wrong, God's Patience is a wonderful thing. But the truth is that Patience is the one area that I probably struggle with the most.

I want things done now. And anyone who knows me will tell you that I'm not the most patient person around. Nonetheless, here I am.

Over the years I've had a lot of people take issue with me on the various things I've said or written. It gets tiresome after a while and I begin to lose my patience.

There's a beautiful scripture in Isaiah 40:31 that says:

> *But they that wait upon the LORD shall renew their strength; they shall mount up with wings as eagles; they shall run, and not be weary; and they shall walk, and not faint.*

When I read the above verse, I have a renewed sense of hope. Despite the potshots that I get on a regular basis, God will give me the strength and energy to do the work that He's called me to do. It's tough to mount up with wings like eagles when you've got a few turkeys trying to tear you down.

I know, I know. I'm not supposed to talk like that. But I'm only human and I know what God has shown me or told me. It's a good thing that God sees the end from the beginning and knows far better than I do.

In truth, God's Patience is more enduring than we can imagine.

> *The Lord is not slack concerning his promise, as some men count slackness; but is longsuffering to us-ward, not willing that any should perish, but that all should come to repentance.* 2 Peter 3:9

The Lord is not slack means that He's not late. It's why God just doesn't slay the wicked on a Friday because Monday they might be coming to Him. It's like the parable of letting the wheat and the tares grow up together.

> *Another parable put he forth unto them, saying, "The kingdom of heaven is likened unto a man which sowed good seed in his field. But while men slept, his enemy came and sowed tares among the wheat, and went his way. But when the blade was sprung up, and brought forth fruit, then appeared the tares also. So the servants of the householder came and said unto him, 'Sir, didst not thou sow good seed in thy field? From whence then hath it tares?' He said unto them, 'An enemy hath done this.' The servants said unto him, 'Wilt thou then that we go and gather them up?' But he said, 'Nay; lest while ye gather up the tares, ye root up also the wheat with them. Let both grow together until the harvest: and in the time of harvest I will say to the reapers, 'Gather ye together first the tares, and bind them in bundles to burn them: but gather the wheat into my barn.'"* Matthew 13:24-29

Tares surround some people but they themselves are actually wheat. Before I knew the Lord, I was one of those, a wheat, and I'm so glad that God was patient enough with me to gather me in His harvest.

Like I said, He doesn't think like you and I do. I, for one, am very grateful for that!

Chapter 15
Our Struggle

But thou, O Lord, art a God full of compassion, and gracious, longsuffering, and plenteous in mercy and truth.

Psalms 86:15

In this H.E.L.P., you'll see that the words, "long-suffering,""patience" and "slow to anger" are all used interchangeably. When we read that God is longsuffering, He's being patient with us. In the parable of the wheat and the tares in the introduction section of the H.E.L.P. of Patience, we saw God waiting to see the nourishment of the grown wheat and then seeing it come to maturity. Wheat is the staff of life. Tares are weeds. They provide no nourishment and steal nutrients from the wheat.

God's desire for our lives is to bring fruitfulness to Himself and because He knows that fruitfulness takes time to mature, He waits patiently. The greatest seed ever given to grow into a harvest is the gospel.

Without patience, you're gonna go whacking tares and harm the young wheat before they're discernable from the tares. When the tares and the wheat grow together, as the wheat matures the weight of the heads make them bow down. The tares are obstinate and grow straight up. But when they both mature, it becomes obvious which is which and that's the time to whack 'em.

Only God knows who is wheat and who are tares. And He's gracious enough, and patient enough, for the wheat to come into their own.

Definitions

I said earlier that we would be using "patience," "longsuffering," and "slow to anger" interchangeably. But what do these words mean?

The word translated as "patience" comes from the Greek word *makrothumia* which means: "patience," "long-suffering" and sometimes "forbearance". It's derived from two words, *makrós* which means "long" and *thymós* which means "passion" or "anger". So *makrothumia* literally means to be "long to anger," or a "long time to anger," and is found thirty-three times in the NT.

"Patience" in the OT is often translated as "longsuffering" and is a combination of the two Hebrew words, *'erekh* and *'appayim*. The combination of these two words literally means "long of nose" or "long of breathing". This is used as a simile for being so angry that your nostrils flare by rapid breaths through your nose. In our modern vernacular "longsuffering" from the Hebrew is best translated "long to anger", "slow to wrath", or "slow to anger".

Here are some of the uses of both the Greek and the Hebrew words:

~ *And refused to obey, neither were mindful of thy wonders that thou didst among them; but hardened their necks, and in their rebellion appointed a captain to return to their bondage: but thou art a God ready to pardon, gracious and merciful, slow to anger ('erekh 'appayim), and of great kindness, and forsookest them not.* **Nehemiah 9:17**

~ *Put on therefore, as the elect of God, holy and beloved, bowels of mercies, kindness, humbleness of mind, meekness, longsuffering (makrothumia). Colossians 3:12*

~ *The LORD is merciful and gracious, slow to anger ('erekh 'appayim), and plenteous in mercy.* **Psalm 103:8**

~ *That ye might walk worthy of the Lord unto all pleasing, being fruitful in every good work, and increasing in the knowledge of God, strengthened with all might, according to his glorious power, unto all patience and longsuffering (makrothumia) with joyfulness. Col 1:10-11*

So as the words apply either to God or man, we see that the same idea is carried over by both the Greek and Hebrew.

Setting Guidelines

Before we go any deeper into what it means for us to be patient, understand that there's a huge difference between being patient and being lazy.

People sometimes substitute apathy, indifference and laziness for patience and claim that they're "waiting on the Lord."

Someone who is patiently waiting on the Lord must still be seriously about the Father's business. They will most certainly continually be on their faces before God, allowing His presence to wash them clean, and His Holy Spirit to speak into their lives. They will also have their nose in the Word like never before. God will be giving them continual revelation and understanding of His Word.

In these situations, it may look like these individuals are doing nothing more than sitting around. On the contrary, they are neck deep in what God has for them. The process takes patience and at the end of this endurance test, they will be changed and that change will be evident. These are individuals that have been truly "waiting on the Lord" and the result of that waiting produces fruit that everyone can eventually see.

Antithetical to this are those people who say they are waiting on the Lord but they spend little time, if any, in prayer and they don't read the Word, nor are they doing even minor things on behalf of our King.

You can't be waiting on the Lord and never read His Word or talk to Him on a continual basis. The lack of these two habits points to someone who is not being patient, but is using patience as a guise for slothfulness. It's a presumptive position, and not a position occupied by the faithful.

His Patience In Our Growth

I've already addressed this issue, but it bears repeating since we are talking about patience and because of what I'm about to share with you.

The reason that people's Words don't come to pass is because they aren't patient enough for them to come to fruition. They become impatient and go to unbelieving brethren who shoot down those Words that God has given them in faith. If you absolutely know that what you heard was from the Lord, whether it be a Word, a dream or a promise out of His Word that the Holy Spirit has applied to your life, why go to people of unbelief to get confirmation or affirmation?

Over the years I've received several Words or impressions by the Holy Spirit regarding God's promises, direction or discipline. I learned a long time ago to be a good steward of those Words.

As an example, as I've shared before, when I came to the Lord all those years ago, I was a real piece of work. But even when we come to the Lord in that state, He still displays His Patience with us. That's because many of the things that we did before we were saved follow us into our newly created life of being His child. We call these things consequences, or to put it in a biblical framework, we reap what we sow.

I remember a time just after I got saved. I was attending a YWAM conference at Mt. Hermon, California. One of the teachers in the morning session talked about how we reap what we sow and how there's a season of reaping for our actions and sin.

I should pause here to point out that when we get saved, God forgives us. But it's like the guy that ends up in jail. God's forgiven him, but he still has to do his time and he still has to pay his dues. There are consequences by man's laws for his illegal actions that require his incarceration.

So the basis of this **YWAM** lesson was that God forgives you for the sin but sometimes there are ramifications for the actions. Even as a brand new Christian, the Holy Spirit quickened my heart to the fact that I could ask God to shorten my time of reaping for the junk that I'd sown in the flesh.

As a caveat, this is different from beating myself up for the stuff I did before I was saved. Sometimes Christians won't come to grips with the fact that God forgives them, and never forgive themselves.

I can't love others until I love myself. I did a lot of junk before I found the Lord and I'm the first to say that I wasn't a nice person.

We all have old patterns of thinking that have to be replaced by correct biblical thinking. False perceptions of ourselves, and others, have to be replaced by correctly seeing ourselves, and them, through God's eyes. All of that takes patience, our patience and the Lord's Patience.

The majority of Christians I know do not love themselves and therefore they cannot love their neighbors as themselves.

> *"Master, which is the great commandment in the law?" Jesus said unto him, "'Thou shalt love the Lord thy God with all thy heart, and with all thy soul, and with all thy mind.' This is the first and great commandment. And the second is like unto it, 'Thou shalt love thy neighbour as thyself.'"* **Matt 22:36-39**

Everyone has issues and those issues have to be resolved in light of God's Word and through the work of His Spirit.

Man! I've still got issues! National Geographic has been around for 130 years and I have more issues than they!

When I told that to the Lord one time, He said, "Yeah Steve, but you're forgetting one thing. I am the Author and Finisher of your faith. And the Lamb's Book of Life has nothing to do with the previous editions of your sin. I am the Author and Finisher of the Lamb's Book of Life".

When we are seeking Him, when we continually wash our minds and our lives with His Word, when we forgive and love others, He is able to change us to be more like Him. All of that takes time and most of all, it takes patience: ours and His.

The Impact of Impatience

What happens when we get impatient? When I'm impatient with God, I get angry. When I get impatient with my brothers, I get angry.

Maybe it's because I live in the future. I've never stopped thinking about that panoramic of history that Jesus showed me at that first meeting with Him. And because I've seen the future, and all that it brings, I always have a sense of urgency. That urgency translates to my work, my relationships and my own spiritual growth. What else does it translate to?

Impatience.

So when I speak of the impact of impatience, the antithesis of patience, I know what I'm talking about.

The lack of patience in any given situation causes a conflict of emotions within us. We can feel anxious, angry, bitter, sad, etc. etc. For growing Christians, it's typical of the war between our spirit and our flesh, or our carnal nature.

The growing Christian is someone who has surrendered his life to the Holy Ghost and His leading, direction and guidance. The carnal Christian is the opposite. He says, "Jesus gave me salvation and I'll take it from here." He would do well to remember what Isaiah wrote:

For my thoughts are not your thoughts, neither are your ways my ways, saith the LORD. For as the heavens are higher than the earth, so are my ways higher than your ways, and my thoughts than your thoughts. ***Isaiah 55:8-9***

God's care for us includes even the most minute aspects of our lives because they too are very important.

Take us the foxes, the little foxes, that spoil the vines: for our vines have tender grapes. ***Song of Solomon 2:15***

Can God really "fix" all the little things in my life that hinder my walk with Him?

But even the very hairs of your head are all numbered. Fear not therefore: ye are of more value than many sparrows. ***Luke 12:7***

See how very much He loves you and how important you are to Him? He knows you better than you know yourself. He knows everything about you. He knows all the good traits that you may have and He also knows all of your faults. But He's still patient with you in order to give you time to become who He knows you can be.

For those of us who long to be something more in the Lord, we can't help but recognize all of our faults. This is very much a mortal state of being. Even the Apostle Paul felt that way.

For we know that the law is spiritual: but I am carnal, sold under sin. For that which I do I allow not: for what I would, that do I not; but what I hate, that do I. ***Romans 7:14-15***

Paul is telling us that no matter how hard we may try, we can never be exactly what we should be on this side of eternity. Nonetheless, we must always remember that it is God's gift through the blood of Christ Jesus that makes us all we need to be in the Father's eyes.

I thank God through Jesus Christ our Lord. So then with the mind I myself serve the law of God; but with the flesh the law of sin. ***Romans 7:25***

And it's through those lenses that God looks at us. Because of that, He's patient enough with us to give us time to walk as we should. If He is patient enough because of Jesus, maybe we should learn to be more patient with ourselves.

So here's the question: Are we realistic in our expectation of where God wants us to be spiritually? Or are we hasty in our assumption that we want to be something that God never meant us to be?

In addition, are we willing to yield to His work in us through His Holy Spirit? This is a tall order because it goes against our basic sinful nature. He's able to help us rise to our patience potential through the fruits of the Spirit.

But the fruit of the Spirit is love, joy, peace, longsuffering, gentleness, goodness, faith. ***Galatians 5:22***

Arm Wrestling with God

As far as patience goes, you can't twist God's arm to make Him speed up His timeline, but God has given us free-will and He will step aside if you insist on going it alone.

Going deeper into surrendering our lives to Him causes us to go deeper into the things of God. In doing so, we inevitably give up long-held carnal positions, desires and wants. In that place of surrender the fruit of the Spirit, including patience, can be manifest. The sooner the surrender, the more we exercise patience, the sooner the other fruit will be seen in our lives. God Himself is waiting patiently for us to come to that place in our walks, in our lives, and in our relationship with Him.

Hearing the phrase "dying to self" sounds so super-spiritual, but I wonder how many Christians truly understand the idea. Certainly if you look across the landscape of the "me, me, me" church these days, you could hardly say that Christians understand what it means to die to self.

The fact is that our flesh is not normally patient.

In Greek, the word for "flesh" in the NT is *sarx* and occurs 147 times. Interestingly, 91 of these occurrences are found in Paul's writings and mostly in Romans and Galatians. Before I tell you exactly what *sarx* means, consider for a moment that Paul was a former Pharisee.

> *For we are the circumcision, which worship God in the spirit, and rejoice in Christ Jesus, and have no confidence in the flesh. Though I might also have confidence in the flesh. If any other man thinketh that he hath whereof he might trust in the flesh, I more: Circumcised the eighth day, of the stock of Israel, of the tribe of Benjamin, an Hebrew of the Hebrews; as touching the law, a Pharisee; concerning zeal, persecuting the church; touching the righteousness which is in the law, blameless. But what things were gain to me, those I counted loss for Christ.* **Phil 3:3-7**

Paul's understanding of the word "flesh" came from the OT's use of "flesh" and he is responsible for further developing the word's use in the NT epistles. This OT scholar based his NT writings upon his conversion to a follower of Jesus as Messiah. So when he talks about the "flesh" we should take notice.

The word flesh, *sarx*, denotes our human nature: our wants, our desires, our will, our rights, and all the things that make up "me" outside of Christ. It's the earthly nature of man apart from God's influence, and therefore prone to sin and opposed to God.

Thank God that you and I don't have to stay in that state. The Holy Spirit inside of us, working on us, is able to change us from the inside out because of Jesus' work on the Cross.

> *I am crucified with Christ: nevertheless I live; yet not I, but Christ liveth in me: and the life which I now live in the flesh I live by the faith of the Son of God, who loved me, and gave himself for me.* **Galatians 2:20**

So dying to ourselves, or dying to our flesh, means to take your "me" off the throne of your life and put Jesus on that throne. In doing so, it is no longer you, or your "me", who controls your motivations; it is the Lord.

> *Therefore if any man be in Christ, he is a new creature: old things are passed away; behold, all things are become new.* **2 Cor 5:17**

Patience produces peace, but the lack of patience produces turmoil. Patience rests in the Lord and what He's going to do in His timing . In most cases, when we get impatient we try to do things to move the hand of God and to hurry everything up. In other words, even though the Bible says:

> Let God arise, let his enemies be scattered: let them also that hate him flee before him. *Psalm 68:1*

We think that WE should arise and our enemies will be scattered. It just doesn't work that way.

Frustration comes when we think God isn't moving as quickly enough. But even our faith takes patience to develop.

> Knowing this, that the trying of your faith worketh patience. But let patience have her perfect work, that ye may be perfect and entire, wanting nothing. *James 1:3-4*

I've seen people who got saved and were on fire for the Lord but weren't patient about their growth in the Lord. They didn't feast on His Word, spend enough time in prayer before the Lord and wouldn't learn from mature Believers. Eventually they blew themselves up and walked away from the Lord.

It could have happened to me had it not been for intensive intercession on my behalf and the Lord putting strong, mature Christians in my life early in my walk to nurture and teach me.

We also have to be patient for the seed of a Word or a promise to develop in God's timing. Mary "hid in her heart" the Word about Jesus that was given to her by the angel.

> But Mary kept all these things, and pondered them in her heart. *Luke 2:19*

She waited patiently for God to do all the things that He said He would do. And we also have Nehemiah making the statement that he didn't tell anyone what God had placed on his heart.

> So I came to Jerusalem, and was there three days. And I arose in the night, I and some few men with me; neither told I any man what my God had put in my heart to do at Jerusalem: neither was there any beast with me, save the beast that I rode upon. *Nehemiah 2:11-12*

One of the key components of King David was that while he was worshipping God, he was also waiting patiently for the Lord.

> I waited patiently for the LORD; and he inclined unto me, and heard my cry. *Psalm 40:1*

Impatience causes your emotions to take charge, whereas faith will cause your emotions to settle down, allowing God's purposes to come to fruition. You and I cannot hurry the purposes of God for our lives. He has a specific timeframe for us to come into our own and we have to trust Him and be obedient during the wait. God is faithful and if you truly heard from the Lord on a given situation or need, He will bring it to pass if you are patient and don't take matters into your own hands .

Patience Through Tears

From time to time, you may have heard people say, "I'm just 'waiting on the Lord.'" But I think that most of the people who use this phrase have no idea what it means.

Waiting on the Lord with regard to patience is more like pouring your heart out before Him and then listening to Him to answer back.

That's right, believe it or not, prayer is a conversation but for most people prayer is a one-way street. People wonder why they talk to God and He doesn't respond. They miss the whole point of the word "cooperation". When we cooperate with the Lord, we work alongside Him and with Him.

When I say that you need to be patient in a situation where you've heard from the Lord, I do know what I'm talking about because I've been there. Sometimes the wait can be painful and we can't help but cry out to God. Often those cries for help are accompanied by real tears, but please know that God sees them and even counts them.

As we read earlier, He's promised to wipe away our tears.

> *And God shall wipe away all tears from their eyes; and there shall be no more death, neither sorrow, nor crying, neither shall there be any more pain: for the former things are passed away.* **Rev 21:4**

I understand this may not help you in this moment if you're feeling the pain of waiting, but there will be no more tears in heaven. Your tears are kept by the Lord, stored up, and He doesn't forget them.

> *Thou tellest my wanderings: put thou my tears into thy bottle: are they not in thy book?* **Psalm 56:8**

The idea of storing up our tears is nothing new to mankind either. In antiquity, as far back as the 1700s, 1800's, people kept, and stored their tears. That's because there's a natural understanding that tears are somehow an emotional memory bank or an emotional storage medium, if you will.

Back in 2017 I wrote a book that, like this one, was a departure from the kind of work that I'm known for. It was called *Tears - An Ocean of Emotion*. In researching for that work, and also by way of my own emotional insight, I was able to uncover and document some very important and fascinating facts about why we weep and what are the ramifications of that weeping.

That's why I can tell you without hesitancy that, for those of you who are weeping in your patience, your tears have not gone unnoticed by God. You are not alone, even though you may feel like you're the only person stranded on a desert island. Yes, the Lord does hear you.

Those tears of patience, or impatience as the case may be, are a liquid hard drive of all of your life's experiences. That's because your tears are as specific to you as your fingerprints or your face scan. They are literally an emotional, biometric data point that is linked to your sorrow or joy.

As this idea applies to the End of the Age, the tears of the redeemed are poured out upon the altar. Those emotional data points are a multiplied and magnified honor to God because of the great thing that He has done in granting salvation to His children by the blood of His Son.

Just think about this in terms of our patience. His people long for His return and have cried in their moments of intercession and travail. He saves up those tears as if they are gold.

But even if we are doing everything right, waiting can take its toll on us. Regarding this kind of patience, the scripture encourages us:

> *And let us not be weary in well doing: for in due season we shall reap, if we faint not. As we have therefore opportunity, let us do good unto all men, especially unto them who are of the household of faith.* **Galatians 6:9-10**

A Question of Timing

Waiting on the Lord is one of the hardest things to do, but there's a difference between waiting anxiously, with anxiety, or waiting with patience. The patience of which I speak is grace imparted to us by the work of the Holy Spirit. In truth, waiting is not, in and of itself, being patient. Waiting is a posture that people adopt in hope, or expectation, of something that may or may not happen. Patience, on the other hand, is a work in us by God.

If I had a "Patience Formula" it would be: Waiting + Patience = Peace. If we've allowed the Holy Spirit to work in us, waiting upon the Lord with His patience will bring peace.

A good example of someone in scripture who was being impatient is Abraham.

Because he and Sarah had no children, they grew impatient waiting on the Lord to give them a child and they took matters into their own hands. Problems arise when we interfere with God's purposes for our lives and often we can do more harm than good. At Sarah's suggestion, Abraham took Hagar so he could have a child . Because of that union, Ishmael was born and now we're dealing with a Mideast problem.

> *Now Sarai Abram's wife bare him no children: and she had an handmaid, an Egyptian, whose name was Hagar. And Sarai said unto Abram, "Behold now, the LORD hath restrained me from bearing: I pray thee, go in unto my maid; it may be that I may obtain children by her." And Abram hearkened to the voice of Sarai. And Sarai Abram's wife took Hagar her maid the Egyptian, after Abram had dwelt ten years in the land of Canaan, and gave her to her husband Abram to be his wife. And he went in unto Hagar, and she conceived: and when she saw that she had conceived, her mistress was despised in her eyes.* **Genesis 16:1-4**

> *And the angel of the LORD said unto her, Behold, thou art with child, and shalt bear a son, and shalt call his name Ishmael; because the LORD hath heard thy affliction. And he will be a wild man; his hand will be against every man, and every man's hand against him; and he shall dwell in the presence of all his brethren.* **Genesis 16:11-12**

When we try to help God advance His plan in our lives, and we've not been invited by Him to do so, we get in trouble. To keep you from making this mistake, remember that when God makes a promise, He's the one Who can bring it to pass with the right results - we cannot.

> *And when Abram was ninety years old and nine, the LORD appeared to Abram, and said unto him, "I am the Almighty God; walk before me, and be thou perfect. And I will make my covenant between me and thee, and will multiply thee exceedingly." And Abram fell on his face: and God talked with him, saying, "As for me, behold, my covenant is with thee, and thou shalt be a father of many nations. Neither shall thy name any more be called Abram, but thy name shall be Abraham; for a father of many nations have I made thee. And I will make thee exceeding fruitful, and I will make nations of thee, and kings shall come out of thee. And I will establish my covenant between me and thee and thy seed after thee in their generations for an everlasting covenant, to be a God unto thee, and to thy seed after thee. And I will give unto thee, and to thy seed after thee, the land wherein thou art a stranger, all the land of Canaan, for an everlasting possession; and I will be their God."* **Genesis 17:1-8**

And the LORD visited Sarah as he had said, and the LORD did unto Sarah as he had spoken. For Sarah conceived, and bare Abraham a son in his old age, at the set time of which God had spoken to him. And Abraham called the name of his son that was born unto him, whom Sarah bare to him, Isaac. **Genesis 21:1-3**

One of the most frustrating things for those of us who have received promises from the Lord is to wait on God's timing for those promises to come to fruition. Abraham, "The Father of Many Nations," struggled with patience in this area; so will we.

As it is written, I have made thee a father of many nations, before him whom he believed, even God, who quickeneth the dead, and calleth those things which be not as though they were. **Romans 4:17**

The Holy Spirit in us is here to help develop our patience in any given situation.

Making Your Petitions Known

Waiting patiently for the Lord to move on your behalf doesn't mean that we sit idly by, wringing our hands. On the contrary, we are told to pursue Him in our need.

And he said unto them, "Which of you shall have a friend, and shall go unto him at midnight, and say unto him, 'Friend, lend me three loaves; For a friend of mine in his journey is come to me, and I have nothing to set before him?' And he from within shall answer and say, 'Trouble me not: the door is now shut, and my children are with me in bed; I cannot rise and give thee.' I say unto you, 'Though he will not rise and give him, because he is his friend, yet because of his importunity he will rise and give him as many as he needeth.' And I say unto you, 'Ask, and it shall be given you; seek, and ye shall find; knock, and it shall be opened unto you.' For every one that asketh receiveth; and he that seeketh findeth; and to him that knocketh it shall be opened. If a son shall ask bread of any of you that is a father, will he give him a stone? Or if he ask a fish, will he for a fish give him a serpent? Or if he shall ask an egg, will he offer him a scorpion? If ye then, being evil, know how to give good gifts unto your children: how much more shall your heavenly Father give the Holy Spirit to them that ask Him? **Luke 11:5-13**

God is not a trickster or a prankster. Many religions have demons that are. They're masquerading spirits that pretend to be something that they are not.

Our Heavenly Father is totally faithful, just and true; there is no shadow of turning with Him.

Every good gift and every perfect gift is from above, and cometh down from the Father of lights, with whom is no variableness, neither shadow of turning. **James 1:17**

When you were a kid, did you ever ask your parents for something only to have their response be, "We'll see"?

You never get that with God. There's no guessing with Him. In that I mean that He will not, and does not, string us along. We may or may not get what we are asking for, but whatever the outcome is, it's always on His terms and for our benefit in the long run.

That's not to say that your parents were stringing you along. They might have had limited resources, didn't want to tell you "No!" outright only to hear you complain, or they just didn't know what the future held.

None of those things apply to God! He has all resources, and knows the future already. Because of that He can tell you with certainty what He'll do, although He's not obliged to answer your requests until He's ready. Beyond your need or want of the moment, His desire is to grow you up into maturity as a Believer.

And in that waiting, we develop patience.

> *In your patience possess ye your souls.* **Luke 21:19**

So what's our expectation when we wait upon the Lord?

We expect an answer to our prayer. But do we expect God to give us exactly what we're asking for? What happens when we don't get exactly what we were praying for? What did Jesus say?

> *Ye ask, and receive not, because ye ask amiss, that ye may consume it upon your lusts.* **James 4:3**

Ouch! So how do we ensure that we are asking in the right way?

> *Thy kingdom come. Thy will be done in earth, as it is in heaven.* **Matt 6:10**

Instead of trying to bend God's will to give us what we think we want, why not ask Him to change your heart to desire the things that He wants? He wants the best for you anyway!

A Tool to Build Our Character

"Potential" is the external manifestation of strengths we may possess. But God doesn't look at those outward strengths, i.e. how we look, how we sound, our upbringing, our intelligence, etc. etc. He looks on the heart. That's not to say that He doesn't choose to use somebody who can speak well, looks good and is intelligent but what it does mean is that He will use somebody regardless of those qualities.

Simply put - He doesn't need them!

David's a perfect example.

His brothers were bigger, stronger, more talented and had been battle-tested. They all had more potential when it came to being able to fight and defeat Goliath.

> *And Samuel said unto Jesse, "Are here all thy children?" And he said, "There remaineth yet the youngest, and, behold, he keepeth the sheep." And Samuel said unto Jesse, "Send and fetch him: for we will not sit down till he come hither." And he sent, and brought him in. Now he was ruddy, and withal of a beautiful countenance, and goodly to look to…* **1 Sam 16:11-12**

David was a scrawny, pretty-boy! He was the youngest and only good for looking after the sheep! But God doesn't look at our outward appearance. In fact, Saul was an impressive man. He was the king. Despite Saul's outward appearance, the Lord wasn't impressed.

> *But the LORD said unto Samuel, "Look not on his countenance, or on the height of his stature; because I have refused him: for the LORD seeth not as man seeth; for man looketh on the outward appearance, but the LORD looketh on the heart."* **1 Sam 16:7**

When it came down to it, only David had the heart to take on Goliath.

> *And David spake to the men that stood by him, saying, What shall be done to the man that killeth this Philistine, and taketh away the reproach from Israel? for who is this uncircumcised Philistine, that he should defy the armies of the living God?* **1 Sam 17:26**

We know the rest of the story. David went to meet the Giant on the battlefield without armor or sword and he took him down. He'd been patient all of his young years while he tended to the sheep. He had honed his skill against the lion and the bear. Patience proved to be his ally and not a hindrance.

Too often we look at God using patience to hone our spiritual development as a hindrance and not an ally. But if we're patient, there comes a point in our lives when God releases our potential and puts those traits into action.

The downside is that if we are not patient, and we take matters into our own hands by using our God-given gifts prematurely, the outcome will not be what He intended.

> *Being confident of this very thing, that he which hath begun a good work in you will perform it until the day of Jesus Christ.* **Phil 1:6**

We have to let His perfect work mature in us before we're able to do His true bidding. Our potential needs to be seasoned with Patience.

Chapter 16
His Being

And the LORD descended in the cloud, and stood with him there, and proclaimed the name of the LORD. And the LORD passed by before him, and proclaimed, "The LORD, The LORD God, merciful and gracious, longsuffering, and abundant in goodness and truth, Keeping mercy for thousands, forgiving iniquity and transgression and sin, and that will by no means clear the guilty; visiting the iniquity of the fathers upon the children, and upon the children's children, unto the third and to the fourth generation." And Moses made haste, and bowed his head toward the earth, and worshipped. And he said, "If now I have found grace in thy sight, O Lord, let my Lord, I pray thee, go among us; for it is a stiffnecked people; and pardon our iniquity and our sin, and take us for thine inheritance."

Exodus 34:5-9

God's very nature is Patience (or longsuffering). We are made in His likeness and therefore have been given the nature of Patience. The preeminent example of the Lord's Patience is that He is not willing that anyone should perish despite our sin. Therefore He waits for people, including you and me, to accept Jesus' work on the Cross through faith.

In this regard, God's longsuffering is associated with God's mercy and goodness, yet they are not exactly the same.

Discerning God's Character

When we think of all the characteristics that make up God's divine nature, for our purposes here, consider His Patience, His mercy and His goodness.

The LORD is merciful and gracious, slow to anger, and plenteous in mercy. *Psalm 103:8*

 The LORD is slow to anger, and great in power, and will not at all acquit the wicked: the LORD hath his way in the whirlwind and in the storm, and the clouds are the dust of his feet. *Nahum 1:3*

I will not execute the fierceness of mine anger, I will not return to destroy Ephraim: for I am God, and not man; the Holy One in the midst of thee: and I will not enter into the city. *Hosea 11:9*

God being "slow to anger" is another way of saying that He's willing to defer due punishment. I say "due" because we know from Romans 3:23:

For all have sinned, and come short of the glory of God.

And we also know that according to Romans 6:23:

The wages of sin is death...

Think about how the Lord is faced daily with such a rebellious world. It is His Patience, or longsuffering, that holds Him back from pouring forth His wrath upon a recalcitrant mankind. Also consider that His Patience is not only demonstrated toward Christians whose lives are now under the blood of Jesus, but that He has restrained Himself from punishing all sinners according to their merits.

When viewed from this perspective, it's easy to see how God's Patience, goodness and mercy are closely related to one another, yet are not strictly synonymous. Here's what I mean: While Patience is a part of His goodness and mercy, it is still unique and different from both.

The definition of patience is:

1. The quality of being patient, as the bearing of provocation, annoyance, misfortune, or pain, without complaint, loss of temper, irritation, or the like; 2) An ability or willingness to suppress restlessness or annoyance when confronted with delay: to have patience with a slow learner; or 3) Quiet, steady perseverance; even-tempered care; diligence.[10]

The definition of goodness is:

1. The state or quality of being good; 2) Moral excellence; virtue; or 3) Kindly feeling; kindness; generosity.[11]

The definition of mercy is:

1. Compassionate or kindly forbearance shown toward an offender, an enemy, or other person in one's power; compassion, pity, or benevolence: Have mercy on the poor sinner;

2. The disposition to be compassionate or forbearing: An adversary wholly without mercy; or 3) The

---

10 Dictionary.com, s.v. "patience," accessed October 27, 2018, https://www.lib.sfu.ca/help/cite-write/citation-style-guides/chicago/encyclopedias-dictionaries

11 Dictionary.com, s.v. "goodness," accessed October 27, 2018, https://www.dictionary.com/browse/goodness?s=t

discretionary power of a judge to pardon someone or to mitigate punishment, especially to send to prison rather than invoke the death penalty.[12]

While the biblical definitions may differ slightly, the understanding of these three words and characteristics have remained constant for millennia. Patience is still patience, goodness is still goodness and mercy is still mercy. Here's how it looks in practical application:

~ **Mercy looks at a person with compassion.**

~ **Patience waits to pass judgment on a person that is guilty.**

~ **Goodness means that whenever God relates to us it will be from the basis of His being absolutely good.**

Paul Mizzi makes the following observations when it comes to the similarities and differences between these three character traits of God.

> *Goodness exhibits God as exercising patience, while this same patience motivates the sinner to flee to God for mercy. That mercy which makes God ready to embrace returning sinners, makes him willing to bear with them in their sins, and wait for their repentance.*
>
> *Patience also may be distinguished from goodness. The object of goodness is every creature, whether they are angels, men, animals, even to the lowest worm that crawls upon the ground. The object of patience is man. The lower creatures are not, strictly speaking, the objects of patience, since they do not injure God.*
>
> *But that same patience which spares man, spares other creatures for man's sake, which were all forfeited because of man's rebellion.*
>
> *The objects of God's goodness, then, is the whole creation, more extensive than that of patience. Goodness brings forth into creation, and supports every creature, while patience views man, particularly, as already created and fallen short of his duty.*
>
> *Had not sin entered, there would be no occasion for patience to be exercised; but from the beginning goodness was evident.*
>
> *The patience of God, being a branch of mercy, is founded in the death of Christ in its exercise.*
>
> *In mercy, God comes to man who is miserable and obnoxious.*
>
> *In patience, God considers him as sinful and provoking to punishment, but withholds that same punishment for a season.*
>
> *In goodness, God views the whole creation as coming from His hand, pronounces it good, and in continuing to care for it, evidences His goodness.[13]*

---

12 Dictionary.com, s.v. "mercy," accessed October 27, 2018, https://www.dictionary.com/browse/mercy?s=t

13 Paul Mizzi, "The Patience, Mercy and Goodness of God." Truth for Today, http://www.tecmalta.org/tft142.htm, (n.d.g.)

Within His Patience, God demonstrates only a portion of His Person toward mankind with Patience being one of His foundational character traits. Since we know that He is love and that love brings about patience, we ultimately know that we can trust God Who has been patient with all of mankind.

The Connection Between Love and Patience

So why is God so patient with us?

You might say, "Well, because He's God. He has to be patient with us!"

Not so. In fact, I distinctly remember a time when He wanted to wipe Israel out for their disobedience and sin, but Moses talked Him out of it.

> And the LORD said unto Moses, "I have seen this people, and, behold, it is a stiffnecked people. Now therefore let me alone, that my wrath may wax hot against them, and that I may consume them: and I will make of thee a great nation." And Moses besought the LORD his God, and said, "LORD, why doth thy wrath wax hot against thy people, which thou hast brought forth out of the land of Egypt with great power, and with a mighty hand? Wherefore should the Egyptians speak, and say, 'For mischief did he bring them out, to slay them in the mountains, and to consume them from the face of the earth?' Turn from thy fierce wrath, and repent of this evil against thy people. Remember Abraham, Isaac, and Israel, thy servants, to whom thou swarest by thine own self, and saidst unto them, 'I will multiply your seed as the stars of heaven, and all this land that I have spoken of will I give unto your seed, and they shall inherit it for ever'." And the LORD repented of the evil which he thought to do unto his people.
> *Exodus 32:9-14*

God basically told Moses, "Move away. I'm going to wipe everybody out and I'll start over new with you!"

There are a couple of really important things going on here. Understand that the sin of Israel was so egregious that they probably should have been killed outright. You might think that sounds harsh but consider what God told Moses about the inhabitants of the Promised Land and why He gave the land to the Hebrews:

> Speak not thou in thine heart, after that the LORD thy God hath cast them out from before thee, saying, "For my righteousness the LORD hath brought me in to possess this land," but for the wickedness of these nations the LORD doth drive them out from before thee. Not for thy righteousness, or for the uprightness of thine heart, dost thou go to possess their land: but for the wickedness of these nations the LORD thy God doth drive them out from before thee, and that he may perform the word which the LORD sware unto thy fathers, Abraham, Isaac, and Jacob. Understand therefore, that the LORD thy God giveth thee not this good land to possess it for thy righteousness; for thou art a stiffnecked people.
> *Deut 9:4-6*

It wasn't because Israel was so righteous that He gave them the land. It was because the inhabitants were so evil. Despite God giving them the Ten Commandments and showing them all of the miracles in the wilderness, the Israelites made the golden calf. That calf and their sin were a direct poke in His eye. I don't know about you, but I sure would be angry if I were God. Unlike man, His longsuffering, or His Patience, enabled Him to step back and listen to Moses and remember His promises to the Hebrews.

That passage was a type of prophecy because Moses interceded for the Israelites just as Jesus intercedes for us.

> *He that spared not his own Son, but delivered him up for us all, how shall he not with him also freely give us all things? Who shall lay any thing to the charge of God's elect? It is God that justifieth. Who is he that condemneth? It is Christ that died, yea rather, that is risen again, who is even at the right hand of God, who also maketh intercession for us.* **Romans 8:32-34**

Jesus was, is, and will forever be the Lamb of God that was slain before the foundation of the world. In his intercession, Moses was a type of Jesus.

Why is God so patient with us?

The simple answer is because He loves us.

> *And we have known and believed the love that God hath to us. God is love; and he that dwelleth in love dwelleth in God, and God in him.* **1 John 4:16**

This could explain in part why He's so patient with us. But could it be that there is a deeper explanation? Yes!

> *Charity suffereth long, and is kind; charity envieth not; charity vaunteth not itself, is not puffed up…* **1 Cor 13:4**

The Greek word for "charity" here is *agapé*, which of course is translated as love. The word for "love" in 1 John 4:16 is also *agapé*, which would indicate that God's very Being is built on the foundation of love. His Everlasting Patience, and His very character being love, makes both of these attributes synonymous. You cannot separate God being love from God being patient.

Scripture tells us that God never changes. He was patient enough not to kill the Israelites and He's patient enough not to kill us.

Patience is truly His virtue.

A Shimmering Illusion

Our patience is based upon our "waiting" in the linear time of our current existence. Albert Einstein theorized that time was an illusion and that the past, present, and the future all existed at the same time.

In one of his more esoteric moments, he said:

> *A human being is a part of the whole called by us universe, a part limited in time and space. He experiences himself, his thoughts and feeling as something separated from the rest, a kind of optical delusion of his consciousness.*

Einstein's comment that time is an optical delusion of our consciousness (or our spirit), may be as an astute observation by the scientist as any of his other theories.

Everyone who has ever driven a car down a hot road has had the experience of seeing the shimmering and twisting illusion of heat coming off the pavement. This mirage bent their view, and caused their eyes to see something different from that which was really there.

Time is like that.

We're traveling down the road of this 3D reality. Rather than heat bending our view, the corruption of sin in this human condition has caused the perspective of our path to look different than it truly is.

This illusion is time.

With the measurement of time we pace the events in our lives. Because these events don't happened instantaneously or quickly, we need patience to see them come to fruition. As we purpose to dwell in God's presence, as we surrender more of our lives to Him, as we become closer to Him, our perspective on time changes and our patience grows.

Going back to the example of the mirage on the road, when you pop up over a ridge, that mirage of time disappears and we see this linear existence of time for what it is - an illusion. Our patience becomes less strained when we increasingly see the world through God's eyes as He changes us from "glory to glory".

> *But we all, with open face beholding as in a glass the glory of the Lord, are changed into the same image from glory to glory, even as by the Spirit of the Lord.* **2 Cor 3:18**

Remember that the illusion of time causes us to need patience but time is only a mirage in eternity. God exists outside of time and space, knows every hair on your head and is able to give you what you need in any given situation. When we focus on this truth, we will have God's Everlasting Patience.

From His Perspective

So how does God demonstrate His Patience or longsuffering toward us?

How about His ultimate act of Patience in sending His own Son to die for people who were still in rebellion?

> *But God commendeth his love toward us, in that, while we were yet sinners, Christ died for us.* **Romans 5:8**

But while this may be the most dramatic example of God showing His Patience toward His children, it certainly wasn't the first. Long before Jesus was born of a virgin, God refrained from punishing His people until He couldn't refrain any long.

You might say, *"Wait a minute. He's God. If He really loves us, He could wait to punish us indefinitely!"*

That wouldn't work because there comes a tipping point in which His forbearance hurts us more than it helps us. He ultimately has to discipline us because of the effect that sin has on His creation.

In addition, if He didn't discipline us, what kind of Father would He be?

> *If ye endure chastening, God dealeth with you as with sons; for what son is he whom the father chasteneth not? But if ye be without chastisement, whereof all are partakers, then are ye bastards, and not sons. Furthermore we have had fathers of our flesh which corrected us, and we gave them reverence: shall we not much rather be in subjection unto the Father of spirits, and live?* **Hebrews 12:7-9**

Nonetheless, God has shown His people Patience time and time again. As an example, despite seeing all that God had done for them, Israel had a propensity to follow other gods.

And the children of Israel did evil in the sight of the LORD, and served Baalim: And they forsook the LORD God of their fathers, which brought them out of the land of Egypt, and followed other gods, of the gods of the people that were round about them, and bowed themselves unto them, and provoked the LORD to anger. And they forsook the LORD, and served Baal and Ashtaroth. And the anger of the LORD was hot against Israel, and He delivered them into the hands of spoilers that spoiled them, and He sold them into the hands of their enemies round about, so that they could not any longer stand before their enemies. Whithersoever they went out, the hand of the LORD was against them for evil, as the LORD had said, and as the LORD had sworn unto them: and they were greatly distressed. Nevertheless the LORD raised up judges, which delivered them out of the hand of those that spoiled them. And yet they would not hearken unto their judges, but they went a whoring after other gods, and bowed themselves unto them: they turned quickly out of the way which their fathers walked in, obeying the commandments of the LORD; but they did not so. And when the LORD raised them up judges, then the LORD was with the judge, and delivered them out of the hand of their enemies all the days of the judge: for it repented the LORD because of their groanings by reason of them that oppressed them and vexed them. And it came to pass, when the judge was dead, that they returned, and corrupted themselves more than their fathers, in following other gods to serve them, and to bow down unto them; they ceased not from their own doings, nor from their stubborn way. And the anger of the LORD was hot against Israel; and He said, "Because that this people hath transgressed my covenant which I commanded their fathers, and have not hearkened unto my voice; I also will not henceforth drive out any from before them of the nations which Joshua left when he died: That through them I may prove Israel, whether they will keep the way of the LORD to walk therein, as their fathers did keep it, or not." Therefore the LORD left those nations, without driving them out hastily; neither delivered He them into the hand of Joshua. ***Judges 2:11-23***

This passage is a perfect example of God's Patience. It's a summary of the Book of Judges and covers over 400 years of Israel's history. This is Israel's recurrent theme:

1. **Walk with God,**

2. **Relapse into idolatry,**

3. **God's discipline,**

4. **Rest and deliverance,**

5. **A brief return to God, and**

6. **A relapse into idolatry again.**

Before we ask, "How could they?" consider how God deals with His people today. We see the same behavior, but He's always slow to punish us, and quick to forgive us.

Yes, we have Jesus' blood covering us, but how many times do you and I fall into sin, and we are slow to repent? God then disciplines us in some way to get our attention. When He does get our attention we repent but then, like Israel, the cycle continues. If we have the Holy Spirit inside of us, the sin that we stumble into should not be as egregious or grievous to the Lord as that of the Hebrews.

And grieve not the holy Spirit of God, whereby ye are sealed unto the day of redemption. ***Ephesians 4:30***

But my point is the same. In spite of Jesus' work on the Cross and in spite of the Holy Ghost living inside of us, we still screw up!

And God is patient with us too.

Even God's Patience Runs Out

When God's Patience does come to an end, He takes action. During all of these millennia He has displayed that forbearance by not wiping out mankind, but scripture gives the example of Him removing man when He has to:

Which sometime were disobedient, when once the longsuffering of God waited in the days of Noah, while the ark was a preparing, wherein few, that is, eight souls were saved by water. **1 Peter 3:20**

Because of the corruption and sin that infested the earth by Fallen Angels, God erased every person from the face of the planet, except eight. Do we really think that He won't do it again? In the very near future, when His Patience runs out, He will bring an end to the history of mankind and we will then exist in the eternal.

But of that day and hour knoweth no man, no, not the angels of heaven, but my Father only. But as the days of Noe were, so shall also the coming of the Son of man be. For as in the days that were before the flood they were eating and drinking, marrying and giving in marriage, until the day that Noe entered into the ark, and knew not until the flood came, and took them all away; so shall also the coming of the Son of man be. **Matt 24:36-39**

Knowing this first, that there shall come in the last days scoffers, walking after their own lusts, and saying, "Where is the promise of his coming? For since the fathers fell asleep, all things continue as they were from the beginning of the creation." For this they willingly are ignorant of, that by the word of God the heavens were of old, and the earth standing out of the water and in the water: Whereby the world that then was, being overflowed with water, perished: But the heavens and the earth, which are now, by the same word are kept in store, reserved unto fire against the day of judgment and perdition of ungodly men. **2 Peter 3:4-7**

But the day of the Lord will come as a thief in the night; in the which the heavens shall pass away with a great noise, and the elements shall melt with fervent heat, the earth also and the works that are therein shall be burned up. **2 Peter 3:10**

God's Patience is not endless; we've already entered into a grace period where the Lord has given us just a little extra time to prepare. This is why I spent so much time on preparation in the last section. Soon, His Patience will run out and your time of prepping will be up.

Patience in Prepping knows that you may not be the ultimate recipient of your foresight, but that someone else will benefit from your prepping efforts, most likely your own family or grandchildren.

I always say that to be able to use life insurance, something bad has to happen, but twenty-five years ago, I came up with the phrase, "Life Assurance", as it applies to preparing for the End Times. With Life Assurance prepping, you get to live and eat the fruit of your labor by providing food for the time when no man can work.

I must work the works of him that sent me, while it is day: the night cometh, when no man can work. **John 9:4**

Because of His Patience, God won't stop warning His people about what's coming. The Word tells us what is about to happen and so do Believers who hear the voice of the Holy Spirit and share with the Body what they hear, see or dream .

> *I will stand upon my watch, and set me upon the tower, and will watch to see what He will say unto me, and what I shall answer when I am reproved. And the LORD answered me, and said, "Write the vision, and make it plain upon tables, that he may run that readeth it. For the vision is yet for an appointed time, but at the end it shall speak, and not lie: though it tarry, wait for it; because it will surely come, it will not tarry."* **Habakkuk 2:1-3**

Life Assurance and the provision of sustenance for life directly contrasts with life insurance that is paid out upon someone's death . When it all hits the fan, will people still be paid on those policies? If the policies are still good, will phony fiat paper buy you something to eat? Your patient preparation ahead of time will bring you peace at a future time when other people are losing their peace.

It's my contention that in the End Times the thing that will rob our peace and our patience is the speed in which the enemy moves to destroy. The Book of Daniel says, "He shall destroy marvelously."

> *And in the latter time of their kingdom, when the transgressors are come to the full, a king of fierce countenance, and understanding dark sentences, shall stand up. And his power shall be mighty, but not by his own power: and he shall destroy wonderfully, and shall prosper, and practice, and shall destroy the mighty and the holy people. And through his policy also he shall cause craft to prosper in his hand; and he shall magnify himself in his heart, and by peace shall destroy many: he shall also stand up against the Prince of princes; but he shall be broken without hand.* **Daniel 8:23-25**

God's End Times witnesses will release God's End Times power and will enable God's End Times people to appropriate God's End Times Patience as they see His Hand moving to complete His-Story.

It isn't just Christians who are feeling a sense of time drawing to an end. The devil is talking to his followers about lying black prophecies and although Christians say that they believe in prophecy, they're trying to minimize it. As it says in Revelation 19:10, *"The testimony of Jesus is the spirit of Prophecy."*

Speaking about the Book of Revelation, I need to mention here that most people have the wrong assumption about it. The Book of Revelation does not stand separate and apart from Jesus. It is the revelation OF Jesus Christ which God the Father gave to His servant John the Apostle on the island of Patmos. Everything that we know as the Book of Revelation, all the imagery, all the interpretation, all the warnings, all of the understanding - is the testimony of Jesus! It's the revelation of Jesus Christ! Only One in all of Heaven was given the authority to open that Book and it was Jesus.

He's been waiting patiently to open that Book for a long time and the wait is almost over. But before we see history's culmination, certain things have to happen, according to scripture.

We must see the Two Witnesses out of Revelation 10:1 – 11:19. It's a fairly long passage and I don't want to include it here, but I would suggest that you read it.

The Two Witnesses will be God's provision. They have been with Him in heaven and they'll be given all the power of Moses and all the prophets to smite the earth. The world is going to embrace the Antichrist at the expense of the Two Witnesses until those Witnesses die in the streets of Jerusalem.

And when they shall have finished their testimony, the beast that ascendeth out of the bottomless pit shall make war against them, and shall overcome them, and kill them. And their dead bodies shall lie in the street of the great city, which spiritually is called Sodom and Egypt, where also our Lord was crucified. And they of the people and kindreds and tongues and nations shall see their dead bodies three days and an half, and shall not suffer their dead bodies to be put in graves. And they that dwell upon the earth shall rejoice over them, and make merry, and shall send gifts one to another; because these two prophets tormented them that dwelt on the earth. And after three days and an half the Spirit of life from God entered into them, and they stood upon their feet; and great fear fell upon them which saw them. And they heard a great voice from heaven saying unto them, "Come up hither. And they ascended up to heaven in a cloud; and their enemies beheld them." Rev 11:7-12

I believe that those Two Witnesses will be the only two people in the Bible who never died: Elijah and Enoch.

But I guess we all are going to have to be patient to see how the Book of Revelation unfolds.

Patience and the Unfolding of History

God is able to give us the Patience we need in our life to walk through even the most trying of circumstances. As He develops that Patience, we find that He's been busy helping us to grow into mature Christians.

King Solomon said in Ecclesiastes that "there's a time…"

To every thing there is a season, and a time to every purpose under the heaven: A time to be born, and a time to die; a time to plant, and a time to pluck up that which is planted; A time to kill, and a time to heal; a time to break down, and a time to build up; A time to weep, and a time to laugh; a time to mourn, and a time to dance; A time to cast away stones, and a time to gather stones together; a time to embrace, and a time to refrain from embracing; A time to get, and a time to lose; a time to keep, and a time to cast away; A time to rend, and a time to sew; a time to keep silence, and a time to speak; A time to love, and a time to hate; a time of war, and a time of peace. Ecclesiastes 3:1-8

God's sense of timing is uncanny.

But when the fulness of the time was come, God sent forth his Son, made of a woman, made under the law, to redeem them that were under the law, that we might receive the adoption of sons. And because ye are sons, God hath sent forth the Spirit of his Son into your hearts, crying, Abba, Father. Wherefore thou art no more a servant, but a son; and if a son, then an heir of God through Christ. Galatians 4:4-7

Regardless of what the future holds or what you may currently be walking in, God is able to give you His Everlasting Patience to see you through.

Softly and Tenderly Jesus is Calling

Softly and tenderly Jesus is calling—
Calling for you and for me;
Patiently Jesus is waiting and watching—
Watching for you and for me!

Come home! come home!
Ye who are weary, come home!
Earnestly, tenderly, Jesus is calling,
Calling, O sinner, come home!

Why should we tarry when Jesus is pleading—
Pleading for you and for me?
Why should we linger and heed not His mercies—
Mercies for you and for me?

Time is now fleeting, the moments are passing—
Passing from you and from me;
Shadows are gathering, death-beds are coming—
Coming for you and for me!

Oh, for the wonderful love He has promised—
Promised for you and for me!
Though we have sinned, He has mercy and pardon—
Pardon for you and for me!

HELP 7

His Everlasting Purity

Behold, what manner of love the Father hath bestowed upon us, that we should be called the sons of God: therefore the world knoweth us not, because it knew Him not. Beloved, now are we the sons of God, and it doth not yet appear what we shall be: but we know that, when He shall appear, we shall be like Him; for we shall see Him as He is. And every man that hath this hope in Him purifieth himself, even as He is pure.

1 John 3:1-3

Purity

This H.E.L.P. of His Everlasting Purity was the most difficult one to write of all the H.E.L.P.s. These are the Lord's words and I felt His Spirit leading me as I wrote, but I too grapple with the conviction of these truths. When compared to God's Purity, all of us should feel incredibly insufficient to His standard.

I don't cheat on my wife, I don't steal, I don't do most of what I know to be sin but I, like you, live in a sullied world and often fall into sin. I lose my temper and I say things I shouldn't. I also don't show the fruits of the Spirit like I should. I'm the last guy you'd expect to write on the Purity of God. But I have no choice here. The Lord has given me this task and I will not shrink from it. Somebody needs to say these things.

Just please know that I don't write about God's Everlasting Purity to tell people that I'm better than anyone. I'm here only to give you the truth of the Word and the words of the Holy Spirit. I may be the messenger, but this is God's message.

We live in a time in the earth's history when everything is basically riddled with filth, corrupted and sinful. Earth is exactly as Jesus said it would be in the days leading up to His return. *"As in the days of Noah…"*

> *But as the days of Noe were, so shall also the coming of the Son of man be. For as in the days that were before the flood they were eating and drinking, marrying and giving in marriage, until the day that Noe entered into the ark, and knew not until the flood came, and took them all away; so shall also the coming of the Son of Man be.* **Matt 24:37-39**

> *And GOD saw that the wickedness of man was great in the earth, and that every imagination of the thoughts of his heart was only evil continually.* **Gen 6:5**

You have to be living under a rock not to see how our culture promotes fornication, idolatry, adultery, same sex relationships and gay "marriage" as the norm. We are taught by the world that impurity is better than God's Everlasting Purity. This is in direct contradiction to the Bible, which calls for followers of Jesus to be separate from the world and to live pure and holy lives that exemplify the Lord.

As I've pointed out earlier, recent polls show that many badge-wearing Christians march in moral lockstep with mainstream American culture. When it comes to practices of divorce, spousal abuse, extramarital sex, pornography consumption, materialism, and racism, just to name a few, there is statistically little moral difference between the Church and the world. We may talk about the importance of purity and holiness, but the sad fact is that most people in our culture don't see us as morally different to non-Christians in any meaningful way.

What do they see us as?

Hypocrites.

Huh, so much for being salt and light.

In this H.E.L.P., we'll explore several aspects of God's Purity. We will see how God's actions, motives and character are pure. We'll also take a look at how His Purity should affect our walk with Him and talk about the life that we live in this flesh-suit and the challenges that the world presents to our purity before the Lord. We'll take a hard look at the ramifications for our ignoring God's call to Purity.

We may be in the world, but we certainly don't have to be of this world. There is a choice to make and as you will see, the wise man chooses God's Everlasting Purity.

Chapter 17

Words Mean Something

For the word of God is quick, and powerful, and sharper than any two-edged sword, piercing even to the dividing asunder of soul and spirit, and of the joints and marrow, and is a discerner of the thoughts and intents of the heart.

Hebrews 4:12

S everal words in Scripture directly relate to God's Everlasting Purity but are not the same thing as purity. We need to take a look at some of these words in their original language.

Holiness

~ *Wherefore gird up the loins of your mind, be sober, and hope to the end for the grace that is to be brought unto you at the revelation of Jesus Christ as obedient children, not fashioning yourselves according to the former lusts in your ignorance, but as He which hath called you is holy, so be ye holy in all manner of conversation. Because it is written, "Be ye holy; for I am holy."* **1 Peter 1:13-16**

Here, "holy" is from the Greek word *hagios*, which means "sacred," "set apart" or "different".

~ *For I am the LORD your God: ye shall therefore sanctify yourselves, and ye shall be holy...* **Leviticus 11:44**

In this verse, "holy" is from the Hebrew word *qadosh* and means "consecrated," "apartness," or "sacredness".

So both the Greek and Hebrew give the same kind of meaning to the word. Living a holy life means that you are set apart from the evil ways of the world and are trying to lead a life of faithful obedience to God's Word.

> *Further more then we beseech you, brethren, and exhort you by the Lord Jesus, that as ye have received of us how ye ought to walk and to please God, so ye would abound more and more. For ye know what commandments we gave you by the Lord Jesus. For this is the will of God, even your sanctification, that ye should abstain from fornication: That every one of you should know how to possess his vessel in sanctification and honour; Not in the lust of concupiscence, even as the Gentiles which know not God: That no man go beyond and defraud his brother in any matter: because that the Lord is the avenger of all such, as we also have forewarned you and testified. For God hath not called us unto uncleanness, but unto holiness. He therefore that despiseth, despiseth not man, but God, who hath also given unto us His Holy Spirit.* **1 Thess 4:1-8**

In the modern-Church, when holiness is discussed at all, it's often associated with what is perceived to be old-fashioned moral behavior such as sexual purity, financial honesty, and commitment to private prayer. The problem is that in trying to cast off old, legalistic notions of holiness, today's Christians have simply replaced them with private, moralistic notions such as political correctness.

Instead of going back to the Word and studying what holiness really is, it's easier for people to come up with a list of dos and don'ts. This legalistic mindset causes Christians to act as if holiness, being set apart for God, is either outdated or something that deserves only our miniscule attention.

Holiness is not purity, but it could be considered a first cousin.

Consecrated

"Consecrated" in Hebrew is *qadash* and is from the same root word as "holy".

"Consecrated" from Greek is *hagiazó*, a derivative of *hagios*, which means "to make holy," "consecrate," "sanctify," "treat as holy" or "set apart as holy". Consecrated and holy are synonymous but are not the same thing as being pure.

Righteousness

> ~ *But seek ye first the kingdom of God, and His righteousness; and all these things shall be added unto you.* **Matt 6:33**

"Righteousness" here is from the Greek word *dikaiosuné*, which means "justice," "justness," or "right-standing."

> ~ *The LORD is my shepherd; I shall not want. He maketh me to lie down in green pastures: He leadeth me beside the still waters. He restoreth my soul: He leadeth me in the paths of righteousness for His name's sake.* **Psalm 23:1-3**

The OT word "righteousness" is taken from the Hebrew word *tsedeq*, which means "accurate," "fairly," "just," "justice," "rightly," "vindication" or simply righteous as in "right-standing".

Interestingly, the etymology, or origin, of its root word *tzadik* means "straightness or "firmness." So the above verse gives the impression that God keeps my path straight.

Again, we see in the two languages a similarity between the OT and NT concepts. But in practicality there is a significant difference in the attribution of righteousness between the OT and the NT.

Righteousness in the OT is the fulfillment of the demands of a relationship, whether that relationship be with men or with God. The fulfillment of such specific demands constituted righteousness. When a man fulfilled the conditions placed on him by that relationship, he was deemed righteous, or in right-standing.

> *Generally, the righteous man in Israel was the man who preserved the peace and wholeness of the community, because it was he who [preserved] fulfilled the demands of communal living. Like Job, he was a blessing to his contemporaries. He cared for the poor, the fatherless, the widow…even defending their cause in the law court (Job 29:16; 31:21; Prov. 31:9)…He was a good steward of his land and work animals…and his servants were treated humanely…he lived at peace with his neighbors, wishing them only good…When he was in authority the people rejoiced, and he exalted the nation (Prov.14:34). He lived in peace and prosperity because he upheld the peace and prosperity. He upheld the physical and psychical wholeness of his community by fulfilling the demands of the communal covenant relationship (Cf. Ps.15:2-5; Isa.33:15).[14]*

So righteousness is attributed to an individual who has done what he needs to do and therefore has achieved "right-standing". This recognition is based upon either the individual's relation to an Israelite law court or based upon his covenant relationship with God founded on the Law, or Torah. In the case of the Law, his standing was only temporary because sacrifice would be needed repeatedly over his lifetime in order to make him "right" before God.

This is in stark contrast to the NT understanding of righteousness.

A follower of Jesus is not provided right-standing, righteousness, before God by his own efforts, i.e. repeated sacrifices. Rather, the NT clearly states that right-standing is afforded to the follower of Jesus through the atoning work of the Lord Himself in His ultimate sacrifice on the Cross.

> *But now the righteousness of God without the law is manifested, being witnessed by the law and the prophets, even the righteousness of God which is by faith of Jesus Christ unto all and upon all them that believe. For there is no difference, for all have sinned, and come short of the glory of God. Being justified freely by his grace through the redemption that is in Christ Jesus, whom God hath set forth to be a propitiation through faith in his blood, to declare his righteousness for the remission of sins that are past, through the forbearance of God. To declare, I say, at this time His righteousness: that He might be just, and the justifier of him which believeth in Jesus.* **Romans 3:21-26**

In other words, this right-standing before God is imparted to the Believer and based upon his faith in Jesus, not by his own efforts. Righteousness is an impartation of the character and the covering of God. The Bible says that the unrighteous will not inherit the kingdom of heaven.

Righteousness is not purity, but they are siblings.

---

14 Art Katz, "Righteousness in the Old Testament." Art Katz Ministries, http://artkatzministries.org/articles/righteousness-in-the-old-testament/, (accessed November 15, 2018).

For all have sinned, and come short of the glory of God, being justified freely by His grace through the redemption that is in Christ Jesus. **Romans 3:23-24**

The Greek word for "justified" is *dikaioó* and is a derivative of the same Greek word for "righteousness". That's because *dikaioó* means "to be shown as righteous," or "to be declared righteous". It's a legalese term of the day in which someone would plead a case for innocence, to acquit or to justify.

I think it was Derek Prince who said that justified was "just as if I've never sinned." It means sinless. "The quality of being morally right or justifiable."

And He made His grave with the wicked, and with the rich in His death; because He had done no violence, neither was any deceit in His mouth. Yet it pleased the LORD to bruise Him; He hath put him to grief: when thou shalt make His soul an offering for sin, He shall see His seed, He shall prolong His days, and the pleasure of the LORD shall prosper in His hand. He shall see of the travail of His soul, and shall be satisfied: by His knowledge shall my righteous servant justify many; for He shall bear their iniquities. **Isaiah 53:9-11**

This is an amazing prophecy out of the OT about Jesus, some 800 years before He was born. Its exactness as to the Messiah's work is astonishing. What's also very interesting about justification in the OT is how scarce the concept is found. There are plenty of examples of righteousness, but for someone to be justified, or declared innocent, the examples are few and far between.

"Justify" here in verse 11 comes from the Hebrew word *tsadeq*, the very same word that is used for "righteous". What the prophet Isaiah is saying here is that when the Messiah comes, 800 years from then, He was going to declare "many" to have "right-standing" before God (which is exactly what Jesus did).

So, the words "justified" and "justification", like "righteousness", are not the same as "purity" but directly related.

Rightly Dividing the Word

Many Christians don't understand the Bible. The previous terms are my case in point. They take what is said from the pulpit as the absolute truth without ever studying the words for themselves. The result is a misunderstanding of what God is showing us in His Word. It's true that we have the Holy Spirit to lead and guide us, but the Holy Spirit alone is only part of God's equation for His people to walk in His ways.

Christians who don't understand the Word unknowingly live their lives founded upon mistruths, or fabricate a belief system based upon their "feelings". "My pastor told me that God loves me so…" Or how many times have you heard someone say, "I believe that…" but the basis of those beliefs are not scriptural. Often they form a convoluted belief system created by slapping together bits and pieces of scriptures or even paganistic and misguided societal mores.

When the Word of God is not absolute in our lives, we become our own god and fool ourselves into thinking that the real God winks at us when we live contrary to His Word.

Before you saw the above definitions of "holiness," "consecration," "righteousness" and "justification," how many times have you mixed up the words with one another? Words mean something.

I have a spirit-filled friend named Daniel who went to Bible College and shared with me one of his great frustrations in sitting in his hermeneutics class. Hermeneutics is the study of how to interpret the Bible.

Daniel was an older student and told me how one of his favorite professors taught the class, but used to drive him crazy. The professor would say, "The Bible can never mean what it never meant." In other words, it was written in an historical, cultural context with specific meaning in mind.

Since Daniel was baptized in the Holy Spirit, and this was a Pentecostal/Charismatic college, he'd disagree with the professor in class and say that the Holy Spirit could do whatever He wanted with His Word. To which the professor would reply, "God said what He meant, and He meant what He said. It's your duty and responsibility as future church leaders to properly interpret the Word if you're going to teach people. You can't play fast and loose with the Word of God and not expect people to get hurt."

Long after he'd left the school, Daniel had lunch with the professor. Out of school, two mature Believers talking over a shared meal, the former student and teacher were able to finally see eye-to-eye on the issue.

Daniel told the professor how his statement, "The Bible can never mean what it never meant" really bothered him. He told him that there'd been plenty of times that he opened the Word and the Holy Spirit took a verse out of context and applied it to his life, with beneficial results.

The professor was now a peer of almost an equal age and not a teacher. He smiled warmly and said, "Of course the Holy Spirit can do that and does, even in my life. But you have to understand, I'm teaching mostly young people that have just graduated high school. These people will be the future pastors and leaders of the Church. I had to give them a firm foundation of responsible study and interpretation because they in turn were going to teach other people. This is God's Word and He can do with it whatever He wants. But we need to start from a right understanding and then let the Holy Spirit be the Holy Spirit."

My point in telling this story is that far too many Christians take the Word and unknowingly misinterpret it or use it. They pull scripture out of context and make a theology on it. We see this all the time with the modern-day Church. Paul cautioned Timothy about this when he said:

> *Study to shew thyself approved unto God, a workman that needeth not to be ashamed, rightly dividing the word of truth.* **2 Timothy 2:15**

Being pure is not being righteous, nor is it being holy, nor is it being consecrated, nor is it being justified. Christian purity stands alone and by itself and is likened to the purification process of gold and silver. Just like with those precious metals, the Holy Spirit's fire burns off the sin, the scum, and the dross in our lives to give us a reflection more like Jesus.

Words mean something.

Cleansed

The word "cleansed" is not a theological term, but understanding the idea is imperative to the discussion of purity. None of those previous attributes (righteousness, etc.) of God makes us pure. Perhaps the closest we get to the idea of purity, as far as cleanliness goes, is God covering us with His righteousness and then justifying us. Yet, neither of those two terms is purity in the full sense. But one of the greatest benefits of walking with God is that He will make a way when there seems to be no way.

My sin and your sin is the case in point. We know that sin cannot even be in God's presence. So although our sin has been forgiven and covered, it would still remain if God didn't wash those sins clean. The question is: How does He do it?

Answer: Through the blood of Jesus!

> *If we confess our sins, he is faithful and just to forgive us our sins, and to cleanse us from all unrighteousness.* **1 John 1:9**

The Greek word for "cleanse" in this verse is *katharizó* and literally means "to make clean" either ceremonially or spiritually. It also means "to make pure by removing all intermingling of filth".

Aha! So what the confession of our sin does is remove our impurities and change our position before God from wrong-standing to being in right-standing before Him.

> *Come now, and let us reason together, saith the LORD: though your sins be as scarlet, they shall be as white as snow; though they be red like crimson, they shall be as wool.* **Isaiah 1:18**

This is one of my favorite verses and one that I've held onto over the years. And although there's not really a Hebrew word here that I can pull out and say, "There! That's the word that says God purifies us", the meaning of the verse is unmistakable. If we go to God and reason with Him, confess our sin in NT vernacular, He will totally change us from bloody red to pure white.

If that's not cleansing like in 1 John 1:9, I don't know what is!

But let's be clear, both of these verses are talking about the action of making us clean. In making us clean, our impurities are initially removed, but we don't stay clean. Why? Because like every kid all over the world, we get our good clothes on and then go out and play in the dirt! We call this the world. Even after we are made clean, pure, we still have to come back and be made clean and forgiven, again and again.

Being cleansed is the mirror image of purity. It is not quite the same, but it's almost the identical thing. Cleansing is the process to purity, but purity is the end result of being cleansed.

Purified

> *Blessed are the pure in heart: for they shall see God.* **Matt 5:8**

The Greek word for "pure" in this verse is *katharos*. It means "to be clean," "pure," "unstained," either literally or ceremonially or spiritually; "guiltless," "innocent," or "upright".

Referring to the above verse, someone who is "pure in heart" is a single-minded individual toward God. Within such a person, you wouldn't find any hypocrisy, guile or hidden motives. They are exactly what they appear to be because their lives, or their pure heart, is transparent and uncompromising in their desire to please God in everything they do. The signs of that external purity are a reflection of their internal purity of soul.

And for the record, I am in no way inferring that this is me. I have a long way to go, but my goal is to give you the truth and give both you and me something to shoot for. I can think of only a handful of people who exemplify the traits above, but it's my hope that my heart looks more like Jesus' every day.

Getting to that place of a pure heart is not something that we can do on our own. We must not only give our lives to Jesus, but we must also ask Him to do His cleansing work in us through His Holy Spirit. That's because it is only God Who can make our hearts pure through the work of the Spirit.

From the OT we read:

> *Who shall ascend into the hill of the LORD? Or who shall stand in his holy place? He that hath clean hands, and a pure heart; who hath not lifted up his soul unto vanity, nor sworn deceitfully.* **Psalm 24:3-4**

"Pure" here is from the Hebrew word *bar*. It means "clean," "innocent" or "pure". Again, we see very acute similarities between OT and NT thoughts on purity. God's work of Purity in our lives as Christians is not works-related nor is it simply imparted to us like righteousness. Purity is a process that the Holy Spirit takes us through as if by fire. More on this in a moment.

Purity and righteousness are not the same. The difference between righteousness and purity is that purity is a quantifiable identifier. Purity is the end product of God's righteousness through the Holy Spirit working it out in our lives. This occurs through the conviction of the Lord through that same Spirit. That conviction should result in repentance. And that repentance is the catalyst that causes our heart's attitude to change in relationship to what God declares as wrong.

Pureness is a condition that either exists, or doesn't exist in our hearts. Sin is an affront to that pureness and is an act that we do in response to the power of sin. The power of sin is what every Christian has to deal with, even the ones who are pure in heart. Even Jesus had to deal with the power of sin trying to take Him out.

The pursuit of Purity is a choice. You can choose to allow the Holy Spirit to refine your life through His work or you can choose to live life on your own terms and ignore His prodding. That said, I think the caution found in Hebrews 10:31 says it best:

It is a fearful thing to fall into the hands of the living God.

I choose God.

Sexual Purity

No discussion on God's Everlasting Purity would be complete without talking about impure sexual relations where Christians are concerned.

I'm a guy and I can only speak from a guy's perspective, but I know that the draw of men to women is powerful. If you're having issues with lusting over the same sex, that's still sexual immorality but it's a whole different kind of animal that I'm not addressing at the moment.

Sexual immorality is exactly what caused King David to fall. We saw in 2 Samuel 11 that David so lusted for Bathsheba he sent her husband off to war to be killed. The impurity of sexual promiscuity in people's lives is a powerful pull. I don't care who you are. Men and women do crazy things to fulfill their impure desires, so we have to be continually vigilant.

Keep in mind who David was. He wasn't some shmuck who didn't know Who God was. He killed giants for Him after all! David knew the presence of God and enjoyed His fellowship. Even a man like that sinned and fell.

Don't fool yourself, man or woman that's reading this, and think that you're not susceptible to this particular attack of the devil. When you feel yourself being baited by the enemy who is trying to lure you into doing something impure, remember this:

> *Wherefore let him that thinketh he standeth take heed lest he fall. There hath no temptation taken you but such as is common to man: but God is faithful, who will not suffer you to be tempted above that ye are able; but will with the temptation also make a way to escape, that ye may be able to bear it.* **1 Cor 10:12-13**

Satan is allowed to tempt you, but you are under no obligation to fall for the temptation. You can choose to run the other way. Joseph did!

If you recall the story, Joseph was in Egypt doing very well and had an excellent reputation. He was staying with Potiphar who was an officer of Pharaoh and captain of the guard. But Joseph was young and probably good-looking. Potiphar's wife was probably feeling neglected. I say so because she came on to Joseph, but the Hebrew would not allow himself to be tempted. We pick up the story there:

> *And it came to pass after these things, that his master's wife cast her eyes upon Joseph; and she said, "Lie with me." But he refused, and said unto his master's wife, "Behold, my master wotteth not what is with me in the house, and he hath committed all that he hath to my hand; There is none greater in this house than I; neither hath he kept back any thing from me but thee, because thou art his wife: how then can I do this great wickedness, and sin against God?" And it came to pass, as she spake to Joseph day by day, that he hearkened not unto her, to lie by her, or to be with her. And it came to pass about this time, that Joseph went into the house to do his business; and there was none of the men of the house there within. And she caught him by his garment, saying, "Lie with me:" and he left his garment in her hand, and fled, and got him out.* **Gen 39:7-12**

No matter how attractive the man's wife was, Joseph would not allow himself to "sin against God." This wasn't just taking advantage of another man's wife; Joseph understood that to yield to such temptation would be an affront to the Most High and would impinge upon his personal purity. Sex is sex and sin is sin. If we saw the sin of sexual immorality, man or woman, like Joseph did, we would never allow the devil to corrupt us in this way.

Don't get me wrong. I'm not saying that sex is bad. Far from it. God instituted marriage in Genesis by making a partnership between husband and wife, with neither being complete without the other. And the natural draw between a husband and wife in a right relationship is a beautiful thing.

After the fall of Adam and Eve, Satan distorted the sexual draw of women toward men and men toward women (and the draw of two people of the same sex together). The enemy knows about this fallen flaw and exploits it whenever he can.

If someone like David, who enjoyed an extremely close relationship to the Lord, could fall into the devil's snare, it's a safe bet that if we're not careful, we can also be caught up in this particular sin.

Adultery is by no means the only snare that people fall into that pollutes our purity. The favorite traps of the enemy are money, power, sex or drugs. Regardless, whatever your weakest link is, we need to be mindful of these attacks if we are to walk upright before God.

Lest Satan should get an advantage of us: for we are not ignorant of his devices. **2 Cor 2:11**

In The Pursuit of Purity

It's only God Who is completely good, transcendently awesome, abundantly adequate, forever holy, and everlastingly pure. We are not, but throughout our lives and walk we can plant good seeds throughout our days in order to see them grow into a life that is reflective of our King. Prayer, repentance and continually dying to ourselves are some of those seeds.

Trying to be pure and holy in our own strength and our own devices only leads to simple (and very temporal) mortal cleanliness, not God's Purity. People who try to become pure apart from the Holy Spirit become pharisaical and trapped in their own perfection. In addition, if you're not baptized in the Spirit, it will be extremely difficult for you to walk in purity. That's because the purification process is the supernatural work of the Holy Spirit in our lives. If you're just doing good in your own strength, you may become purer, but it is a purity developed in your own flesh, not of the Spirit.

It's the blood of Jesus that cleanses us, but what does the blood of Jesus cleanse us from? Our impurity of sin, but nowhere in scripture does it say that His blood purifies us once and for all. I'll get into that in a minute.

With that said, it doesn't mean that we can do whatever we want to do and just go back to the Lord and ask Him to forgive us and cleanse us! There is far too much of this going on in the Church today and I've already addressed the issue in depth earlier. But my point is that even though it is ultimately Messiah's blood that cleanses us, our own practical purity is paramount and it is our responsibility.

Here's what I mean: Guys, you can't visit strip clubs without spiritual consequence and then go back to the Lord to simply ask Him to forgive you and cleanse you. The Holy Spirit inside of you, if indeed He lives inside of you, would have hounded you before, during and after to get the heck out of there.

Ladies, the Holy Ghost inside of you would have interrupted you during your diatribe to your friends in which you denigrated or gossiped about another person.

In both of these examples, God leads us to take action against impurity but we still have to choose not to participate in the sin. This is a simple fact. Not participating in sin doesn't make us pharisaical. Not sinning and then patting ourselves on the back and acting like we're the best thing next to sliced bread makes us pharisaical.

You to have the right perspective about Purity in order to draw near to Him. First: It isn't your Purity. It's His. Second: If we long to be in His presence and spend as much time with Him as we can, we'll naturally avoid the vast majority of sin and thus maintain our purity.

But frankly clean hands and a pure heart, as mentioned in Psalm 24:3-4, are beyond the experience of most Christians. They're so busy trying to figure out what they can get away with, but they take little to no practical steps to maintain a healthy relationship with the Father

Stop thinking about walking in Purity before God in human terms, and start thinking about it from God's perspective. Our basis for drawing near to Him can't be what we do or don't do. All of our righteousness has to come from God. This is exemplified by what He's done for us on the inside and what He'll do for us on the outside.

So what's your particular blemish that hinders your relationship with God? Is it porn? Gossip? Sleeping around? Drugs? A filthy mouth? Hatefulness? Unforgiveness? You name it; all of these things cause us to be impure before God.

> *Now the works of the flesh are manifest, which are these; Adultery, fornication, uncleanness, lasciviousness, idolatry, witchcraft, hatred, variance, emulations, wrath, strife, seditions, heresies, envyings, murders, drunkenness, revellings, and such like: of the which I tell you before, as I have also told you in time past, that they which do such things shall not inherit the kingdom of God.* **Gal 5:19-21**

And because many of these are entrenched habits in our lives, we can't shake them. We know that they are sin and cause us to be impure. So we try in our own strength to stop our particular fleshiness, but in doing so, we are trying to walk in our own purity.

First, God always wants to hear from us, even when we're in sin. You don't need to be perfect; you just need to be repentant. Second, when we acknowledge our sin and honestly confess it before Him, He covers it. Third, when we cry out to Him for deliverance, we give Him permission to intervene. This is a powerful tool. He will not interfere with your life unless you allow Him to do so.

You can wallow in your sin all you want. Or you can try to fix it on your own. But ultimately you need His supernatural deliverance to overcome that sin and to make you pure.

Chapter 18

Consequences and Repercussions

There was a certain rich man, which was clothed in purple and fine linen, and fared sumptuously every day. And there was a certain beggar named Lazarus, which was laid at his gate, full of sores, and desiring to be fed with the crumbs which fell from the rich man's table: moreover the dogs came and licked his sores. And it came to pass, that the beggar died, and was carried by the angels into Abraham's bosom: the rich man also died, and was buried; and in hell he lift up his eyes, being in torments, and seeth Abraham afar off, and Lazarus in his bosom. And he cried and said, "Father Abraham, have mercy on me, and send Lazarus, that he may dip the tip of his finger in water, and cool my tongue; for I am tormented in this flame." But Abraham said, "Son, remember that thou in thy lifetime receivedst thy good things, and likewise Lazarus evil things: but now he is comforted, and thou art tormented. And beside all this, between us and you there is a great gulf fixed: so that they which would pass from hence to you cannot; neither can they pass to us, that would come from thence." Then he said, "I pray thee therefore, father, that thou wouldest send him to my father's house for I have five brethren; that he may testify unto them, lest they also come into this place of torment." Abraham saith unto him, "They have Moses and the prophets; let them hear them." And he said, "Nay, father Abraham: but if one went unto them from the dead, they will repent." And he said unto him, "If they hear not Moses and the prophets, neither will they be persuaded, though one rose from the dead.

Luke 16:19-31

The contemporary Church, for the most part, denies the existence of Hell. When Jesus talked about Lazarus, that's a specific case, not a general case. He's not talking metaphorically. He's not generalizing. He's talking specifics, but eternal damnation is something that most people simply can't accept.

How many times have you heard someone say, "Oh, I don't believe in Hell."

My first response is: What is your belief system based on? In most cases it's simply denial. If they can deny the existence of Hell, or even God, then they can live life any way they want to without consequence. The fact is that God has given us supernatural evidence of His existence and His expectations in His Word. We ignore that evidence and those expectations to our own peril.

When it comes to God's Everlasting Purity, there is also the antithesis of purity. If someone is pursuing a life full of God's Purity, the opposite of that pursuit is someone pursuing a life of sin or worldliness. The consequences of such a pursuit are eternally dangerous because you will eventually find yourself… in Hell.

Overwhelming Evidence

In order to fully consider what the eternal repercussions are of a life in rebellion against God, it's important for people to understand the validity of the Bible. That's because within the Bible lies the truth of the infinite future.

Here is a very short list of the evidence for the validity of God's Word:

- *There are 16 total historians apart from Scripture who reference (Jesus) Christ.*
- *Almost everything about (Jesus) Christ we can find without ever going to the NT.*
- *There's more evidence that Jesus lived than Julius Caesar, yet no one doubts Caesar existed.*
- *John said, "What our eyes have seen, what our ears have heard, what our hands have handled is what we're declaring to you." In other words, they were eyewitnesses.*
- *The Bible is more accurate than any other ancient document because the closer the manuscript to the original, the less chance of error or miscopy.*
- *We've got manuscripts and fragments that show up within 35 or 40 years of the time when they were written.*
- *Current surviving Bible manuscripts get closer to the original work than any other manuscripts from the ancient world.*
- *It means there's not enough time for error and mythology to corrupt the message of what's going on there.*
- *When you look at Greek and Roman historians like Herodotus and Tacitus and Livy, those (oldest surviving manuscripts) are hundreds of years later - 500, 600, 700 years after the fact.*
- *When it comes to the Bible, the surviving ancient copies or pieces of it way outnumber all other ancient works.*
- *There are approximately 66,420 manuscripts and scrolls of the Bible.*
- *A distant second place goes to Homer's The Illiad, with just 1,827. Most ancient works have far few intact remnants.[15]*

---

15 Paul Strand, "Incredible Proof for Why You Should Have Faith in the Bible." CBN News, http://www1.cbn.com/cbnnews/us/2016/march/incredible-proof-for-why-you-should-have-faith-in-the-bible, (April 1, 2018).

As I said, this is just a short list. The fact is that books and books have been written outlining factual proof of the Bible's validity. So if the Bible is true, then its numerous statements about Hell must equally be true.

And if the Bible is true, should we not heed the things in the Bible that God told us to do? As an example: Within those pages He calls on His people to not only believe in Him, but to die to themselves and seek His Purity. So why do the vast majority of people who call themselves Christians not seek His Purity?

The reason, of course, is that the vast majority of Christians think that getting saved gives them all they need to be pure. After all, they are new creations and they have Holy Spirit inside them.

> *Therefore if any man be in Christ, he is a new creature: old things are passed away; behold, all things are become new.* **2 Cor 5:17**

Here's a newsflash - Even after His blood cleanses us initially, we're still told that we are to be conformed to the image of Jesus (Rom 8:29). We're also prompted by the Holy Spirit to continue to change into mature Believers who reflect the image of Jesus.

> *But we all, with open face beholding as in a glass the glory of the Lord, are changed into the same image from glory to glory, even as by the Spirit of the Lord.* **2 Cor 3:18**

That is the purification process of God.

So let me be clear: When we come to the Lord and truly repent, we are saved and therefore "qualified" to go to heaven to be with Him. Jesus' blood initially cleanses our sin, purifies us, and then covers us. We are given right-standing before Him and all He sees is His Son's blood. So it's as if we never sinned.

But wait… you and I still sin!

Positionally we're seated in heavenly places, but we are literally still here in this world of scum/dross. This is why there is a purification process where we work out our own salvation with fear and trembling.

> *Wherefore, my beloved, as ye have always obeyed, not as in my presence only, but now much more in my absence, work out your own salvation with fear and trembling. For it is God which worketh in you both to will and to do of his good pleasure.* **Phil 2:12-13**

If Jesus did all those things for us when we got saved, what is there to work out if we are "qualified" to be with Him? And why are we being conformed to the image of Christ?

That's because the working out of our salvation and our being conformed is a process, the purification process!

Earlier you read about what it means to die to ourselves. I've also talked about dealing with trials. Both of these things, and more, are parts of that same purification process. After we get saved, God is still working on us! He's prompting us to become more like His Son Jesus and the work of the Holy Spirit in our lives is designed to make us pure.

Don't get me wrong, when I got saved and then filled with the Holy Spirit that night, God radically changed me. It wasn't like I had to try to be different, I just was. He really did make me into a new creation, but there was, and still is, a ton of things that He continually works on in my life. He continually refines me, and you, to look like His pure Son.

It is to this end that we have choices when it comes to a relationship with God.

1. We can accept what Jesus did on the Cross and ask Him to come into our lives. After that we can yield to the work of the Holy Spirit in us as He continues to make us purer and purer until we reflect our Lord;

2. We can accept what Jesus did on the Cross and ask Him to come into our lives, but not yield to the work of the Holy Spirit to make us pure. We will have to answer for that at the Bema Seat judgment, more on that in a minute; or

3. We can ignore God's call for repentance and live life on our own terms.

We only have three choices. And by the way, saying that you don't believe in God or the Bible is you simply taking door number three.

All of these positions have consequences and repercussions. It is my sincere prayer that you choose well.

Punishment and Principle

Go back to the scripture at the beginning of this chapter, Luke 16:19-31, and consider the following:

~ **The rich man was in torment.**

~ **The rich man had a memory.**

~ **He knew that he had brothers and he knew that they would end up there too.**

In other words, he was totally self-conscious in Hell. He didn't cease to exist. It was not a case of Nihilism.

> *Nihilism is a non-Christian belief that, in the end, "nothingness" prevails in a world that is totally meaningless. Nihilism teaches that God does not exist or that He is dead. Nihilism says there is no higher purpose in life, that life is simply futile. The word nihilism comes from nihil, a Latin root meaning "nothing" or "that which does not exist." Interestingly enough, this same root is found in the word annihilate, which means "to destroy something completely, especially so that it ceases to exist."[16]*

The damned live with the continual memory of every sound, every sight, every taste and every pleasure that they had in their life on earth. Everything of their lives will be a continual reminder to them about their rejection of God and His forgiveness. Worse, there is no covering for their sin because they have already rejected Jesus. Judgment has been pronounced.

At this point, I feel compelled to clear up a misunderstanding about the fate of people who reject Jesus' work on Calvary and the Holy Spirit's purification process in our lives.

How many times have you heard someone say, "Well, if God was so loving, how could He send people to Hell?"

---

16 Got Questions, "What is nihilism?" GotQuestions.org, https://www.gotquestions.org/nihilism.html, (accessed November 11, 2018).

To be clear, God doesn't send anyone to Hell; you send yourself by your rejection of the Truth.

He's given everyone throughout history a level playing field. Because I know His character, I know that He is fair and just. He has, and will, give everyone the opportunity to accept Jesus or reject Him. I don't know how exactly, but I have heard some wild stories about missionaries coming upon tribes in the jungle that had no contact with the outside world. In the case I'm thinking about, their chief had a dream or a vision about "a man with a book" that was going to come and give them Jesus. Years later, the missionary shows up and the dream was fulfilled and these previously ignorant villagers got saved.

However He does it, everyone gets a **chance to choose.**

Heart Action

This is the choice that I'm talking about. If you accept Him and live for Him, you'll be with Him forever. If you reject Him, and only give Him lip service and live like Hell, you will go to Hell regardless of what you may have said. Or you can outright reject Him and go to Hell. Those are your choices.

By the way, being saved is not lip action - it's heart action, "action" being the operative word.

Someone may want to take issue with this stance. I can hear them now, "But the Bible says that if I confess with my mouth, I'll be saved."

Really? So all I have to do is repeat a prayer in church, or at a revival, or in a meeting and I'm set for life? Let's take a look at this because if that's all there is to being a Christian, I'm feeling pretty dumb.

The verse in question is Romans 10:9, but since I mentioned practicing good Bible study skills, let's look at the verse in context and then at the original language.

> *But what saith it? The word is nigh thee, even in thy mouth, and in thy heart: that is, the word of faith, which we preach; That if thou shalt confess with thy mouth the Lord Jesus, and shalt believe in thine heart that God hath raised him from the dead, thou shalt be saved. For with the heart man believeth unto righteousness; and with the mouth confession is made unto salvation.* **Romans 10:8-10**

First, let's look at this confessing thing in context.

- Verse 8 says that the Word is near you, even on the tip of your tongue. So that means that it's in your heart and swims around in your conscience. If this were you, His Word would always be at the forefront of your mind.

- With the Word permeating your heart and mind that way, do you really think you'd live any way you want? Do you think that your verbal confession would give you a pass?

- Verse 9 is the confessing with your mouth part.

- But it also says that you have to believe in your heart.

- If you really believed that God is Who He says He is, and that there are real consequences for your sin, can you do whatever you want?

- ~ If you think that way, I'd submit to you that you don't believe. Otherwise we'd be back to that fear and trembling thing.
- ~ Verse 10 says that it's not just moving your mouth that gives you righteousness, or right-standing, with God, it's your heart, i.e. heart-action.

But to be sure, let's look at the Greek.

The Greek word translated as "confess" in verse 9 is the word *homologeó*. It literally means "to be of one mind with someone else," as well as "to declare," "to praise," "to speak in conclusion together," "to profess," "to align yourself" or "to endorse".

So it's not just what I say that saves me, it's much deeper than lip service. It's my direct mental attachment to Jesus Himself, i.e. the mind of Christ in Phil 2:5.

The other word in verse 9 that we need to look at is "believe". This is the Greek word *pisteuó* from the root word *pístis*, which means "faith". To believe in this context is "to entrust in," or "to trust in". In other words, believing is not just believing. It is fully giving yourself over to something or someone.

Can you fully give yourself over to the Lord in this way and then take yourself back? I would say that anything is possible. But my thought would be that if you gave your heart to Him at all, how could it be so easy to take it back?

Confessing with our mouths and believing in Him is not as simple as some people would make it sound. I would submit to you that you cannot make yourself of one mind with Christ, and give Him your heart, and then go out and live like Hell. It just isn't possible. If this were the case, your confession of Jesus as your Messiah would be only lip service.

So back to my earlier point. All of us will get a chance to choose Jesus or not.

For those people who choose poorly, it might be important for them to understand what Hell is.

The Many Faces of Hell

In the NT of the KJV of the Bible, the word Hell is used 23 times. In the OT and NTs, the word Hell is used 54 times.

To understand Hell, we have to understand what Jesus meant when He said:

> *And fear not them which kill the body, but are not able to kill the soul: but rather fear him which is able to destroy both soul and body in hell.* **Matt 10:28**

In truth, the word "Hell" is only one name for this place of punishment. The Bible contains several others.

- ~ **Hell**
- ~ **Hades**
- ~ **Tartarus**
- ~ **Gehenna**

The Greek term "Hades" is translated as Hell 10 times in the KJV. Many newer translations use the term Hades directly from the original language. Like Hell, Hades is the place of internment of the spirits of the dead. Jesus says in Revelation 1:18 that He has the keys of Death and Hades.

I am He that liveth, and was dead; and, behold, I am alive for evermore, Amen; and have the keys of hell and of death. **Rev 1:18**

In **Revelation 6:8**, the apostle John saw Hades as one of the four horsemen of the apocalypse, the pale horse. What most people miss is that Hades will be emptied at the time of the judgment, **Revelation 20:13-14.** That's because after the Great White Throne Judgment, an unbeliever's place of eternal punishment will be the Lake of Fire.

Another lesser-known term for Hell is *tartarus.*

"God spared not angels when they sinned, but cast them down to hell, and committed them to pits of darkness, to be reserved unto judgment . . ." **2 Peter 2:4**

In this verse, Hell is from the Greek term *tartarosas,* the noun form of which is *tartarus.* This is the word's only appearance in the NT.

Another term for Hell is the word *gehenna.* It's found 12 times in the Greek of the NT. It's the transliteration of the OT Hebrew expression of *"the valley of Hinnom,"* which was a literal ravine on the south side of Jerusalem. Unbelieving Hebrews offered their own children in ritual sacrifice to pagan gods and eventually it became a garbage dump where the trash was burned continually. The sacrifice of children brought to mind the idea of weeping and gnashing of teeth. The picture of garbage on fire continually brought the idea of eternal torment. It's easy to see the symbolism.

Hell is talked about in Revelation four times. One of those is one of the four horses of the apocalypse, which is called Hell. The original language renders this word as Hades.

Hell is real and the Bible clearly talks about what it's like.

Know Your Adversary.

So, why all this talk about Hell? Especially when we're supposed to be talking about God's Everlasting Purity?

Hell Is Anything but Pure

And Jesus Himself made it clear that Hell is a very real place. Just because people want to whistle past the graveyard doesn't mean it's not real.

It is a fearful thing to fall into the hands of the living God. **Hebrews 10:31**

And the sea gave up the dead which were in it; and death and hell delivered up the dead which were in them: and they were judged every man according to their works. And death and hell were cast into the lake of fire. This is the second death. And whosoever was not found written in the book of life was cast into the lake of fire. **Rev 20:13-15**

Notice that Death and Hell are entities. You can't cast a place into the lake of fire.

> *And when he had opened the fourth seal, I heard the voice of the fourth beast say, Come and see. And I looked, and behold a pale horse: and his name that sat on him was Death, and Hell followed with him. And power was given unto them over the fourth part of the earth, to kill with sword, and with hunger, and with death, and with the beasts of the earth.* **Rev 6:7-8**

Most people who actually believe in Hell still think that it's just a place. But in reality it's also a place where the king of Hell comes from. There is a ruler over Hell. In the context above, Hell is that entity.

> *Son of man, take up a lamentation upon the king of Tyrus, and say unto him, "Thus saith the Lord GOD; Thou sealest up the sum, full of wisdom, and perfect in beauty. Thou hast been in Eden the garden of God; every precious stone was thy covering, the sardius, topaz, and the diamond, the beryl, the onyx, and the jasper, the sapphire, the emerald, and the carbuncle, and gold: the workmanship of thy tabrets and of thy pipes was prepared in thee in the day that thou wast created. Thou art the anointed cherub that covereth; and I have set thee so: thou wast upon the holy mountain of God; thou hast walked up and down in the midst of the stones of fire. Thou wast perfect in thy ways from the day that thou wast created, till iniquity was found in thee. By the multitude of thy merchandise they have filled the midst of thee with violence, and thou hast sinned: therefore I will cast thee as profane out of the mountain of God: and I will destroy thee, O covering cherub, from the midst of the stones of fire. Thine heart was lifted up because of thy beauty, thou hast corrupted thy wisdom by reason of thy brightness: I will cast thee to the ground, I will lay thee before kings, that they may behold thee. Thou hast defiled thy sanctuaries by the multitude of thine iniquities, by the iniquity of thy traffick; therefore will I bring forth a fire from the midst of thee, it shall devour thee, and I will bring thee to ashes upon the earth in the sight of all them that behold thee. All they that know thee among the people shall be astonished at thee: thou shalt be a terror, and never shalt thou be any more."* **Ezekiel 28:12-19**

Now connect the above scripture to Isaiah 14:12-22 to see the full picture of what entity we are talking about:

> *How art thou fallen from heaven, O Lucifer, son of the morning! how art thou cut down to the ground, which didst weaken the nations! For thou hast said in thine heart, "I will ascend into heaven, I will exalt my throne above the stars of God: I will sit also upon the mount of the congregation, in the sides of the north. I will ascend above the heights of the clouds; I will be like the most High." Yet thou shalt be brought down to hell, to the sides of the pit. They that see thee shall narrowly look upon thee, and consider thee, saying, "Is this the man that made the earth to tremble, that did shake kingdoms, that made the world as a wilderness, and destroyed the cities thereof; that opened not the house of his prisoners?" All the kings of the nations, even all of them, lie in glory, every one in his own house. But thou art cast out of thy grave like an abominable branch, and as the raiment of those that are slain, thrust through with a sword, that go down to the stones of the pit; as a carcase trodden under feet. Thou shalt not be joined with them in burial, because thou hast destroyed thy land, and slain thy people: the seed of evildoers shall never be renowned. Prepare slaughter for his children*

for the iniquity of their fathers; that they do not rise, nor possess the land, nor fill the face of the world with cities. For I will rise up against them, saith the LORD of Hosts, and cut off from Babylon the name, and remnant, and son, and nephew, saith the LORD. I will also make it a possession for the bittern, and pools of water: and I will sweep it with the besom of destruction, saith the LORD of Hosts.

With those two pieces of scripture in the back of your mind, go to 1 Peter 5:8 where it says:

Be sober, be vigilant; because your adversary the devil, as a roaring lion, walketh about, seeking whom he may devour.

Satan acts like a lion, but he is not. One day the world will look upon him and say (I'm paraphrasing here out of Isaiah 14:16-17), "This is the one that scared everybody to death? This puny guy?" As Christians really begin to understand who they are in Jesus, and purpose to have the Holy Spirit purify their lives, some amazing things will happen at the End of the Age.

And the seventy returned again with joy, saying, "Lord, even the devils are subject unto us through thy name." And he (Jesus) said unto them, "I beheld Satan as lightning fall from heaven. Behold, I give unto you power to tread on serpents and scorpions, and over all the power of the enemy: and nothing shall by any means hurt you. Notwithstanding in this rejoice not, that the spirits are subject unto you; but rather rejoice, because your names are written in heaven." Luke 10:17-20

Don't get me wrong, you don't want to tangle with Satan or the demonic without the direction or protection of the Lord, but my point is that he isn't what he appears to be.

Chapter 19
Reality Check

And we know that we are of God, and the whole world lieth in wickedness.

1 John 5:19

The Lake of Fire was prepared for Satan and the Fallen Angels and when people reject God, unbelievers will join the devil and his angels in their eternal torment in that fiery tomb. That is the reality.

We live in a world that is pervasive with sin. That ugliness and impurity impacts everything and everyone around us, Christian or unbeliever. How people deal with that sin and the devil will ultimately determine where they'll spend eternity.

In this chapter, you're going to see just how bad things have gotten in both the Church and the world. God's creation appears to be in full rebellion and that rebellion is a direct affront to His Everlasting Purity. Such a perspective helps us to really understand why the Lord said that if God didn't shorten the days, there would be no flesh left alive.

The Oxymoronic

Someone once said that the phrase "nominal Christian" is the ultimate oxymoron. I would agree. These are those badge-wearing Christians in name only. And just so you know, I'm not judging here. Here's the principle:

Beware of false prophets, which come to you in sheep's clothing, but inwardly they are ravening wolves. Ye shall know them by their fruits. Do men gather grapes of thorns, or figs of thistles? Even so every good tree bringeth forth good fruit; but a corrupt tree bringeth forth evil fruit. A good tree cannot bring forth evil fruit, neither can a corrupt tree bring forth good fruit. Every tree that bringeth not forth good fruit is hewn down, and cast into the fire. Wherefore by their fruits ye shall know them. **Matt 7:15-20**

This begs the question: What fruits? We've already addressed this, but it's worth revisiting. The fruit of the Spirit is exemplified in our lives.

But the fruit of the Spirit is love, joy, peace, longsuffering, gentleness, goodness, faith, meekness, temperance: against such there is no law. **Gal 5:22-23**

This fruit grows in us as the Holy Spirit's purification process continues to work in us. Just because people call themselves a Christian, or says they "believe" in God doesn't mean that they belong to Him. In fact, the opposite is true.

Jesus said unto them, "If God were your Father, ye would love me: for I proceeded forth and came from God; neither came I of myself, but he sent me. Why do ye not understand my speech? Even because ye cannot hear my word. Ye are of your father the devil, and the lusts of your father ye will do. He was a murderer from the beginning, and abode not in the truth, because there is no truth in him. When he speaketh a lie, he speaketh of his own: for he is a liar, and the father of it. And because I tell you the truth, ye believe me not. Which of you convinceth me of sin? And if I say the truth, why do ye not believe me? He that is of God heareth God's words: ye therefore hear them not, because ye are not of God." **John 8:42-47**

The harsh reality is that nominal Christians, or badge-wearing Christians in name only, do not display the Fruit of the Spirit, or very little of it. It's that fruit that's the evidence of someone who truly belongs to God! NO, it doesn't mean Christians are perfect and never sin.

What it does mean is that those attributes out of Galatians 5 are the evidence of someone's ongoing relationship with God, someone who is being purified. The lack of that fruit indicates someone offering lip-service to their relationship. While lip-service may work on this side of Hell, it certainly won't save them from the judgment of the Lake of Fire.

Enter ye in at the strait gate: for wide is the gate, and broad is the way, that leadeth to destruction, and many there be which go in thereat. Because strait is the gate, and narrow is the way, which leadeth unto life, and few there be that find it. **Matt 7:13-14**

It's not enough to say you know Jesus. The real question is: Does He know you?

Not every one that saith unto me, "Lord, Lord," shall enter into the kingdom of heaven; but he that doeth the will of my Father which is in heaven. Many will say to me in that day, "Lord, Lord, have we not prophesied in thy name? And in thy name have cast out devils? And in thy name done many wonderful works?" And then will I profess unto them, "I never knew you: depart from me, ye that work iniquity." **Matt 7:21-23**

Christians in name only, CINOs, are people who claim to believe in God and who have supposedly gotten saved. Yet, these same supposed Christians are embracing Artificial Intelligence, A.I., promoting homosexual lifestyles, advocating abortions and more.

Some CINOs are even trying to rewrite scripture as they rid the Bible of all the things their lifestyles disagree with. Despite their claims, they denigrate the Son of God and declare Jesus' specific statements to be metaphors or allegory. But remember what John said in Revelation about taking away or changing the Word:

> And if any man shall take away from the words of the book of this prophecy, God shall take away his part out of the book of life, and out of the holy city, and from the things which are written in this book. *Rev 22:19*

They will argue that this is only talking about The Book of Revelation, but they fail to see that it's a principle. The words of the Bible are not their words, and these precepts are not theirs to change. Besides, we also see this same emphasis on not changing God's Word in the OT.

> Ye shall not add unto the word which I command you, neither shall ye diminish ought from it, that ye may keep the commandments of the LORD your God which I command you. *Deut 4:2*

> What thing soever I command you, observe to do it: thou shalt not add thereto, nor diminish from it. *Deut 12:32*

One part of scripture that CINOs love to try to change is **Galatians 6:9-10:**

> Know ye not that the unrighteous shall not inherit the kingdom of God? Be not deceived: neither fornicators, nor idolaters, nor adulterers, nor effeminate, [Homosexual] nor abusers of themselves with mankind, nor thieves, nor covetous, nor drunkards, nor revilers, nor extortioners, shall inherit the kingdom of God.

CINOs are so deceived that they justify their sin and are unwilling to die to their flesh, or to allow the Holy Spirit to purify their lives.

Speaking of people trying to justify their sin, I once saw an interview on TV with a pair of supposed Christians. This couple had a Bible study in their home. Wonderful, right?

They also shared in this interview that at the end of the Bible study, they swapped mates!

What?!

I heard about another couple who went to a Spirit-filled church and encouraged the Pastor and his wife to use pornography in their sexual relations to "spice up" their marriage. The pastor didn't do it and had some strong words for the couple. A perfect example of CINOs, these people do not believe in living by the Word of God. They are willingly being deceived.

This reminds me of the section of scripture out of **2 Peter 3:3-5:**

> Knowing this first, that there shall come in the last days scoffers, walking after their own lusts, and saying, "Where is the promise of his coming? For since the fathers fell asleep, all things continue as they were from the beginning of the creation." For this they willingly are ignorant of, that by the word of God…"

You cannot be willingly ignorant and not have known at one time. In other words, nominal Christians, or CINOs will choose to believe in the lie over the truth of God's Word. This is deception.

But to truly fear the Lord and walk with Him is to hate evil.

Supernatural Accountability

The problem is, as I said earlier, there is no fear of the Lord anymore. But if there's no fear of God, then there's also no understanding of the coming judgment.

But make no mistake. Everyone will be judged.

Non-Christians will stand before the Great White Throne Judgment.

> *And I saw a great white throne, and Him that sat on it, from whose face the earth and the heaven fled away; and there was found no place for them. And I saw the dead, small and great, stand before God; and the books were opened: and another book was opened, which is the book of life: and the dead were judged out of those things which were written in the books, according to their works. And the sea gave up the dead which were in it; and death and hell delivered up the dead which were in them: and they were judged every man according to their works. And death and hell were cast into the lake of fire. This is the second death. And whosoever was not found written in the book of life was cast into the lake of fire.* **Rev 20:11-15**

Christians will stand before the judgment seat of Christ, which comes from the Greek word *bema*, also known as the Bema Seat Judgment.

> *But why dost thou judge thy brother? Or why dost thou set at nought thy brother? For we shall all stand before the judgment seat of Christ. For it is written, As I live, saith the Lord, every knee shall bow to me, and every tongue shall confess to God. So then every one of us shall give account of himself to God.* **Romans 14:10-12**

> *For I know nothing by myself; yet am I not hereby justified: but he that judgeth me is the Lord. Therefore judge nothing before the time, until the Lord come, who both will bring to light the hidden things of darkness, and will make manifest the counsels of the hearts: and then shall every man have praise of God.* **1 Cor 4:4-5**

> *For we must all appear before the judgment seat of Christ; that every one may receive the things done in his body, according to that he hath done, whether it be good or bad.* **2 Cor 5:10**

There's a huge difference between The Great White Throne Judgment for unbelievers and The Bema Seat Judgment for Christians. The Bema Judgment is a reward of the faithful, as in "What have you done with what I've given to you?" Think about Jesus' parable of the servants and the talents.

Juxtaposed to this is The Great White Throne Judgment, which will send people to the Lake of Fire for rejecting Jesus.

> *He (Jesus) answered and said unto them, "He that soweth the good seed is the Son of man; the field is the world; the good seed are the children of the kingdom; but the tares are the children of the wicked*

one. The enemy that sowed them is the devil; the harvest is the end of the world; and the reapers are the angels. As therefore the tares are gathered and burned in the fire; so shall it be in the end of this world. The Son of man shall send forth his angels, and they shall gather out of his kingdom all things that offend, and them which do iniquity; and shall cast them into a furnace of fire: there shall be wailing and gnashing of teeth. Then shall the righteous shine forth as the sun in the kingdom of their Father. Who hath ears to hear, let him hear. Matt 13:37-43

Although it's not a popular sentiment in seeker-friendly churches today, the fact is that people will be cast into the Lake of Fire. The vast majority of those claimants of Christianity, those CINOs and nominal Christians, will also end up in that judgment.

Poisoned Culture

We see in the world today that many people want nothing to do with God. The culture of our day negates God and embellishes evil. Hollywood and the music industry promote this dichotomy with movies and entertainment designed by the devil himself to lead the masses away from their Creator.

Woe unto them that call evil good, and good evil; that put darkness for light, and light for darkness; that put bitter for sweet, and sweet for bitter! Woe unto them that are wise in their own eyes, and prudent in their own sight! Woe unto them that are mighty to drink wine, and men of strength to mingle strong drink which justify the wicked for reward, and take away the righteousness of the righteous from him! Therefore as the fire devoureth the stubble, and the flame consumeth the chaff, so their root shall be as rottenness, and their blossom shall go up as dust: because they have cast away the law of the LORD of hosts, and despised the word of the Holy One of Israel. Isaiah 5:20-24

Nothing changed the world more than the sexual revolution and rock-n-roll. Rock was the vehicle to launch Satanism and the occult. That music vehicle brought those practices out from the secret societies that had practiced them since after the flood.

"Give me the beat boys to free my soul, I want to get lost in your rock-n-roll and drift away..."

Yeah, drift away to spend eternity in Hell!

This onslaught against mankind and our culture started in the early sixties with the introduction of rock-n-roll and the development of the early entertainment industry. Today, this two-pronged attack on American culture has matured into a blunt, brute force influence that is anything but subtle.

Before you think me a prude, remember that I grew up in that culture. I was the guy in a garage band and rock was a big part of my life. God delivered me out of that lifestyle and I'm more than qualified to give you an honest perspective.

So it's with confidence when I say that this culture has been promulgated in the cause of Satan for the purpose of corrupting mankind away from God's Purity.

As an example, in researching for this section I found a list of over 100 popular songs that promote Hell, or at least spin it in a positive light: *Highway to Hell, Hell's Bells, Heaven and Hell, Run Like Hell, Bat Out of*

Hell and the list goes on! I also did a quick search and found forty songs with demon in the title: *Demons - Imagine Dragons, Demon Days - Gorillaz, Tiny Demons - Todd Rundgren, Occasional Demons - Jethro Tull, Mind Demons - Suzi Quatro* to name just a few. Those songs which extol Satan are even more disturbing.

Well-known musicians with ties to the devil have had many "hits" over the years. In several interviews, Bob Dylan bragged about how he literally sold his soul to the devil for the price of stardom. But such direct embellishment of Lucifer isn't always necessary. Most of the time those performers simply sing about Satan. Popular songs from back in the day like *Sympathy for the Devil* by the Rolling Stones, *Running With The Devil* by Van Halen, *Shout at the Devil* by Motely Crew and *The Devil Went Down To Georgia* by Charlie Daniels all memorialized Satan. But it's no better today. The popular group Shinedown has a new song out called *Devil*, wildly successful Wolfgang Gartner, a.k.a. Skrillex has a hit called *The Devil's Den* and The Watson Twins put out *Run Devil Run* in 2006.

There are dozens and dozens of songs referencing the devil, demons or Hell. That's because the disturbing truth is that in our culture, focusing positively on the devil sells entertainment.

Why?

We're living in a time when the world is calling evil good and good evil. God's call to Purity is not only falling on deaf ears, but Purity is openly shunned and denounced as old fashioned and even bigoted.

Words are containers and words have power. These entertainers rewrite Hell to belittle it, deny it and deride it and thus desensitize mankind to the very real peril that lies in front of an unbelieving generation.

Talk about impurity, most of this music extols the demonic influence of Fallen Angels and their entities as if it's something to be desired. In fact, one mega pop star of the modern era, Beyoncé, assumes an alter ego in her performances named Sasha Fierce. Before and after video of her performances are startling. There are distinct physical changes that she undergoes as she transforms on stage into this "spirit guide". Oh yeah, she's also reported to be a Satanist so it's safe to say that she is not only promoting demonic influence in her music but is demonically possessed herself.[17]

She's a mega-star and has a great deal of influence on her audience, most of whom are youth. But Beyoncé is not alone in her demonic lifestyle when it comes to entertainers. Many celebrities are reportedly also closely aligned with the Illuminati.

Names like Katy Perry, Jay Z, Brad Pitt, Angelina Jolie, Kanye West, Eminem, Lady Gaga and J.K. Rowling, of Harry Potter fame, have all been closely tied to the Illuminati, or Satan worship, or both. And the list goes on. At least twenty-one stars of just the music industry reportedly have this affiliation and use their music to influence the masses against the Living God.[18]

Even more amazing is the fact that secular music is not alone in its embracing of the Illuminati. There are numerous Contemporary Christian Music artists that also promote Illuminati imagery in their music.[19]

---

17 Mark Shrayber, "Breaking: Beyonce Is Possessed, Sasha Fierce Is Satan". Jezebel, https://jezebel.com/breaking-beyonce-is-posessed-sasha-fierce-is-satan-1589577846, (June 12, 2014).

18 Mike Rothschild, "21 Musicians Who Are (Supposedly) in the Illuminati". Ranker, https://www.ranker.com/list/illuminati-in-the-music industry/mike-rothschild?ref=rltdlsts&l=2090532&li_source=LI&li_medium=desktop-also-saw, (accessed November 12, 2018).

19 David Stewart, "New World Order Occult Images in Contemporary Christian Music (CCM)". Jesus is Savior.com, https://www.jesus-is-savior.com/Evils%20in%20America/CCM/nwo_images_in_ccm.htm, (September 2010).

The light of the body is the eye: therefore when thine eye is single, thy whole body also is full of light; but when thine eye is evil, thy body also is full of darkness. **Luke 11:34**

The society in which we live is directed by its eyes and ears, and that direction is toward entertainment. Is it any wonder that we've morphed into an entertainment consumable society? We have movies that promote sexual promiscuity, mainstream media that promotes abhorrent sexual deviance and the killing of innocents, a video game industry that promotes violence, and a music industry that promotes demonic lifestyles.

As an example, within the last few years we have seen very popular movies come out in which the devil wins! This is disgusting but the fact is that the world is promoting Satan and elevating him to the place of god. Movies like *Skellig: The Owl Man* from 2009, *The Blackcoat's Daughter* from 2015, *The Witch* from 2015, *Along Came The Devil* from 2018, *Darkness Reigns* from 2018, *Paranormal Activity* from 2007 and *The Last Exorcism Part II* from 2013 are just a few modern movie examples in which the devil is hailed as a hero.

We also see in our modern era a gaming industry that has burgeoned into a juggernaut in the entertainment sector. Once the pastime of children, adults of all ages now spend countless hours playing in front of their game consoles.

I will refrain from speaking about how these games are designed to rewire player's brains and the countless hours of useless time wasted on this form of entertainment.

Rather, in terms of purity or the lack thereof, here's a list of some of the most popular violent or sexual games that users are playing. Names like *PlayerUnknown's Battlegrounds, Bulletstorm: Full Clip Edition, Conan Exiles, Dark Souls III: The Ringed City and Dead by Daylight* to name just a few.

Entertainment productions on sex are omitted from the above lists. The sad fact is that the list of movies and music that promote sexual immorality are too numerous to write out, but their influence on society is extremely powerful and detrimental.

For where your treasure is, there will your heart be also. **Luke 12:34**

You've heard the phrase, "Garbage in, garbage out"? All of this leads to the corruption of mankind's biblical morality and is a direct assault against God's Purity.

And He said, "That which cometh out of the man, that defileth the man. For from within, out of the heart of men, proceed evil thoughts, adulteries, fornications, murders, thefts, covetousness, wickedness, deceit, lasciviousness, an evil eye, blasphemy, pride, foolishness. All these evil things come from within, and defile the man." **Mark 7:20-23**

A Personal Glimpse

In spite of seeing Jesus just after I got saved, in spite of what He showed me about that panorama of history and in spite of Him giving me a Joseph's ministry to prepare for the End of the Age, I initially had a very difficult time believing in Hell.

Instinctively I knew that something was wrong with my point of view so one day early in my walk I was kneeling in prayer before the Lord with tears in my eyes. I said to the Lord, "God, I want to believe, but I don't believe in Hell."

Instantly I was yanked out of my body away from that place.

It was pitch black all around me and I was falling. I heard screams, hopelessness and despair. I never saw the devil, I never saw anybody in Hell, but the one thing that the Lord allowed me to see was the eternal and complete separation that Hell brings. I saw that it separates a person from all that is good and that it also exists in absolute darkness, absent of any light. It was like black tar was all around me and black tar was inside me. I knew that there was no escaping from it.

The worst thing that I took away from that experience was an idea that God implanted in me during that time. That separation, that darkness, that hopelessness, was forever.

I've never forgotten about that experience and you better believe that I now know there's a Hell.

At a different time, the Lord told me what people's torment in Hell would be like. He said, "As to their specific sin, so shall their judgment be."

Hell is real and it is ugly.

Chapter 20
Purity Found

The words of the LORD are pure words: as silver tried in a furnace of earth, purified seven times.

Psalm 12:6

The statutes of the LORD are right, rejoicing the heart: the commandment of the LORD is pure, enlightening the eyes.

Psalm 19:8

But the wisdom that is from above is first pure, then peaceable, gentle, and easy to be intreated, full of mercy and good fruits, without partiality, and without hypocrisy.

James 3:17

Every part and every characteristic of God is absolutely pure. God is pure energy, pure power and pure light. God is pure love and God is purely just. God is purely holy and God's motives are absolutely pure. I could go on, but you get the picture.

In fact, God is so pure that He can't even look on our sin.

Thou art of purer eyes than to behold evil, and canst not look on iniquity... **Habakkuk 1:13**

Because of Who He is, everything that He does is based upon His person of Purity. Whether it be dealing with creation or dealing with mankind, He is the very essence of Purity.

Purity Found in Creation

God's Purity can be seen in the Book of Genesis in some very specific language. When we read phrases such as "image and likeness" and "after their kind", we see that God designed His original creation to procreate with the same species. In other words, their offspring would be purely made up of the same kind of genetic material as the original creation, man included.

This is a perfect example of God's Everlasting Purity in the creation process.

And God said, Let the earth bring forth the living creature after his kind, cattle, and creeping thing, and beast of the earth after his kind: and it was so. And God made the beast of the earth after his kind, and cattle after their kind, and every thing that creepeth upon the earth after his kind: and God saw that it was good. And God said, "Let us make man in our image, after our likeness: and let them have dominion over the fish of the sea, and over the fowl of the air, and over the cattle, and over all the earth, and over every creeping thing that creepeth upon the earth." So God created man in his own image, in the image of God created He him; male and female created He them. And God blessed them, and God said unto them, "Be fruitful, and multiply, and replenish the earth, and subdue it: and have dominion over the fish of the sea, and over the fowl of the air, and over every living thing that moveth upon the earth." And God said, "Behold, I have given you every herb bearing seed, which is upon the face of all the earth, and every tree, in the which is the fruit of a tree yielding seed; to you it shall be for meat. And to every beast of the earth, and to every fowl of the air, and to every thing that creepeth upon the earth, wherein there is life, I have given every green herb for meat:" and it was so. And God saw every thing that He had made, and, behold, it was very good. And the evening and the morning were the sixth day. **Gen 1:24-31**

In man's life before the fall, we see peace, stability and most importantly God's Purity within their relationship and their existence. Although we have no idea how long that period of time lasted, God gave Adam and Eve very specific guidelines in order to maintain their carefree life.

And the LORD God took the man, and put him into the garden of Eden to dress it and to keep it. And the LORD God commanded the man, saying, "Of every tree of the garden thou mayest freely eat, but of the tree of the knowledge of good and evil, thou shalt not eat of it. For in the day that thou eatest thereof thou shalt surely die." **Gen 2:15-17**

And out of the ground the LORD God formed every beast of the field, and every fowl of the air; and brought them unto Adam to see what he would call them: and whatsoever Adam called every living creature, that was the name thereof. And Adam gave names to all cattle, and to the fowl of the air, and to every beast of the field; but for Adam there was not found an help meet for him. And the LORD God caused a deep sleep to fall upon Adam, and he slept: and He took one of his ribs, and closed up the flesh instead thereof and the rib, which the LORD God had taken from man, made he a woman, and brought her unto the man. And Adam said, "This is now bone of my bones, and flesh of my flesh: she shall be called Woman, because she was taken out of Man." **Gen 2:19-23**

And they were both naked, the man and his wife, and were not ashamed. **Gen 2:25**

Despite God's warning about what would happen if they disobeyed Him, we read how Adam and Eve were tempted. They chose to break God's command and eat from the tree of the knowledge of good and evil. The result of that disobedience was:

1. **The loss of their purity and their innocence,**

2. **Their physical death, and**

3. **Their spiritual death.**

Although the Bible lists spiritual death after their physical death, in reality it was flipped around. When God gives His word, He's true to His word.

> **Loss of Purity and Innocence** - *And they heard the voice of the LORD God walking in the garden in the cool of the day: and Adam and his wife hid themselves from the presence of the LORD God amongst the trees of the garden. And the LORD God called unto Adam, and said unto him, "Where art thou?" And he said, "I heard thy voice in the garden, and I was afraid, because I was naked; and I hid myself." And He said, "Who told thee that thou wast naked?"* **Gen 3:8-11**

> **Physical Death** - *Unto the woman He said, "I will greatly multiply thy sorrow and thy conception; in sorrow thou shalt bring forth children; and thy desire shall be to thy husband, and he shall rule over thee." And unto Adam He said, "Because thou hast hearkened unto the voice of thy wife, and hast eaten of the tree, of which I commanded thee, saying, Thou shalt not eat of it: cursed is the ground for thy sake; in sorrow shalt thou eat of it all the days of thy life; thorns also and thistles shall it bring forth to thee; and thou shalt eat the herb of the field. In the sweat of thy face shalt thou eat bread, till thou return unto the ground; for out of it wast thou taken: for dust thou art, and unto dust shalt thou return.* **Gen 3:16-19**

> **Spiritual Death** - *And the LORD God said, "Behold, the man is become as one of us, to know good and evil: and now, lest he put forth his hand, and take also of the tree of life, and eat, and live forever. Therefore the LORD God sent him forth from the garden of Eden, to till the ground from whence he was taken." So He drove out the man; and He placed at the east of the garden of Eden Cherubims, and a flaming sword which turned every way, to keep the way of the tree of life.* **Gen 3:22-24**

Within all of the beauty and purity in God's creation in Genesis, we see His Hope. That Hope was, as it still is today, delayed by the sin of Adam and Eve. Despite that sin, there remains redemption at the end of trial. This theme is duplicated several times in the Bible. Another place we see the fulfillment of God's plan of purity is in the account of Noah.

Preserving Purity

One of the greatest illustrations of God's Everlasting Purity is the length He would go in order to keep His creation pure. I'm speaking specifically about that which occurred in Genesis 6 with the inbreeding of Fallen Angels and mankind.

And it came to pass, when men began to multiply on the face of the earth, and daughters were born unto them, that the sons of God saw the daughters of men that they were fair; and they took them wives of all which they chose. And the LORD said, "My spirit shall not always strive with man, for that he also is flesh: yet his days shall be an hundred and twenty years." There were giants in the earth in those days; and also after that, when the sons of God came in unto the daughters of men, and they bare children to them, the same became mighty men which were of old, men of renown. **Gen 6:1-4**

As you probably know, I've written and spoken extensively on the subject of Giants and I don't want to necessarily rehash the issue here. To do so would be a distraction from the purposes of this book and in particular this Hope of God's Everlasting Purity. For a deeper discussion on Giants, I would refer you to my book entitled *Genesis 6 Giants* which can be found on my website, but we do need to briefly address the Genesis 6 issue here.

We see from the above passage that Fallen Angels, the "sons of God", in their rebellion, had forced themselves upon the human gene pool by mating with human women. The title of "sons of God" in the OT prior to Jesus' resurrection in the NT was used solely in reference to angels. Only after Jesus rose from the dead are His followers called the sons of God. Therefore, we know that these entities were not human, but the Fallen who had chosen to leave their first estate.

And the angels which kept not their first estate, but left their own habitation, he hath reserved in everlasting chains under darkness unto the judgment of the great day. **Jude 1:6**

Further, we also know from Genesis 6:4 that the word "giants" translated in the KJV is actually the word Nephilim, which were Fallen Angels. In addition we see that the offspring that the human mothers bore became "mighty men". This phrase is from the Hebrew word *gibbor* or *gibborim,* which in fact are giants, or later referred to as Rephaim.

So what we see are Fallen Angels corrupting the human gene pool by infusing their genetic material into mankind's genome, thus polluting God's creation. And that corruption didn't stop with mankind. We know this because we see a very interesting comment in the following verse:

And the LORD said, I will destroy man whom I have created from the face of the earth; both man, and beast, and the creeping thing, and the fowls of the air; for it repenteth me that I have made them. **Gen 6:7**

Why would God want to destroy not only mankind, but also all the animals, and even insects? We see the answer here:

And God looked upon the earth, and, behold, it was corrupt; for all flesh had corrupted his way upon the earth. **Gen 6:12**

That word "corrupted" in the Hebrew is the word *shachath*, which literally means "to go to ruin".

When God says that the whole earth, His creation, is corrupted, He's really saying that it's ruined! And as we can see, it wasn't just man that was ruined; it was everything. Man could be ruined by sin because they rebelled, but how could flowers and trees and the air and the insects be ruined?

In our modern day vernacular, the opposite of pure is impure. Since impurity is something that's been mixed with extraneous matter, especially something of an inferior or contaminating nature, it means that the item's purity has been corrupted. So the opposite of purity is corruption.

That which God had created in His Everlasting Purity was made corrupt, ruined, by… Fallen Angels.

And it is because of that corruption on a global scale that God purposed to destroy what He had created in love. At the same time, He also purposed to preserve some of that creation by finding someone who had yet to be corrupted by Satan and his minions.

He found Noah.

> *But Noah found grace in the eyes of the LORD. These are the generations of Noah: Noah was a just man and perfect in his generations, and Noah walked with God.* **Gen 6:8-9**

Notice the sequence here:

a   In verse 7 God says He would destroy everything and everyone from the face of the earth.

b   In verse 8 Genesis says that Noah found grace in God's eyes.

c   At the beginning of verse 9 it mentions the "generations" of Noah.

d   Then at the end of the same verse it says that Noah was "perfect" in those generations.

First, you have to ask yourself, "What generations of Noah is verse 9 talking about?" The answer can be found in Genesis 5 in the following verses:

~   *v 3 - And Adam lived an hundred and thirty years, and begat a son in his own likeness, after his image; and called his name Seth: (130 yrs)*

~   *v 6 - And Seth lived an hundred and five years, and begat Enos: (105 yrs)*

~   *v 9 - And Enos lived ninety years, and begat Cainan: (190 yrs)*

~   *v 12 - And Cainan lived seventy years, and begat Mahalaleel: (170 yrs)*

~   *v 15 - And Mahalaleel lived sixty and five years, and begat Jared: (165 yrs)*

~   *v 18 - And Jared lived an hundred sixty and two years, and he begat Enoch: (162 yrs)*

~   *v 21 - And Enoch lived sixty and five years, and begat Methuselah: (65 yrs)*

~   *v 25 - And Methuselah lived an hundred eighty and seven years and begat Lamech: (187 yrs)*

~   *v 28 - And Lamech lived an hundred eighty and two years, and begat a son: (182 yrs)*

~   *v 29 - And he called his name Noah,…*

When you add all Noah's generations years together, 130 + 105 + 90 + 70 + 65 + 162 + 65 + 187 + 182, it equals 1056 years.

The second part of Gen 6:9 says that Noah was a "just" man and "perfect" in all of those generations. The word "just" comes from the Hebrew word *tsaddiq* which means "just" or "righteous".

Keep in mind that this was long before the Cross and long before Moses. So the idea of God attributing righteousness, or right-standing, to someone before the Abrahamic covenant is a little different than our understanding today. Noah's belief in God, his justness or righteousness, was the lone light in a very dark place. It reminds me of someone else who was attributed righteous without a covenant in place.

> *And he (Abraham) believed in the LORD; and he counted it to him for righteousness.* **Gen 15:6**

Consider the world at the time of Noah. Not only was it corrupt, it was evil and violent.

> *The earth also was corrupt before God, and the earth was filled with violence. And God looked upon the earth, and, behold, it was corrupt; for all flesh had corrupted his way upon the earth.* **Gen 6:11-12**

The next word out of Gen 6:9 is what I really need to point out. The word that the KJV translates as "perfect" is translated as "blameless" in most other translations, but perfect or blameless is not what the Hebrew really says. The Hebrew word is *tamim* and could be better rendered as "complete" or "unblemished"! Consider this in light of Gen 6:12. If Noah is *tamin*, "unblemished," then he is not *shachath*, "ruined".

In all of those generations prior to Noah, ten generations and 1056 years, there had not been any time in which his forefathers' genome had been corrupted or ruined, with angelic DNA. Noah was genetically pure, unblemished, in all of his generations. This is why God spared him and his family. His DNA was a lifeline to the Messiah Jesus, Who would not be born for thousands of years after the time Noah was born.

Satan and the Fallen Angels tried to ruin mankind's seed by not staying in their own heavenly realm, thereby polluting that which God created in His Everlasting Purity. Despite their efforts, the Lord sustained that seed through the purity of eight souls, Noah and his family.

The other thing to remember is that it was God who led the animals to the Ark instead of Noah. That's because only the Lord knew which animals hadn't been genetically corrupted.

> *Of clean beasts, and of beasts that are not clean, and of fowls, and of every thing that creepeth upon the earth, there went in two and two unto Noah into the ark, the male and the female, as God had commanded Noah.* **Gen 7:8-9**

God's Everlasting Purity is a principle by which He operates the universe. The Lord will give you the ability to remain pure in your walk and He will ensure, as He did with Noah, that we continue in that physical purity if we will listen to Him and yield to His Holy Spirit.

Purity Through Fire

> *Wherefore we receiving a kingdom which cannot be moved, let us have grace, whereby we may serve God acceptably with reverence and godly fear for our God is a consuming fire.* **Hebrews 12:28-29**

This is absolutely critical for people to understand: The closer you walk to the light; the more the light burns off the dross in your life.

Being pure in heart involves having a singleness of heart toward God. A pure heart has no hypocrisy, no guile, no hidden motives. The pure heart is marked by transparency and an uncompromising desire to please God in all things. It's more than an external purity of behavior; it's an internal purity of soul.

"Refining" is the final stage of gold and silver production. This process involves removing impurities within the gold and silver that remain after the smelting process. Refiners will superheat the metals until they achieve a molten state. They used to add fullers soap to the molten metal, but these days borax and soda ash are applied to remove impurities. The heat in combination with the borax and soda ash cause the pure gold or silver to separate from the impurities within the molten liquid. Those impurities float to the top of the liquid as a layer of scum and then the scum is skimmed off and discarded. What you're left with is at least 99.9% gold or silver. This is what's known as pure gold or silver.

This percentage is a quantification of the purity of that which is being refined. God also uses a refining process like this in our lives as Believers. He then quantifies our purity in the process. But that quantification isn't a percentage like we use with metals. His quantification of our purity is how much we look like His Son.

Think of the sin in our lives like that scum, that dross. It's the Holy Spirit that brings heat to our lives in order to separate the fruit of the Spirit from the sin, the dross, which still remains in us.

> *And I will bring the third part through the fire, and will refine them as silver is refined, and will try them as gold is tried: they shall call on my name, and I will hear them: I will say, It is my people: and they shall say, The LORD is my God.* **Zech 13:9**

> *Behold, I have refined thee, but not with silver; I have chosen thee in the furnace of affliction.* **Isaiah 48:10**

> *The fining pot is for silver, and the furnace for gold: but the LORD trieth the hearts.* **Proverbs 17:3**

> *For thou, O God, hast proved us: thou hast tried us, as silver is tried.* **Psalm 66:10**

> *And he said, "Go thy way, Daniel: for the words are closed up and sealed till the time of the end. Many shall be purified, and made white, and tried; but the wicked shall do wickedly: and none of the wicked shall understand; but the wise shall understand."* **Daniel 12:9-10**

> *That the trial of your faith, being much more precious than of gold that perisheth, though it be tried with fire, might be found unto praise and honour and glory at the appearing of Jesus Christ.* **1 Peter 1:7**

Silver is the most reflective element that there is. Refiners knew that they had pure silver when they could see their unwavering reflection in the metal. Our lives are a lot like that. When we are refined and all of the dross, the scum of our sin, is skimmed off our lives, we reflect the image of our Master - Jesus. This is the purpose of our purification process. God's goal for our lives is that we look more like His Son and less like the world. That process can be painful, but it is absolutely necessary in developing our purity. John the Baptist told people that Jesus would baptize with the Holy Spirit and with fire.

> *I indeed baptize you with water unto repentance: but he that cometh after me is mightier than I, whose shoes I am not worthy to bear: he shall baptize you with the Holy Ghost, and with fire.* **Matthew 3:11**

Malachi speaks of the coming Messiah as being like a "refiner's fire".

> *But who may abide the day of His coming? And who shall stand when He appeareth? For He is like a refiner's fire, and like fullers' soap. And He shall sit as a refiner and purifier of silver…* **Malachi 3:2**

The idea of fire gives us a vivid picture of the work of the Holy Spirit. Consider that the Spirit's like a fire in at least three ways. He brings God's presence, He shows God's passion for our purposes, He causes God's Purity.

For the grace of God that bringeth salvation hath appeared to all men, teaching us that, denying ungodliness and worldly lusts, we should live soberly, righteously, and godly, in this present world, looking for that blessed hope, and the glorious appearing of the great God and our Saviour Jesus Christ; Who gave Himself for us, that he might redeem us from all iniquity, and purify unto Himself a peculiar people, zealous of good works. **Titus 2:11-14**

Remember, the blood of Jesus cleanses our sin, thus rendering us initially pure when we accept Him. We are then afforded righteousness, or right-standing, before God and justified, declared to be innocent, of sin. Because we live in the world and continue to sin, the purification of our lives is also the ongoing work of the Holy Spirit.

This call to Purity is something that all Christians must heed, including me. I am the least person who should bring this call to you. After writing this section of the book, I can absolutely relate to Isaiah when he said:

Then said I, "Woe is me! For I am undone; because I am a man of unclean lips, and I dwell in the midst of a people of unclean lips: for mine eyes have seen the King, the LORD of hosts." **Isaiah 6:5**

I fall far short of the Purity that God requires of us, but if I can communicate anything to you, it's the fact that this is a process and none of us is where we should be. We always need to remember that it's God's Holy Spirit Who will bring His Purity to pass in our lives if we simply trust and obey the Lord's leading.

The purification process is absolutely necessary for Christians who desire to reflect the light of the Savior in their lives. It's also a process that we willingly embark on for the sake of His Everlasting Purity.

Purer In Heart, Oh God

Purer in heart, O God, help me to be;
May I devote my life wholly to Thee:
Watch Thou my wayward feet,
Guide me with counsel sweet;
Purer in heart, help me to be.

Purer in heart, O God, help me to be;
Teach me to do Thy will most lovingly;
Be Thou my friend and guide,
Let me with Thee abide;
Purer in heart, help me to be.

Purer in heart, O God, help me to be;
Until Thy holy face one day I see:
Keep me from secret sin,
Reign Thou my soul within;
Purer in heart, help me to be.

HELP 8

His Everlasting Proclamation

I am the LORD, and there is none else, there is no God beside me:

I girded thee, though thou hast not known me.

That they may know from the rising of the sun, and from the west, that there is none beside me.

I am the LORD, and there is none else.

Isaiah 45:5-6

Proclamation

The power of God's Everlasting Proclamations reverberates throughout the universe for eternity. The sound of those Proclamations is one of the universe's most powerful forces.

Scientists and researchers have experimented with water to illustrate the impact of sound. What they've discovered is amazing. There is structure to water and water has a memory.

In their analysis, these researchers spoke (proclaimed) lovingly and kindly to plain samples of water. They then flash-froze it and observed it under a microscope. They saw structure, continuity and unimaginable beauty. In a second sample, they cursed the water and shouted at it (proclaimed). When it was flash-frozen, the water was darkened and only a blob. In the third test, they completely ignored the water (no proclamations) and then quickly froze it. That water had no structure at all and was black under the microscope. Interestingly, they also found that the cursed water literally dies and plants can't even grow in it.

They also did experiments with music, with similar results. Classical music had distinct patterns of beauty, which altered depending on which composer was played i.e., Bach, Mozart, Beethoven, etc. The same experiments with heavy metal music again produced blobs of dark unstructured ugliness.

If you consider for a moment that sound is a form of proclamation, the results of these experiments have important implications.

In the creation of the universe, sound preceded light; God said (proclaimed) *"let there be light"*. He called something into being that was hidden, shielded or not in the form it had been before. God spoke with a voice, an audible tone.

Light waves are examples of electromagnetic waves and sound waves are mechanical waves. Physicists have postulated that at the fundamental level those sound waves must be fluctuations of the electromagnetic field propagating through matter. In other words, sound is a form of electromagnetic radiation, which is the basis for light. God's Proclamations are not just sound, they are light and life.

In him was life; and the life was the light of men. John 1:4

The Bible says that God created man in His image (Gen 1:26) and part of that creation was our ability to speak. Mankind's ability to co-create is our ability to communicate. Again, this is based upon sound and our ability to hear, or to process the information and act upon it.

Without man's ability to proclaim or to speak, there would be no communication. Proclamation is essential for our communication process. Without the ability to communicate, mankind could not accomplish all that we have accomplished, for good or bad.

The tower of Babel is a good example. The devil knew that if he could control the speech of the world, our proclamations, he could direct the outcome of the world by manipulating how mankind spoke.

Of course God also understood this and had no choice but to stop man from being able to communicate, to proclaim, with a single understandable language, and therefore scattered their language of rebellion.

And the whole earth was of one language, and of one speech. Gen 11:1

And the LORD said, "Behold, the people is one, and they have all one language; and this they begin to do: and now nothing will be restrained from them, which they have imagined to do. Go to, let us go down, and there confound their language, that they may not understand one another's speech." **Gen 11:6-7**

Proclamation in scripture and through the audible voice of God or the inaudible voice of the Holy Spirit is a powerful weapon. This is why God gives us His Word to substitute for our doubt and our fears. With it, we're able to align our will with God.

And in that co-creation of lining up our words and Proclamations with His Words and Proclamations, He infuses our lives with His presence and His power.

That infusion was demonstrated in Moses when he made proclamations on God's behalf to Egypt to demand that the children of Israel be set free. As Pharaoh found out, God's Proclamations establish Who He is versus who we are. When He proclaims, who can stand against Him?

Thus saith the LORD the King of Israel, and His redeemer the LORD of hosts; "I am the first, and I am the last; and beside me there is no God. And who, as I, shall call, and shall declare it, and set it in order for me, since I appointed the ancient people? And the things that are coming, and shall come, let them shew unto them. Fear ye not, neither be afraid: have not I told thee from that time, and have declared it? Ye are even my witnesses. Is there a God beside me? Yea, there is no God; I know not any." **Isaiah 44:6-8**

God proclaims to the hosts of heaven, the redeemed of the Lord. As you will find in this H.E.L.P., every single Proclamation of God is as eternal as His creative power is eternal.

There is no limit to God's Everlasting Proclamations.

Chapter 21

The Power of Proclamation

And God said, "Let there be light:" and there was light.

Genesis 1:3

*E*x nihilo is Latin and means "from nothing". We know from the Word, that only God Himself can create something out of nothing. That's pretty much how He created the universe.

The earth and everything in it and on it; the heavens and every piece of light that you see in the sky; the universe and its vast expanse which is way beyond what you and I can see or even imagine, was all created by a Being Who existed independently before everything else was created.

Linear time and space as we understand it has not always existed, but God has always existed. Simply by proclaiming it to be so, He caused everything else to come into being (Col 1:16-17).

Believers accept this creative fact but science still struggles with the reality. Rather than attributing creation to God, science develops theories like "the big bang" to explain the universe's linear beginning.

Despite the big bang sounding an awful lot like what happened when God pronounced, *"Let there be light"*, their theorizing is a testimony to man's desire to grasp and explain the unfathomable. The describing of creation from a solely scientific worldview causes intellectuals and academics alike to exclude the Creator of all things. Now, how smart is that?

There's a standard based upon the uniqueness and attributes of God as Creator that is unbendable to anything and everyone. That's because His Word is holy and it's pure. It's the quintessential measuring rod for all that's right and contrasts against all that's wrong.

I will worship toward thy holy temple, and praise thy name for thy lovingkindness and for thy truth: for thou hast magnified thy word above all thy name. **Psalm 138:2**

With that assurance, we know that by God simply speaking the Word, proclaiming creation, He created everything including light. But even light's creation is a challenge for those big-brained scientists who try to reason away such a supernatural magnificent eruption of power in the illumination of the universe. Their problem, in a nutshell, is that since light was the third thing that was created according to the scripture, it's very old. Because of that, those secular scientists struggle to understand light's origin.

> *When we look out at the Universe today, highlighted against the vast, empty blackness of the sky are points of light: stars, galaxies, nebulae and more. Yet there was a time in the distant past before any of those things had formed, just after the Big Bang, where the Universe was still filled with light. If we look in the microwave part of the spectrum, we can find the remnants of this light today in the form of the Cosmic Microwave Background (CMB). But even the CMB is relatively late: we're seeing its light from 380,000 years after the Big Bang. Light, as far as we know it, existed even before that. After centuries of investigating the origins of the Universe, science has finally uncovered what physically happened to "let there be light" in space.[20]*

> *So where did this light — the first light in the Universe — first come from? It didn't come from stars, because it predates the stars. It wasn't emitted by atoms, because it predates the formation of neutral atoms in the Universe. If we continue to extrapolate backwards to higher and higher energies, we find some strange things out: thanks to Einstein's $E = mc2$, these quanta of light could interact with one another, spontaneously producing particle-antiparticle pairs of matter and antimatter![21]*

While science continues to try to find answers outside of the Bible, we know that this idea of the origin of light was purposed from the very beginning with God's own Proclamation, *"Let there be light…"* God spoke the world into existence and that creative force of God's love, purpose, intention, design and desire is echoing throughout eternity, for eternity.

> *By the word of the LORD were the heavens made; and all the host of them by the breath of His mouth.* **Psalm 33:6**

The truth of these words and His Proclamations are made evident in the creation around us.

This is the power of His Everlasting Proclamation.

Thinking Outside The Box

I said at the beginning of this book that I wanted to help you to think differently about the Word and to challenge what mainstream Church calls Christianity. I wanted to be real, vulnerable and literal.

For more than 400 years, since the KJV Bible came out, far too many Christians have just taken at face value what they "think" the Bible is saying. As I lamented earlier, pastors and teachers are doing the same thing and teaching their flocks in that way. The Bible says, *"My people are destroyed for lack of knowledge…"*

---

20 Ethan Siegel, "Science Uncovers The Origin Of The First Light In The Universe." Forbes, https://www.forbes.com/sites/startswithabang/2017/06/30/science-uncovers-the-origin-of-the-first-light-in-the-universe/#73412dd63487, (June 30, 2017).

21 Ibid.

(Hosea 4:6). It's apparent to me that some of that destruction is self-imposed because we fail to study the Word to show ourselves approved.

In the following section you'll find that I've done some extensive investigative study on the original language of these portions of scripture. Much of what you hear may be absolutely foreign to you if you've taken what has been taught from the pulpit, TV or radio at face value and never looked at the scriptures deeply.

But don't just take my word for it. In our modern era, you don't need to go to seminary, or Bible college to see what the original languages of the Hebrew, Greek and Aramaic are saying. There are a plethora of online lexicons and expository dictionaries you can access for free.

When you see what God's Proclamations are in their original languages, it's like adding color and depth to a plain black-and-white sketch. The results can be very illuminating.

To help you see what I'm driving at, let's break down the different words that are used for the word "proclamation".

Declaring

Moreover, brethren, I declare unto you the gospel which I preached unto you, which also ye have received, and wherein ye stand; by which also ye are saved, if ye keep in memory what I preached unto you, unless ye have believed in vain. **1 Cor 15:1-2**

The word "declare" in the verse above comes from the Greek word *gnórizó* and means "to make known" or "to inform". Notice that "declaring" is not "proclaiming" as some people might think. Declaring is akin to "teaching" or even "showing". For instance, The Declaration of Independence was a visual notice to the British that the Colonies had had enough.

The heavens declare the glory of God; and the firmament sheweth His handywork. **Psalm 19:1**

This is an interesting verse in that the word used here in the KJV for "declare" comes from the Hebrew word *saphar* which literally means to "recount" or "relate to". Again, it gives the idea of informing all creation about God's awesome creative power simply by looking up at the sky.

Then we see the word "sheweth". This word is from the Hebrew *nagad*, which means "to make conspicuous" or "to declare", or "make known".

Both the Greek and the Hebrew carry the same idea. Declaring is to inform but it is not the same as proclaiming.

Confessing

Confession means, "to say the same as". So when we are confessing as Christians we are saying the same things with our mouths as God already said in His Word.

That if thou shalt confess with thy mouth the Lord Jesus, and shalt believe in thine heart that God hath raised Him from the dead, thou shalt be saved. For with the heart man believeth unto righteousness; and with the mouth confession is made unto salvation. **Romans 10:9-10**

This is a physical action by Believers to make their mouths, and the words coming out of them, agree with the Word of God. This is in itself a proclamation. By saying what God says , we put ourselves in the position of receiving the full backing and authority of God.

I recently saw a movie where an advisor to the President said, *"I speak for the President on this matter. I have his full authority. If you're talking to me, you're talking to him."* This is the idea we get with the word "confession". The Bible says that Jesus is the High Priest of our confession.

> *Wherefore, holy brethren, partakers of the heavenly calling, consider the Apostle and High Priest of our profession, Christ Jesus.* **Heb 3:1**

He's our High Priest in respect to what we confess. When it comes to our confessions of the Word, it's like Jesus saying, "Devil, if you're talking to him, you're talking to Me."

> *And Jesus came and spake unto them, saying, "All power is given unto me in heaven and in earth. Go ye therefore, and teach all nations, baptizing them in the name of the Father, and of the Son, and of the Holy Ghost: Teaching them to observe all things whatsoever I have commanded you: and, lo, I am with you always, even unto the end of the world. Amen."* **Matt 28:18-20**

If we do not confess those things in the Word but we remain silent, we shut off any connection to our High Priest through our silence. It's not enough to "believe". Our belief must be accompanied by faith action, either in Word or in deed. Silence, inaction and complacency are the equivalent of disregarding our confession, or proclamation, of the Word which results in our disconnection to Jesus and His victory.

Believe me when I tell you that God is serious about our proclamation of Him. One day I was extremely frustrated and upset with supposed Christians who will not speak up or acknowledge Jesus in their lives. The Lord immediately broke into my thoughts and asked me this simple question: *"Steve, how many people believe when I said, "Whosoever will confess me before men, will I also confess before my Father in heaven?"'*

I thought about this for a second and answered Him, *"Lord, evidently not many or they would be doing so."*

Most people who claim to be Christians do not even mention the name of Jesus because they're too scared or intimidated because of simple social pressure.

Give me a break!

The Lord is "dead serious" about our verbal acknowledgment of our relationship and our identification with Him - eternally "dead serious" if you know what I mean.

> *Whosoever therefore shall confess me before men, him will I confess also before my Father which is in heaven. But whosoever shall deny me before men, him will I also deny before my Father which is in heaven.* **Matt 10:32-33**

It appears to me that people don't take Jesus seriously or at His word. If you're a Christian, let there be no doubt in your mind, Jesus means what He says.

That's not to say that we can use the Word on our own accord and act or speak without God's direction. Rather, via the prompting of the Holy Spirit, we will have the words or actions needed to act at the time we need them.

> *Also I say unto you, "Whosoever shall confess me before men, him shall the Son of man also confess before the angels of God: But he that denieth me before men shall be denied before the angels of*

God. And whosoever shall speak a word against the Son of Man, it shall be forgiven him: but unto him that blasphemeth against the Holy Ghost it shall not be forgiven." And when they bring you unto the synagogues, and unto magistrates, and powers, take ye no thought how or what thing ye shall answer, or what ye shall say: For the Holy Ghost shall teach you in the same hour what ye ought to say. **Luke 12:8-12**

If you're continually thinking about His Word and are walking and talking with the Lord throughout your day, in the moment you need to represent Him, your words will be His words. This is our confession, or our proclamation.

Heralding and Preaching

Proclaiming is closely related to the activity of heralding. In the old days, a herald was also known as an "officer of arms" and was an officer of a monarch or government official. He was someone who was given the official duty of making announcements, or a messenger, especially in a time of war. A Herald was also a crier, "Hear ye, hear ye…" and was the person responsible to announce news or give official proclamations, which normally preceded or foreshadowed an event.

Closely related to heralding is the word "preach" or "preaching". As an example, Jesus says in **Matt 24:14**:

And this gospel of the kingdom shall be preached in all the world for a witness unto all nations; and then shall the end come.

The word for "preached" is the Greek word *kérussó*, which means "to herald," "proclaim" or "preach".

So someone who preaches the Word of God is someone who is heralding the Word of God, "Hear ye, hear ye…"

There's a huge difference between proclaiming the Word of God and teaching the Word of God. Teaching is passive. Proclaiming is assertive. Teaching imparts knowledge and understanding. There's a lot of Bible teaching going on today. There's teaching in mega-churches, teaching on the radio, teaching on television and teaching on the internet.

So why, with all this Bible "teaching", don't we see a perceivable change in the hearers' lives? People go into the buildings, sit for an hour, and walk out the same.

Contrarily, in the past we saw men and women of God proclaiming, declaring, heralding and preaching the Word. Through their proclamations, revival happened. People, who sat under those declarations, would fall under the conviction of the Holy Spirit, repent and be changed. There was power in those messages because they are designed to be assertive, in your face and to the point.

Don't get me wrong; there was plenty of hogwash that went on in the pulpit even back then. People would be dramatic without the power of the Spirit, only to generate an emotional response through theater. While preaching by itself is not necessarily godly, preaching under the anointing of the Holy Ghost is life-changing and dynamic.

I'm not saying that teaching doesn't have a place in the Church's message. There is a time to teach, but my point is that most pastors and teachers have shied away from preaching or proclaiming because of their own self-consciousness or laziness, or the lack of palpability by the audience. In fear of empty church seats, pastors continue to speak to empty hearts based upon their own lack of relationship with the Lord Jesus. The end result of failing to deliver the anointed message of God is that the people remain in bondage.

That seeing they may see, and not perceive; and hearing they may hear, and not understand; lest at any time they should be converted, and their sins should be forgiven them. **Mark 4:12**

This know also, that in the last days perilous times shall come. For men shall be lovers of their own selves, covetous, boasters, proud, blasphemers, disobedient to parents, unthankful, unholy, without natural affection, trucebreakers, false accusers, incontinent, fierce, despisers of those that are good, traitors, heady, highminded, lovers of pleasures more than lovers of God; Having a form of godliness, but denying the power thereof: from such turn away. For of this sort are they which creep into houses, and lead captive silly women laden with sins, led away with divers lusts, ever learning, and never able to come to the knowledge of the truth. **2 Tim 3:1-7**

Conviction under God-appointed and Holy Ghost-anointed preaching is a powerful thing. God's Word is supernatural power and our proclamation of it has extra-dimensional effects in ways that we cannot see.

Proclamation

There is power in Proclamation.

The word "proclaim" comes from the Greek word *kérussó*, and appears in the NT sixty times. We've already seen this word for preach. It means "to be a herald," or "to officiate as a herald" or "to proclaim like a herald". It always suggests an air of formality, gravity and authority, which must be listened to and obeyed. It also means "to publish," or "proclaim openly something that must be done". Lastly, it's used as in a public proclamation of the gospel and issues pertaining to it.

We see the word translated in the following manner in the NT: Made proclamation 1x, preach 16x, preached 10x, preacher 1x, preaches 2x, preaching 11x, proclaim 8x, proclaimed 6x and proclaiming 6x.

"Proclaim" from the Hebrew is more diverse because there are a few different words used in the OT for its meaning.

The first comes from the Hebrew word *qara*, which means "to call," "to read" or "to proclaim". This is the same word that's repeated in Genesis. **Gen 1:8** says:

And God called the firmament Heaven. And the evening and the morning were the second day.

God "called" the firmament Heaven or He proclaimed it to be Heaven.

Qara is used 734 times in the OT and in many more ways than just proclaiming.

The next transliteration of the word proclaim comes from the Hebrew *tsaaq* which means to "cry out", "to cry" or "to call". This word is used 55 times.

Apaggelló is another word translated as proclaim in the OT where it's used 47 times. It means "to report", "to announce" and "to declare".

Life and Death in The Tongue

God's people are also supposed to proclaim. Life and death is in the tongue.

Death and life are in the power of the tongue: and they that love it shall eat the fruit thereof. **Proverbs 18:21**

By our words we shall be justified and by our words we shall be condemned.

O generation of vipers, how can ye, being evil, speak good things? For out of the abundance of the heart the mouth speaketh. A good man out of the good treasure of the heart bringeth forth good things: and an evil man out of the evil treasure bringeth forth evil things. But I say unto you: That every idle word that men shall speak, they shall give account thereof in the day of judgment. For by thy words thou shalt be justified, and by thy words thou shalt be condemned. **Matt 12:34-37**

The proclamation of our testimony reminds all the principalities and powers, spiritual wickedness in heavenly places, the devils, and all forms of evil that God rules and reigns.

Who is like unto thee, O LORD, among the gods? Who is like thee, glorious in holiness, fearful in praises, doing wonders? **Exodus 15:11**

The physical action of moving our lips and speaking out loud about the glory of God is a powerful way to interact with the world around us. Notice I said the "physical action" of doing so. It's not enough to simply think to God, or think about God. To only think about Him leaves those thoughts and words bound up in your head. You have to let those words out, because it is in proclaiming verbally Who He is that we interact with the world around us.

When you are verbal, two important parties hear your proclamations of God's greatness:

- ~ **The devil and his minions hear you. As a consequence, they're put on notice of your allegiance and adherence to His Word;**

- ~ **You hear those proclamations with your own ears. In doing so, your faith is reinforced and your spirit strengthened.**

This is why praise and worship is so important. I spoke briefly about praise and worship in Chapter 11, but when it comes to proclaiming God and the inter-dimensional effects that heartfelt praise and worship have, it is worth revisiting. A perfect example of this is Jesus' triumphal entry into Jerusalem.

Remember the scene:

And they brought him to Jesus: and they cast their garments upon the colt, and they set Jesus thereon. And as He went, they spread their clothes in the way. And when He was come nigh, even now at the descent of the mount of Olives, the whole multitude of the disciples began to rejoice and praise God with a loud voice for all the mighty works that they had seen, saying, "Blessed be the King that cometh in the name of the Lord: peace in heaven, and glory in the highest." **Luke 19:35-38**

It's important to recognize that although the Greek word for proclaiming isn't here, the people are definitely proclaiming Him to be King by their actions and who could blame them? They'd longed for their Messiah to come. They'd been under Roman rule for more than sixty years. They knew that the OT promised them a Savior. Based upon the miracles they saw and the power of God that was evident everywhere that Jesus went, they proclaimed Him to be the King and Messiah they had long awaited!

"Hosanna, Lord!" "Hosanna in the highest!"

But they were looking for an earthly kingdom to be reestablished in Israel and this was not what the Messiah was supposed to do at all. Jesus' goal was to ensure that His message of salvation went everywhere in the world and only then the end would come (Matt 24:14). The Lord further understood that He would have to die in order to kick over that earthly kingdom into an eternal, supernatural kingdom.

But this is the part that doesn't quite make sense.

Even with all that understanding, He still let them proclaim Him King?

In fact, that proclamation was extremely important. So much so that we read in the next verses the following:

> *And some of the Pharisees from among the multitude said unto Him, "Master, rebuke thy disciples." And He answered and said unto them, "I tell you that, if these should hold their peace, the stones would immediately cry out."* **Luke 19:39-40**

Wow! Talk about an example of Proclaiming God's Glory! Even the very rocks would proclaim that Jesus is King!

The whole idea of the rocks crying out makes me ask a few questions about the text:

~ **Translation:** What does the phrase "rocks cry out" really mean? Would they cry out in joy? Are we talking about a sorrowful cry? Is it a cry at all, or is it just that they would make a sound?

~ **Inanimate Objects Crying Out From Scripture:** Are there other examples in the Word where inanimate objects "cried" out?

~ **Did He Know:** What was the significance to the rocks crying? Would it have been a proclamation? If so, to what or whom would those rocks be proclaiming?

1…The Translation: When Jesus said that the very rocks would "cry out", we see in the Greek that the word used is *krazó*, which literally means "to scream" or "cry out". What's interesting about the translation is that it goes even further than that. *Krazó* is an onomatopoetic term, as in onomatopoeia.

An onomatopoeia is not a word at all, but a sound that people make to represent a word. It's like you saying, "And all of a sudden the gun went off, **bang!**" Or, "Her heels clicked on the sidewalk, **click, click, click.**"

Krazó is the sound of a raven's piercing cry like "caw, caw!" It's the sound of an urgent scream or shriek, which is designed to express deep emotion.

In addition, the KJV translates the verse as, *"…if these should hold their peace…"*; but in reality in the original language Jesus wasn't referring to the people at all. What He intimates is more like, *"If this event didn't occur..."* meaning the worship and proclamation, *"then the stones would shriek like ravens!"*

Now, you're probably scratching your head and wondering what this is all about. It'll become clear with my third point on this scripture.

2...Inanimate Objects Crying Out From Scripture: There are several examples where declarations, proclamations, warnings or cryings have been heard from inanimate objects in scripture. Could it be that Jesus was using this type of illustration so the Pharisees understood the weight of what was happening? Because those pharisaical leaders were pious, arrogantly so, and well-studied in the OT, their minds would probably have immediately remembered the following instances:

> *And Cain talked with Abel his brother: and it came to pass, when they were in the field, that Cain rose up against Abel his brother, and slew him. And the LORD said unto Cain, "Where is Abel thy brother?" And he said, "I know not: Am I my brother's keeper?" And He said, "What hast thou done? The voice of thy brother's blood crieth unto me from the ground. And now art thou cursed from the earth, which hath opened her mouth to receive thy brother's blood from thy hand. When thou tillest the ground, it shall not henceforth yield unto thee her strength; a fugitive and a vagabond shalt thou be in the earth."* **Gen 4:8-12**

This incident was so important that it's mentioned later in the Book of Hebrews:

> *And to Jesus the mediator of the new covenant, and to the blood of sprinkling, that speaketh better things than that of Abel.* **Hebrews 12:24**

Joshua made a covenant with the people to serve God and said that a stone would be a witness against them:

> *So Joshua made a covenant with the people that day, and set them a statute and an ordinance in Shechem. And Joshua wrote these words in the book of the law of God, and took a great stone, and set it up there under an oak, that was by the sanctuary of the LORD. And Joshua said unto all the people, "Behold, this stone shall be a witness unto us; for it hath heard all the words of the LORD which He spake unto us: it shall be therefore a witness unto you, lest ye deny your God."* **Joshua 24:25-27**

We also see another example of stones crying out in Habakkuk where it talks about a wall crying out against those who had plotted greedy plans.

> *Woe to him that coveteth an evil covetousness to his house, that he may set his nest on high, that he may be delivered from the power of evil! Thou hast consulted shame to thy house by cutting off many people, and hast sinned against thy soul. For the stone shall cry out of the wall, and the beam out of the timber shall answer it.* **Habakkuk 2:9-11**

Throughout scripture inanimate objects are crying out or proclaiming against someone. Jesus knew all of these examples and the Pharisees should have, which leads me to my third point.

3...Did He Know: When it comes to Jesus' triumphal entry, could His reference to the rocks crying out denote a proclamation to the Pharisees about the Lord's foreknowledge of events that would soon transpire in Jerusalem?

263

When everyone reads this excerpt from Luke and then they read about the sourpuss comments by the Pharisees trying to shut the people up, they automatically think Jesus is telling them, *"Are you kidding me? They're so excited to see their promised Messiah that there's no way anyone could contain that excitement!"*

But this isn't what His discourse with the Pharisees was about at all.

On numerous occasions the people sought to proclaim Him Messiah and King, but He declined because He understood that His kingdom was a supernatural one and not a physical one.

> *Then those men, when they had seen the miracle that Jesus did, said, "This is of a truth that prophet that should come into the world." When Jesus therefore perceived that they would come and take Him by force, to make Him a king, He departed again into a mountain himself alone.* **John 6:14-15**

> *Jesus answered, "My kingdom is not of this world: if my kingdom were of this world, then would my servants fight, that I should not be delivered to the Jews: but now is my kingdom not from hence."* **John 18:36**

Let me go back to the word *krazó* from **Luke 19:40** and the whole idea that the rocks would shriek like a raven if He tried to stop the people from celebrating Him.

Think about a raven and what it's symbolic of.

Death. Ravens hang around dead carcasses to pick at their bodies.

With that analogy of the ravens that He Himself used, it signifies that He's not basking in the warmth of the people's praises and finally succumbing to their desire to proclaim Him King. His inaction to stop them is not His acquiescence as if to say, *"Alright, alright. You got me. I'll be your king."*

Such acquiescence would be contrary to the previous dissuasions by Him in not letting the people proclaim Him as king.

> *And when they wanted wine, the mother of Jesus saith unto Him, "They have no wine." Jesus saith unto her, "Woman, what have I to do with thee? Mine hour is not yet come."* **John 2:3-4**

So my question is: Why, all of a sudden, did He allow the people to proclaim Him Messiah and King during His triumphal entry into Jerusalem? What changed?

The answer is: Nothing changed!

As we know in hindsight, it was His death on the Cross and His resurrection that changed everything. And it wasn't until just before His arrest that He said the following:

> *And Jesus answered them, saying, "The hour is come, that the Son of man should be glorified."* **John 12:23**

Prior to this passage, we don't see any catalyst for this change of heart from Jesus. And if He didn't change His mind on letting them call Him King, did He have an unknown motive for allowing their actions?

Every Believer at that time, and the vast majority of Believers in our day, view His going into Jerusalem as a "triumphal entry," a coronation of sorts.

I would submit to you that in the Lord's mind, this was not a triumphal entry at all.

Rather, I believe that Jesus saw it for what it was: A funeral procession!

I would further submit to you that since He knew that He was going to die a horrible death on a Cross, that His reference to the raven's cry of the rocks was in and of itself a proclamation.

Remember that even though they couldn't be seen, Satan and his demonic cohorts were present on that road that day. They heard the people's proclamation of Jesus as King and they laughed. They laughed because they knew their own plans to have Him killed and they were salivating at the prospect.

Jesus allowed those arrogant Fallen Angels and demons to believe that the people were idiots. Satan knew that he would dash their hopes and dreams with the killing of their Messiah.

Jesus also allowed the people to proclaim His name and His personage as a siren call to those devils about what would soon happen. There was a reason He would have allowed the rocks and the people to proclaim His name at this funeral procession.

He knew that although He had to die, His Father would raise Him from the dead in resurrection power. We know this because early on in His earthly ministry, just after He turned the water to wine, He told us that the Father would raise Him.

> Then answered the Jews and said unto him, "What sign shewest thou unto us, seeing that thou doest these things?" Jesus answered and said unto them, "Destroy this temple, and in three days I will raise it up." Then said the Jews, "Forty and six years was this temple in building, and wilt thou rear it up in three days?" But He spake of the temple of His body. When therefore He was risen from the dead, his disciples remembered that He had said this unto them; and they believed the scripture, and the word which Jesus had said. **John 2:18-23**

The Lord knew that the procession into Jerusalem was the final leg before He would be killed. In His mind, it wasn't celebratory: He was on a mission.

He also knew that after He was raised from the dead, He would then show up at the devil's doorstep to yank the keys of Hell and death from his hand.

Very simply, the proclamation of the people and the raven's cry of the rocks were a warning, a gauntlet, by our Lord in which He declared:

I'm coming for you, devil!

Hallelujah!

A Damning Proclamation

The most damning proclamation in the Bible is the one God made against Satan in Genesis 3. This happened when the serpent deceived Eve and caused God's newest creation to fall. It's this Proclamation of God that sets everything else in motion when it comes to the Lord's judgment against the devil.

Back in 2017, I coauthored a book with Tom Horn called *Unearthing The Lost World Of The Cloudeaters*. This book had to do with ancient angelic technology and evidence, which is often overlooked by the mainstream. It's an excellent resource and one I'd recommend if you were interested in such things. You can get a copy on my website.

In laying the background about who Satan is and what he's been trying to do for millennia, I did extensive research into the Garden account regarding his interaction with Adam and Eve. That work is an important stepping-stone to understanding God's Proclamations against him.

I'm including that segment of the book here for your benefit. When you're finished reading, we'll pick up with this discussion in the next chapter.

Clipped Wings

(Begin Excerpt)

As previously discussed, although the Angels were free to leave the place or dimension wherein they were created to exist, an exit from that habitation had consequences. We have a general idea when they got their wings clipped, but was limitation set on the Angels before the Pre-Adamic era, or after? Are there some Angels who are more limited than others?

Pseudepigraphal writings like the *Book of Enoch* give us some answers, but perhaps the best place to start is with humanity's beginning in the Bible itself. If we dig into the original language of **Genesis 3:11-15**, we find some puzzle pieces from the account of what happened in the Garden:

> And he said, "Who told thee that thou was naked? Hast thou eaten of the tree, whereof I commanded thee that thou shouldest not eat?" And the man said, "The woman whom thou gavest to be with me, she gave me of the tree, and I did eat." And the LORD God said unto the woman, "What is this that thou hast done?" And the woman said, "The serpent beguiled me, and I did eat. And the LORD God said unto the serpent, "Because thou hast done this, thou art cursed above all cattle, and above every beast of the field; upon thy belly shalt thou go, and dust shalt thou eat all the days of thy life."

A casual reading of this passage in any translation from other than the original Hebrew overlooks the deeper meaning of the words, such as the word translated "serpent". That word in Hebrew is *nachash*, נָחָשׁ, Strong's #H5175. *Nachash* comes from an "unused" root. This is an interesting point of Hebrew grammar, which Messianic Jewish scholar Dr. Arnold Fruchtenburg explains this way:

> What is meant by "unused" root is that though the root of the word has a specific meaning, you will not find that root meaning in literature. Only its derived meanings will be found. Knowing the root meaning of a word, then, is only the first step. The root meaning of a word may be exactly as it says, but that root may not even be used in biblical literature. Only derived meanings might be used, and, therefore, you must learn to distinguish between the root meaning and its derived meanings.[22]

Hebrew roots are usually three letters, which can be used to make other words of related meanings. Sometimes all that distinguishes the different forms of the root are the vowel sounds, but this is where it gets interesting – and confusing. Hebrew has no written vowels, so vowel sounds are depicted with the use of special marks called "points". If the vowel points are not written, as often happens in Hebrew, then the translator is left to guess what the actual word means. It's an educated guess, of course; there are only so

---

22 Dr. Arnold Fruchtenbaum, "Biblical Answers to Tough Questions: Hebrew Language", http://www.ariel.org/qa/qhebrew.htm, (December 26, 2016).

many meanings for each word, but this explains how the same passage in ancient Hebrew can be translated several different ways.

The word serpent, *Nachash* (שָׁחָנ, Strong's #H5175), comes from the root *nachash* (שָׁחָנ, Strong's #H5172). In writing the two words are virtually identical, differing only by one vowel point, but the meanings are very different. The root word means, *"to practice divination or observe signs."*

Divination is also translated as witchcraft, and witchcraft implies working magic, perhaps by casting spells. This is how we get the connection from the root word, nachash, to its nearly identical derivative. The Strong's definition of the root is, "to hiss, i.e., whisper a (magic) spell". That hissing sound that is made by the witch, diviner, or conjurer is the link to the snake, an animal which makes no sound from its throat other than hissing.

What does this do for our understanding of Genesis 3? It explains the link between *nachash* the serpent and *nachash* the diviner; the one possessing hidden power or knowledge. The translators of the KJV, and most other translations for that matter, adopt the meaning of nachash as being a serpent, snake, or reptile. However, the word by itself does not specifically say that the being in Genesis 3 is a serpent. We could just as easily translate it as, *"the one who hisses and practices witchcraft."*

As we learn from other passages in the Bible (such as Ezekiel 28:1-19), this creature is Lucifer, or Satan. According to 2 Corinthians 11:14, Satan masquerades as an angel of light. That is definitely not a slithering snake. He can make himself appealing, which is one of his greatest powers. Why would Eve, or any of us today, listen to Satan if he appeared as an ugly serpent?

It does seem, though, that Satan likes the moniker of snake or serpent. As an example, the Mayans and other ancient civilizations of Central and South American worshiped a plumed or feathered serpent named Quetzalcoatl. Perhaps Quetzalcoatl was one of a number of demonic manifestations as snakes or serpents recorded throughout human history. It may be that Satan's apparent fondness for the form of a serpent is an effort at spiritual propaganda: turning a negative feature into something positive. We humans may not like snakes, but we do like dragons. Quetzalcoatl and his kin from China and other cultures are essentially glorified snakes with wings. All of them fall into the category of serpent.

In our investigation, this "serpent" of Genesis 3 is not some kind of reptile, but a practitioner of enchantment. Does this stand up to scrutiny elsewhere in the Bible? We find the answer in I Samuel 15:23, where the prophet Samuel defines the sin of King Saul by saying,

"For rebellion is as the sin of witchcraft, and stubbornness is as iniquity and idolatry."

Rebellion in God's eyes is like witchcraft. This is very important and it sheds some light on how God must have seen Lucifer's leadership of the angelic rebellion. Remember that Satan said he wanted to be "like the Most High" (Isaiah 14;14), and that his rebellion apparently started long before his appearance in the Garden of Eden. The Creator was intimately familiar with Satan's rebellious attitude, and recognized it in him before it manifested in actions against Him. The passage in Isaiah 14 and the parallel in Ezekiel 28 address this rebellious pride and haughtiness. Clearly God was not talking to a simple serpent in Genesis 3:14.

In the previous verse, according to the KJV, Eve said that the serpent "beguiled" her. This word beguiled is *nasha*, (אָשָׁנ), from Strong's # H5378. It is translated as "deceived", but it means much more than that. This word literally means "to make someone a debtor". This is the consequence of the sin of Adam and Eve in the Garden, a consequence that continues to bear bitter fruit in our own sin to this day. The act of rebellion against the Creator's command put humanity into such debt that it could only be satisfied by the blood of Jesus Christ. But Satan was the banker who wrote the note!

The point of this chapter is to make the case that the Fallen Angels, after having their wings clipped, had to resort to technology to accomplish their goals. The translation of Genesis is germane to that discussion, as we see in the curse God pronounced on the devil in **Genesis 3:14**:

> And the LORD God said unto the serpent,

> "Because thou hast done this, thou art cursed above all cattle, and above every beast of the field; upon
> thy belly shalt thou go, and dust shalt thou eat all the days of thy life."

"All cattle" in Hebrew is *behemah*, (בְּהֵמָה), Strong's #H929, which is also derived from an unused root. A better translation is "beast", and that is how the KJV renders the term in most of the 189 instances where it appears in the OT.

This is where it gets interesting. Remember God had put man over all the beasts He created, as we see in **Genesis 1:26**:

> And God said, "Let us make man in our image, after our likeness: and let them have dominion over
> the fish of the sea, and over the fowl of the air, and over the cattle, and over all the earth, and over every
> creeping thing that creepeth upon the earth."

Here again the KJV translators use "cattle" for *behemah*. Think what this means in regard to that curse in Genesis 3:14. What God is telling this arrogant angel – the one He had created to be over the other Angels, and the most beautiful of them all – is that He had just lowered his position not only to a place beneath mankind, but under all the animals!

Imagine the devil's indignation. As a consequence of tricking Adam and Eve into rebellion and putting mankind in bondage, he was now even lower than the creeping things. In God's eyes, he was lower than a bug!

The curse goes on to say, "upon thy belly". The Hebrew term translated as belly is *gachon*, (גָּחוֹן), Strong's #H1512, a word considered to be derived from the root word *giach*, (גִּיחַ), Strong's #H1518. *Giach* means "bursting forth" or "gushing forth", such as waters breaking forth (**Job 38:8**), something or someone breaking out (**Ezekiel 32:2**), or the breaking forth from the womb (**Psalm 22:9; Micah 4:10**). This is the way the devil is to move, as God says, "upon thy belly shalt thou go, and dust shalt thou eat all the days of thy life." "Shalt thou go" in Hebrew is *halak*, (הָלַךְ), Strong's #H1980, which means: "to go", "to come" or . . . "TO WALK"!

Now we arrive at the last part of the curse, a very important phrase translated as, "dust shall thou eat." There is nothing controversial in this translation. "Eat" means just what is says: eat, devour, consume. "Dust" also means what we would expect: dust, powder, dry earth. Where it interests us is in the implications we draw from the devil's new purpose "all the days of thy life". Instead of ruling over the Creator's angelic dominion, he gets to consume the refuse of creation.

When we consider these deeper meanings of the Hebrew text, we see that Genesis 3:14 is not telling us about a serpent at all. It is addressing the relationship between the Creator and His most prized creation – the one who, because of his pride and jealousy, caused Adam and Eve to fall. Read it like this:

> *"For doing this (making the man and woman, My newest prized creation, a debtor to sin) you have become small in My eyes. You are even lower than an ant! Your pride has broken out and you are going to have to eat your rebelliousness. I don't care how beautiful you think you are! From this point on, your wings are clipped and you are going to have to walk the earth and eat my dust."*

Maybe it would have been better to be just a serpent.

(End Excerpt)

Chapter 22
Treading On Serpents

Behold, I give unto you power to tread on serpents and scorpions, and over all the power of the enemy: and nothing shall by any means hurt you.

Luke 10:19

G od's Everlasting Proclamations are also designed to illustrate the victory we have in Jesus over the enemy. It's His way of saying, *"Don't trust your eyes, use your faith."* This illustration leads us back to our discussion from Genesis 3.

Proclamation Against The Serpent

And the LORD God said unto the serpent, "Because thou hast done this, thou art cursed above all cattle, and above every beast of the field; upon thy belly shalt thou go, and dust shalt thou eat all the days of thy life. And I will put enmity between thee and the woman, and between thy seed and her seed; it shall bruise thy head, and thou shalt bruise his heel. **Genesis 3:14-15**

I want to focus on the phrase, "between thy seed and her seed".

The Hebrew word for seed is *zera* and it simply means "offspring", but has also been translated as "descendants". This is where we as readers of the Bible are presented a challenge.

We know that the rest of humanity is considered Eve's offspring, her seed or her descendants. We further know that Jesus was part of that offspring because the Bible goes to great lengths in Luke 3:23-38 to show exactly how Jesus' lineage traced all the way back to Adam and Eve.

It also says in Genesis 3:15 that God put enmity between Eve's offspring, us and specifically Jesus, and… the serpent's seed.

So who are the serpent's seed?

To clarify a doctrine that was made popular in the early 1930's and persists even today, Satan DID NOT have sex with Eve, nor did she have his children. As the excerpt from *Cloudeaters* clearly points out, the original language of the text says nothing about sex, but that the devil made her a debtor to sin through his deception and her willing participation.

So again, who are the serpent's seed if not human offspring?

Part of the answer lies in this interaction between Jesus and the religiously minded people of His day:

> *Jesus said unto them, "If God were your Father, ye would love me: for I proceeded forth and came from God; neither came I of myself, but He sent me. Why do ye not understand my speech? Even because ye cannot hear my word. Ye are of your father the devil, and the lusts of your father ye will do. He was a murderer from the beginning, and abode not in the truth, because there is no truth in him. When he speaketh a lie, he speaketh of his own: for he is a liar, and the father of it. And because I tell you the truth, ye believe me not."* **John 8:42-45**

He told them *"You are of your father the devil,"* so we know that at least spiritually those people who reject Jesus are the offspring of the devil, or in other words the seed of the serpent. But this is only part of the answer.

Satan's rebellion occurred long before the incident in the Garden. Through his smooth talking and good looks, he'd coerced the other angels to join his rebellion. In their joining him, those Fallen Angels also became the serpent's seed.

I can even imagine how the devil must have made his own proclamations to the angels in order to get them to follow him. Everything that the devil does is in a question form, everything that God says is in a declarative certain form. The devil can't proclaim and create out of nothing. He can only impugn [Argue] and challenge the word of God to get people to doubt and lock themselves out of receiving the promises of God in faith. God declares things and there is no other.

Keep in mind that this fight with Satan has always been because he wanted to be like the Most High God. We know from the devil's character that such a devastating proclamation from God, a curse really, would have enraged him.

Later we see him acting out on that rage as he prompted his Fallen cohorts, the Nephilim, to impregnate women thus corrupting the human genome. The offspring of those Fallen Angels with women were the Rephaim. These creatures could also be considered the serpent's progeny. And, we could say that demons, the disembodied spirits of those Rephaim, are also the serpent's seed.

The Lasting Impact Of Proclamations

But of the cities of these people, which the LORD thy God doth give thee for an inheritance, thou shalt save alive nothing that breatheth, but thou shalt utterly destroy them; namely, the Hittites, and the Amorites, the Canaanites, and the Perizzites, the Hivites, and the Jebusites; as the LORD thy God hath commanded thee. That they teach you not to do after all their abominations, which they have done unto their gods; so should ye sin against the LORD your God. **Deut 20:16-18**

People who dispute the validity of the Bible somehow always gravitate toward the above scripture or a section like it as evidence that God is not a fair or a loving God and therefore can't be real. They contend that no so-called God would call for mass genocide.

On the contrary, if you study the Bible and history, you'll begin to see the wisdom of God's Proclamation to the Israelites when He said, *"thou shalt save alive nothing that breatheth"*.

First, we have an indication within the passage itself that if these peoples were to remain in the land, they would corrupt God's people with their abominations. Second, they wouldn't take too kindly to a whole new people coming into their land to make it home. Most likely, the resulting strife would make the Israelites' lives very difficult. And third... oh yeah, there were giants in the land!

That's right, it's those same people-groups that possessed Fallen Angel DNA mixed with human DNA. If God destroyed the earth with the flood to rid it of that corruption, do we really think He would spare a people who interbred with the serpent's seed?

What if you could peer into the future and know that Enver Pasha of Turkey would be responsible for 2.5 million deaths in the Armenian genocide; that Pol Pot of Cambodia would order the killing of 2.4 million people in the Cambodian genocide; that over the course of years Saddam Hussein would murder 2 million people; that Yahya Khan of Pakistan would be directly responsible for up to 12 million deaths in the Bangladesh genocide; that the infamous Adolf Hitler would have the blood of up to 12 million deaths on his hands; that Joseph Stalin could be directly or indirectly linked to 62 million deaths; or that Mao Tse-tung of China would eradicate 75 million human beings? If you could take preemptive action against them and take them out before they killed anybody, would you do it? Of course you would.

As I've pointed out repeatedly, God lives outside of time and space. He knows what's going to happen. It is for this reason that I believe that there's a practical reason why God proclaimed that the previous inhabitants of the Promised Land should be killed.

Look at the "enmity" (Gen 3:15) there has been throughout the centuries with, say, the Canaanites.

More than 90 percent of the genetic ancestry of modern Lebanese is derived from ancient Canaanites, according to a paper published today in the American Journal of Human Genetics.

Researchers supported by The Wellcome Trust were able to sequence the Canaanite genome from the remains of five individuals buried in the ancient port city of Sidon (modern Saïda, Lebanon) around 3,700 years ago. The results were compared against the DNA of 99 modern-day Lebanese residents.

According to the results, Canaanite ancestry is a mix of indigenous populations who settled the Levant (the region encompassing much of modern Syria, Lebanon, Jordan, Israel, and the Palestinian territories) around 10,000 years ago, and migrants who arrived from the east between 6,600 and 3,550 years ago.[23]

It's interesting to note that in English, "enmity" is a derivative of the word "enemy". Where this verse is concerned, it gives the idea of perpetual enmity and is equated with war. So what we see is that unless Israel would do away with these people as commanded, they would be perpetually at war with them!

While this isn't a popular position in the modern-day, politically-correct Church, God had instructed the Israelites to eliminate all the inhabitants of the Promised Land. Obviously, Israel didn't follow God's instructions; even today, thousands of years later, there is still enmity between Israel and her neighbors.

My larger point is that all of these, the Fallen Ones, the Rephaim, demons and people with corrupted DNA according to the Bible, are the serpent's seed who would be crushed by Jesus' heel.

Wherefore God also hath highly exalted Him, and given Him a name which is above every name: that at the name of Jesus every knee should bow, of things in heaven, and things in earth, and things under the earth; and that every tongue should confess that Jesus Christ is Lord, to the glory of God the Father.
Phil 2:9-11

Understanding exactly who and what we're battling against, *"For we wrestle not with flesh and blood..."* (Eph 6:12) is extremely important in understanding the power of God's Proclamations in our lives.

Proclaiming The End From The Beginning

As human beings we tend to see things from our time-sensitive, straight forward linear point of view. But this is not how God sees things.

Remember the former things of old: for I am God, and there is none else; I am God, and there is none like me, declaring the end from the beginning, and from ancient times the things that are not yet done, saying, "My counsel shall stand, and I will do all my pleasure." **Isaiah 46:9-10**

We say that God is eternal, but do we understand what that really means?

It's not just that God lives on forever. It means that God has always existed and is also present at every point in time: past, present and future.

Before the mountains were brought forth, or ever thou hadst formed the earth and the world, even from everlasting to everlasting, thou art God. **Psalm 90:2**

Because of His perspective outside of time and space, He's already seen what the future holds for mankind (you and me included).

It's because of this that He tells you, His child, what will happen in your unique, individual future. And

---

23 Kristin Romey, "Living Descendants of Biblical Canaanites Identified Via DNA". National Geographic, https://news.nationalgeographic.com/2017/07/canaanite-bible-ancient-dna-lebanon-genetics-archaeology/, (July 27, 2017).

God specifically declares the events of the End of the Age as a warning to His people so that they will not be destroyed.

Throughout my life, I've listened to some of the most powerful End Time proclamations from people like A.A. Alan, A.C. Valdez, Daisy Osborn, Dumitru Duduman, Henry Gruver and David Wilkerson. God gave His gifts and callings to men without repentance for our future benefit.

For the gifts and calling of God are without repentance. **Romans 11:29**

Their message, which is ultimately God's message coupled with my own personal view of the Last Days, has made me acutely aware of the fact that God's Proclamations regarding the End of the Age are all soon to be fulfilled.

As an example, God proclaims several things in the Book of Revelation about the Two Witnesses.

And I will give power unto my two witnesses, and they shall prophesy a thousand two hundred and threescore days, clothed in sackcloth. These are the two olive trees, and the two candlesticks standing before the God of the earth. And if any man will hurt them, fire proceedeth out of their mouth, and devoureth their enemies: and if any man will hurt them, he must in this manner be killed. These have power to shut heaven, that it rain not in the days of their prophecy: and have power over waters to turn them to blood, and to smite the earth with all plagues, as often as they will. And when they shall have finished their testimony, the beast that ascendeth out of the bottomless pit shall make war against them, and shall overcome them, and kill them. And their dead bodies shall lie in the street of the great city, which spiritually is called Sodom and Egypt, where also our Lord was crucified. And they of the people and kindreds and tongues and nations shall see their dead bodies three days and an half, and shall not suffer their dead bodies to be put in graves. And they that dwell upon the earth shall rejoice over them, and make merry, and shall send gifts one to another; because these two prophets tormented them that dwelt on the earth. And after three days and an half the Spirit of life from God entered into them, and they stood upon their feet; and great fear fell upon them which saw them. And they heard a great voice from heaven saying unto them, "Come up hither." And they ascended up to heaven in a cloud; and their enemies beheld them. And the same hour was there a great earthquake, and the tenth part of the city fell, and in the earthquake were slain of men seven thousand: and the remnant were affrighted, and gave glory to the God of heaven. **Rev 11:3-13**

At the same time that the Antichrist appears, so do the two witnesses. God will not allow a supernatural Antichrist to do signs and wonders in a vacuum without having His two witnesses around to offset the devil's deception.

...In the mouth of two or three witnesses shall every word be established. **2 Cor 13:1**

I believe that the Two Witnesses are Elijah and Enoch. These are the only two men in biblical history who have never died, but they will die in the streets of Jerusalem, forty-two months after their appearance. God will bring forth Elijah and Enoch in order to proclaim to the people His ultimate and everlasting power.

I mention these things because when we get to the Book of Revelation and you begin to see God's Proclamations over and over again, you understand that we've come full circle back to the Garden of Eden.

With each unveiling in Revelation of the seven seals, the seven trumpets and the seven bowls, we see another Proclamation from God about events leading up to the end. Here's an example:

> *And I saw another angel fly in the midst of heaven, having the everlasting gospel to preach unto them that dwell on the earth, and to every nation, and kindred, and tongue, and people, saying with a loud voice, "Fear God, and give glory to Him; for the hour of His judgment is come: and worship Him that made heaven, and earth, and the sea, and the fountains of waters. And there followed another angel, saying, "Babylon is fallen, is fallen, that great city, because she made all nations drink of the wine of the wrath of her fornication." And the third angel followed them, saying with a loud voice, "If any man worship the beast and his image, and receive his mark in his forehead, or in his hand, the same shall drink of the wine of the wrath of God, which is poured out without mixture into the cup of His indignation; and he shall be tormented with fire and brimstone in the presence of the holy angels, and in the presence of the Lamb, and the smoke of their torment ascendeth up for ever and ever: and they have no rest day nor night, who worship the beast and his image, and whosoever receiveth the mark of his name." Here is the patience of the saints: here are they that keep the commandments of God, and the faith of Jesus.* **Rev 14:6-12**

These declarations in Revelation are really end-from-the-beginning Proclamations. God is telling everyone who will listen how things are going to play out.

> *Saying, "I am Alpha and Omega, the first and the last: and, what thou seest, write in a book, and send it unto the seven churches which are in Asia; unto Ephesus, and unto Smyrna, and unto Pergamos, and unto Thyatira, and unto Sardis, and unto Philadelphia, and unto Laodicea."* **Rev 1:11**

There's a ton of God's Everlasting Proclamations in Revelation, but we don't have time to go into all of them. God speaks to us in Proclamations about those things that have occurred, that are occurring and that will occur. His intention, His design, His warning, His commandments, His expectations, His sentencing, His beckoning to come reason together, His declaration of future intent are all examples of His declaring the end from the beginning and proclaiming to us those things that we need to know.

Just think about how the OT prophets would declare, *"Thus, saith the Lord!"* They were giving godly Proclamations as prompted by God about something that was going to happen. To proclaim means "to declare verbally". You cannot have silent proclamations because God's Proclamations never leave any doubt about His position.

Elijah's encounter with the 450 prophets of Baal is a good example. While formed as a question, the proclamation from the prophet's lips was very clear.

> *And Elijah came unto all the people, and said, "How long halt ye between two opinions? If the LORD be God, follow Him: but if Baal, then follow him." And the people answered him not a word. Then said Elijah unto the people, "I, even I only, remain a prophet of the LORD; but Baal's prophets are four hundred and fifty men. Let them therefore give us two bullocks; and let them choose one bullock for themselves, and cut it in pieces, and lay it on wood, and put no fire under: and I will dress the other bullock, and lay it on wood, and put no fire under. And call ye on the name of your gods, and I will call on the name of the LORD: and the God that answereth by fire, let him be God." And all the people answered and said, "It is well spoken."* **1 Kings 18:21-24**

"How long will you be between two opinions?" In other words, *"Make up your mind, will you?!"* How's that for a proclamation? The false prophets wailed, they cried, they demanded, they beat their chests, they even cut themselves, but there was no fire.

And Elijah took twelve stones, according to the number of the tribes of the sons of Jacob, unto whom the word of the LORD came, saying, "Israel shall be thy name. And with the stones he built an altar in the name of the LORD: and he made a trench about the altar, as great as would contain two measures of seed. And he put the wood in order, and cut the bullock in pieces, and laid him on the wood, and said, "Fill four barrels with water, and pour it on the burnt sacrifice, and on the wood." And he said, "Do it the second time. And they did it the second time." And he said, "Do it the third time." And they did it the third time. And the water ran round about the altar; and he filled the trench also with water. And it came to pass at the time of the offering of the evening sacrifice, that Elijah the prophet came near, and said, "LORD God of Abraham, Isaac, and of Israel, let it be known this day that thou art God in Israel, and that I am thy servant, and that I have done all these things at thy word. Hear me, O LORD, hear me, that this people may know that thou art the LORD God, and that thou hast turned their heart back again." Then the fire of the LORD fell, and consumed the burnt sacrifice, and the wood, and the stones, and the dust, and licked up the water that was in the trench. And when all the people saw it, they fell on their faces: and they said, "The LORD, he is the God; the LORD, he is the God." 1 Kings 18:31-39

God's Proclamations never leave you in doubt.

Jesus Proclaimed

Ye men of Israel, hear these words; Jesus of Nazareth, a man approved of God among you by miracles and wonders and signs, which God did by Him in the midst of you, as ye yourselves also know: Him, being delivered by the determinate counsel and foreknowledge of God, ye have taken, and by wicked hands have crucified and slain: Whom God hath raised up, having loosed the pains of death: because it was not possible that he should be holden of it. For David speaketh concerning Him, "I foresaw the Lord always before my face, for he is on my right hand, that I should not be moved: Therefore did my heart rejoice, and my tongue was glad; moreover also my flesh shall rest in hope: Because thou wilt not leave my soul in hell, neither wilt thou suffer thine Holy One to see corruption. Thou hast made known to me the ways of life; thou shalt make me full of joy with thy countenance." Men and brethren, let me freely speak unto you of the patriarch David, that he is both dead and buried, and his sepulchre is with us unto this day. Therefore being a prophet, and knowing that God had sworn with an oath to him, that of the fruit of his loins, according to the flesh, He would raise up Christ to sit on his throne; He seeing this before spake of the resurrection of Christ, that His soul was not left in hell, neither His flesh did see corruption. This Jesus hath God raised up, whereof we all are witnesses. Therefore being by the right hand of God exalted, and having received of the Father the promise of the Holy Ghost, He hath shed forth this, which ye now see and hear. For David is not ascended into the heavens: but he saith himself, "The LORD said unto my Lord, 'Sit thou on my right hand, until I make thy foes thy footstool.'" Therefore let all the house of Israel know assuredly, that God hath made that same Jesus, whom ye have crucified, both Lord and Christ. Acts 2:22-35

Whether it be in prophecies before He was born, during His time on earth or after He ascended to be with the Father, the Proclamation of Jesus is a key theme throughout the whole Bible. We see in Jeremiah how the Lord proclaimed ahead of time that He would send the Messiah with a new covenant:

> *"Behold, the days come," saith the LORD, "that I will make a new covenant with the house of Israel, and with the house of Judah: Not according to the covenant that I made with their fathers in the day that I took them by the hand to bring them out of the land of Egypt; which my covenant they brake, although I was an husband unto them," saith the LORD. "But this shall be the covenant that I will make with the house of Israel; After those days," saith the LORD, "I will put my law in their inward parts, and write it in their hearts; and will be their God, and they shall be my people. And they shall teach no more every man his neighbour, and every man his brother, saying, 'Know the LORD:' for they shall all know me, from the least of them unto the greatest of them," saith the LORD: "for I will forgive their iniquity, and I will remember their sin no more." Jeremiah 31:31-34*

God's Proclamations always come true. We see the fulfillment of the above prophecy proclamation in several places in the NT.

> *For this is my blood of the New Testament, which is shed for many for the remission of sins. Matt 26:28*

> *But now hath He obtained a more excellent ministry, by how much also He is the mediator of a better covenant, which was established upon better promises. For if that first covenant had been faultless, then should no place have been sought for the second. Heb 8:6-7*

> *And to Jesus the mediator of the new covenant, and to the blood of sprinkling, that speaketh better things than that of Abel. Heb 12:24*

Jesus' own Proclamations told the people what He would accomplish during His ministry on earth:

> *The Spirit of the Lord GOD is upon me; because the LORD hath anointed me to preach good tidings unto the meek; he hath sent me to bind up the brokenhearted, to proclaim liberty to the captives, and the opening of the prison to them that are bound. Isaiah 61:1*

> *And there was delivered unto Him the book of the prophet Esaias. And when He had opened the book, He found the place where it was written, "The Spirit of the Lord is upon me, because He hath anointed me to preach the gospel to the poor; He hath sent me to heal the brokenhearted, to preach deliverance to the captives, and recovering of sight to the blind, to set at liberty them that are bruised, to preach the acceptable year of the Lord." And He closed the book, and He gave it again to the minister, and sat down. And the eyes of all them that were in the synagogue were fastened on Him. And He began to say unto them, "This day is this scripture fulfilled in your ears." Luke 4:17-21*

God's Proclamation about Jesus left little doubt as to Who He was, as the Most High declared Jesus to be His beloved Son:

> *And it came to pass in those days, that Jesus came from Nazareth of Galilee, and was baptized of John in Jordan. And straightway coming up out of the water, He saw the heavens opened, and the Spirit like*

a dove descending upon Him: and there came a voice from heaven, saying, "Thou art my beloved Son, in whom I am well pleased." **Mark 1:9-11**

God's Proclamations work like this in our lives as well. He proclaims His love and salvation to us through His Word, He proclaims our deliverance through His Son Jesus and He proclaims that He not only knows about every detail of our lives but that He has plans for our good.

Before I formed thee in the belly I knew thee… **Jer 1:5**

"For I know the thoughts that I think toward you," saith the LORD, "thoughts of peace, and not of evil, to give you an expected end. Then shall ye call upon me, and ye shall go and pray unto me, and I will hearken unto you. And ye shall seek me, and find me, when ye shall search for me with all your heart." **Jer 29:11-13**

Ask, and it shall be given you; seek, and ye shall find; knock, and it shall be opened unto you: For every one that asketh receiveth; and he that seeketh findeth; and to him that knocketh it shall be opened. **Matt 7:7-8**

Yes, it's true: God loves you and He thinks about you all the time.

How precious also are thy thoughts unto me, O God! how great is the sum of them! **Psalm 139:17**

For those people who are truly His, God's Proclamation for their eternal future is encompassed in His great love for us.

The Proclamation to Hear and Obey

Hear, O Israel: The LORD our God is one LORD. **Deut 6:4**

This verse is a great example of why I love to get to the original language behind a translation. When we read this proclamation in our English versions and we think it simply is God saying, *"Hear me!," "Listen!"* But while it certainly is a Proclamation of God telling His people to listen, there's so much more behind this single-sentence verse.

The word for "hear" comes from the Hebrew word *shama*, pronounced 'shaw-mah', and is a cultural concept that even Jews today would be very familiar with. It literally means, *"to hear and obey!"*

That is some proclamation. In fact, every time you see God say, *"Hear me," "Pay attention," "Listen"*, these are all proclamations. We see this thread of not just hearing but obeying in several places in the NT.

But be ye doers of the word, and not hearers only, deceiving your own selves. **James 1:22**

But he said, Yea rather, blessed are they that hear the word of God, and keep it. **Luke 11:28**

When it comes to God's Proclamations, there are two contrasts: There are those who listen and those who don't. He even made the following statement when it comes to those contrasts:

Hear now this, O foolish people, and without understanding; which have eyes, and see not; which have ears, and hear not: **Jer 5:21**

Having eyes, see ye not? And having ears, hear ye not? And do ye not remember? **Mark 8:18**

Although this response may seem harsh, Jesus' Proclamations are always creative in their nature. The previous scripture is a perfect example.

Think about how long he'd been with the people when those religious Jews came up to challenge Him. In this instance, scripture acts like a spiritual body scanner. You could see into their hearts and no matter how many miracles they'd seen, no matter how many times they saw Him fulfill prophecy and no matter how many circumstances showed them that He was the promised Messiah, they refused to believe.

Notice what I said: His Proclamation about them not seeing or hearing was a result of "their refusal" to believe the evidence of His Messiahship. But here is what I mean by His Proclamations being creative in nature. His rebuke to those religious unbelievers is recorded in the NT. As a consequence, you and I read it today and that recounting of the event in scripture spurs us on to believe and CREATES faith and hope in us. What was tough love two thousand years ago is an anchor for us today.

That said, we sure could use His to-the-point Proclamation in the Church today. The evangelical Church today is pathetic, apostate, apathetic, indifferent, compromised, neutralized, sanitized and castrated because they will not speak the Word of God or adhere to His Proclamations. They won't declare those Proclamations or the gospel.

They may give lip service to declaring God's Proclamations and they may even donate a little bit of money. But for the most part, they are happy to sit on their pews and sing about how God loves them - the world be damned. Literally!

For some reason, these people seem to think that God is blind to their life choices and willfully ignorant toward their inaction and sin. As they will soon find out, God is anything but ignorant.

He that planted the ear, shall he not hear? He that formed the eye, shall he not see? He that chastiseth the heathen, shall not He correct? He that teacheth man knowledge, shall not He know? **Psalm 94:9-10**

God's Proclamations are power and if the Church wants to regain that power they've lost, we will need to go back to the basics: proclaiming the message of the gospel and the Name of Jesus!

Can you hear the cry of the Holy Spirit across the globe?

O that there were such an heart in them, that they would fear me, and keep all my commandments always, that it might be well with them, and with their children for ever! **Deut 5:29**

Oh that my people had hearkened unto me, and Israel had walked in my ways! **Psalm 81:13**

I have sent also unto you all my servants the prophets, rising up early and sending them, saying, "Return ye now every man from his evil way, and amend your doings, and go not after other gods to serve them, and ye shall dwell in the land which I have given to you and to your fathers: but ye have not inclined your ear, nor hearkened unto me." **Jer 35:15**

O Jerusalem, Jerusalem, which killest the prophets, and stonest them that are sent unto thee; how often would I have gathered thy children together, as a hen doth gather her brood under her wings, and ye would not! **Luke 13:34**

*Jesus answered and said unto her, "If thou knewest the gift of God, and who it is that saith to thee, 'Give me to drink;' thou wouldest have asked of Him, and He would have given thee living water." **John 4:10***

Come unto me, all ye that labour and are heavy laden, and I will give you rest. Take my yoke upon you, and learn of me; for I am meek and lowly in heart: and ye shall find rest unto your souls. For my yoke is easy, and my burden is light. **Matt 11:28-30**

All of these verses are Proclamations in one form or another. God has called, and is, calling His people to Himself. Without the challenge from the standard that God creates, mankind could not turn from his wicked ways.

It says in Genesis that the Holy Spirit moved upon the face of the waters. Today, that same Holy Spirit moves across the face of the earth proclaiming that time is short. We see in the Word in 1 Tim 4:1 that the Holy Spirit proclaims what these days would look like, in that *"in the last days men will depart from the faith giving seed to seducing spirits".*

These Proclamations by God and the conviction of His voice, whether written or by an impression of the Holy Spirit, show us that what we are doing is wrong and contrary to God's desire and will. But God doesn't stop there in His Proclamations and declarations. His pleadings and Proclamations call us to repentance. No man comes to the Father lest the Spirit draws him (John 6:44).

So how are we drawn to the Father? We hear the Word of God, or we read the Word of God, and the Holy Ghost convicts us.

Then they cry unto the LORD in their trouble, and He saveth them out of their distresses. He sent His word, and healed them, and delivered them from their destructions. **Psalm 107:19-20**

God is the author and finisher of our faith (Heb 12:2). He's the ultimate record keeper and author of the Lamb's Book of Life. And each page in the Book of Life has a Proclamation in which we are ordained to walk.

And there shall in no wise enter into it any thing that defileth, neither whatsoever worketh abomination, or maketh a lie: but they which are written in the Lamb's Book of Life. **Rev 21:27**

Proclamation Of Life Over The Believer

Look, it was King David who proclaimed: Let the man whom the Lord hath redeemed, declare so, proclaim so and say so!

Let the redeemed of the LORD say so, whom he hath redeemed from the hand of the enemy.
Psalm 107:2

I will declare thy name unto my brethren: in the midst of the congregation will I praise thee.
Psalm 22:22

Proclamation is our confession made assertively or aggressively. When we use God's Word as Proclamations, the fireworks begin! Our Proclamation vested in the authority of God becomes a lightning bolt of spiritual warfare.

Let me pause here to set up this word-picture for you.

We know from Ephesians 6:16 that the devil lobs fiery darts, or arrows at us in the course of our run-ins with him:

Above all, taking the shield of faith, wherewith ye shall be able to quench all the fiery darts of the wicked.

Most of the time, these burning spears are in the form of thoughts, which he places in our heads in order to seed doubt or pain. He's really good at telling you that you're no good, or reminding you of things that you did that he says "disqualifies" you from being a child of God. These efforts are designed to cripple you into becoming placid and ineffectual in the Kingdom of God.

And sometimes those words can come from people we trust or value,such as a friend, a fellow Believer or a family member. Although it's a familiar face speaking, keep in mind that their thoughts that generated the piercing ember originated from the enemy. If they are tearing you down, the devil may well have planted that thought in their head. If this is the case, its design was intended to wound you. Remember that the devil doesn't play fair.

Still other fiery implements are more ruthless and physical attacks can be attempted on you from direct demonic or Fallen Angel cohorts. These napalm projectiles are designed to do more than just wound you mentally or spiritually. Those violent weapons can be an attempt to kill, or seriously maim you.

But we are not unaware of the devil or his schemes (2 Cor 2:11), nor do we have to sit back and take the garbage that he dishes out.

Your godly Proclamations from the Word are like thrusting lightning bolts at the enemy in time of warfare. They turn mere words into aggressive weapons of spiritual warfare against an enemy who would rather have you come to the battlefield empty-handed and naked.

But! You are not empty-handed and naked! Your effectual, positive proclamations from the Word of God are tactical nuclear weapons against the enemy when you use them with the leading of the Holy Spirit. These Word-based Proclamations release the power of God, and the devil has no effective counter.

Don't get me wrong, that doesn't mean he won't try. You just need to know about the positive proclamation power the Lord has placed in your arsenal so you can use it if you need to. The reason so many Christian ministries are aborted and lives destroyed is because Believers do not understand that Proclamation power, or that the power of death and life is in the tongue. This ignorance is to our detriment because the Word also says, *"And we eat the fruit thereof"* (Prov 18:21).

A lot of people say or pray, *"If God wills."* Although that's true, if you're walking close with Him through

His Holy Spirit, He will tell you what His will is. Wisdom does need to be foremost followed by knowledge and understanding. Faith is likened to wisdom, but it's not exactly the same.

Now faith is the substance of things hoped for, the evidence of things not seen. **Hebrews 11:1**

"Faith is the substance of things hoped for…" Again, by our words we're justified or by our words we are condemned (Matt 12:37). Believing in faith and proclaiming those beliefs with our mouths is a potent weapon against an enemy who would rather that you shut up!

And they overcame him by the blood of the Lamb, and by the word of their testimony; and they loved not their lives unto the death. **Rev 12:11**

"And they overcame him by the WORD of their mouth," the proclamation of their faith. We'll either starve by the lack of fruit of our words or we'll overcome by the fruit of our words.

As an aside, and at the risk of sounding like a macho male chauvinist, I'm a guy that likes a firm handshake. Handshaking with women is different, but between guys I just believe it should be firm. But have you ever gone to another guy to shake his hand and his shake was limp, like a loose, wet-noodle that made it feel like his hand was going to slip out of yours? Yuck.

Our prayers are kind of like that. Loose, limp-wristed, wet-noodled questioning prayers are not proclamations! They have no power, nor are they infused with faith.

It's not the wisest prayer to pray *"If it be thy will…"* The wisest prayer is to find out what God's will is like, *"None should perish,"* and say, *"Lord, I proclaim with authority Your promise over that person, etc."*

When we have God-given authority, it takes Proclamation for it to be exercised.

Moving Mountains By Proclamation

And Jesus answering saith unto them, "Have faith in God. For verily I say unto you, 'That whosoever shall say unto this mountain, "Be thou removed, and be thou cast into the sea;" and shall not doubt in his heart, but shall believe that those things which he saith shall come to pass; he shall have whatsoever he saith.' Therefore I say unto you, 'What things soever ye desire, when ye pray, believe that ye receive them, and ye shall have them.'" **Mark 11:22-24**

When Jesus said, *"…whosoever shall say (proclaim) unto this mountain, 'Be thou removed, and be thou cast into the sea…'"* He was instructing His disciples to proclaim in faith those things that God led them in.

Let me be clear: This is not "name it and claim it". The idea of proclaiming those things that God has, by His Spirit, revealed to you is a very powerful principle for Believers. Using this principle correctly will give you ammo that 99% of Christians fail to realize. But that utilization must be for the benefit of the Kingdom. It cannot be used for selfish gain. In other words, just because I want a brand new Bugatti, I can't use this mountain-moving principle to make it happen. Again, it has to be directed by the Lord and for His benefit.

Here's an example of a mountain-moving proclamation:

Early in my Christian walk, about forty years ago, a river in Bozeman, Montana, was rising and flooding all the other adjacent streams and creeks. Unfortunately a friend of mine had a house and property on one of those very creeks. The result was that this normally tranquil creek became an angry river. Because of the rising water, everyone said, and everything pointed to the fact thathis house and property would end up being four feet underwater when all was said and done.

Then the Lord spoke to me. He said, *"Go out and draw a line on the side of the creek bed and speak to the water saying, 'Thus saith the Lord, so shall this water not go beyond this boundary!'"*

I thought, *"Well, I'm either crazy or I heard from God."* So I went out as instructed, drew a line on the side of the creek bed with my foot and spoke to the water as the Lord told me to.

Then the most astonishing thing happened.

The water had been coming directly toward the house and there was no way it was going to miss. It suddenly took a hard left turn, went straight, and then took a hard right turn and continued on its path. It was like some unseen water diversion had been deployed! This rushing, violent and raging tributary went around the house!

The entire property where I'd drawn the line DID NOT flood. It was absolutely mind-blowing.

The difference between God's direct decrees and our proclamations is that we need to be sure we make decrees that line up our will with God's will. There are men and women of God that come directly against evil. They do this when God gives them discernment that a strongman or principality is over a city; as an example, a spirit of suicide. Then God says rebuke the spirit of suicide and come against it and come against the blood-guiltiness of the land. That's what my friend Henry Gruver does.

According to God's prompting, Henry will remit the sins of those who shed innocent blood and then will release the forgiveness of God. By releasing God's forgiveness, the redeeming purpose and plan, and the authority of the blood of Jesus, God's degree as proclaimed by Henry dissolves and takes away the curse that was on the land. This enables God to freely move to grant conviction and repentance. The decrees take the blinders off and also put our minds and hearts into a faith mode rather than a questioning mode.

Speaking of a questioning mode, the Lord asked me a very interesting question a while back. It had to do with **1 Cor 2:9**:

> *But as it is written, "Eye hath not seen, nor ear heard, neither have entered into the heart of man, the things which God hath prepared for them that love Him."*

The Lord asked, *"Have you ever applied that to the (spiritual) war that you are fighting now or will fight in the days to come?"*

I had to honestly answer Him that I hadn't.

He told me that we only think of this verse as it pertains to eternity, but humanly we don't think of it for the Last Days.

Many people talk about a great outpouring of the Holy Spirit in the Last Days. The fact is that we'll be stunned at what God will do with His people if we trust and believe Him.

The Bride Proclaimed

First, let me just point out that I'm not an emotional, touchy-feely kind of guy. So from my perspective, God's Proclamations about us being His bride don't invoke the same kind of emotions as it would in other people, or women in particular. But that doesn't mean that God proclaiming the Church as His Bride is lost on me.

The Bible is full of the examples of marriage between Jesus and the true body of Believers known as His Church. As we've discussed at length, that Church, the real Church, is comprised of Believers who have not only trusted in Jesus Christ as their personal Savior, but also seek to walk in His ways daily. That real relationship with the Lord is evidenced by the observance of the fruit of the Spirit in their lives. All of us fall short and we sin, but we get on our face before Him, we experience heartfelt repentance and then we continue to go about His business: no excuses, no pious pretending, no self-centered, anything-goes, I-can-get-forgiven attitude. It's not enough to say *"I know Jesus."* The question is: Does He know you?

For those who are indeed His, Jesus proclaims Himself as the Church's Bridegroom Who has sacrificially and lovingly chosen us to be His bride.

> *For thy Maker is thine husband; the LORD of hosts is His name; and thy Redeemer the Holy One of Israel; The God of the whole earth shall He be called.* **Isaiah 54:5**

> *Husbands, love your wives, even as Christ also loved the church, and gave Himself for it; That He might sanctify and cleanse it with the washing of water by the Word, that He might present it to Himself a glorious church, not having spot, or wrinkle, or any such thing; but that it should be holy and without blemish.* **Eph 25:25-27**

It's important to understand that the Church being the Lord's Bride is more than just symbolism or imagery. Consider who it is that came first; God or us? Why would God simply give us an example of something that we would participate in here on earth, i.e. an engagement, then a ceremony and then a life with our spouse?

Could it be that it's the other way around? Could it be that our biblical relationships here on earth are supposed to mirror a God-based, factual relationship in eternity? Could it be that we are not the example, but that He is the example for us? I think so.

When we consider His Proclamations about the wedding feast and marriage in that light, this so-called symbolism takes on a deeper meaning. God is proclaiming to the entire universe that WE are His beloved. WE are more important to Him than anything else. And WE are the ones who have captured His heart.

Now that is a powerful Proclamation!

Paul understood this analogy better than most.

> *For I am jealous over you with godly jealousy: for I have espoused you to one husband, that I may*

present you as a chaste virgin to Christ. But I fear, lest by any means, as the serpent beguiled Eve through his subtilty, so your minds should be corrupted from the simplicity that is in Christ. **2 Cor 11:2-3**

The idea that we're supposed to be chaste to Jesus before our wedding feast is a tradition that has been carried on since biblical times. Back then, the bride and groom were separated until the wedding. During that separation they made themselves ready for the wedding and spending the rest of their lives together. This idea also harkens back to the previous H.E.L.P. of Purity.

If I may be blunt, as His pure Bride, we can't go whoring around: not physically, not emotionally and not spiritually. In other words, we can't allow ourselves to become defiled by the world, as we discussed in the last section.

Then shall the kingdom of heaven be likened unto ten virgins, which took their lamps, and went forth to meet the bridegroom. And five of them were wise, and five were foolish. They that were foolish took their lamps, and took no oil with them: But the wise took oil in their vessels with their lamps. While the bridegroom tarried, they all slumbered and slept. And at midnight there was a cry made, "Behold, the bridegroom cometh; go ye out to meet him." Then all those virgins arose, and trimmed their lamps. And the foolish said unto the wise, "Give us of your oil; for our lamps are gone out." But the wise answered, saying, "Not so; lest there be not enough for us and you: but go ye rather to them that sell, and buy for yourselves." And while they went to buy, the bridegroom came; and they that were ready went in with him to the marriage: and the door was shut. Afterward came also the other virgins, saying, "Lord, Lord, open to us." But he answered and said, "Verily I say unto you, I know you not." Watch therefore, for ye know neither the day nor the hour wherein the Son of man cometh. **Matt 25:1-13**

This engagement between the Lord and us seems to have gone on for a very long time. We've been waiting for His return for centuries, but in the expanse of eternity, it's only been a drop in the bucket. Soon, as God's Everlasting Proclamation has put us on notice, the marriage will be at hand.

And I heard as it were the voice of a great multitude, and as the voice of many waters, and as the voice of mighty thunderings, saying, "Alleluia: for the Lord God omnipotent reigneth. Let us be glad and rejoice, and give honour to Him: for the marriage of the Lamb is come, and His wife hath made herself ready. And to her was granted that she should be arrayed in fine linen, clean and white: for the fine linen is the righteousness of saints." And he saith unto me, "Write, 'Blessed are they which are called unto the marriage supper of the Lamb.'" And he saith unto me, "These are the true sayings of God." **Rev 19:6-9**

And I saw a new heaven and a new earth: for the first heaven and the first earth were passed away; and there was no more sea. And I John saw the holy city, new Jerusalem, coming down from God out of heaven, prepared as a bride adorned for her husband. **Rev 21:1-2**

We are destined for so much more than just this earthly existence of sin, pain and trouble. But in order to become that bride, we must lean on the Everlasting Proclamations of our King to pull us through.

My advice?

Make sure you are truly His and that you too are counted as worthy to attend the Marriage Supper of the Lamb.

All Hail The Power of Jesus' Name

All hail the power of Jesus' name!
Let angels prostrate fall;
bring forth the royal diadem,
and crown him Lord of all.
Bring forth the royal diadem,
and crown him Lord of all.

Ye chosen seed of Israel's race,
ye ransomed from the fall,
hail him who saves you by his grace,
and crown him Lord of all.
Hail him who saves you by his grace,
and crown him Lord of all.
Sinners, whose love can ne'er forget
the wormwood and the gall,
go spread your trophies at his feet,
and crown him Lord of all.
Go spread your trophies at his feet,
and crown him Lord of all.

Let every kindred, every tribe
on this terrestrial ball,
to him all majesty ascribe,
and crown him Lord of all.
To him all majesty ascribe,
and crown him Lord of all.

Crown him, ye martyrs of your God,
who from his altar call;
extol the Stem of Jesse's Rod,
and crown him Lord of all.
Extol the Stem of Jesse's Rod,
and crown him Lord of all.

O that with yonder sacred throng
we at his feet may fall!
We'll join the everlasting song,
and crown him Lord of all.
We'll join the everlasting song,
and crown him Lord of all.

HELP 9

His Everlasting Peace

Peace I leave with you, my peace I give unto you:
not as the world giveth, give I unto you. Let not your heart be troubled,
neither let it be afraid.

John 14:27

Peace

God's Everlasting Peace is not necessarily the kind of peace that you may think.

For most people "peace" can be defined as the condition of life as it should be, an emotional response to a satisfactory environmental situation. This is essentially, what the world thinks of as peace.

Peace can mean one thing for me, but you can think peace is something entirely different. So if peace only depends on what the circumstances are in our own unique situation as individuals, it's easy to understand why peace is so fleeting. Not only that, but think about the chaos that such a subjective, self-centered mindset peace brings.

In the Middle East, Israelis think that peace means that they don't have to worry about the Arabs dropping rockets on their heads. For the Arabs, peace is when there is no such thing as Israel and it's wiped off the map!

Or how about the young, unmarried, teenage, girl who had sex with someone and is now pregnant. She thinks that peace would be restored to her life if she terminated the baby in her womb. If she had an abortion before she started showing, and anyone found out, she could go on with her life as if the pregnancy never happened.

To the baby, being killed wouldn't be peaceful. In addition, those of us who believe in the sanctity of life don't find abortion peaceful at all. For us, peace in this land would be restored if abortion were made illegal!

In both of these two cases, peace is at polar opposites. So who has the right to determine what peace should or shouldn't mean? Is there an absolute decision maker when it comes to the definition and application of peace? If all of us could get the kind of peace we wanted, wouldn't it be an imposed peace? Wouldn't it also be peace at the expense of someone else?

As you can see, the definition of peace cannot be determined by our own biased viewpoints, or selfish wants and needs. Neither can we set the standard for peace according to the norms of a turbulent society whose mores twist and turn with every manipulation of an evil enemy, the devil. Therefore, if we can't look to society or ourselves to define peace, where do we find the criteria to delineate true peace?

In a world where there are no absolutes, not even in the Church, we look to the only place that has the longevity and legitimacy to determine what real peace is:

We look to God's Everlasting Peace.

Chapter 23

Back To The Garden

The LORD bless thee, and keep thee. The LORD make his face shine upon thee, and be gracious unto thee. The LORD lift up his countenance upon thee, and give thee peace.

Numbers 6:24-26

The definition of peace in Webster's dictionary focuses on two primary ideas:

1. The cessation of hostilities or conflict between individuals or groups.

2. A mindset that's free from inner turmoil, also known as "peace of mind".

Everyone likes the idea of peace. If you listen to the newscasters, politicians, and religious leaders of every denomination and religion, they all say that they want peace. So if most people aren't against it, why is peace in our world and lives so elusive?

Perhaps it's because when it comes to peace, people aren't talking the same language. Peace means different things to different people.

Peace according to people who follow Eastern religions, comes only "through the obliteration of the individual personality when we become part of the universe with no awareness of self." But what they're really saying is that they're seeking serenity.

Peace is what the senior citizen says he wants when he's living next door to a noisy teenage neighbor practicing on the drums. What he really wants is quiet.

 Peace is what the worried storeowner who can't pay her bills says she wants. What she really wants is not to lose everything.

 Peace is what the anxious patient says he wants while he waits for medical exam results. What he really wants is not to die.

 Peace is what the detective wants while on the trail of a serial killer. Peace for him really means that no one else is murdered.

Peace outside of Jesus, whether it be forced political peace, false religious peace, the temporary elimination of physical or mental discomfort or the fulfillment of temporary pleasure - is a lie. That's because there's no lasting, purposeful peace until the Prince of Peace is seated on His throne in your life and in eternity.

When you understand the power and purpose of a relationship with Him, you'll be able to continually walk in God's Everlasting Peace.

First Fruits

When you look at the world today, the crime, the sin and the ugliness, it's hard to imagine an earth that wasn't a representation of this contemporary fallen "miasma" (an oppressive or unpleasant atmosphere that surrounds or emanates from something).

For Christians with eyes wide open, we know that all of this degradation is a direct result of sin. We further understand that this sin is a result of the fall of man, which occurred long ago in the Garden of Eden.

In the last section we spoke about the circumstances leading up to the fall, and the repercussions of that fall. So I won't rehash them here. Rather, I'll simply point out that the degrading environment of our current world is the outcome of too many people who love, "...*the darkness rather than the light...*" (John 3:19).

The Bible does talk about a pristine and sinless world that existed in the first fruits of peace. Can you imagine how peaceful the Garden, and the world, would have been back then?

But there went up a mist from the earth, and watered the whole face of the ground. Gen 2:6

An uncorrupted earth would have been a climate paradise that was full of lush, green vegetation. It didn't need to rain because a mist came up from the ground and watered it. Storms didn't rage around the planet, the earth didn't quake and the very air that they breathed was filled with peace. At the end of Day Six, this was the kind of world that God Almighty created. It was so perfect that it caused Him to pronounce it "very good".

> *And God saw every thing that he had made, and, behold, it was very good. And the evening and the morning were the sixth day.* Gen 1:31

God saying that His creation was "very good" shows us that Adam and Eve lived in an environment of perfect temperature and humidity. It was a world without pests or diseases. That world didn't include any stresses or problems to distract the couple from enjoying each other, enjoying their environment and enjoying their Creator. They were at peace, they were whole and they were innocent in the paradise.

> *And they were both naked, the man and his wife, and were not ashamed.* **Gen 2:25**

Adam and Eve had never sinned so they had no idea of the concepts of guilt and shame. They had clean hearts and clean consciences. This was a land before sin and ugliness. It was a land of peace.

> *So God created man in his own image, in the image of God created he him; male and female created he them.* **Gen 1:27**

> *Therefore shall a man leave his father and his mother, and shall cleave unto his wife: and they shall be one flesh.* **Gen 2:24**

The above two verses give us a perfect example of the first marriage. In verse 24 we understand that no matter how worldly or corrupt our culture has made sexual relations between men and women, God's original intention was for it to be a beautiful thing between a husband and a wife. This deep, open and resplendent connection was an unblemished expression of their human sexuality. We also see in the verse that our Creator purposed husband and wife to be sexual in the purest sense. There was no such thing as strife between them and they enjoyed an uninhibited and unhindered relationship with God.

> *And they heard the voice of the LORD God walking in the garden in the cool of the day...* **Gen 3:8a**

> *And the LORD God called unto Adam, and said unto him, "Where art thou?" And he said, I heard thy voice in the garden...* **Gen 3:9-10a**

It's also apparent that they were at peace with the animals.

> *And God blessed them, and God said unto them, "Be fruitful, and multiply, and replenish the earth, and subdue it: and have dominion over the fish of the sea, and over the fowl of the air, and over every living thing that moveth upon the earth."* **Gen 1:28**

They weren't afraid or threatened by the animals, nor were the animals afraid or threatened by Adam and Eve. That's because both man and animals ate plants and not each other. We know this because it wasn't until Noah that we see the mention of eating meat.

> *And God blessed Noah and his sons, and said unto them, "Be fruitful, and multiply, and replenish the earth. And the fear of you and the dread of you shall be upon every beast of the earth, and upon every fowl of the air, upon all that moveth upon the earth, and upon all the fishes of the sea; into your hand are they delivered. Every moving thing that liveth shall be meat for you; even as the green herb have I given you all things."* **Gen 9:1-3**

In the midst of this peace, Adam and Eve also had purpose.

> *And the LORD God took the man, and put him into the garden of Eden to dress it and to keep it.* **Gen 2:15**

> *And the LORD God said, It is not good that the man should be alone; I will make him an help meet for him.* **Gen 2:18**

Adam tended the Garden and Eve helped him and because the ground hadn't been cursed yet (Gen 3:17), the work was probably easy and enjoyable.

This perfect lifestyle had been instituted for man in a pre-fallen world. It was a world of provision and of joy. Adam and Eve's lives were whole and as pure as God's Everlasting Peace.

Completeness

The LORD will give strength unto his people; the LORD will bless his people with peace. **Psalm 29:11**

As you've seen, the word "peace" is used for what we want that we do not have.. In turn, this use makes the definition and application of the idea of peace extremely subjective. The Hebrew word for peace is *shalom* and its definition is much more than simple peace. It means completeness, soundness, welfare, or wholeness.

This is exactly what we saw in the Garden of Eden. Adam and Eve were complete and whole. Their welfare was assured and they certainly were of sound mind.

Hebrew is still spoken in Israel today. Greeting someone or saying goodbye to someone with the word *shalom* communicates much more than simply saying "peace to you". In saying *shalom*, you're literally saying, "may you be full of well-being", "may health and prosperity be upon you," or "may you be whole, full and complete."

Shalom in the OT has been translated in the KJV in the following manner: a greeting 6x, peaceful 2x, peacefully 3x, safe 2x, safely 7x, safety 6x, welfare 14x, well 17x, well-being 5x and peace 153x.

Peace I leave with you, my peace I give unto you: not as the world giveth, give I unto you. Let not your heart be troubled, neither let it be afraid. **John 14:27**

It's important to understand that the NT understanding of peace comes directly from the OT understanding of peace. And although we see the Greek word *eiréné* used for peace, the NT ties the word's use directly back to the OT.

Eiréné comes from the root word *eirō* and literally means "to join," or "tie together into a whole". It gives the idea of "wholeness" as in when all essential parts are joined together to make something complete.

As you can see, the English translation for the simple word "peace" leaves us with a diminished description of what God is trying to communicate to us in His Word. How can this happen?

Peace vs. Shalom

The common English translation of the word "peace" comes from the Latin word *pax*. *Pax* to the Romans literally meant a cessation of hostilities between the conqueror and the vanquished. Normally Rome was the conqueror so it's easy to understand how *pax* is one-sided.

While interesting, it is a far cry from the *shalom* that the Bible is talking about. Using the Latin definition shows us how the peace of the world is so fleeting in our modern culture. In the Roman sense, *pax* was always temporary because it depended on one party being in the position of strength over the other party. This is not the case with true biblical peace.

 Pax is a temporary pact based upon a victor. Shalom is a permanent agreement so long as you stay in the Lord.

 Pax is an instrument, a treaty or a paper. Shalom is the persistent, intangible and ubiquitous condition of the heart.

 Pax rests on the negative condition of defeat in a war or conflict. Shalom is a positive condition within us regardless of the circumstance.

 Pax is partial because it's only good until the next conflict breaks out. Shalom is whole and complete because it's based upon our King Who has come.

Worldly peace, or *pax*, can be dictated by one party to another, but *shalom* is by mutual agreement between you and the Lord. God says, *"If you will then I will."*

The Source

Shalom rests with God. For the Believer, we know that God Almighty is our Creator and that He's established a standard for His people based upon His Word. Living by that Word and being in right-standing with God, or walking in righteousness, will give you a life that is whole or complete and one that is full of calmness, provision, hope and purpose. The Christian who is actively seeking the Father's will understands that God is not angry with the sinner all the day long.

We see that this wholeness is different from just a cessation of hostilities with an enemy. As Christians we're in the midst of a war with the enemy and a cessation of hostilities between the devil and God's people will not occur until Jesus comes to rule and reign in His Kingdom. It's in the midst of this war, through a relationship with Jesus, that God gives us real wholeness and Peace which goes far beyond a halting of conflict between two parties.

Biblical shalom refers to an inward sense of completeness or wholeness, which has been imparted to us through the indwelling of the Holy Spirit. Although it can describe the absence of war, the vast majority of biblical references point to the inner completeness and tranquility that occur as we enter into a relationship with God. So by correctly understanding biblical Peace, many verses in the Bible take on new meaning.

Let's take a look at some of these verses and substitute biblical shalom in place of the word "peace".

~ Col 3:15 - *And let the* **wholeness, calmness, well-being and completeness** *of God rule in your hearts, to the which also ye are called in one body; and be ye thankful.*

~ Phil 4:7 - *And the* **wholeness, calmness, well-being and completeness** *of God, which passeth all understanding, shall keep your hearts and minds through Christ Jesus.*

~ Rom 12:18 - *If it be possible, as much as lieth in you, live in* **wholeness, calmness, well-being and in the completeness** *of God with all men.*

~ Psalm 34:14 - *Depart from evil, and do good; seek the* **wholeness, calmness, well-being and in the completeness** *of God, and pursue it.*

~ Isaiah 55:11-12 - *So shall my word be that goeth forth out of my mouth: it shall not return unto me void, but it shall accomplish that which I please, and it shall prosper in the thing whereto I sent it. For ye shall go out with joy, and be led forth in* **wholeness, calmness, well-being and completeness***: the mountains and the hills shall break forth before you into singing, and all the trees of the field shall clap their hands.*

Peace with God

Back a few sections I went through the appearances of the "Angel of the Lord" in the OT and concluded that these appearances were, in fact, Jesus in what theology calls "Christophanies". Even before He came to earth in bodily form, Jesus was paving a way for mankind back to the Father. Because of this, we must remember that real Peace is always in the context of faith in Jesus Christ. It does not exist apart from Him. Yet, people still seek peace without Him.

God's provided a way to be free from the muck and mire of sin, guilt, shame and the pain of mental suffering that we have to wade through in this fallen world. He sent His Son Jesus to die on a Cross to pay the penalty for our sins, forever changing our peace-less state.

There's a huge difference between the peace that many of the world's religions offer and the Peace that the one true God provides for His people. As an example, while many Muslims will say that Islam is a religion of peace, the Qur'an contains commands for both peace and for undirected violence.

I say "undirected violence" because there's a significant disparity between the commands of the OT to clean out the Promised Land of specific people and the calls for modern day violence from the Qur'an against any non-Muslim. Within the Qur'an, it appears that non-violent commands and violent commands for militant Muslims appear equally justified. For some unfortunate people, the peace that their god offers is through the sword. For others, that peace is found in unbounded mercy.

The Islamic principle of *taqiyya* is taught by Muslim scholars and says that Muslims should generally be truthful to each other, unless the purpose of lying is to "smooth over differences" or "gain the upper-hand over an enemy". And in one of their commentary-like teachings, Sahih Bukhari states in 49:857 the following:

> *"He who makes peace between the people by inventing good information or saying good things, is not a liar." Lying is permitted when the end justifies the means.*[24]

How can true Peace occur on the back of deception? In addition, the Qur'an specifically calls for violence as opposed to peace.

~ The servants of the All-merciful are those who walk in the earth modestly and who, when the ignorant address them, say, 'Peace'. *Q 25:63*

~ Fight them, and god will chastise them at your hands and degrade them, and he will help you against them, and bring healing to the breasts of a people who believe. *Q 9:14*

Compare the above verse to this directive of the apostle Paul out of Romans:

---

24 What Makes Islam So Different? "What Does Islam Teach About: Deception, Lying and Taqiyya". The Religion of Peace, https://www.thereligionofpeace.com/pages/quran/taqiyya.aspx, (last accessed December 16, 2018).

If it be possible, as much as lieth in you, live peaceably with all men. **Rom 12:18**

Even supposed peaceful Buddhists in the 969 Movement have a history of violence. No doubt this violence somehow is justified in helping them reach Nirvana.

The Peace that's afforded to the Christian is through God's Holy Spirit and is not predicated on us warring with the rest of the world. That's because we're born from above and translated out of the kingdom of darkness and into the kingdom of God's own dear Son.

> *That ye might walk worthy of the Lord unto all pleasing, being fruitful in every good work, and increasing in the knowledge of God, strengthened with all might, according to his glorious power, unto all patience and longsuffering with joyfulness, giving thanks unto the Father, which hath made us meet to be partakers of the inheritance of the saints in light: Who hath delivered us from the power of darkness, and hath translated us into the kingdom of His dear Son in whom we have redemption through His blood, even the forgiveness of sins.* **Col 1:10-13**

As I mentioned before, this is called super-positioning in quantum theory because the Bible says that we ARE already seated with the King of Glory in heavenly places.

> *But God, who is rich in mercy, for his great love wherewith he loved us, even when we were dead in sins, hath quickened us together with Christ, (by grace ye are saved;) and hath raised us up together, and made us sit together in heavenly places in Christ Jesus:* **Eph 2:4-6**

Through Jesus we have Peace with God and are no longer at war with Him as a result of our sin. Other religions, including Judaism, don't have that liberty.

> *For, brethren, ye have been called unto liberty; only use not liberty for an occasion to the flesh, but by love serve one another.* **Gal 5:13**

God now writes His Word on our hearts and we have become living stones in the Kingdom of God.

> *For I will take you from among the heathen, and gather you out of all countries, and will bring you into your own land. Then will I sprinkle clean water upon you, and ye shall be clean: from all your filthiness, and from all your idols, will I cleanse you. A new heart also will I give you, and a new spirit will I put within you: and I will take away the stony heart out of your flesh, and I will give you an heart of flesh. And I will put my spirit within you, and cause you to walk in my statutes, and ye shall keep my judgments, and do them.* **Ezekiel 36:24-27**

> *Ye also, as lively stones, are built up a spiritual house, an holy priesthood, to offer up spiritual sacrifices, acceptable to God by Jesus Christ.* **1 Peter 2:5**

This direct connection to God through Jesus Christ is our bridge to Peace.

The Agent of Peace

We find peace with God through Jesus. He's the only true agent of true Peace that exists.

> *Thou wilt keep him in perfect peace, whose mind is stayed on thee: because he trusteth in thee. Trust ye in the LORD for ever: for in the LORD JEHOVAH is everlasting strength.* **Isaiah 26:3-4**

The first step in obtaining this promised Peace is recognizing and trusting the agent of that Peace. Trusting in God means that we not only recognize Him, but we must also give Him His rightful place in our lives. This agent is the Messiah Jesus, the Christ. Long before He came to be born on earth, God told us that He would send Him.

> *For unto us a child is born, unto us a Son is given: and the government shall be upon His shoulder: and His name shall be called Wonderful, Counseller, The mighty God, The everlasting Father, The Prince of Peace. Of the increase of His government and peace there shall be no end, upon the throne of David, and upon his kingdom, to order it, and to establish it with judgment and with justice from henceforth even for ever. The zeal of the LORD of hosts will perform this.* **Isaiah 9:6-7**

In order to help us understand how Jesus would bring Peace, God used the prophet Isaiah to tell us what to expect.

> *Surely He hath borne our griefs, and carried our sorrows: yet we did esteem him stricken, smitten of God, and afflicted. But He was wounded for our transgressions, He was bruised for our iniquities: the chastisement of our peace was upon Him; and with His stripes we are healed.* **Isaiah 53:4-5**

God poured out all of His judgment on Jesus at the Cross. The blood of the Lamb is what made Peace with God possible. That appeasement allows us as individuals to be reconciled back to the Father through the Son. It's also humanity's long road back to the Peace that we once experienced in the Garden: a road paved through Jesus' sacrifice.

Jesus is the Prince of Peace and the antidote to the war that started in Eden. The enmity that God put between His followers and Satan's followers, who have ravaged the world's peace with perpetual war, will be removed when the Prince of Peace comes to do away with evil once and for all.

The problem in our current fallen state is that people have the misunderstanding that peace is the absence of war. Nothing could be further from the truth. That illusion, a delusion, is fueled by self-preserving cowardice. Evil clearly exists in the world and that evil won't rollover and stop stealing, killing, and destroying on his own. The Bible clearly shows us that Jesus, as that antidote, didn't come to bring Peace to this age as mankind defined peace.

> *And I saw heaven opened, and behold a white horse; and He that sat upon him was called Faithful and True, and in righteousness He doth judge and make war. His eyes were as a flame of fire, and on His head were many crowns; and He had a name written, that no man knew, but He himself. And He was clothed with a vesture dipped in blood: and His name is called The Word of God. And the armies which were in heaven followed Him upon white horses, clothed in fine linen, white and clean. And out of His mouth goeth a sharp sword, that with it He should smite the nations: and He shall rule them with a rod of iron: and He treadeth the winepress of the fierceness and wrath of Almighty God. And He hath on His vesture and on His thigh a name written, KING OF KINGS, AND LORD OF LORDS.* **Rev 19:11-16**

This begs the question: Why would Jesus be called the Prince of Peace and God is called the Lord of Hosts of the Armies of Heaven? Jesus answers this question for us.

> *Think not that I am come to send peace on earth: I came not to send peace, but a sword.* **Matt 10:34**

Consider for a moment that I'm a husband, a son, a father and a grandfather. There are many parts of Steve Quayle. In the same way, Jesus relates to different people or entities differently. He certainly isn't Peace to the devil and to people who will not accept Him. In those cases, He'll be their judge.

Ultimately, we're the ones who choose how He will relate to us. We can accept His Peace that surpasses all understanding or we can reject it. If we choose to reject it, we're also choosing to relate to Him in a different way than our Prince of Peace.

Suppose ye that I am come to give peace on earth? I tell you, Nay; but rather division: For from henceforth there shall be five in one house divided, three against two, and two against three. The father shall be divided against the son, and the son against the father; the mother against the daughter, and the daughter against the mother; the mother in law against her daughter in law, and the daughter in law against her mother in law. **Luke 12:51-53**

The LORD said unto my Lord, Sit thou at my right hand, until I make thine enemies thy footstool. **Psalm 110:1**

Even when Jesus is seated on His throne, the Bible says that He will rule with a "rod of iron".

And out of his mouth goeth a sharp sword, that with it he should smite the nations: and he shall rule them with a rod of iron: and he treadeth the winepress of the fierceness and wrath of Almighty God. **Rev 19:15**

In the end, it's His kingship that becomes the foundation for an everlasting Peace.

That at the name of Jesus every knee should bow, of things in heaven, and things in earth, and things under the earth and that every tongue should confess that Jesus Christ is Lord, to the glory of God the Father. **Phil 2:10-11**

He's a fair, just and loving King Who will, and does, impart true Peace to His followers.

The Trying of Men's Souls

Candid words from the English writer Thomas Paine remind us that even though Jesus has already won the peace, we still have to fight the war. In our day and age, we face a bloodthirsty, supernatural, evil enemy who won't stop inflicting pain because he knows his time is short.

The following essay, entitled The Crises, was set against the backdrop of the freezing winter of 1776 in the darkest days of the Revolutionary War. General George Washington was trying to regroup with his troops from the relentless British who had inflicted heavy casualties on the American colonists. Times were desperate and many people wondered, perhaps like you, if they could make it through the war to find real peace.

These are the times that try men's souls. The summer soldier and the sunshine patriot will in this crisis shrink from the service of their country. But they that stand it now, deserve the love and thanks of men and women. Tyranny, like hell, is not easily conquered. But the harder the conflict, the more glorious the triumph. Heaven knows how to put a proper price on its goods. It would be strange indeed if so celestial an article as freedom should not be highly rated.[25]

So how much more should we persevere in service to our King? Satan will throw everything at you to try to disrupt your life and your peace. God has given us the weapons of our warfare to overcome the enemy, but it doesn't mean that the battle is not ugly. Something greater than the birth of an earthly nation is at stake. Your peace and spiritual freedom are in the devil's sight and if he can discourage you enough to give up - he wins. "Hell is not easily conquered," but it is conquered.

I think we're at the end and have entered into the final act of mankind's history. I am NOT setting a date here. I'm only pointing out that events around the world are lining up with biblical prophecy. There are still prophecies to be fulfilled, but I think that some of those are stacked up on top of one another and you'll see a bunch of them fulfilled all at the same time. All I know for sure is that with the help of the Fallen, mankind has corrupted the earth and our DNA. They will not stop until we are destroyed, but God will not allow us to be destroyed completely.

> *And except those days should be shortened, there should no flesh be saved: but for the elect's sake those days shall be shortened.* **Matt 24:22**

If we are at the End of the Age, then we're also at the beginning of eternity. As a consequence, many of us will be stepping into the presence of the Lord at the time of His choosing. Such a statement may shake your peace, but I'm here to tell you that God is able to sustain you even in the worst, life-ending, circumstances.

It's extremely difficult to speak to the issue of peace at the moment that Believers lose their lives. I've never experienced that scenario, and people who have don't come back to tell us that they had peace in the middle of their dying experience, but I have heard stories and I know what the Word says.

I think, only think, that they may not be experiencing the supernatural Peace that surpasses all understanding. I think that what they are experiencing is the Prince of Peace Himself because He's there with them at the time of their death.

> *When they heard these things, they were cut to the heart, and they gnashed on him with their teeth. But he, being full of the Holy Ghost, looked up stedfastly into heaven, and saw the glory of God, and Jesus standing on the right hand of God and said, "Behold, I see the heavens opened, and the Son of Man standing on the right hand of God." Then they cried out with a loud voice, and stopped their ears, and ran upon him with one accord, and cast him out of the city, and stoned him: and the witnesses laid down their clothes at a young man's feet, whose name was Saul. And they stoned Stephen, calling upon God, and saying, "Lord Jesus, receive my spirit." And he kneeled down, and cried with a loud voice, "Lord, lay not this sin to their charge." And when he had said this, he fell asleep.* **Acts 7:54-60**

I've witnessed family who were dying and knew the Lord. At the moment of the death, they appeared to have seen Jesus. I've also talked to other Believers who've been present when Christians died and they have also witnessed this phenomenon.

Other contemporary examples of Christians' persecution and death indicate that God's Everlasting

---

25 Thomas Paine, "The Crises". USHistory.org, http://www.ushistory.org/paine/crisis/c-01.htm, (last accessed December 16, 2018).

Peace is present at the time of the faithful's demise. I'm specifically thinking about the example of those Coptic Christians who were beheaded by ISIS in 2015. They would not recant their faith, they verbally forgave their killers and they sang to the Lord. The Peace that they appeared to experience in that moment indicates that the Lord and His angels were standing with them. I've been in His presence and I can tell you that it brings immediate Peace.

Remember, peace is not the absence of conflict. Peace is the presence of the Way, the Truth, and the Life. When they're in the presence of the King, that's when they sing.

Luke even says that when we go to be with Him, He sends His angels to see us home.

And it came to pass, that the beggar died, and was carried by the angels into Abraham's bosom. **Luke 16:22a**

If you're seeking Him, if you love Him more than your own life, if you're obeying Him and if you're truly His, He will be at your side as you step into glory. On this, you can have Peace.

Peace-less, Raging Nations

I mentioned earlier that I thought we were at the End of the Age; however long that takes. Things are changing very quickly now and becoming more volatile by the day. In society, in politics, in genetics, in robotics, in technology and in earth changes, all around you can feel the building pressure of birthpangs (Matt 24:8).

With changes of this scale and speed, it's easy to have your personal peace wane and to feel overwhelmed. Nonetheless, we know that regardless of the reason or the season, God's Everlasting Peace can be a constant anchor for our lives.

There are signposts that we can look at on this End Time journey which show how close we're getting. The Bible says that we'll hear people proclaiming peace and safety in the very near future but then disaster will come:

For when they shall say, Peace and safety; then sudden destruction cometh upon them, as travail upon a woman with child; and they shall not escape. **1 Thess 5:3**

We also see in the Word that in the Last Days, Jerusalem will become a cup of trembling.

Behold, I will make Jerusalem a cup of trembling unto all the people round about, when they shall be in the siege both against Judah and against Jerusalem. And in that day will I make Jerusalem a burdensome stone for all people: all that burden themselves with it shall be cut in pieces, though all the people of the earth be gathered together against it. "In that day," saith the LORD, "I will smite every horse with astonishment, and his rider with madness: and I will open mine eyes upon the house of Judah, and will smite every horse of the people with blindness. And the governors of Judah shall say in their heart, 'The inhabitants of Jerusalem shall be my strength in the LORD of hosts their God.'" **Zechariah 12:2-5**

We certainly see more and more of the world's attention being focused on Jerusalem. With the recent moving of the American Embassy to the city, it's a good guess that sometime in the very near future,

Jerusalem will become a "burdensome stone" for the world. Maybe that's why we're told to pray for the peace of Jerusalem:

> *Pray for the peace of Jerusalem: they shall prosper that love thee.* **Psalm 122:6**

We also know that as we get closer to the end, peace will be removed from the earth and the nations will rage.

> *Why do the heathen rage, and the people imagine a vain thing? The kings of the earth set themselves, and the rulers take counsel together, against the LORD, and against His anointed, saying, "Let us break their bands asunder, and cast away their cords from us." He that sitteth in the heavens shall laugh: the Lord shall have them in derision. Then shall He speak unto them in His wrath, and vex them in His sore displeasure. Yet have I set my King upon my holy hill of Zion. I will declare the decree: the LORD hath said unto me, "Thou art my Son; this day have I begotten thee. Ask of me, and I shall give thee the heathen for thine inheritance, and the uttermost parts of the earth for thy possession. Thou shalt break them with a rod of iron; thou shalt dash them in pieces like a potter's vessel." Psalm 2:1-9*

Another signpost toward the culmination of time is the red horse out of Revelation 6 whose job it is to "take peace from the earth".

> *And when he had opened the second seal, I heard the second beast say, "Come and see." And there went out another horse that was red: and power was given to him that sat thereon to take peace from the earth, and that they should kill one another: and there was given unto him a great sword. Rev 6:3-4*

In the above passage, the next thing you know, everyone starts killing one another: "it was given unto him (the Red Horse) a great sword." I think that there's a direct correlation here to the "Restrainer" being removed from the earth.

And now ye know what withholdeth that he might be revealed in his time. For the mystery of iniquity doth already work: only he who now letteth will let, until he be taken out of the way. 2 Peter 2:6-7

For the record, I don't believe that the Restrainer, or the one that "withholdeth" in the KJV, is the Holy Spirit. In fact, if Jesus said, *"Lo, I am with you even until the end of the age"* (Matt 28:20) how could the Holy Spirit be removed?

I do believe that this Restrainer is the Archangel Michael. Michael was warring against the "Prince of Persia" who withstood him for twenty-one days. So it stands to reason that it is also Michael who's holding back this evil.

> *But the prince of the kingdom of Persia withstood me one and twenty days: but, lo, Michael, one of the chief princes, came to help me; and I remained there with the kings of Persia.* **Daniel 10:13**

If all of this talk about rushing to the End of the Age is upsetting your peace, I challenge you to change your perspective. For the Christian, Peace is knowing that what God said in His Word is true. The very fact that these things are coming to pass gives His words legitimacy. If He's telling you the truth about what has happened, what is happening, and what will happen, shouldn't we accept as true His statement that He will give us "Peace that surpasses all understanding"?

In this way, the acceptance of God's Everlasting Peace is a choice.

The Freedom of Friendship

Peace with God is the most life-freeing thing that there is. His Peace is based upon a life- nourishing relationship, with Jesus at the center, and where we are called His friend.

> *Henceforth I call you not servants; for the servant knoweth not what his lord doeth: but I have called you friends; for all things that I have heard of my Father I have made known unto you.* **John 15:15**

Have you ever had a good friendship, a friend that you've had for years, who can be candid with you and you with them? This is a friend that doesn't judge you because of your actions or motives. You don't have to have your defenses up around this friend. You two interact in perfect peace. This is the kind of friendship that Jesus wants to have with you.

The fact that Jesus would call us friends is the most mind-blowing thing in scripture! That friendship can only come through Peace, but there are some limits to the example of comparing Jesus to our earthly friends. That's because even our friends don't know our deepest, darkest thoughts and feelings. This is human nature. We always hold back part of ourselves from other people as a defense mechanism. There are things in my head that I would rather not have other people hear or know. No, I don't want to go around killing, raping or stealing but like you, my private thoughts are private for a reason. Maybe I don't want to hurt someone else's feelings. Maybe if I said what's in my head I would alienate myself to someone. Maybe I don't trust the other person on an issue. All of these thoughts are normal.

Many people are hindered by the idea that if God really knew who they were, knew what their lives were like, and knew their thoughts and motives, He wouldn't want to be their friend. But the fact is that He already knows you better than you know yourself and yet, He still wants to call you His friend!

> ~ *LORD, thou hast searched me, and known me. Thou knowest my downsitting and mine uprising, thou understandest my thought afar off. Thou compassest my path and my lying down, and art acquainted with all my ways. For there is not a word in my tongue, but, lo, O LORD, thou knowest it altogether.* **Psalm 139:1-4**

> ~ *For if our heart condemn us, God is greater than our heart, and knoweth all things.* **1 John 3:20**

> ~ *For the word of God is quick, and powerful, and sharper than any twoedged sword, piercing even to the dividing asunder of soul and spirit, and of the joints and marrow, and is a discerner of the thoughts and intents of the heart.* **Heb 4:12**

> ~ *But the LORD said unto Samuel, Look not on his countenance, or on the height of his stature; because I have refused him: for the LORD seeth not as man seeth; for man looketh on the outward appearance, but the LORD looketh on the heart.* **1 Sam 16:7**

> ~ *And He that searcheth the hearts knoweth what is the mind of the Spirit, because He maketh intercession for the saints according to the will of God.* **Rom 8:27**

In spite of all of this, He still loves us with an unfathomable love and He can't stop thinking about us!

*How precious also are thy thoughts unto me, O God! How great is the sum of them! If I should count them, they are more in number than the sand: when I awake, I am still with thee. **Psalm 139:17-18***

Wow! Talk about Peace in a relationship! He knows all of our thoughts and He thinks about us constantly. And He thoroughly loves us! This is mind-blowing:

 God's thoughts toward us are more numerous than the sea,

 He knows everyone who has ever been created or will be created,

He knows our thoughts and knows everything about us,

 He knows what we are like now and what we will be like if we surrender to Him.

He's the Lord who calls the end from the beginning (Isaiah 46:10).

It is this God who offers Peace. It's the Lord Almighty Who knows you better than you know yourself. It's this God Who gives His people His Peace and eternal life through direct relationship made possible by His Son. No other god or religion offers eternal life or that kind of Peace. It makes me wonder: What do you want to do, practice meditation forever and still not have the free gift of what God is offering?

*And this is the record, that God hath given to us eternal life, and this life is in His Son. He that hath the Son hath life; and he that hath not the Son of God hath not life. **1 John 5:11-12***

When we surrender our lives to the Lord, the number one thing that happens, after His forgiveness, is that a supernatural Peace envelops us and the burden of our sin rolls away. That doesn't meant that we won't sin again, we are still in this world full of yuck. What it does mean is that when we do, we have an advocate with the Father.

*My little children, these things write I unto you, that ye sin not. And if any man sin, we have an advocate with the Father, Jesus Christ the righteous: and He is the propitiation for our sins: and not for ours only, but also for the sins of the whole world. **1 John 2:1-2***

There's no other religion out there that has the gift of life and friendship that's offered through the Lord Jesus Christ.

Chapter 24
The Trenches

These things I have spoken unto you, that in me ye might have peace. In the world ye shall have tribulation: but be of good cheer; I have overcome the world.

John 16:33

There've been times in my life when I've had great mental or emotional pain or distress and cried out to the Lord and instantly He gave me Peace. At those times, my situation might not have changed, but a calmness appeared in the midst of the circumstance. It still hurt, I still had to live through it, but Jesus giving me Peace in the middle of the situation enabled me to walk through it.

Nonbelievers do not have that calm in the middle of the storm. They have to go through painful and stressful situations alone. They can meditate, they can medicate, they can repeat mantras, and they can try every gimmick you can imagine, but Peace, real Peace, only comes with the presence of the Lord.

Yea, though I walk through the valley of the shadow of death, I will fear no evil: for thou art with me; thy rod and thy staff they comfort me. **Psalm 23:4**

The Plight

In a world where the majority of the created have turned their backs on their Creator, a lack of Peace is humanity's plight. Peace for the Christian is supposed to be not only accessible, but also part of their daily lives through the fruit of the Spirit.

> *But the fruit of the Spirit is love, joy, peace, longsuffering, gentleness, goodness, faith, meekness, temperance: against such there is no law.* **Gal 5:22**

Understanding Who the imparter of this peace is and what we need to do to walk in it, is something that the mainstream Church fails to communicate. It's apparent that even the leadership doesn't comprehend the true impetus of God's Everlasting Peace. If true, how can they adequately communicate it to their congregations? It's no wonder that the mental health crisis is even battering Christians!

Historically, this hasn't always been the case. The early Church knew full well Who was the source of their Peace. This fact is evident in the greetings of the epistles of the NT.

> *Unto Timothy, my own son in the faith: Grace, mercy, and peace, from God our Father and Jesus Christ our Lord.* **1 Tim 1:2**

But it's not enough to intellectually understand who imparts this Peace. Rather than dying to ourselves and seeking the Lord with our whole hearts, the mainstream Church is still fixated on the idea of "what's in it for me?" I've already addressed the self-centered attitude of most Christians so I won't revisit it here. If our lives are not our own and we are bondservants to Jesus, why are we always so focused on ourselves?

Sitting in His presence, repenting on a regular basis, studying His Word and worshiping Him daily will go a long way to providing you that elusive Peace. The vast majority of so-called Believers don't do any of this and we wonder why we don't have Peace?

Now, you may be read this, scratch your head and think, "I don't get all of this spiritual mumbo jumbo at all! 'Fruit of the Spirit' whatever! I just need some peace!"

As I pointed out at the beginning of this section, peace means different things to different people. To better help you understand what real Peace can do in your life, let's look at real issues where there is no peace to be had.

Anxiety/Fear

Anxiety is the number one sign pointing to a lack of the peace of God. It's an emotional and mental indication that causes you to believe that your circumstance is beyond your ability to cope.

Being fearful/anxious about a situation is not an indication that you actually can't deal with it; you only feel like it's too big for you to handle. And it's this lack of confidence in yours, or God's, ability that is the center of the anxiety. If you're a Christian, and full of anxiety, where God's ability is concerned you don't trust Him to help you, to protect or deliver you. This lack of trust, either in yourself or in God, makes you feel insecure and that insecurity aggravates the anxiety that you feel.

For the record, feeling anxious about a minor situation like a job interview or test in school is not necessarily anxiety. Having a concern about the unknown outcome of a situation is normal. However, when anxiety becomes a hindrance to your life or even debilitating, this is a sure sign that the Peace of God is absent from the situation or the individual.

Some of the signs of real fear/anxiety are:

~ Excessive Worry

~ Agitation with Physical Symptoms

~ Restlessness

~ Fatigue

~ Difficulty in Concentrating

~ Irritability

~ Tense Muscles

~ Sleeplessness

~ Panic Attacks

~ Purposeful Avoidance of Social Situations

~ Irrational Fears[26]

Again, everyone has probably experienced one or more of these symptoms in their lifetime. But the continual, ongoing and persistent reoccurrence of one or more of these symptoms indicates a distinct lack of peace and the presence of fear/anxiety.

As an indication of the times in which we find ourselves, anxiety is snowballing, especially in the West. It's estimated that 1 in 5 people in the U.S., almost 40 million, experience some form of anxiety disorder. And it's reported that 300 million people worldwide are struggling with the affliction.[27]

Earlier in this book, I spoke specifically to the issues of mental health in the Church. While the statistics for Christians are slightly better than non-Christians, anxiety and the effects thereof are also drastically affecting Believers.

Does it surprise you that our adversary, the devil, seeks to mentally torment all of mankind? The antidote to that torment is God's perfect Peace. But somehow that supernatural Peace eludes the majority of His people. This is in spite of our being partly supernatural creations with Holy Spirit living in us to combat that torment.

> *But if the Spirit of Him that raised up Jesus from the dead dwell in you, He that raised up Christ from the dead shall also quicken your mortal bodies by His Spirit that dwelleth in you.* ***Rom 8:11***

Eating Disorders

Another symptom of a lack of peace and the anxiety that builds up in people are eating disorders. For some people who don't know how to handle that peace-lessness, their anxiety causes them to resort to eating uncontrollably, while others have no appetite at all and become severely malnourished. In either case, this lack of peace eventually causes health problems, some which are life threatening.

---

26 Erica Julson, "11 Signs and Symptoms of Anxiety Disorders". Healthline Red, https://www.healthline.com/nutrition/anxiety-disorder-symptoms, (April 10, 2018).

27 Tim Newman, "Anxiety in the West: Is it on the Rise?" Medical News Today, https://www.medicalnewstoday.com/articles/322877.php, (September 5, 2018).

~ At least 30 million people of all ages and genders suffer from an eating disorder in the U.S.

~ Every 62 minutes at least one person dies as a direct result of an eating disorder.

~ Eating disorders have the highest mortality rate of any mental illness.

~ Eating disorders affect all races and ethnic groups.

Specific to the disorder, we see the following:

Anorexia Nervosa:

~ 0.9% of American women suffer from anorexia in their lifetime.

~ 1 in 5 anorexia deaths is by suicide.

~ 33-50% of anorexia patients have a *comorbid mood disorder, such as depression. Mood disorders are more common in the binge/purge subtype than in the restrictive subtype. (*In medicine, comorbidity is the presence of one or more additional diseases or disorders co-occurring with a primary disease or disorder.)

~ About half of anorexia patients have a comorbid anxiety disorder, such as obsessive-compulsive disorder and
social phobia.

Bulimia Nervosa:

~ 1.5% of American women suffer from bulimia nervosa in their lifetime.

~ Nearly half of bulimia patients have a comorbid mood disorder.

~ More than half of bulimia patients have comorbid anxiety disorders.

~ Nearly 1 in 10 bulimia patients have a comorbid substance abuse disorder, usually alcohol use.

Binge Eating Disorder (BED):

~ 2.8% of American adults suffer from binge eating disorder in their lifetime.

~ Nearly half of BED patients have a comorbid mood disorder.

~ More than half of BED patients have comorbid anxiety disorders.

~ Nearly 1 in 10 BED patients have a comorbid substance abuse disorder, usually alcohol use.[28]

And the lack of peace in people's lives has far-reaching effects.

Lifestyle Instability

We've all known someone who can't hold down a job, is strung out on drugs or alcohol, has had several marriages or relationships, can't keep friends or is always at odds with family and coworkers. The fact is that a lack of peace of mind can lead to that kind of instability.

Often times people are unknowingly searching for peace and the above behaviors are the negative byproducts of that search. People who are desperate for peace will go from place to place, addiction to addiction, and relationship to relationship to try to find that elusive peace.

---

28 ANAD, "Eating Disorder Statistics". Anad.org, https://anad.org/education-and-awareness/about-eating-disorders/eating-disorders-statistics/, (last accessed December 14, 2018).

All the while God waits on the sideline so that He can be their peace. In order to make that happen, the person must surrender to Him first.

Depression

As I said, we all deal with these issues at one time or another in even minute ways. We live in a broken world. Sorrow and depression are part of the muck that we wade through in this life.

If you haven't experienced it yet, you will at one time in your life have someone close to you who dies , perhaps a horrible death. I think of the mighty men and women of God whom I've known throughout the years who have died in this way, wonderful people like Greg Evenson, Sue Bradley and others.

Honestly, it's one of the most perplexing things in life. Why were their deaths painful or their lives cut short early? Why can we not consistently work the works of Him Who died for us and rose again? We do see miracles from time to time, but they don't manifest routinely like they did in the NT. Certainly, with these losses, my peace has come under assault and yours will too.

You might find yourself in a situation where you've been treated unfairly or hurt in some other way and were heartbroken. When that happens, we will be sorrowful, sad, hurt, angry and depressed. It's inevitable. For a time, our peace is stolen or misplaced.

To find it again, we can lean on the Lord Who is more than able to mend our hearts.

Come unto me, all ye that labour and are heavy laden, and I will give you rest. **Matt 11:28**

Most people will be able to work through their grief, perhaps with counseling, to come out of the sorrow and depression. Some people never seem to dig themselves out of that hole.

I am not a doctor but I will tell you that God is capable, all by Himself, to heal you and to give you the Peace that you lack. I believe this with my whole heart and I wouldn't tell you if it were not so. However, neither am I here to judge you if you're taking prescriptions or if you're imprisoned by a cycle of depression. I'm only here to remind you of what God has said, and done, for each of us.

At the core of depression is hopelessness. This ought not to be. God's Peace can fill the void you're feeling if you only let Him. He is our hope. He is our Peace. The devil comes to steal, kill, and destroy (John 10:10). If Satan has stolen your peace and hope, God can, and will, give them back to you if you lean on Him.

Casting all your care upon him; for he careth for you. **1 Peter 5:7**

In particular I need to speak to you if you're considering suicide.

If there was ever an example of the devil's torment, it's in this area. The Fallen Ones, or a demon, may well come to you to whisper these thoughts into your mind. You know exactly which thoughts I'm talking about. It's when you have a thought that you think is your own, but it's not. They are tormenting thoughts disguised as "self-speak" which try to convince you to end it all. They might sound like this in your head:

"I'm never going to be good enough…" "No one cares…" "I'll show him, I'll just kill myself…" "It's never going to get better…" "I'm so tired of all of this…" etc. etc.

The common denominator in all of these thoughts is that they end up with you thinking you want to kill yourself. You may think it's your own thoughts, but it's not. It's a demon - remember that. It is the voice of Hell that puts the thoughts in your mind and tries to get you to agree with it that you need to end your life.

If this is you, and you're a Christian, the next time you think those thoughts - rebuke them aloud in Jesus' name. There is power in that Name that the demonic can't stand up against.

You may feel helpless, hopeless and that peace is far from you. You may think that there's no way out. For both the Christian and the unbeliever, I'm here to tell you that God is your way out. His Peace, here and now, in this life, is available to you if you only cry out to Him.

Toward the end of this section, I'll provide some specific things that you can do to pull yourself out of this pit, so please - don't stop reading. God loves you, deeply, constantly and without end. Nothing you feel or think can separate you from His love (**Romans 8:35-39**). His Holy Spirit can mend your broken heart and give you Peace.

Suicide is the 10th leading cause of death in the United States and the rate is increasing. In the age group of 15 to 25, it's the 3rd leading cause of death. This is an End Times epidemic as the demonic onslaught increases, Christians and non-Christians alike will be in Satan's crosshairs.

People say that they want peace. They say that they need peace.

The real question is: Are they willing to accept the One who paid the price of Peace for us? **Jesus is that Peace.**

The Struggle is Real

Struggling with peace happens when we try to fight the leftovers from our past, or contemporary attacks, in our own strength.

> *Finally, my brethren, be strong in the Lord and the power of HIS might.* **Eph 6:10**

For those of us who were raised in a cold, sterile, scientific and/or analytical environment, we try to figure everything out instead of letting God work it out. Trying to use your head and think through issues is great, except when you let that reasoning supersede God's hand. At times, this imbalance in my walk hinders me and leads to a loss of peace.

As an example, have you ever been in the presence of people who are calm on the outside, but you see a tension underneath the surface that indicates they are anything but calm? They seem to be seething and at a moment's notice they could uncork and blow?

I must confess that at times, I can even be like that. I wish that I had the Peace of God that surpasses all understanding - all of the time. Sometimes I do, but candidly, I don't always walk in it.

So here's my disclaimer: Because I know me and my own struggles, I feel like I'm the last guy to try to give you solutions for your own lack of peace. The truth is the truth. The Word is the Word. It's by the Holy Spirit that I share these things with you and not because I have it all together. Please take these words at face value and understand that I'm certainly not in the position to judge you. I've got my own issues.

God tells us in His Word that He's going to walk through the mess with us. Here's a candid, real life example from my own experience. For your benefit, I've cleaned up the language a bit.

A while back, I was having a hard time about something and was praying during my private quiet time. Now, keep in mind that no one else was around. In my frustration, I said, *"Lord, I'm tired of having to walk through the dung on this earth! I'm just tired of it!"* (This is the cleaning up part. I didn't say dung. Use your imagination.)

I meant no disrespect to the Lord. I was fed up and I was just being real with Him.

Out of the blue, either that day or the next, I received a word from a woman who intercedes in prayer for me regularly.

She said plainly, *"Son, Jesus wants me to tell you that you will walk through dung in this life but that He's walking through it with you. In fact, He will carry you through it until you go to be with Him."*

Here's the thing: She didn't say dung either! She used the exact words that I used in my quiet time!

Now, you might be offended by my candor. But God isn't offended. He knows our thoughts even before we have them. The Bible is full of references to dung. If you search the literal meaning of that word in the original language, you'll find that it means either human or animal excrement. I didn't say anything that He's not already said in His Word. Our struggle with Peace is real. When we approach God, we have to be real with Him too.

> *And he said unto me, "My grace is sufficient for thee: for my strength is made perfect in weakness." Most gladly therefore will I rather glory in my infirmities, that the power of Christ may rest upon me. Therefore I take pleasure in infirmities, in reproaches, in necessities, in persecutions, in distresses for Christ's sake: for when I am weak, then am I strong.* **2 Cor 12:9-10**

Scorched Earth

Trying to communicate God's Peace to a nonbeliever isn't something that just anyone can do. No man can go and do a work for God until God first works in that man. Neither will God work through him until he's in the position and place where He can work through Him; that is, until His Spirit can flow through the man to other thirsty hearts. In essence, we become a ladle of Living Water to thirsty souls who are dying in their trespasses and sins. Until those souls come to know Jesus, they will not know peace, real Peace.

Likewise, for the Believer who's going through a difficult time and has no peace, ministering to them can also be challenging. I can hear some of them now, *"How do you know, Steve? Your life is perfect! You're on the radio, people listen to you, you have a good income, and there's no way that you can understand what I'm going through!"*

Maybe I don't know your exact situation, but Peace in my life, or the lack thereof, is something that I'm deeply familiar with. And the only way that I'm able to communicate anything of value about Peace is:

    a. By the Holy Spirit, and...

b. Because God has done His work in me because I too have struggled and searched for God's Everlasting Peace.

This reminds me of something a friend of mine says. One of his favorite sayings is: *"We are the sum of our own personal histories."* I would wholeheartedly agree with that statement.

Please don't misunderstand. As the Word says, when we come to Jesus and ask Him into our hearts, and are filled with the Holy Ghost, we instantly become new creations - but we still have a history. All of our experiences and memories don't magically disappear. Somehow, and I don't know how, God makes it possible in that instant for us to be forever changed, but at the same time we remember what we were like and what we did prior to that supernatural conversion.

For some of us, that landscape of our personal history prior to Jesus is like a scorched earth. I became an alcoholic at the young age of 13. At that pubescent stage, most teenagers' hormones are raging, making them sexually active. I was no different. I hate to admit it but I was virtually addicted to sex and porn from that time until Jesus delivered me when I got saved.

To me, alcohol and sex were the only way to sooth the inner rage and abandonment that I felt throughout my whole life.

As you'll recall, I mentioned that I went to MSU to go to film school. What I didn't say earlier was that my whole goal in going to film school was to learn how to make porn-science fiction movies!

I remember reading Hugh Hefner's biography in the early 70's and determined to model my life after him. I know, I know, sick right? But I figured that life in the fast lane -- getting drunk, fast women, fast cars and the motto "eat, drink and be merry for today's another party"-- was the best way to try to find some peace and happiness.

I mention these things not to boast on the ugliness of my past. The fact is that now, after Jesus, I'm embarrassed by that life. But peace was the one thing that I needed desperately because I couldn't find anything that could fill that hole in my life. The moment Jesus saved me I understood that there was Peace in Him and a larger purpose for my life that went beyond pleasure and a hedonistic lifestyle.

People all over the world search for peace in all kinds of areas: New Age, transcendental meditation, Buddhism, Hinduism, sex, drugs and rock n roll and more. But I know first-hand that they can party, they can live life on their own terms, they can have a good time and they can do everything to run from God, but they won't find real peace, the Peace of God, in the world.

There is no peace, saith the LORD, unto the wicked. **Isaiah 48:22**

The wicked are those who do not know God. The wicked are those who reject God. The wicked are those who make war against God. Because there's no peace in them, there's no peace on earth. As I pointed out in the last H.E.L.P. of Proclamation, enmity means perpetual war. There is no real Peace between the devil and his followers and God's people, according to Genesis 3:15.

But the overriding ironic thing about the unbeliever's search for peace is that the devil just needs to remove his hand and stop tormenting his followers to give them peace. He's the one causing the torment and the lack of peace in the first place! As I've mentioned, he absolutely hates us, so fat chance of him voluntarily stopping the torment.

The Lord is able to immediately stop that torment and give us His Everlasting Peace when we surrender our wills and lives to Him.

And, having made peace through the blood of his cross, by him to reconcile all things unto himself; by him, I say, whether they be things in earth, or things in heaven. **Col 1:20**

Peace, real Peace, is a settled knowing that I have a purpose in life. I don't have to just react to circumstances anymore. My life has a greater meaning than the pure pleasure of the moment.

Flee also youthful lusts: but follow righteousness, faith, charity, peace, with them that call on the Lord out of a pure heart. **2 Tim 2:22**

The life I led before Jesus helps me to understand that the key to Peace is always to set your eyes on Him. When I have my eyes on Jesus, I have Peace. When I take my eyes off of Jesus, I lose my Peace.

And the same day, when the even was come, He saith unto them, "Let us pass over unto the other side." And when they had sent away the multitude, they took Him even as He was in the ship. And there were also with Him other little ships. And there arose a great storm of wind, and the waves beat into the ship, so that it was now full. And He was in the hinder part of the ship, asleep on a pillow and they awake Him, and say unto Him, "Master, carest thou not that we perish?" And He arose, and rebuked the wind, and said unto the sea, "Peace, be still." And the wind ceased, and there was a great calm. And He said unto them, "Why are ye so fearful? How is it that ye have no faith?" And they feared exceedingly, and said one to another, "What manner of man is this, that even the wind and the sea obey Him?" **Mark 4:35-41**

When you think of this verse, you have to think of the calmness that Jesus brings with His presence. Just like He stilled that storm, He can still your nerves and anxiety. And believe me, I know what anxiety is.

Under the Gun

Many people in life, Believers and unbelievers, feel so under-the-gun that their nerves are strung tighter than a Great Wallenda tightrope. I also know this feeling of being under-the-gun, but under a literal gun. I've had numerous death threats and attempts on my life over the years. Those were nearly as dangerous as growing up in our house when I was a kid.

My father was an alcoholic and would get drunk and shoot into my bedroom! I remember as a young man, thirteen or fourteen, sitting in my Ethan Allen rocking chair, crying and waiting for my dad to come into my room to shoot me. At the same time, I remember holding my gun at the ready because if he came in to my room, I might have to shoot him before he tried to kill me. There certainly was no peace in that situation.

Years later, after I'd gotten married and my daughter was older, I took my wife and daughter into the basement of our old house where my room had been. Despite my stories of my dad shooting into my room, my wife and my daughter never really believed me. That was until they looked in the closet and saw the bullet holes for themselves!

Alcoholic rage was a routine part of my life. My kid brother Clayton was two years younger than me.

313

One time my dad was so angry at him that he pistol-whipped him with the butt of a .45! He almost killed Clayton and would have if my mother and I didn't pull him off of my brother.

Clayton survived that attack but living in that dysfunctional family also took a toll on his life as well. He ran hard in the other direction from the Lord for most of his life. Talk about generational curses, he too was a raging alcoholic. Thank God that he accepted Jesus six months before he was murdered.

Like you, my personal history has affected my life and my peace. My grandfather, my father's father, was an abusive and angry man. My alcoholic father had raged as a result of his upbringing by cold, indifferent and non-loving parents. Because of this I was the peace-less fruit of a very hurt and damaged man.

How's that for an illustration about the devil stealing someone's peace, instilling fear and warping my understanding of God the Father? While I'm certainly not defending my lifestyle choices prior to coming to know Jesus, there is a reason why people do the things they do. I was a product of my upbringing: angry, a drunk, lonely, etc. etc.

When Hal Lindsey pointed at me that night and said that Jesus loved me, I was shocked to hear that anyone could love me. When he told me Who Jesus was, I knew that if I ever had a chance for real Peace in my life, this was it! To be able to stand in the presence of Jesus and feel the kind of Peace that flowed right through my body and spirit, I knew that He was the only Way, the only Truth and the only Life.

God delivered me from many of the things of my past that very first night. When He filled me with His Holy Spirit, my perspective of the world instantly changed as He gave me Peace. But don't think for a second that the devil doesn't still try to bait me with my personal history from time to time and steal my Peace.

Every time I get a death threat (Yes! I still do!) the devil tries to reassert fear into my life. But he can only be as successful in that attack as I let him. The fact is that we all have things in our pasts that he tries to use against us. But it's always God's sustaining power that keeps us, and His Holy Spirit who fills us with His Peace.

> *My sheep hear my voice, and I know them, and they follow me: And I give unto them eternal life; and they shall never perish, neither shall any man pluck them out of my hand. My Father, which gave them me, is greater than all; and no man is able to pluck them out of my Father's hand. I and my Father are one. John 10:27-30*

In the midst of this constant battle, the ebb and flow of spiritual warfare is all around us. You may not be able to see the bloodthirsty demonic forces, but they would like nothing more than to turn you into emotional and mental mush, or even cause you to take your own life.

The Everlasting Peace of God is your counter to that onslaught.

I know, I've lived it.

Forgiveness

There's a direct connection between forgiveness and Peace. And forgiving is something that most people have a hard time doing. I know I did.

I told you the story about my father and gave you a snippet of the junk that I had to live with. That junk followed me my whole life, causing me to be angry and unforgiving toward my father.

But unforgiveness is a poison. It will ruin virtually every part of your life if you don't deal with it. When I found Jesus, I had no idea this was the case. I just thought I was screwed up and had no clue why but if we Christians hang onto unforgiveness, we will face consequences.

> *For if ye forgive men their trespasses, your heavenly Father will also forgive you: But if ye forgive not men their trespasses, neither will your Father forgive your trespasses.* **Matt 6:14-15**

God is gracious and He will give us time and opportunity to get right with others, thereby getting right with Him where unforgiveness is concerned. Even after I got saved, even though I physically saw Jesus and spoke to Him, even though He gave me a commission of a Joseph's ministry and even though He showed me that panoramic of history, I was still steeped in unforgiveness. Jesus knows me better than I know myself so He was acutely aware of this but didn't address it with me right away.

I went to a Christian retreat one weekend within the first year after I got saved. There my pastor, Wayne Snyder, laid hands on me and prayed over me that God would break the hold of unforgiveness over my life. He prayed, "God, release Steve from the hurt and the hatred of his father."

Now here's the thing. Pastor Wayne was the Campus Pastor for the people of my age group. I learned a lot from him and spoke to him often. But he had no idea of all the stuff that went on with my father. He was led by the Holy Spirit to pray as he did and I knew that God was dealing with me about forgiving my dad for all of that junk that I had to grow up with.

At that point I had a choice about what I would do. The very first part of the following week I wrote my dad a long letter telling him that I loved him and forgave him for all the years of hatred and abuse. I also took responsibility for my part in not being as good of a son as I could have been. The very act of my willingness to forgive my father in the letter set me free from all of that junk that I'd been feeling. But here is the astonishing thing. My dad had been living in the Yak River Country in a rugged part of Montana. Roads are winding and steep and traverse numerous cliffs. That very week my father was going down one such road when his car went off the embankment and plunged into the freezing Yak River. Even though people stopped and saw his car going under, no one helped him. He drowned.

This is why I share with you: My father's position with the Lord had nothing to do with me. The Lord knew when his life would end. But because He loves me, God worked on my heart and gave me the opportunity to be released from all of that unforgiveness while my father was still alive. God showed me the problem through His Holy Spirit and used Pastor Wayne to prompt me to take action to bring me peace.

By the way, my father never read my letter. When we went through his belongings after he died, the letter had reached his home after the accident and was with other unopened mail. The letter wasn't for my dad after all - It was for me so that God could restore His Everlasting Peace to my life

Lack of forgiveness brings torment in your own life. How many Christians today are still suffering at the hands of the tormentors (demons) because they just can't forgive? Maybe you've been abused by someone mentally, physically or even sexually and you just can't forgive that person. Maybe you've been lied to, cheated on, done wrong or even been ruined by someone and you can't forgive them. Maybe someone you love was murdered or injured by someone and you can't find it in yourself to forgive the perpetrator.

Neither could I until someone prayed over me and asked God to break the unforgiveness and hatred in my life. I pray now that God will break the unforgiveness in your life too. If the peace in your life is bound up by unforgiveness, God wants to restore that peace if you will forgive and let Him.

In the years since then, another important lesson I've learned is our need to forgive people over and over again.

> *Then came Peter to Him, and said, "Lord, how oft shall my brother sin against me, and I forgive him? Till seven times?" Jesus saith unto him, "I say not unto thee, 'Until seven times:' but, 'Until seventy times seven.'"* **Matt 18:21-22**

> *Take heed to yourselves: If thy brother trespass against thee, rebuke him; and if he repent, forgive him. And if he trespass against thee seven times in a day, and seven times in a day turn again to thee, saying, "I repent;" thou shalt forgive him.* **Luke 17:3-4**

We also need to be careful about judging others and to forgive them as well.

> *Judge not, and ye shall not be judged: condemn not, and ye shall not be condemned: forgive, and ye shall be forgiven.* **Luke 6:37**

And, as tough as it is, we also need to forgive people regardless of what they've done to us.

> *And they stoned Stephen, calling upon God, and saying, "Lord Jesus, receive my spirit." And he kneeled down, and cried with a loud voice, "Lord, lay not this sin to their charge." And when he had said this, he fell asleep.* **Acts 7:59-60**

I'm not saying for a second that I have this forgiving thing down. In fact, sometimes I struggle. There's also a big difference between forgiving and forgetting. If someone has harmed you or someone you love, you can forgive them but you don't have to subject yourself to future pain by them.

Alexander Pope said, *"To err is human to forgive is divine."* That spark of divine, the Holy Spirit, lives inside of us and enables us to walk as Jesus walked. Jesus forgave, and forgives, us. In God's forgiveness of us, we come into peace and that peace enables us to extend the same benefit and the same offer to those around us. This is what the gospel is.

Standing in the Gap

Walking uprightly and continually before God and forgiving others helps us to maintain our Peace, but we are also called to support others through prayer in their own quest for peace.

Intercessory prayer is an essential part of the peace process. I believe that for every earthly battle, there's a supernatural fight in the heavenlies that ensues before it takes place on earth. If we're functioning as part of the Body, then interceding on behalf of other people will bring us peace. Our direct intervention through the power of prayer opens the door for peace for others. The greatest victories that I've gotten in my own life were not a result of my own prayers, but someone else touching God on my behalf.

~ *Is any sick among you? Let him call for the elders of the church; and let them pray over him, anointing him with oil in the name of the Lord and the prayer of faith shall save the sick, and the Lord shall raise him up and if he have committed sins, they shall be forgiven him. Confess your faults one to another, and pray one for another, that ye may be healed. The effectual fervent prayer of a righteous man availeth much. James 5:14-16*

~ *I exhort therefore, that, first of all, supplications, prayers, intercessions, and giving of thanks, be made for all men. 1 Tim 2:1*

~ *Two are better than one because they have a good reward for their labour. For if they fall, the one will lift up his fellow: but woe to him that is alone when he falleth, for he hath not another to help him up. Again, if two lie together, then they have heat, but how can one be warm alone? And if one prevail against him, two shall withstand him; and a threefold cord is not quickly broken. Ecclesiastes 4:9-12*

God addressed the issue of intercessory prayer when He looked for a man to stand in the gap and couldn't find any.

And I sought for a man among them, that should make up the hedge, and stand in the gap before me for the land, that I should not destroy it, but I found none. Ezekiel 22:30

Our interactive participation through intercessory prayer will cause us to draw closer to God and bring us Peace in this war. Our intercession also gives us a positive and godly influence in other people's lives. Thus, we can lead a larger spiritual life than even we ever thought was possible.

Prayer works.

Not Simple Religion

There is no fear in love; but perfect love casteth out fear: because fear hath torment. He that feareth is not made perfect in love. 1 John 4:18

You can't have peace if you don't have hope.

Those of us raised with poor self-images battle the lack of positive confessions and I still struggle with this even to this day. Unfortunately, this is the environment of our fallen world. When we meet Jesus, He heals us and gives us His peace. Then we go back out to the world where we interact with a real devil and his entities and they do their very best to tear us down again. It's the cycle of war.

In the middle of that war, as I've already discussed, we've been given weapons that enable us to fight and win against the enemy. But what about those times when our fear, our anxiety or our lack of peace feels like it will absolutely crush us?

For the vast majority of Christians who absolutely surrender their lives to Jesus, are filled with His Holy Spirit, continually wash their minds with His Word and purpose to live an interactive prayer life, you'll be able to walk in His Peace for much of your earthly life. You'll also be able to be used by Him mightily.

Sometimes, for some people, the attack of the enemy is so fierce that no matter how much we pray, or seek God, we never seem to experience that sense of Peace that surpasses all understanding. With that lack of peace comes that sense of hopelessness that I spoke about earlier.

I mentioned that I intended to give you some information that will help you to overcome that feeling of hopelessness. Understand that this is beyond simple religion and I am not, nor do I present myself to be, a mental health counselor.

It's apparent to me that at the very core of this country's mental health crisis is a supernatural assault by Satan on the minds and hearts of God's people and unbelievers.

> *… He was a murderer from the beginning, and abode not in the truth, because there is no truth in him. When he speaketh a lie, he speaketh of his own: for he is a liar, and the father of it.* **John 8:44b**

Because the impetus of this hopelessness and internal strife is supernatural, you must use the supernatural weapons that God has given you to fight this battle. There are times when the lack of peace, or continual issues in our lives, are a result of supernatural generational curses in our family tree.

> *And the LORD passed by before him, and proclaimed, "The LORD, The LORD God, merciful and gracious, longsuffering, and abundant in goodness and truth, keeping mercy for thousands, forgiving iniquity and transgression and sin, and that will by no means clear the guilty; visiting the iniquity of the fathers upon the children, and upon the children's children, unto the third and to the fourth generation."* **Exodus 34:6-7**

Those curses are the fruit of an egregious sin by an ancestor and you as their descendant could very well be paying the price for their sin. A lot of times people have to go through Deliverance in order to break these family curses.

I know what you're thinking, "More spooky, spiritual, mumbo jumbo." Wrong - Not only is it scriptural, I've seen the results of these curses on people's lives first-hand and I've seen what happens when they're broken.

I spoke earlier on this subject, but it's important that we talk about Deliverance in the context of breaking off continual hopelessness, anxiety and depression.

Again, I can hear some of you now, "I don't believe in that deliverance stuff! All you need is Jesus and He can fix you."

It's only you and God who know you're reading this book right now. You may well not want to believe in Deliverance for doctrinal reasons. I don't care! The facts are the facts.

As we rush toward the End of the Age, demonic possessions and exorcisms are at an all time high all over the world. And although I don't believe in the validity of the Catholic Church performing those rites, there are spirit-filled men and women of God who have been given this ministry.

I'm not saying that if you feel hopeless or suicidal that you're possessed. I'm only pointing out that at their core, those feelings could be a demonic attack and it can't be business as usual to deal with it.

Ask yourself: Why is it that good people, Christians, struggle their whole lives? They flounder with issues even though they know the Word, they read their Bible, they go to Church and they go about the work of the Lord, but the things of their past drag them down. Are you or I any better than they? Of course not! They just need help to be set free from a binding generational curse or a direct demonic attack. These things must be broken by the power of the Word and the Holy Spirit in order for these individuals to find real, lasting Peace.

So what can you do if you think you fall into this category?

Here's a brief list to start the process. It's not designed to give you every tool and every ministry. My goal is to simply get you thinking differently in order to combat the assault on your peace.

Surrender - This is one of those phrases that sounds super-spiritual and I really don't mean it to be. It's a simple concept.

First, if you don't know the Lord, or if you've walked away, surrender your life, your will, your wants, your desires and your baggage to Jesus. Get on your knees or even lie prone before Him and tell Him that.

Second, if you do know the Lord but are struggling with some of these issues, surrender the things to Him that are causing you anxiety or depression. For instance, if you're suffering from an eating disorder that's a result of a poor self-image, surrender whatever it is that caused you to feel that way: "My parents didn't love me", "I'm not pretty enough", "I was molested" etc. etc.

Take an honest look at your heart and mind to see what it is that's causing you to feel the way you do. Don't make excuses or try to avoid the subject. It's just you and the Lord anyway and He already knows what it is. He's waiting for you to come around and surrender it to Him.

The disorder, or the anxiety, or the depression is only a byproduct of something else in your past or your heart. Surrender those things to Jesus and continue to surrender them until you are free from them. At that point you can begin to heal.

Pray - I don't mean pray as in, "Now I lay me down to sleep…" I mean pray! Pray like your life depends on it. Be persistent with God. Bug Him! Pour your heart out to the Lord in your prayer closet. Repent. Go back to Him again and again asking Him to fill you with His Peace and to remove whatever encumbrance is pulling you down.

> And I say unto you, "Ask, and it shall be given you; seek, and ye shall find; knock, and it shall be opened unto you." For every one that asketh receiveth; and he that seeketh findeth; and to him that knocketh it shall be opened. *Luke 11:9-10*

Fast - Fasting is a powerful weapon against the enemy. This is used in conjunction with praying.

> Moreover when ye fast, be not, as the hypocrites, of a sad countenance: for they disfigure their faces, that they may appear unto men to fast. Verily I say unto you, "They have their reward." But thou, when thou fastest, anoint thine head, and wash thy face, that thou appear not unto men to fast, but unto thy Father which is in secret: and thy Father, which seeth in secret, shall reward thee openly. *Matt 6:16-18*

Read and Study the Word - I'm not talking daily devotional here. You need to pour over His Word like never before and commit it to memory. Use some of those study tools that I spoke about earlier and dig into the Word, letting it wash you. This too is in conjunction with praying and even fasting.

Be Baptized In The Holy Spirit - If you've never been baptized in the Holy Spirit, you need to seek it right away. That direct connection with God will cause many of the entanglements in your life to fall right off. You'll begin to see things differently and God will no longer be just a distant icon of religious belief to you. He will become real, personal and available in ways that you can't even imagine.

Break Generational Curses - I get so many emails from people that deal with this issue. Often times I'll point them in the direction of Derek Prince's, *Breaking Generational Curses*. Again, study through the Word and search through your local Christian bookstore or online for other resources. The breaking of Generational Curses can, and often is, done in conjunction with Deliverance.

Seek Deliverance - I personally think that the vast majority of Christians need to go through Deliverance in one form or another. All of us have junk in our past that hangs on even after we get saved. Deliverance deals with these issues, both great and small.

A word of caution here: Just because someone says that their "ministry" is Deliverance doesn't mean that it's the real thing or of God. Some of those ministries can do more harm than good. Do your homework. A good place to start is with Russ Dizdar's site: http://www.russdizdar.com/. But it's only a start. You'll learn a lot there and you may be able to find a legitimate Deliverance ministry in your area. And for the record, if someone wants you to pay for Deliverance, run the other way. If it's God's ministry, He certainly wouldn't charge you. Unsolicited offerings and donations for the ministry are fine.

There may be other tools that I'm not including, but I'm confident that if you seek the Lord and ask Him how to help you overcome your particular situation, He is faithful.

Walking Daily

People have to understand that Peace is reconciliation to God and being welcomed back into the family of God. There is no welcoming into the heart of God, without the Son of God. For those people who strive to find real Peace outside of that relationship, His Peace eludes them.

That's because Peace is the redemption of a loving God who intervenes in the entire rebellion of His creation and then takes His people out of this.

> *If the world hate you, ye know that it hated me before it hated you. If ye were of the world, the world would love his own: but because ye are not of the world, but I have chosen you out of the world, therefore the world hateth you.* **John 15:18-19**

> *Love not the world, neither the things that are in the world. If any man love the world, the love of the Father is not in him. For all that is in the world, the lust of the flesh, and the lust of the eyes, and the pride of life, is not of the Father, but is of the world. And the world passeth away, and the lust thereof: but he that doeth the will of God abideth for ever.* *1 **John 2:15-17***

Given all the junk that we as Believers have to see and walk through here on earth, sometimes I feel like I'm of the world. That's because, like you, I lose track because I'm so focused on my personal situation, but when I set my heart upon Him, my true super-positioning, in the world but not of it, comes into focus.

The stark reality is that most Christians today are oblivious to how the world really is, versus what they want it to be. The problem is that philosophically shallow people, who know not their God, nor the power of their God, try to lay claim to the name of God.

There's no magic wand to wave to change the war we find ourselves in. There's this misnomer that Jesus is some kind of warm, fuzzy teddy bear - That He came to love all of humanity and to bring Peace to the whole world. Typically this is a message propagated by those aforementioned seeker-friendly churches trying to fill their comfy seats.

It's accurate to equate Jesus' Peace to God's love. But it's a lie from the pit of Hell to think and teach that, since Jesus loves me so, "I can do whatever I want" and I still have God's Peace. Jesus did come to bring Peace but it was a specific Peace between the sinner who was doomed to eternal damnation and the Living God through His Son's blood.

God's love sent His Son to die on Calvary and be raised from the dead, thereby bringing Peace and reconciliation. Peace is never separated from reconciliation with God in the context of scripture. If we take ourselves out of His hands through sin and rebellion, we place our own selves in the danger zone.

Therefore, pursue God. Love Him. Obey Him.

And God's Everlasting Peace which surpasses all understanding will be with you.

I've Got Peace Like a River

I've got peace like a river,
I've got peace like a river,
I've got peace like a river in my soul.
I've got peace like a river,
I've got peace like a river,
I've got peace like a river in my soul.
I've got joy like a fountain,
I've got joy like a fountain,
I've got joy like a fountain in my soul.
I've got joy like a fountain,
I've got joy like a fountain,
I've got joy like a fountain in my soul.
I've got love like an ocean,
I've got love like an ocean,
I've got love like an ocean in my soul.
I've got love like an ocean,
I've got love like an ocean,
I've got love like an ocean in my soul.

HELP 10

His Everlasting Promise

The Lord is not slack concerning His promise,

as some men count slackness;

but is longsuffering to us-ward,

not willing that any should perish,

but that all should come to repentance.

2 Peter 3:9

Promise

When the Lord showed me the concept for *Jesus - The Premise of the Promise*, He also showed me all ten H.E.L.P.s at the same time, in the order that I've given them to you. It was not my intention to place this last H.E.L.P. of His Everlasting Promise at the end of the list. This was done only by the inspiration and design of the Holy Spirit. It is by that supernatural design, the H.E.L.P. of "Promise" is included at the end of the list to reinforce this one principle - Jesus is our Promise!

So what is a promise? In the dictionary a "promise" is defined as "a declaration that one will do or refrain from doing something specified".

You hear people all the time say, "I'm going to…" or "I promise you…" But the real question is, will they follow through with what they say they will or will not do?

As Christians, our lives should be based upon God's Word. But do we believe that God is who He says He is and do we believe that He will do what He says He'll do?

In this context, I think of a promise as an oath: I will, if you will.

There are two types of oaths: There's the oath where the greater person binds themselves to the lesser with no conditions. Then there's the oath where the greater says, "I will, if you will." There are many examples of this kind of Godly oath in the Bible.

> *If my people, which are called by my name, shall humble themselves, and pray, and seek my face, and turn from their wicked ways; then will I hear from heaven, and will forgive their sin, and will heal their land.* **2 Chron 7:14**

And it is here, within the oath of God, where we find the foundation for God's Everlasting Promise.

Chapter 25
The Promisor

God is not a man, that He should lie; neither the son of man, that He should repent. Hath He said, and shall He not do it? Or hath He spoken, and shall He not make it good?

Numbers 23:19

H ave you ever wondered why Jesus said the following?

…Nevertheless when the Son of man cometh, shall he find faith on the earth? Luke 18:8b

I must admit that I've scratched my head over this question at times. I suppose that what He's really trying to ask us is whether or not we believe that God means what He says. In other words: Will He do what He said He would do as His people fulfill our obligation to believe?

But without faith it is impossible to please Him: for He that cometh to God must believe that He is, and that He is a rewarder of them that diligently seek Him. Heb 11:6

"Faith on the earth" pertains to Believers because the world doesn't believe that God is, and therefore, they don't believe His promises.

So let me ask you:

Do you believe in God's Everlasting Promises?

Trusting Him to Make Good on His Promises

In order for a promise to have strength, there has to be a record of performance. Can you trust God's performance with regard to His promises?

~ *And they that know thy name will put their trust in thee: for thou, LORD, hast not forsaken them that seek thee.* **Psalm 9:10**

~ *Some trust in chariots, and some in horses: but we will remember the name of the LORD our God.* **Psalm 20:7**

~ *Trust in the LORD with all thine heart; and lean not unto thine own understanding. In all thy ways acknowledge Him, and He shall direct thy paths.* **Proverbs 3:5-6**

~ *Then was the king exceeding glad for him, and commanded that they should take Daniel up out of the den. So Daniel was taken up out of the den, and no manner of hurt was found upon him, because he believed in his God.* **Daniel 6:23**

~ *And He that sat upon the throne said, "Behold, I make all things new." And he said unto me, "Write: for these words are true and faithful."* **Rev 21:5**

We all go through this mental exercise when evaluating someone who makes a promise to us:

1. **Is the person who is promising you something prone to lie?**

2. **Does he say he's going to do something and then not do it?**

Jesus said that it's not about those people who say they will do something and then don't do it. It's about those people who say they won't do something, but then do it.

> *But what think ye? A certain man had two sons; and he came to the first, and said, "Son, go work to day in my vineyard." He answered and said, "I will not:" but afterward he repented, and went. And he came to the second, and said likewise. And he answered and said, "I go, sir:" and went not. Whether of them twain did the will of his father? They say unto him, "The first..."* **Matt 21:28-31a**

Talk is cheap. It's what the promisor actually does that matters.

Fulfillment of a Promise

The same King of Glory Who by the sheer Word of His power, spoke into existence both the worlds that we know and the unseen realms that we don't know, has set His affection on us. We are the apple of His eye.

> *For thus saith the LORD of hosts; "After the glory hath he sent me unto the nations which spoiled you: for he that toucheth you toucheth the apple of His eye."* **Zech 2:8**

For the value that God the Father saw in us, Jesus was willing to go to Calvary. There, He would cover our lives with His blood and transform us from the kingdom of darkness into the Kingdom of Light.

"That was the true Light, which lighteth every man that cometh into the world. He was in the world, and the world was made by Him, and the world knew Him not. He came unto His own, and His own received Him not. But as many as received Him, to them gave He power to become the sons of God, even to them that believe on His name: Which were born, not of blood, nor of the will of the flesh, nor of the will of man, but of God." **John 1:9-13**

But the thing that gets me is that He wasn't prejudicial about it. He went to Calvary's Cross for both the saved and unsaved alike, for everyone's sins, even the people who "received Him not". The difference in our salvation is our acceptance of the Promise of that "power to become the sons of God".

Surely He hath borne our griefs, and carried our sorrows: yet we did esteem Him stricken, smitten of God, and afflicted. But He was wounded for our transgressions, He was bruised for our iniquities: the chastisement of our peace was upon Him; and with His stripes we are healed. **Isaiah 53:4-5**

When the scripture says, "the chastisement of our peace was upon Him," I can't help but imagine how we humans get overwhelmed with three or four emotions all at the same time. That sense of emotional burden must have overwhelmed Jesus on the Cross. Every single sin and thought was poured out upon Him to the point that Jesus bore the sin of the world, not just the current sin of the world, but all past, present and future sin as well! The consciousness of sin and its effects on all of us who have been created in God's image rested on the shoulders of Jesus as the sacrificial lamb.

Jesus was the "promissory note" that paid for our sin, up front and in full.

For even the Son of Man came not to be ministered unto, but to minister, and to give His life a ransom for many. **Mark 10:45**

He is our "Kinsman-Redeemer".

Jesus - Our Promise

Not only does God keep His Promises, but He also gives us examples in His Word of those Promises to help us to understand His heart.

As I've tried to show you throughout this book, the whole NT is built upon the foundation of the OT. Jesus, His disciples, the apostles and all the Believers that you read about in the NT based their faith on the fundamentals of the OT. This is why we read excerpts from the OT as they are reiterated in the NT. One of those fundamental concepts can be found in the Book of Ruth.

Ruth was King David's great-grandmother and the book was written sometime between 1160 B.C. and 1100 B.C., more than a thousand years before Jesus came to earth.

Within the book there is a very important Promise of God called the "Kinsman-Redeemer". Jesus is an exact representation of this person. Understanding how Jesus is our Kinsman-Redeemer will help you to understand how God keeps His Promises to His people. The way you understand Revelation 5 will change when you grasp this concept because, as the "Kinsman-Redeemer", Jesus is the only one Who is worthy to open the book.

I've solicited an article from the late Chuck Missler to help explain the concept. I'm only including part of the article for the sake of expediency but it's worth a full read. I'd also recommend that you read the entire Book of Ruth for yourself.

The Background

The family of Elimelech, due to a local famine, leaves its home in Bethlehem and immigrates to Moab. The two sons marry local girls, but the father and the two sons subsequently pass away, leaving his wife, Naomi, and her two daughters-in-law destitute. Hearing that things are now better back home, Naomi decides to return to her native Bethlehem. She urges the two young girls to remain in their homeland and begin new lives, but Ruth refuses and insists on accompanying Naomi.

The Law of Gleaning

One of the values of this book is to highlight the operation of the laws of ancient Israel. As a landowner, you were permitted to reap on one pass only: what was missed, or left behind, was available to be gleaned by the widows or the destitute.

Naomi and Ruth are, of course, in that situation, and Ruth, in her support of the household, goes out to glean after the reapers and happens onto the field of Boaz, one of the wealthy landowners and the hero of our story. Boaz arranges for his reapers to drop handfuls on purpose to assure Ruth an abundant gathering. When Naomi learns of Ruth's good fortune, she is especially delighted since it turns out that Boaz is a kinsman of the family, and that leads to the opportunity that is the crux of the tale.

To properly understand what follows, it is necessary to be familiar with several other laws operative from the Torah.

The Law of Redemption

When property is sold in our culture, title is usually passed in fee simple, in perpetuity to the buyer. However, Israel's land was granted, in the days of Joshua, to the tribes to be retained within the family. (That's one of the reasons genealogies were so important.)

When someone sold a property "to pay debts, or whatever" the transaction was what we would view as a lease: there were provisions for the land to eventually return to the family. A title deed included the terms that a kinsman of the family could perform to redeem the property to the family.

The Law of Levirate Marriage

There was also an unusual procedure to assure the continuation of a family in the event of the death of a husband without issue. If a widow had no son, she could request the next of kin to take her and raise children to continue the family bloodline.

It is from this background that we understand Naomi's opportunity in Ruth Chapter 3. She realizes that Boaz is a kinsman; therefore, there was an opportunity to regain the family properties lost by her deceased husband 10 years earlier and also a chance for Ruth to have a new life. Naomi instructs Ruth on how to proceed.

The Threshing Floor

The harvest included winnowing the wheat at a threshing floor, a parcel of ground where there was a prevailing wind. The grain was tossed into the air and the grain would fall downwind a small distance;

the chaff, being lighter, would be carried further downwind. When done properly, two piles would result: the furthest would be burned as trash; the closer one would be bagged for the marketplace.

The harvest was, of course, also a time for celebration, and the evenings were accompanied by festivities for having made payroll another season, etc. After the celebration, the owners typically would sleep near the grain to preclude theft. Ruth is instructed by Naomi to approach Boaz privately at the threshing floor. What follows is widely misunderstood by the uninitiated reader.

The Request

Ruth approaches Boaz while he is sleeping and requests him to spread his skirt over her as he is a near kinsman. This is not the kind of proposition many people assume it to be.

The shul (skirt), or hem, was the emblem of rank or authority in Israel, much like the stripes on the sleeve of a naval officer or airline pilot in our culture. (This insight is essential to really understand David's cutting Saul's hem, or why the woman with the issue of blood touched Christ's hem, etc.)

Ruth was asking Boaz to put the authority of his house over her. She is invoking her right under the laws of Israel for him to take her to wife. Boaz was delighted to accommodate her, but there remained an obstacle to be overcome.

A Nearer Kinsman?

It seems that there is a nearer kinsman who would have to first step aside for Boaz to assume his role. This is a cloud over the otherwise joyous proceedings. Boaz takes on the task of confronting this nearer kinsman, in front of the city council, to force the issue.

When a widow requested the next of kin to perform the role of the goel, or kinsman-redeemer, he wasn't forced to. In fact, there were three conditions to be met:

He had to be qualified as a kinsman;

He had to be able to perform;

He had to be willing.

There were two issues at stake: the redeeming of the land for Naomi and the taking of Ruth to wife. As far as the land is concerned, the man appears to be willing. But for some undisclosed reason, he is unable to perform where Ruth is concerned. That clears the way for our hero, Boaz, to fulfill his role as the goel.

The giving of the shoe needs an explanation. If the nearer kinsman declined the responsibility, he would have to yield one of his shoes and could also suffer the indignity of being spit upon. When he declined, he performed the traditional gesture by yielding his shoe to Boaz. The shoe was intended to be a symbol of disgrace, but to Boaz it was a marriage license!

(It may seem remarkable that Boaz, a wealthy Jew, would take a Gentile to wife. Remember who his mother was: Rahab, the harlot of Jericho. Both Rahab and Ruth are in Christ's genealogy.)

A Closer Look

This elegant love story is a classic in literature, and it also gives us some interesting insights into the life of ancient Israel.

But if we look more closely, we will discover that it is much more than that. The plan of God appears to be hidden among its colorful symbols and roles. The Bible frequently deals in symbols, models, or types. As we examine the role of Boaz as the goel, or kinsman-redeemer, we can easily see how he, in some ways, pre-figures our own kinsman-redeemer, Jesus Christ. Through his act of redemption, Boaz returns Naomi (Israel) to her land, and also takes Ruth (a Gentile) as his bride. This suggests a parallel with the Church as the Gentile bride of Christ.

The parallels between Boaz, Naomi, and Ruth with Christ, Israel, and the Church have been widely recognized, and it is remarkable to notice how many additional details of the story are consistent with this viewpoint.

The Unnamed Servant

Who first introduces Boaz to Ruth? An unnamed servant. This is suggestive of the role of the Holy Spirit, and it is interesting that in every example that the Holy Spirit is viewed in such a role, He is always the unnamed servant. In Genesis 24, Abraham, as the Father, sent his eldest servant to gather a bride for his son Isaac. This unnamed servant seems to be mentioned elsewhere as Eliezer, which means Comforter. Why does the Holy Spirit always appear as the unnamed servant? Because Jesus said He would never testify of Himself.

It is interesting that, no matter how much Boaz wanted Ruth, as a gentleman there was nothing he could do until she declared herself. It was her move. No matter how much Jesus loves us, He awaits our response. How about you? Have you asked your Goel to do His kinsman-redeemer part for you?

The Nearer Kinsman

What does the nearer kinsman symbolize? Most scholars view him as the Law. What the Law could not do, Jesus has already done for us. It is also significant that at the confrontation with the nearer kinsman, it was Ruth's position to confront the nearer kinsman; however, Boaz stood in Ruth's place and took the entire burden upon himself.[29]

Sound familiar?

That's exactly what Jesus did for us! Jesus is our Kinsman-Redeemer and God's Everlasting Promise!

An Intentional Walk

Early on in my Christian walk, I began to understand how powerful God's Promises were. I also gleaned that it might be possible to participate in the Promises of God that had been given to someone else in His Word. Here's what I mean:

---

[29] Chuck Missler, "The Kinsman-Redeemer: A Story of Bethlehem." Koinonia House, https://www.khouse.org/articles/2006/683/, (December 1, 2006).

Back when I was a new Christian, I was seeking God with all my heart. I was attending that YWAM conference in Mount Hermon, California, that I mentioned earlier. During a morning session there, the speaker was teaching on how Elisha received a double portion of Elijah's mantle.

> *And it came to pass, when they were gone over, that Elijah said unto Elisha, "Ask what I shall do for thee, before I be taken away from thee." And Elisha said, "I pray thee, let a double portion of thy spirit be upon me." And he said, "Thou hast asked a hard thing: nevertheless, if thou see me when I am taken from thee, it shall be so unto thee; but if not, it shall not be so." And it came to pass, as they still went on, and talked, that, behold, there appeared a chariot of fire, and horses of fire, and parted them both asunder; and Elijah went up by a whirlwind into heaven. And Elisha saw it, and he cried, "My father, my father, the chariot of Israel, and the horsemen thereof." And he saw him no more: and he took hold of his own clothes, and rent them in two pieces. He took up also the mantle of Elijah that fell from him, and went back, and stood by the bank of Jordan; And he took the mantle of Elijah that fell from him, and smote the waters, and said, "Where is the LORD God of Elijah? and when he also had smitten the waters, they parted hither and thither: and Elisha went over."* **2 Kings 9-14**

It's that particular promise of Elijah to Elisha, *"if thou see me when I am taken from thee, it shall be so unto thee"* that I was focused on.

I thought that if Elisha could receive a "double portion" of Elijah's spirit, why couldn't I ask God to give me a double portion.

We broke for lunch after that 10:00 session and it was during that time that I went into the forest and began to earnestly petition God for a "double portion". But I wasn't asking Him for a "double portion" of Elijah's spirit. I was asking for a "double portion" of Elisha's spirit. Remember, Elisha got a double portion of Elijah spirit, so I was asking for even more than Elisha got.

In this part of the Californian forest there were huge Sequoia trees. They're very old and the woods were dense with them. There was one particular tree there that was absolutely gigantic. As I was worshipping and praying for this double portion, I heard the Lord tell me, *"Walk around that tree two times."* What else was I going to do? If someone saw me they might think I was crazy. Heck, I wondered if I was just imagining what I thought I heard. Nonetheless, I wanted to be obedient so I walked around that huge tree two times.

Here's something that you need to understand: I was a brand new Christian, who'd never been to Church or sat in a Sunday School class. I'd never read the story of Jericho or what it meant to walk around the walls to see God make them fall down. I had no idea what it meant for me to walk around that tree. All I knew was to do what He said.

After I walked around the tree, I went back to praising and worshiping Him as I had been doing before He told me about the tree. Following the retreat schedule, I went back to the afternoon session. That session broke for dinner and then the evening session started. The speaker for the session was a powerful woman of God named Joy Dawson. I didn't know who she was at the time, but she had a worldwide ministry and was very well known.

This was a meeting of several hundred people and I was just someone in the audience. So as I was sitting there, minding my own business, Joy looked at me, pointed and out of the blue said, *"Young man, go get me a glass of water."*

I had no idea why she singled me out, but I was eager to help. The problem was that I had no clue how the camp was laid out and the evening was dark. When I say evening, I'm talking sun gone down and dark, really dark. This was in the High Sierras and it was pitch-black out. It was also in the early 70's so the camp didn't have the fancy lighting that's available these days. Back then, all they had were bare light bulbs hanging outside of the buildings for light. I wanted to help so I ran out of the auditorium into the dark looking for water without a clue of where to find it.

In the distance I saw a light and thought, "Maybe where there's a light, there's water." Now that I think about it, that's got to be a spiritual principle as well.

Anyway, sure enough the light led me to the kitchen where I found several large plastic cups. I filled two of the cups with water because I figured with my clunkiness, I had a good chance of dropping one or spilling it. To my own amazement, I didn't spill a drop. What that meant was that I walked back into the auditorium with two full cups of water.

I was a brand new Christian and wasn't very familiar with people operating in the gifts of the Spirit. But in the previous sessions I saw how Joy operated powerfully in the gifts as she gave word after word to people in those meetings.

It was because of this that I was very concerned that she was going to do that to me as I walked up to the podium with her water. The reason I was concerned was because I was such a scoundrel, I thought that through the Holy Spirit she was going to call me out in front of the whole world and tell everyone how bad I was.

Sure enough, she did give me a word, but it was nothing that I could have ever imagined. As I walked up to her with the two cups of water, to my astonishment she said, *"Young man, I only asked you for one cup of water and you've brought me two. Let this night mark the rest of your life, that God will give you what you have asked for!"*

I pause here to remind you of what I asked for after that morning session. I asked for a double portion of Elisha's spirit.

She continued, *"And he'll always give you double. The reason you have experienced such frustration is because you must seek Him with all of your heart. And just as you brought me two cups of water, so will the Lord double unto you the blessing, so much so that the angels in heaven will say, 'That young man means business with God.'"*

I share this story with you as an example because by the Holy Ghost, I was prompted to latch onto a Promise from God. But please don't misunderstand what I'm saying. I'm in no way inferring that I'm Elisha or a prophet. If you think this, you're missing the point.

What God did for me that night was to supernaturally demonstrate how He answered prayer and made good on His Promise to me via the Holy Spirit.

I'm just a fallible guy trying to walk with the Lord as best I can. I'm no different than you and God is no respecter of persons (Acts 10:34). I know that there's nothing good in me, in and of myself. I have no room to brag because I know who I am and what I've done, and I know my shortcomings better than anyone except for the Lord. In spite of my shortcomings, God does what He does with me and things really do happen.

If you're seeking Him, you are no different. Just as God Promised me a double portion, He can Promise you the same, or something else that the Lord has put on your heart. But you have to seek Him.

Notice I said to "seek Him" and not seek it. Our affection for Him and our relationship with Him cannot be based upon what He can do for us. I know that some of you may be shocked to hear this. God is not our sugar-daddy or our gravy train. He's the Alpha and Omega, the beginning and the end. He's the Creator of all things.

His Person is worthy of our praise just for Who He is. Set your affection on Him just as He's already set His affection on you and then walk with Him throughout your life. You'll be amazed to see how He makes and keeps His Everlasting Promises to you too.

Where Your Treasure Is

What, or who, you love is where you spend time.

For where your treasure is, there will your heart be also. **Matt 6:21**

When I fell in love with Jesus, I spent every waking hour listening to teachers and preachers about the Bible about how to grow in Him. People say that they desire to walk with God but they don't want to give up what's got their attention in the world. Walking with the Lord is more than just having intent. Here's what I mean:

I'm not, but let's say that I was severely overweight.

Let's say that I know I'm overweight and it's obvious by my appearance. So let's pretend that you're my good friend, and I told you, "I'm going to start exercising, eating right and lose some weight."

You might be happy for me and encouraging, "I think that's great, Steve. Good for you."

So let's say that we don't see each other for a while, months, and when I do see you again I'm the same size, maybe even a little larger. Clearly I've done nothing about my weight. Regardless, I still tell you, "Yeah, I'm going to lose weight. I'm going to get on this so I can get healthy."

You, might say, "Good luck. I'm rooting for you." But realistically, you can't help but be less convinced of my intent.

Again, what if months go by and we don't see each other for a while. But when we do - I look exactly the same. So what happens when this conversation occurs again and again? Would you think that I was serious about losing weight?

Of course not! The evidence of my lack of intent is the weight that I carry with no measurable change. It doesn't matter what I say, it only matters what I do.

It's the same way for our spiritual walk.

We do what we want to do. If you want to grow in the Lord, you'll turn off the television, put down the video game, get off of Facebook, shut off your phone, or do whatever you need to do so you can be alone and undisturbed with God. You'll also stick your nose in His Word and fast like your life depended on it. You'd pray all the time, even though you may not feel like He's listening and you would be on your face before Him asking Him to forgive you for the junk in your heart and your life. You'd continually ask Him to make you more like Jesus. You'd run after Him seeking a fresh infilling of His Holy Spirit.

As I said, we do what we want to do. No excuses - truth.

Even the fulfillment of a carnal goal or lust is whatever your soul lusts after. Your soul is your mind, will, intellect and emotions but your spirit hungers for God. People suppress their spirit. The soul and the spirit are not the same.

We're triune beings created in the image of a triune God. God formed Adam out of the clay of the earth, then the Bible says that God breathed into his nostrils the breath of life and Adam became a living soul.

> And the LORD God formed man of the dust of the ground, and breathed into his nostrils the breath of life; and man became a living soul. **Gen 2:7**

The key here is that God "breathed". It was the Spirit of God coming into contact with the clay body of man. When that happened it was the interaction of the Spirit of God, which is unique to each and every person who is co-created in God's image.

Our mind, intellect, will and emotions are how our spirit communicates with the physical world as it's contained in a physical body.

> And the very God of peace sanctify you wholly; and I pray God your whole spirit and soul and body be preserved blameless unto the coming of our Lord Jesus Christ. Faithful is He that calleth you, who also will do it. **1 Thess 5:23-24**

The only way you're going to be able to run this race is to acknowledge the prize that you're running for. But do you really believe in that prize, or the Promise of that prize?

> Brethren, I count not myself to have apprehended: but this one thing I do, forgetting those things which are behind, and reaching forth unto those things which are before, I press toward the mark for the prize of the high calling of God in Christ Jesus. **Phil 3:13-14**

Today, people believe, or are taught, that they can live however they want and still be forgiven by the Lord for their actions. This is true in the case of real repentance. Repentance, heartfelt repentance, brings forgiveness. It is the intent of your heart that will be known by the Lord and based upon that intent, He'll know if you're really repentant and not just sorry. There's a huge difference.

Being sorry about your actions is to dislike the situation or outcome of those actions without any meaningful change in your life. **It's like saying:**

- **I'm sorry that I drink too much (because it cost me my job).**
- **I'm sorry that I cheated on my wife (because now I'm getting a divorce).**
- **I'm sorry I stole that stuff at the department store (because I got caught and now have a record).**

But then you go back and do the same thing again when no one is looking. Being sorry isn't the same as being repentant.

Specifically, to repent means to "turn away" from something that offends a righteous and holy God. We don't repent because God will strike us dead if we don't. We repent because our action is an offense against our good and loving Creator.

Repentance brings a conscious decision to change our behavior away from a sinful action or lifestyle to a biblical action or lifestyle. It means that you're willing to move from immaturity in the Lord to a mature walk with Him. To turn from listening to whatever thoughts come into your mind (remember, they are not always our own) and turn to listening only to thoughts that agree with God. In other words, it's a purposeful decision to walk out of dysfunction and toward spiritual health.

More to the point, being truly repentant and not just sorry unbinds us from the sin that has dragged us down and frees us to live a more joyful life because we are no longer being held captive by that destructive behavior.

In addition, the attitude of repentance (and yes, it is an attitude) indicates that we understand that our lives are no longer our own, but God's. Placing Jesus in that rightful Kingship position in our lives produces another byproduct: we are released from the shame and guilt of that sin.

Here's the catch: None of this can happen unless we have a willingness to let something go. We have to die to self , at least in this area of sin. It's that death of our self-centered tendencies, with humility, that is a genuine indicator of true repentance.

There's more to repentance than just saying, "I did it," or "I'm sorry." True repentance transforms our character from the inside out. Everyone has character traits that we had lacked when young in the Lord but which begin to surface as we mature spiritually. We become more humble, less self-centered and selfish and more compassionate, just to name a few.

Repentance, real repentance, will change your life. We are Promised as much in God's Word.

> Now I rejoice, not that ye were made sorry, but that ye sorrowed to repentance: for ye were made sorry after a godly manner, that ye might receive damage by us in nothing. For godly sorrow worketh repentance to salvation not to be repented of: but the sorrow of the world worketh death. *2 Cor 7:9-10*

Believe it or not, there are also negative Promises of God for our actions. This is when He says, "If you do this, I Promise you this will happen."

In one particular case, no matter how much we "repent", that repentance will fall on deaf ears. It was Jesus Himself Who said that He doesn't allow a free pass regarding blasphemy of the Holy Spirit.

> Verily I say unto you, All sins shall be forgiven unto the sons of men, and blasphemies wherewith soever they shall blaspheme. But he that shall blaspheme against the Holy Ghost hath never forgiveness, but is in danger of eternal damnation. *Mark 3:28-29*

From time to time I will hear of people fretting over this verse, worrying that they've somehow blasphemed the Holy Ghost. My thinking is that if you're actually worried that you've blasphemed the Holy Spirit, then you probably haven't. That's because for you to do such a thing would mean that your mind, heart and most importantly, your spirit would have been given over to Satan, never to return to the Lord. Such an immersion in that kind of evil would sear your conscious and you wouldn't even care about repenting.

> And even as they did not like to retain God in their knowledge, God gave them over to a reprobate mind, to do those things which are not convenient. Being filled with all unrighteousness, fornication, wickedness, covetousness, maliciousness; full of envy, murder, debate, deceit, malignity; whisperers, backbiters, haters of God, despiteful, proud, boasters, inventors of evil things, disobedient to parents,

without understanding, covenant breakers, without natural affection, implacable, unmerciful. Who knowing the judgment of God, that they which commit such things are worthy of death, not only do the same, but have pleasure in them that do them. Rom 1:28-32

The Lord isn't a "gotcha god" or a "trickster". He isn't trying to ensnare you or cause you to stumble. It's His overriding hope that you'll repent and come to accept His Promise of eternal life in Jesus.

Feed My Sheep

All this talk about repentance, true repentance, and humility makes me think about how Christians should act. I've come face-to-face with many so-called Believers who demonstrate biting attitudes that shouldn't be in Christians. As I've already said I'm far from perfect, but that kind of behavior reminds me about a conversation that I had with the Lord one day. It had to do with Jesus telling Peter to feed His sheep.

So when they had dined, Jesus saith to Simon Peter, "Simon, son of Jonas, lovest thou me more than these?" He saith unto Him, "Yea, Lord; thou knowest that I love thee." He saith unto him, "Feed my lambs." John 21:15

As I was thinking about this verse, I heard the Lord clearly say to me, *"Steve, if you love me feed my sheep."*

I try to listen to, and talk with, the Lord throughout the day so it wasn't hearing Him tell me this that bothered me. It was what He asked me to do.

I said, *"But Lord, they're Sabre Tooth Tiger Sheep! Why do your sheep have to have Sabre Tooth Tiger teeth?"*

Immediately He replied, and said, *"Steve, what makes you think that those people are my sheep?"*

We're promised in the Word that the Holy Spirit working in our lives will make us different if we walk with the Lord.

But ye are not in the flesh, but in the Spirit, if so be that the Spirit of God dwell in you. Now if any man have not the Spirit of Christ, he is none of His. And if Christ be in you, the body is dead because of sin; but the Spirit is life because of righteousness. But if the Spirit of Him that raised up Jesus from the dead dwell in you, he that raised up Christ from the dead shall also quicken your mortal bodies by His Spirit that dwelleth in you. Therefore, brethren, we are debtors, not to the flesh, to live after the flesh. Rom 8:9-12

Just saying that you accept God's Promises at face-value but not letting Him change you from glory to glory through the work of the Holy Spirit is akin to not accepting the Promises at all.

Promises Hindered

Some people stagger at the Promises of God. The reason is because they take their eyes off of Jesus and put them on themselves. I know this because, it happens to me at times.

And Peter answered him and said, "Lord, if it be thou, bid me come unto thee on the water." And He said, "Come." And when Peter was come down out of the ship, he walked on the water, to go to Jesus. But when he saw the wind boisterous, he was afraid; and beginning to sink, he cried, saying, "Lord, save me."

And immediately Jesus stretched forth His hand, and caught him, and said unto him, "O thou of little faith, wherefore didst thou doubt?" **Matt 14:28-31**

Sometimes people who have had an immense amount of rejection have the hardest time accepting God's unconditional love and His Promises. It's the idea of love, or the lack thereof, that permeates people's trust in Him to fulfill His Promises. But a relationship with the Lord is based upon His Promises and enables us to grow into maturity in Him. We were all at one time alienated from God but because of Jesus, we are no longer distant.

And you, that were sometime alienated and enemies in your mind by wicked works, yet now hath He reconciled in the body of his flesh through death, to present you holy and unblameable and unreproveable in His sight, if ye continue in the faith grounded and settled, and be not moved away from the hope of the gospel, which ye have heard, and which was preached to every creature which is under heaven; whereof I Paul am made a minister. **Col 1:21-23** *According as His divine power hath given unto us all things that pertain unto life and godliness, through the knowledge of Him that hath called us to glory and virtue: Whereby are given unto us exceeding great and precious promises: that by these ye might be partakers of the divine nature, having escaped the corruption that is in the world through lust.* **2 Peter 1:3-5**

Often times people's view of God's Promises are warped by their experience with their earthly parents. Unfortunately, a parent's promises are based upon variables that may limit their ability to fulfill those promises. They can have meaning and intent, but lack capability. A guy that says, "I'm going to send my kid to college," but loses his job and is working for minimum wage had the desire and intent but due to earthly conditions, lacked the capability to carry through. None of those things apply to God. What God has declared He will do, He will do. Not only is God able to conceive, He's able to fulfill His Promises.

And being fully persuaded that, what He had promised, He was able also to perform. **Romans 4:21**

If we lean on God's Promises, then we don't have to be fearful about the future. Perfect love casts out fear.

Whosoever shall confess that Jesus is the Son of God, God dwelleth in him, and he in God. And we have known and believed the love that God hath to us. God is love; and he that dwelleth in love dwelleth in God, and God in him. Herein is our love made perfect, that we may have boldness in the day of judgment: because as He is, so are we in this world. There is no fear in love; but perfect love casteth out fear: because fear hath torment. He that feareth is not made perfect in love. We love Him, because He first loved us. **1 John 4:15-19**

Trusting God and trusting His Word in faith doesn't come naturally. As Believers, we have to continually exercise our "faith muscle" if we want it to become strong. When it comes to helping us walk in faith, a couple of important scriptures come to mind.

But my God shall supply all your need according to His riches in glory by Christ Jesus. **Phil 4:19**

And whatsoever ye shall ask in my name, that will I do, that the Father may be glorified in the Son. If ye shall ask any thing in my name, I will do it. **John 14:13-14**

All of God's Promises are based upon His love. The problem is that some people have a hard time believing that God really loves them even after accepting Jesus. It's one thing to hear that God loves you and it's another thing to know that God loves you.

Now faith is the substance of things hoped for, the evidence of things not seen. **Heb 11:1**

"Faith is the substance of things hoped for." I have faith because I believe that God is Who He says He is. I have faith because I've read about Him in the Bible and see how He dealt with people. I have faith because of the many times that I know how I should've been killed or hurt, but miraculously escaped through His intervention. These experiences in our lives build our faith muscle.

People think that having faith is some spooky, supernatural big deal. But it's much simpler than that. The closer we are to the heart of Jesus, the easier it is to love Him. And the easier it is to love Him, the easier it is to believe Him. What does the scripture say? Faith works by love.

For in Jesus Christ neither circumcision availeth any thing, nor uncircumcision; but faith which worketh by love. **Gal 5:6**

Exercise your faith muscle by spending one-on-one time with Jesus. If you do that, your faith will grow and His Promises will come alive.

Promises Where You Least Expect Them

Every single prophetic utterance is a Promise.

God, who at sundry times and in divers manners spake in time past unto the fathers by the prophets. **Heb 1:1**

God has purposeful intent and He is jealous over His Word.

As it is written, "I have made thee a father of many nations," before him whom he believed, even God, who quickeneth the dead, and calleth those things which be not as though they were. Who against hope believed in hope, that he might become the father of many nations; according to that which was spoken, "So shall thy seed be." And being not weak in faith, he considered not his own body now dead, when he was about an hundred years old, neither yet the deadness of Sara's womb, he staggered not at the promise of God through unbelief; but was strong in faith, giving glory to God; And being fully persuaded that, what He had promised, He was able also to perform. **Rom 4:17-21**

For as the heavens are higher than the earth, so are my ways higher than your ways, and my thoughts than your thoughts. For as the rain cometh down, and the snow from heaven, and returneth not thither, but watereth the earth, and maketh it bring forth and bud, that it may give seed to the sower, and bread to the eater, so shall my word be that goeth forth out of my mouth: it shall not return unto me void, but it shall accomplish that which I please, and it shall prosper in the thing whereto I sent it. **Isaiah 55:9-11**

Jesus said that He came that we might have life and life more abundantly, but the devil comes to steal, kill, and destroy.

The thief cometh not, but for to steal, and to kill, and to destroy: I am come that they might have life, and that they might have it more abundantly. ***John 10:10***

Interestingly the word "kill" in the above verse is the word *thuó*, which literally means "to kill and offer as a sacrifice". It gives the impression that the thief, Satan, sees spiritual significance in your demise.

The word "destroy" is from the word *apollumi*, which means "to utterly destroy," "decimate" or "obliterate as in a permanent destruction".

Think about that for a moment. It's not enough for the devil to end or ruin your life, and potentially cause you to die spiritually as well as physically, but he thinks that in doing so he's won a spiritual victory and is honored by your death and destruction. How sick is that?

Contrast that to the second part of John 10:10 when Jesus said that His primary purpose for His coming was to give us life! The original language gives the impression that this life is both physical and spiritual and that He wants us to possess it as if it were ours alone. It's like a pair of shoes that have molded to your unique feet out of all the people in the world, He's chosen this unique life for you.

We are given the qualifier of this life as being "abundant" from the word *perissos*. This word means "beyond what is anticipated" or "exceeding our expectation". It's going past the expected limit and is more than enough.

So the devil's destructive goals are preempted by God's purposes in your life if you truly walk with Him. What a wonderful Promise!

Promises for the End

No matter what promise you need for any occasion, all of God's promises are in His Word and are complete. God's Promises have foretold End Time events in places like Matthew 24, Luke 21 and Mark 10. But you do have a choice to believe His prophets or not.

~ *And they rose early in the morning, and went forth into the wilderness of Tekoa: and as they went forth, Jehoshaphat stood and said, Hear me, O Judah, and ye inhabitants of Jerusalem; Believe in the LORD your God, so shall ye be established; believe his prophets, so shall ye prosper.* ***2 Chron 20:20***

~ *...I am thy fellowservant, and of thy brethren that have the testimony of Jesus: worship God: for the testimony of Jesus is the spirit of prophecy.* ***Rev 19:10b***

~ *Remember the former things of old: for I am God, and there is none else; I am God, and there is none like me, declaring the end from the beginning, and from ancient times the things that are not yet done...* ***Isaiah 46:9-10a***

Through the Holy Spirit, we also have contemporary people who have seen or heard about End Times events. Regarding these things, people always ask me, "When is all this stuff going to happen?"

I tell everyone the same thing, "Just like in Egypt, when the money fails, that's when the children of

Israel left Egypt and went into the Promised Land." When our money fails, and Christians aren't allowed to conduct any type of commerce because they won't take the mark, that's when we all go into the wilderness.

The thought of those things that are coming upon the earth can be scary. There are times when even I tremble and am terrified. Not necessarily for losing my life, but for what's coming on the earth. I saw it, remember? As a firsthand witness to the future, I can tell you that it's terrifying.

If you'll recall, when God gave that vision of the future to me, He only allowed me to remember parts of it. Then, as some of those things are about to come to pass, He reminds me of what I saw. Can you imagine what would have happened to me if I remembered it all at once? I couldn't handle it. It was God's way of protecting me.

We may be looking at our End of the Age, but there were times that King David felt like his whole world was ending. We can take a cue from how he handled the situation.

> *Be merciful unto me, O God: for man would swallow me up; he fighting daily oppresseth me. Mine enemies would daily swallow me up: for they be many that fight against me, O thou most High. What time I am afraid, I will trust in thee. In God I will praise His word, in God I have put my trust; I will not fear what flesh can do unto me. Every day they wrest my words: all their thoughts are against me for evil. They gather themselves together, they hide themselves, they mark my steps, when they wait for my soul. Shall they escape by iniquity? In thine anger cast down the people, O God. Thou tellest my wanderings: put thou my tears into thy bottle: are they not in thy book? When I cry unto thee, then shall mine enemies turn back: this I know; for God is for me. In God will I praise His word: in the LORD will I praise His word. In God have I put my trust: I will not be afraid what man can do unto me. Thy vows are upon me, O God: I will render praises unto thee. For thou hast delivered my soul from death: wilt not thou deliver my feet from falling, that I may walk before God in the light of the living?* **Psalm 56**

Like David, the thing that will keep us in the days to come will be knowing that nothing can pluck us out of God's hand.

> *My sheep hear my voice, and I know them, and they follow me: and I give unto them eternal life; and they shall never perish, neither shall any man pluck them out of my hand. My Father, which gave them me, is greater than all; and no man is able to pluck them out of my Father's hand. I and my Father are one.* **John 10:27-30**

We're supernatural beings experiencing a mortal episode in eternity as we live a linear life in this flesh-suit. In the end, we will all die physically. We may even die by a literal sword during the End Times, but our deaths can also be a victory. And that too is a Promise.

> *And the great dragon was cast out, that old serpent, called the Devil, and Satan, which deceiveth the whole world: he was cast out into the earth, and his angels were cast out with him. And I heard a loud voice saying in heaven, "Now is come salvation, and strength, and the kingdom of our God, and the power of His Christ: for the accuser of our brethren is cast down, which accused them before our God day and night. And they overcame him by the blood of the Lamb, and by the word of their testimony; and they loved not their lives unto the death."* **Rev 12:9-11**

His Promise to Protect

Our potential demise by the sword is by no means assured. We have also been given Promises as individuals that 1) He'll never leave us or forsake us, and 2) We aren't to be afraid of him who can kill our body, but we are to be afraid of Him who can cast us into Hell.

...for He hath said, I will never leave thee, nor forsake thee. **Heb 13:5b**

And fear not them which kill the body, but are not able to kill the soul: but rather fear Him which is able to destroy both soul and body in hell. **Matt 10:28**

When Jesus is telling us these things, He's putting our physical, temporal situation into an eternal framework. Most people only care about the here and now and don't even give a thought about eternity. The fact is that there are worse things than death.

He's also telling us that He'll never abandon us and that we won't be left to the powers and the evil of the day.

Take therefore no thought for the morrow: for the morrow shall take thought for the things of itself. Sufficient unto the day is the evil thereof. **Matt 6:34**

In declaring that the days are evil, Jesus directly speaks to His Promise to never leave us or forsake us. He substitutes His power, the power of the resurrection, the power of the Living God that He possesses, and He gives us the power to become the sons of God. This is not just mental assent. It's a transformation that has to take place through God, with the greater (God) moving on behalf of the weaker (man) through the blood of Jesus.

Those individual Promises are woven into a beautiful tapestry of a Father's love for His creation. Since it's His creation, of course, He will protect us if we yield our lives to Him.

Speaking of creation, I need to go back to Genesis for a moment and to a passage that we examined earlier in depth.

And the LORD God said unto the woman, "What is this that thou hast done?" And the woman said, "The serpent beguiled me, and I did eat." And the LORD God said unto the serpent, "Because thou hast done this, thou art cursed above all cattle, and above every beast of the field; upon thy belly shalt thou go, and dust shalt thou eat all the days of thy life. And I will put enmity between thee and the woman, and between thy seed and her seed; it shall bruise thy head, and thou shalt bruise his heel." **Genesis 3:13-15**

As I was writing this H.E.L.P. of Promise, the Holy Spirit quickened my heart to a connection in this section with scripture in latter parts of the Bible. Specifically, it deals with the portion of verse 15 that says:

And I will put enmity between thee and the woman, and between thy seed and her seed; it shall bruise thy head, and thou shalt bruise his heel.

While this is certainly a curse on Satan for causing the downfall of man, it's also a Promise to us. Here's what I mean.

If you'll recall, when Jesus had sent out the seventy-two disciples in Luke, they came back with glowing reports of how even "the devils" were subject to them.

And the seventy returned again with joy, saying, "Lord, even the devils are subject unto us through thy name." And He said unto them, "I beheld Satan as lightning fall from heaven. Behold, I give unto you power to tread on serpents and scorpions, and over all the power of the enemy: and nothing shall by any means hurt you." Luke 10:17-19

I believe that the Lord's statement, *"I give unto you power to tread on serpents and scorpions"* is a direct connection to the curse/promise found in Genesis 3:15. This is evident by the effect that the disciples had in Luke 17. These two verses are also pertinent to our walks as we move headlong into the End of the Age. That promise in Gen 3:15 comes alive to us when we read Rev 9:1-6 and see what happens at the Fifth Trumpet.

And the fifth angel sounded, and I saw a star fall from heaven unto the earth: and to him was given the key of the bottomless pit. And he opened the bottomless pit; and there arose a smoke out of the pit, as the smoke of a great furnace; and the sun and the air were darkened by reason of the smoke of the pit. And there came out of the smoke locusts upon the earth: and unto them was given power, as the scorpions of the earth have power. And it was commanded them that they should not hurt the grass of the earth, neither any green thing, neither any tree; but only those men which have not the seal of God in their foreheads. And to them it was given that they should not kill them, but that they should be tormented five months: and their torment was as the torment of a scorpion, when he striketh a man. And in those days shall men seek death, and shall not find it; and shall desire to die, and death shall flee from them. Rev 9:1-6

When it says, *"And there came out of the smoke locusts upon the earth: and unto them was given power, as the scorpions of the earth have power,"* understand that according to Gen 3:15, those same locusts-like scorpions will not have power over you! We know this because it also says *"And it was commanded them that they should not hurt the grass of the earth, neither any green thing, neither any tree; but only those men which have not the seal of God in their foreheads."*

Those people who are truly the Lord's will not only be able to live during that time without fear of being stung, but according to Genesis 3:15 the followers of Jesus will be able to subdue those creatures!

How's that for a Promise?!

Chapter 26
The Heart of God

For all the promises of God in Him are yea, and in Him Amen,
unto the glory of God by us.

$2Cor\ 1:20$

I have the feeling that we're gonna find out that God's heart is bigger than our limited imagination. That's because everything that we read and hear from the Lord is based upon His character.

> *For I am the LORD, I change not; therefore ye sons of Jacob are not consumed.* **Malachi 3:6**

It's based upon His holiness.

> *Follow peace with all men, and holiness, without which no man shall see the Lord.* **Heb 12:14**

It's also based upon His perfect balance between truth and justice. The Cherubim on the top of the Ark of the Covenant is a perfect example.

> *And thou shalt make a mercy seat of pure gold: two cubits and a half shall be the length thereof, and a cubit and a half the breadth thereof. And thou shalt make two cherubims of gold, of beaten work shalt thou make them, in the two ends of the mercy seat. And make one cherub on the one end, and the other cherub on the other end: even of the mercy seat shall ye make the cherubims on the two ends thereof. And the cherubims shall stretch forth their wings on high, covering the mercy seat with their wings, and their faces shall look one to another; toward the mercy seat shall the faces of the cherubims be. And thou shalt put the mercy seat above upon the ark; and in the ark thou shalt put the testimony that I shall give thee. And there I will meet with thee, and I will commune with thee from above the mercy seat, from between the two cherubims which are upon the ark of the testimony, of all things which I will give thee in commandment unto the children of Israel.* **Exodus 25:17-22**

Those Cherubim are an illustration of the perfect balance of justice and mercy, with the mercy seat in the middle and the blood of the Lamb on the altar. Even though the Ark was made thousands of years before the Lord came to earth, we now know it represents Jesus as God's Everlasting Promise. God's demand for perfect justice and His desire to show perfect mercy can only be fulfilled through the Blood of Jesus on the Mercy Seat.

A Favorite Promise

One of my favorite Promises out of the Word can be found in Romans.

> *Who shall separate us from the love of Christ? Shall tribulation, or distress, or persecution, or famine, or nakedness, or peril, or sword? As it is written, "For thy sake we are killed all the day long; we are accounted as sheep for the slaughter." Nay, in all these things we are more than conquerors through Him that loved us. For I am persuaded, that neither death, nor life, nor angels, nor principalities, nor powers, nor things present, nor things to come, nor height, nor depth, nor any other creature, shall be able to separate us from the love of God, which is in Christ Jesus our Lord.* **Romans 8:35-39**

This picture of the End Times environment shows us how God will fulfill His promises to us, even in the worst of circumstances. If we go to the original Greek language, we can see how this passage is dealing with an End of the Age in which the supernatural is erupting all around us. Verse 35a asks the question, *"Who shall separate us from the love of Christ."* The very first word in the verse as translated in the KJV is "who". However, in the Greek the word is the interrogative pronoun *tis* and can equally be translated as "who", "which", "why" or "what".

Understanding this is very important to comprehend the scenario painted by the author Paul as the Holy Spirit is leading him. I believe it is the Holy Spirit trying to warn us of a time when we will absolutely have to depend and trust on God's Everlasting Promises.

Also, when you look at the word translated as "separate" we also see a different picture being painted. That's because this word is the Greek word *chorizo*, which can mean "separate" but can also can mean "divide".

Next we need to focus on the word for "love" which is the familiar word *agapé*. A*gapé* of course means "love," but it can also mean "goodwill".

So if I may, let's look at the translation of this verse a little differently before we dissect the rest of the passage. Based upon the original language, verse 35 could easily have been translated as the question:

"What shall try to divide us from the goodwill of the Messiah Jesus?"

In order to answer that question of "what" you have to know the primary mission of the Messiah Jesus. And while it sounds elementary, remember that there are many things that Jesus accomplished when He came. Even with everything that He did while He was physically here, there is still one main mission out of which His entire ministry flowed.

The answer is simple, but it has many ancillary benefits. Within the primary reason of Jesus' advent we see all the Promises of God wrapped up in the personage and appearance of His Son on earth. Of Himself, Jesus said:

I am come that they might have life, and that they might have it more abundantly. **John 10:10b**

The whole reason that Messiah Jesus came was because without His sacrifice, we were separated from God, which is spiritual death. The only way to bridge that chasm was through His blood. And everything that He did while on earth, and will do in the future, will be for that very purpose. The goodwill, or God's perfect will, in the work of Messiah Jesus was to give us life. Keep this essential truth in the back of your mind as we continue to breakdown Romans 8:35-39.

The second part of verse 35 asks the question:

Shall tribulation, or distress, or persecution, or famine, or nakedness, or peril, or sword?

Tribulation is from the word *thlipsis*, which can mean "persecution," "affliction," or "tribulation". In other words, a whole host of bad, uncomfortable stuff!

But the word translated as "distress" is interesting in that it comes from the Greek word *stenochória*. This word literally means "narrowness of space" as in the sense of being confined or hindered by a small, narrow place.

Immediately my mind goes to the Matthew 7:13 which says:

Enter ye in at the strait gate: for wide is the gate, and broad is the way, that leadeth to destruction, and many there be which go in thereat.

In modern English, this verse would say enter by way of the "narrow" gate, and broad is the way of destruction.

And that verse makes me think of what Jesus Himself said a few verses later:

Not every one that saith unto me, "Lord, Lord," shall enter into the kingdom of heaven; but he that doeth the will of my Father which is in heaven. Many will say to me in that day, "Lord, Lord, have we not prophesied in thy name? And in thy name have cast out devils? And in thy name done many wonderful works?" And then will I profess unto them, I never knew you: depart from me, ye that work iniquity. **Matt 7:21-23**

Before I drift too far from verse 35b, in the original Greek, the word "famine" means to be "hungry". The word "nakedness" literally means "to be without clothes" and "naked" and the word translated as "peril" means "danger". Lastly from this verse, the word translated as "sword" is from the word *machaira* which was a short sword or dagger mainly used for stabbing. It was often called a "slaughter-knife" and used as an instrument for exacting retribution.

So, when we look at the totality of verse 35, Paul is really asking:

"What shall try to divide us from the goodwill and the life that the Messiah Jesus brought? These circumstances will cause you severe distress. Will you allow yourself to be divided from Him because of that distress? Contrary to what most of the world thinks, the path of a relationship with Jesus is narrow. Will that narrow path hinder you? You will be hungry, you will be naked and you will be in great danger. Moreover, there will be those who will try to exact retribution upon you and kill you because of your faith in Jesus. Will any of these things divide us from a life that is more abundant?"

We see in verse 36 a reference to Psalm 44, which pretty much says the same thing. More importantly it alludes to people being compared to sheep which are unassuming and docile animals that are easily led to slaughter. In contrast, we're also told in 2 Corinthians 2:11 that we shouldn't be unassuming and ignorant about the devil's activities.

> Lest Satan should get an advantage of us: for we are not ignorant of his devices. *2 Corinthians 2:11*

I specifically point this out because in verse 37, we see the following KJV translation:

> Nay, in all these things we are more than conquerors through him that loved us. *Romans 8:37*

This is one of my favorite verses in the whole Bible. Interestingly, the phrase "more than conquerors" comes from the word *hupernikaó*, which literally means to "prevail mightily". The rest of the verse in Greek reads *dia agapaó* (a form of the word *agapé*), which, if we are to be consistent, would be better translated as *"through God's goodwill or perfect will for us."*

The following verses are why I've taken the time to breakdown this passage, because if you look closely, things get really interesting.

There is a lot of information packed in verse 38 and 39 and I will lay it all out for you in the translation and then put it together at the end. Please read this carefully. In the KJV, the verses read as follows:

> For I am persuaded, that neither death, nor life, nor angels, nor principalities, nor powers, nor things present, nor things to come, nor height, nor depth, nor any other creature, shall be able to separate us from the love of God, which is in Christ Jesus our Lord. *Romans 8:38-39*

"Persuaded" comes from the Greek word *peithó*, which means "to persuade" or "to have confidence." So if we look at this verse in its context, perhaps it would be better to translate it as an exhortation from Paul trying to persuade readers about what God is capable of doing in their lives. So instead of saying that he is "persuaded," what if he's really trying to persuade us by saying, *"Listen to me! I promise you..."*

That translation would better fit the context of the rest of the verses. That's because we see the next word that he uses is the conjunction *oute* which literally means "neither" or "and not".

The next word is *thanatos* and is correctly translated as "death," either physical or spiritual. Again we see the conjunction *oute* and then the word "life" which comes from *zóé* and means life either a present physical life or a future spiritual existence.

Let's pause to consider what we're being told here. Why would Paul say, *"Hey! Listen to me! I promise you that neither death nor life in a future spiritual existence..."*? Why start a sentence like that? The answer lies in the rest of the verse.

He then says, *"and not angels..."* This is a curious statement because at first reading, you may wonder, "Why should I be worried about angels?" But the word for angels here is *aggelos* and the real question is: Which angels? This isn't defined for us outright and it should make you ask the question: The good angels or the bad angels?

Given the other exhortations in the verse, I believe that Paul's talking about Fallen Angels here, or the bad angels. After all, why would we be concerned about God's angels trying to separate us from Jesus?

346

I'm also led to this conclusion because of the next thing he says, *"and not principalities…"* This is a telling word because it comes from the Greek word *arché*, which doesn't mean principalities at all.

The literal translation of *arché* is "beginning" or "origin". It gives the impression of someone, or something that has existed from the beginning of time or at least earth's time. The word also lends itself to the idea of *arché* being a "chiefdom", a foremost being, who has priority because he came before the rest.

With the words *aggelos* (angels) and *arché* (from the beginning) I'm reminded of the following passage out of Job when God rebuked him:

> Then the LORD answered Job out of the whirlwind, and said, "Who is this that darkeneth counsel by words without knowledge? Gird up now thy loins like a man; for I will demand of thee, and answer thou me. Where wast thou when I laid the foundations of the earth? Declare, if thou hast understanding. Who hath laid the measures thereof, if thou knowest? Or who hath stretched the line upon it? Whereupon are the foundations thereof fastened? Or who laid the corner stone thereof, when the morning stars sang together, and all the sons of God shouted for joy?" **Job 38:1-7**

As we've discussed in an earlier section in this book, those beings that were there when God laid the foundations of the earth were in fact the angels. These are the sons of God that are mentioned.

It's Paul's understanding of the actions and motives of these Fallen Angels which prompts his exhortation in this passage. That exhortation is even more intriguing when you consider the timeframe that Paul is trying to warn us about. This too is contained within the passage.

"…nor things present, nor things to come…" in verse 38b comes from the Greek word for "present" which is *enistémi* and means "to be at hand" or impending and *"things to come…"* is from the word *melló* which means "to be about to".

This particular portion of the passage seems to be saying something like *"the things that are impending or that will happen."* In addition, we understand from Ephesians 6:12 that this struggle with the Fallen Angels is a battle that is occurring in the present tense:

"For we wrestle not against flesh and blood, but against principalities, against powers, against the rulers of the darkness of this world, against spiritual wickedness in high places."

The impression from Paul in this section is that something much bigger than our current struggle is coming.

I need to pause here and point out that the next thing in the original language is our translated word of "powers". It's important to note that in the KJV, the word "powers" is rendered just before "principalities" as if to say "those powerful devils". This is not how the original writing reads.

Powers is listed after those things that are "present" and "to come" and it comes from the familiar word *dunamis*, which means a "miraculous power," "might" or "strength". So when we read the verse in the context of current opposition and future opposition by the Fallen Angels, it gives the impression of a great releasing of power at some point in the future - As in the End of the Age. This is consistent with various things read in the Book of Revelation like Rev 13:4-7:

> And they worshipped the dragon which gave power unto the beast: and they worshipped the beast, saying, "Who is like unto the beast? Who is able to make war with him?" And there was given unto

him a mouth speaking great things and blasphemies; and power was given unto him to continue forty and two months. And he opened his mouth in blasphemy against God, to blaspheme His name, and His tabernacle, and them that dwell in heaven. And it was given unto him to make war with the saints, and to overcome them: and power was given him over all kindreds, and tongues, and nations.

Could it be that in 2 Corinthians 2 Paul is warning of a time in the future when the supernatural goes ballistic and that supernatural power, *dunamis*, begins to spread all across the globe?

I believe so. This is further clarified when he says, *"nor height, nor depth, nor any other creature…"*

"Height" is the word *hupsóma*, which can be defined as simply "height," but also literally means "that which is lifted up"! This translation contextually flows with the idea of an evil *dunamis* being released at the End of the Age as we saw in that excerpt from Revelation. And it appears that those Fallen Angels, or at least their representatives, are being lifted up or worshiped! Sound familiar?

The word "depth" comes from the word *bathos*, which can mean "depth" and even "deep water". It can also mean "to meet", "to have fullness", "to be immense", or "something that is to an extreme degree" or it can also mean "deep-laid plans".

This is particularly important when you consider that the enemy has been planning for mankind's downfall for millennia. How much more "deep-laid plans" can there be?

Therefore rejoice, ye heavens, and ye that dwell in them. Woe to the inhabiters of the earth and of the sea! For the devil is come down unto you, having great wrath, because he knoweth that he hath but a short time. **Rev 12:12**

Paul then says, *"nor any other creature"*. The word rendered as "creature" is from the word *ktisis*, which is the word for "creation," as in divine creation. Those Fallen Angels were created beings and it appears that Paul is telling us that even they will not *"be able to separate us from the love of God, which is in Christ Jesus our Lord."*

So we've come full circle with this last sentence. Again, the word "separate" comes from the word *chorizo*, which means to "divide," and "the love" is *agapé*, which can also be translated as "the goodwill" that God has for us in Jesus.

— Romans 8:35 —39

So to sum it all up in our modern day vernacular, Paul is telling us something like this:

v35 - *What shall try to divide us from the goodwill and the life that the Messiah Jesus brought? These circumstances will cause you severe distress. Will you be divided from Him because of that distress? Contrary to what most of the world thinks, the path of a relationship with Jesus is narrow. Will that narrow path hinder you? You will be hungry, you will be naked and you will be in great danger. Moreover, there will be those that will try to exact retribution on you and kill you because of your faith in Jesus. Will any of these things divide you from a life that is more abundant?*

v36 - *Like it says in the OT, they think of you as dumb sheep and that they can slaughter you. But you don't need to be like dumb sheep.*

v37 - *Despite all of these things, we will prevail mightily through God's perfect will for us of an abundant life.*

v38 & 39 - *Listen to me! I promise you that neither death nor life in a future spiritual existence nor the Fallen Angels, the ones that have been here since the very beginning with deep-laid scheming plans, nor the bad things that are impending or that will happen, nor any other created creature that displays supernatural powers against us, will divide us from God's perfect will which is a more abundant life in Jesus!*

When you translate Romans 8:35-39 like this, I'm sure you'll agree - **That is some Promise!**

A Life Beyond

There was a man of the Pharisees, named Nicodemus, a ruler of the Jews. The same came to Jesus by night, and said unto Him, "Rabbi, we know that thou art a teacher come from God, for no man can do these miracles that thou doest, except God be with him." Jesus answered and said unto him, "Verily, verily, I say unto thee, 'Except a man be born again, he cannot see the kingdom of God.'" Nicodemus saith unto Him, "How can a man be born when he is old? Can he enter the second time into his mother's womb, and be born?" Jesus answered, "Verily, verily, I say unto thee, 'Except a man be born of water and of the Spirit, he cannot enter into the kingdom of God. That which is born of the flesh is flesh; and that which is born of the Spirit is spirit.' Marvel not that I said unto thee, 'Ye must be born again.' The wind bloweth where it listeth, and thou hearest the sound thereof, but canst not tell whence it cometh, and whither it goeth. So is every one that is born of the Spirit." **John 3:1-8**

We always hear that people need to be "born again" or that they said a prayer and were born again. But the fact is that this phrase, taken out of the passage above, has only come into popularity in our modern era. It's become a catch-phrase, or a movement, that started in the early 60's and was made popular in the 70's with the Jesus Movement.

Don't get me wrong; people do need to be born again. But even Jesus specifically said, *"Marvel not that I said unto thee, 'Ye must be born again.'"* So why do we marvel? Why do we fixate? Why do we need a tagline or an experience in order to come into a relationship with Him while His Holy Spirit makes us into new creations?

I came out of the Jesus Movement in the early 70's when the power of the Holy Spirit was displayed mightily. And I can tell you from firsthand experience that the thing that caused the Jesus movement to explode was true *charismata*, or the real endowment of the Holy Spirit of the Living God. It was powerful and life changing, but what it wasn't - was a slogan or box to check on your spiritual checklist.

In fact, I'll go one-step farther and say that people don't need a "born again" experience - They need a real, living, transformative encounter with the resurrected Son of the Living God, Jesus Christ. His Holy Spirit living inside of us is what literally transforms us into a new creation. That's what the initial born again and Jesus movements accomplished. It wasn't about a catch-phrase.

Contrarily, these days we are so "civilized" in church, i.e. "Yes, I see that hand." We have a generation of church goers who believe they've had an encounter with the Living God, but all they've done is checked a box on their religious checklist. This is why we need Jesus, the real Jesus, as our Promise!

God is eternal. Men who are born on earth instinctively know that they have a beginning and that they have an end. For those who choose to live life on their own terms without the Lord, they may try and prolong death, they may try and escape death, they may even think that they can download their consciousness into a computer and live forever.

Despite their desperate efforts, eternity confronts every finite mortal who refuses to believe in an eternal life after death for the sake of expediency. In the understanding of a final judgment from a real, eternal God, man comprehends the limitlessness of his existence. With that comprehension comes the realization that their decision here on earth impacts their immortal souls. In vain, they do whatever they can to postpone the realization by futilely adhering to manmade belief systems like the "annihilation of the soul".

Annihilationism is also known as extinctionism or destructionism. It's a modern belief that has been made popular by people because they can't bear the truth of God's eternal judgment of casting people into the Lake of Fire. They believe that after the final judgment, unrepentant human beings and all Fallen Angels will not meet their fate in the Lake of Fire, but instead will be obliterated and totally destroyed. They believe that it will be as if they never existed. Their spirits and consciousness will be extinguished instead of suffering everlasting torment in Hell. In other words, God will eventually destroy the wicked, leaving only the righteous to live on eternally.

The only problem is that annihilationism is not biblical. This is one of those negative Promises by God that He will live up to. You don't get a pass if you won't follow Him. You will be judged and you will meet your end in Hell. It's as simple as that.

If you can't believe God when His Word clearly says that people will go to Hell, how are you supposed to believe in all of the good stuff that He's Promised you as a Christian? You can't have it both ways.

That doesn't mean that we don't try.

Pedal to the Metal

Earlier I mentioned my fondness for speed and even though I've matured over the years, both in the Lord and chronologically, I still like to go fast.

In fact, a few years after I'd gotten saved, I was driving on a straight, long and empty road outside of Columbus, Montana, between Bozeman and Billings, in a European model Porsche 928 S sports car. I had that sleek machine roaring down the road at 150 mph. I know, I know, stupid, I shouldn't have. But I did and what happened next would be a lesson that I would never forget.

I wasn't being especially spiritual in that moment. I wasn't worshiping the Lord or thinking of Bible verses or anything. I was just driving for the sheer love of driving.

Suddenly I was snatched out of that car and I found myself in the presence of Jesus the King as He sat at a white alabaster judge's bench, which I assume was the previously mentioned Bema Seat.

The bench or podium was large and tall, because I'm 5'10" and as I stood in front of it, my head just barely cleared the top of it.

The Lord looked exactly as I remembered Him; He leaned forward on His elbows and looked at me face-to-face. My head was bowed because of the sheer weight of His presence and His Holiness. As He spoke to me, I looked up into His eyes. What He said to me in that moment would stay with me the rest of my life.

All He said was, *"Steve, why have you done so little when I have given you so much?"*

I was ashamed and humbled by the fact that I'd let Him down. I bowed my head again and said, "Forgive me, Lord. Give me another chance."

Then, bam! I found myself back in my car without missing a beat. I was traveling down the same road at the same speed.

Just before I had been snatched away, I looked at my watch. When I got back, I looked at it again. I had only been gone for a few seconds but it seemed like a long time.

I told this story to a friend who calculated how far I went in that short time. It turns out my car sped down the road about 10 miles without me being behind the wheel! In eternity all time stops but my car was in our 3D world's time and space and kept going. I've joked that maybe my guardian angel liked to go fast too. Just another miracle in my life done by our incredible God!

Here's the lesson that sticks with me to this day: At the time, I thought that I was on fire for Jesus. I was doing everything that I thought I should have been doing (except speeding). But the experience made me acutely aware of our responsibility as Believers to the calling that God gives each of us. We are all going to have to stand before the Lord and give account for what we have done, or not done, with what He's given us. And He's given us all something. We're only on this earth for the briefest of times when compared to the vastness to eternity. We have a job to do and whether you feel like it or not, God is depending on you to fulfill your calling.

We all have a calling and we all have a responsibility to Him to do what He's given us to do. Getting saved is not about our being rescued as individuals from Hell. Getting saved should be about our entry into the Kingdom of God where we are instantly conscripted into His army with a purpose.

My advice?

Find out what your purpose is, your calling, and pursue it with all of your time and energy. You certainly don't want to be called on the carpet in front of the Lord like me.

As much as the damned get their eternal reward of separation from God in the Lake of Fire, the righteous will be judged on our faithfulness to God's calling on our lives. As I mentioned earlier, all real Christians will stand before the Bema Seat Judgment. Those rewards for your faithful work on His behalf are His Promise to you. Never forget that.

He Will Take You Back

When I was inspired to write this book, the Holy Spirit impressed upon me the need to address those individuals who had known the Lord but had walked away from Him. This is a subject that I'm intimately familiar with. Perhaps the greatest example of God's Promise of forgiveness for those who have backslid can be found in the story of the prodigal son. It's a little long, but worth reviewing.

And He (Jesus) said, "A certain man had two sons. And the younger of them said to his father, 'Father, give me the portion of goods that falleth to me.' And he divided unto them his living. And not many days after the younger son gathered all together, and took his journey into a far country, and there wasted his substance with riotous living. And when he had spent all, there arose a mighty famine in that land; and he began to be in want. And he went and joined himself to a citizen of that country; and he sent him into his fields to feed swine. And he would fain have filled his belly with the husks that the swine did eat: and no man gave unto him. And when he came to himself, he said, 'How many hired servants of my father's have bread enough and to spare, and I perish with hunger! I will arise and go to my father, and will say unto him, "Father, I have sinned against heaven, and before thee and am no more worthy to be called thy son: make me as one of thy hired servants."' And he arose, and came to his father. But when he was yet a great way off, his father saw him, and had compassion, and ran, and fell on his neck, and kissed him. And the son said unto him, 'Father, I have sinned against heaven, and in thy sight, and am no more worthy to be called thy son.' But the father said to his servants, 'Bring forth the best robe, and put it on him; and put a ring on his hand, and shoes on his feet, and bring hither the fatted calf, and kill it; and let us eat, and be merry. For this my son was dead, and is alive again; he was lost, and is found. And they began to be merry.' Now his elder son was in the field: and as he came and drew nigh to the house, he heard musick and dancing. And he called one of the servants, and asked what these things meant. And he said unto him, 'Thy brother is come; and thy father hath killed the fatted calf, because he hath received him safe and sound.' And he was angry, and would not go in: therefore came his father out, and intreated him. And he answering said to his father, 'Lo, these many years do I serve thee, neither transgressed I at any time thy commandment: and yet thou never gavest me a kid, that I might make merry with my friends. But as soon as this thy son was come, which hath devoured thy living with harlots, thou hast killed for him the fatted calf.' And he said unto him, 'Son, thou art ever with me, and all that I have is thine. It was meet that we should make merry, and be glad: for this thy brother was dead, and is alive again; and was lost, and is found.'" Luke 15:11-32

So too does God yearn for you to return to Him if you've walked away. I know this because I'm ashamed to admit that I once walked away from Him. In this book I've tried to be transparent with you to show you that God can use anyone, even someone as fallible as yours truly. This experience is a perfect example.

In the mid to late 80's I had an experience that absolutely crushed and wounded me. For your purposes, it really doesn't matter what happened, only the results of the incident. I was a "man of God". These types of things weren't supposed to happen to me. I was angry at the situation and frustrated and in my frustration, I walked away from the Lord for a couple of years.

You've read my testimony about how I got saved, how the Lord appeared to me and baptized me in His Holy Spirit, how He showed me the future and how He personally gave me a Joseph's ministry. In spite of all those powerful, life-changing, palpable and awe-inspiring experiences, it took only one incident, one stumble, one moment of looking away from the Lord, to cause me to leave Him.

That's where some of you are right now. You've messed up, been crushed like me, or just lusted after the things of the world. Now you too are estranged from your first love and you wonder, even doubt, if you could ever go back to Jesus. I can relate. When I had backslid, in my heart I had been crying out to God even though I was in sin and away from Him.

I am living proof that God is bigger than your poor choices and bigger than your sin.

This is why I think that Isaiah 1:18 is the greatest of God's Everlasting Promises:

Come now, and let us reason together, saith the LORD: though your sins be as scarlet, they shall be as white as snow; though they be red like crimson, they shall be as wool.

I fell and I fell hard. When I came to my senses, I desperately needed Him to wash me. He can wash you too. God loves you. And if we come to Him in honest, heartfelt and determined repentance - He will forgive you. He forgave me.

If we confess our sins, he is faithful and just to forgive us our sins, and to cleanse us from all unrighteousness. **1 John 1:19**

My little children, these things write I unto you, that ye sin not. And if any man sin, we have an advocate with the Father, Jesus Christ the righteous. **1 John 2:1**

That advocate doesn't walk away from us even though we might walk away from Him. On the contrary, He waits patiently for our hearts to turn back to Him.

That's not to say that you can live any old way you want and then, like using your fire insurance policy, come back to Jesus and give Him lip-service about your repentance. He knows your heart and your life better than you do and if you're still anchored to the world, He'll know. True heartfelt repentance with a deliberate turning away from sin and yielding your life once again to the Master will provide the renewed relationship you seek.

You just have to take the first step. **And that's a Promise.**

Full Circle

We find that we've come full circle with *Jesus - The Premise of the Promise.*

A lot of ground has been covered and I trust that you've found at least one nugget within these pages that will make your relationship with the Living God stronger and more purposeful.

In review, here are the H.E.L.P.s as listed in the book:

Preeminence - Where He is for eternity; we will be with Him for eternity.

{God} Who hath delivered us from the power of darkness, and hath translated us into the kingdom of his dear Son in whom we have redemption through his blood, even the forgiveness of sins, who is the image of the invisible God, the firstborn of every creature. For by Him were all things created, that are in heaven, and that are in earth, visible and invisible, whether they be thrones, or dominions, or principalities, or powers: all things were created by Him, and for Him. And He is before all things, and by Him all things consist. And He is the head of the body, the church: who is the beginning, the firstborn from the dead, that in all things He might have the preeminence. **Colossians 1:13-18**

And I heard a great voice out of heaven saying, "Behold, the tabernacle of God is with men, and He will dwell with them, and they shall be His people, and God Himself shall be with them, and be their God. And God shall wipe away all tears from their eyes; and there shall be no more death, neither sorrow, nor crying, neither shall there be any more pain: for the former things are passed away." **Rev 21:3-4**

Power - Ye shall receive power.

He spreads out the northern skies over empty space. He suspends the earth over nothing. He wraps up the waters in his clouds, yet the clouds do not burst under their weight. He covers the face of the full moon, spreading his clouds over it. He marks out the horizon on the face of the waters for a boundary between light and darkness. The pillars of the heavens quake, aghast at his rebuke. By His power He churned up the sea, by His wisdom He cut Rahab to pieces. By His breath the skies became fair, His hand pierced the gliding serpent. And these are but the outer fringe of His works, how faint the whisper we hear of Him! Who then can understand the thunder of His power?" **Job 26:7-14**

But ye shall receive power, after that the Holy Ghost is come upon you: and ye shall be witnesses unto me both in Jerusalem, and in all Judaea, and in Samaria, and unto the uttermost part of the earth. **Acts 1:8**

Presence - I am with you even until the end of the age.

Thou wilt shew me the path of life. In thy presence is fulness of joy. At thy right hand there are pleasures for evermore. **Psalm 16:1**

And Jesus came and spake unto them, saying, "All power is given unto me in heaven and in earth. Go ye therefore, and teach all nations, baptizing them in the name of the Father, and of the Son, and of the Holy Ghost: Teaching them to observe all things whatsoever I have commanded you: and, lo, I am with you alway, even unto the end of the world. Amen." **Luke 28:18-20**

Let not your heart be troubled: ye believe in God, believe also in me. In my Father's house are many mansions: if it were not so, I would have told you. I go to prepare a place for you and if I go and prepare a place for you, I will come again, and receive you unto myself; that where I am, there ye may be also. **John 14:1-3**

Protection - Behold I give you power to tread on serpents and scorpions.

The angel of the LORD encampeth round about them that fear him, and delivereth them. **Psalm 34:7**

Behold, I give unto you power to tread on serpents and scorpions, and over all the power of the enemy: and nothing shall by any means hurt you. **Luke 10:19**

Provision - My God shall supply all your needs.

But my God shall supply all your need according to his riches in glory by Christ Jesus. **Philippians 4:19**

Now unto Him that is able to do exceeding abundantly above all that we ask or think, according to the power that worketh in us, unto Him be glory in the church by Christ Jesus throughout all ages, world without end. Amen. **Eph 3:20-21**

Patience - He is able to keep those in perfect peace whose minds are stayed upon Him.

Thou wilt keep him in perfect peace, whose mind is stayed on thee: because he trusteth in thee. **Isaiah 26:3**

Commit thy way unto the LORD; trust also in Him; and He shall bring it to pass. And He shall bring forth thy righteousness as the light, and thy judgment as the noonday. Rest in the LORD, and wait patiently for Him: fret not thyself because of Him who prospereth in his way, because of the man who bringeth wicked devices to pass. **Psalm 37:5-7**

Purity - Though your sins be red as scarlet I'll make them white as wool.

Come now, and let us reason together, saith the LORD: though your sins be as scarlet, they shall be as white as snow; though they be red like crimson, they shall be as wool. **Isaiah 1:18**

Behold, what manner of love the Father hath bestowed upon us, that we should be called the sons of God: therefore the world knoweth us not, because it knew Him not. Beloved, now are we the sons of God, and it doth not yet appear what we shall be: but we know that, when He shall appear, we shall be like Him; for we shall see Him as He is. And every man that hath this hope in Him purifieth himself, even as He is pure. **1 John 3:1-3**

Proclamation - Behold I am the Lord thy God and there is no other.

I am the LORD, and there is none else, there is no God beside me: I girded thee, though thou hast not known me. That they may know from the rising of the sun, and from the west, that there is none beside me. I am the LORD, and there is none else. **Isaiah 45:5-6**

Peace - My peace I give unto thee, not as the world gives.

Peace I leave with you, my peace I give unto you: not as the world giveth, give I unto you. Let not your heart be troubled, neither let it be afraid. **John 14:2**

Promise - All the Promises of God are yea and amen according to God the Father.

For all the promises of God in Him are yea, and in Him Amen, unto the glory of God by us. **1 Corinthians 1:20**

I'm so grateful to the Lord for all that He's taken me through and all that He's taught me. I'm also thankful for you and for my being able to share these H.E.L.P.s with you. Always remember that our God is bigger than anything you may come up against in this life and that He stands ready to H.E.L.P.

His Ever Lasting Preeminence

That's a Promise you can count on.

Blessed Assurance

Blessed assurance, Jesus is mine! O what a foretaste of glory divine!
Heir of salvation, purchase of God, born of his Spirit, washed in his blood.

This is my story, this is my song, praising my Savior all the day long.
Perfect submission, perfect delight, visions of rapture now burst on my sight;
angels descending bring from above echoes of mercy, whispers of love.

Perfect submission, all is at rest; I in my Savior am happy and blest,
watching and waiting, looking above, filled with his goodness, lost in his love.

Conclusion

H.O.P.E.

(His Overwhelming Power Everyday)

Now the God of hope fill you with

all joy and peace in believing,

that ye may abound in hope,

through the power of the Holy Ghost.

Rom 15:13

I can take little credit for the things that you've read in this book because it was the Lord Who provided the richness of this content. Many times I felt like a bystander listening, yielding and writing what the Holy Spirit impressed upon me and I too was convicted by some of the truths that came out. Because of this process, this project has been one of the most rewarding and challenging that I've ever undertaken.

Those H.E.L.P.s are the very character manifestations of the Living God. With our limited, human understanding we try, and fail most of the time, to define Who God really is, what infinity really is. Whatever grasp on eternity we may have comes from the Eternal God. And what's even more mind-blowing is that by design, He's put eternity in our hearts.

He hath made every thing beautiful in His time: also He hath set the world in their heart, so that no man can find out the work that God maketh from the beginning to the end. **Eccles 3:11**

Each of those H.E.L.P.s is a confirmation of the One in Whom we put our trust, and each was given to help us understand our purpose in Him.

> *For in him we live, and move, and have our being; as certain also of your own poets have said, "For we are also his offspring." Acts 17:28*

That God-inspired foundation brings us to the ultimate realization that our H.O.P.E. is secure when it's placed in the Son of the Living God.

The Foundational Hope

There are fundamental beliefs that Christians possess that define where their H.O.P.E. is based:

 The Word of God

 Our acceptance of Him as our Lord and Savior

 Our experiences in Him in our individual lives

 The revelations about Him throughout history

 The prophesies in the Word that have, are now and will yet come to pass.

When we embrace these foundational tenets we are armed to deal with whatever may come our way. We understand that He is with us, in us and leading us.

> *Fear none of those things which thou shalt suffer. Behold, the devil shall cast some of you into prison, that ye may be tried and ye shall have tribulation ten days. Be thou faithful unto death, and I will give thee a crown of life. He that hath an ear, let him hear what the Spirit saith unto the churches. He that overcometh shall not be hurt of the second death. Rev 2:10-11*

As we approach the supernatural atmosphere and events of the End of the Age, it's not enough to just make it through life as a Christian. God wants us to overcome with victory, which is best defined as triumphing over the enemy and defeating him completely.

> *And having spoiled principalities and powers, He (Jesus) made a shew of them openly, triumphing over them in it. Col 2:15*

Through Jesus' death and resurrection, which totally decimated the devil and his minions, we partake in that victory. Step-by-step, those H.E.L.P.s are the key to living that victorious life. Yes, you do have a choice in the level of your participation in this victory but not the battle. You must fight to defeat the literal devil or he will steamroll right over you.

Unfortunately because far too many Christians don't understand the principles contained herein, they give the devil the win by simply lying down for him without a fight. Believers will admit to an early defeat by thinking things like, "Okay, you're right devil, I'm going to die early..." or, "I'm going to lose everything..." or "I'm going to..." whatever. It's then, at your weakest moment, that the devil pounces to claim victory over you. But it's a lie. He hasn't won and you aren't done.

Consider that hope is built upon the anticipation of something good, or better, that will come in the future. You can't hope for something that you already have, but you can hope that something that you have continues or ends.

For instance, God's people hope that, as it says in Matt 6:10, God's will is done on earth as it is in heaven. That may sound like a tall order given the current state of the earth where the devil is the "ruler of this world", but hope says that there is something greater and better to come in the future. For the Christian, that future is one where Jesus reigns supreme, the devil is bound, and all of the junk that we currently deal with is gone. The Believer hopes for the fruition of what began when Jesus declared that the Kingdom of God was at hand.

> *Now after that John was put in prison, Jesus came into Galilee, preaching the gospel of the kingdom of God, and saying, "The time is fulfilled, and the kingdom of God is at hand. Repent ye, and believe the gospel." **Mark 1:14-15***

It's through that lens of hope that we can see right through life's struggles and opposition. This hope looks forward, past these temporal issues to the promised Kingdom of God. That Kingdom and our hope are anchored in the reality of the resurrection of Jesus. Hope is a byproduct of the love that God Himself puts in our hearts.

> *(Love) Beareth all things, believeth all things, hopeth all things, endureth all things. **1 Cor 13:7***

Through His love, Jesus granted us total forgiveness. That forgiveness draws us closer to the Lord and our relationship with God transforms us from rebel to child of God. In this supernatural act, our hope is justified.

Even as the world around us destroys itself in rebellion against God, the gift of H.O.P.E. shines into the hearts of people who will reach out and accept Jesus as Savior. In doing so, we all find that regardless of the oppression, this hope shows us that it's not so bleak after all. God's already won the victory and because of that, in the end, so have we.

Wielding the Sword

> *And take the helmet of salvation, and the sword of the Spirit, which is the word of God. **Eph 6:17***

By shifting our focus to overcoming the enemy through these H.E.L.P.s, we find H.O.P.E. in our daily walks. In the Word, there are scriptures that speak about overcoming. They are extremely important to living a victorious life and I would strongly suggest that you go back to them, commit them to memory and use them throughout your day.

We live in a season in the twenty-first century where people are walking away from God. This has caused a supernatural vacuum in people's hearts. Because they will not look to the One True God, they search to fill that spiritual emptiness in a variety of ways. More people are turning to the Book of Incantations and fewer people believe in the Bible. The devil is releasing his End Time power in his followers. God's own people don't understand God's greater power that is available to them that He also wants to release. It's called the power of the Holy Ghost.

But ye shall receive power, after that the Holy Ghost is come upon you: and ye shall be witnesses unto me both in Jerusalem, and in all Judaea, and in Samaria, and unto the uttermost part of the earth. **Acts 1:8**

Abiding continually in His Word is the key to understanding His End Time battle strategy which He's designed for your victory. The devil attacks all people, and his greatest attack is on Jesus as the Word of God. Most Christians don't believe the scripture that says, "Greater is He in you than he that is in the world."

Ye are of God, little children, and have overcome them: because greater is he that is in you, than he that is in the world. **1 John 4:4**

If they did, they would practice it victoriously.

God is tired of His people succumbing to a lying, thieving, murdering impostor in Satan. He's calling on you to rise up and be the people that He created you to be.

He that hath an ear, let him hear what the Spirit saith unto the churches; To him that overcometh will I give to eat of the tree of life, which is in the midst of the paradise of God. **Rev 2:7**

With the above passage, we've come right back to the Garden of Eden where man's innocence was lost and sin entered the world. As tough as it is to comprehend, there's something greater than the Garden that is being prepared for those who overcome.

In my Father's house are many mansions. If it were not so, I would have told you. I go to prepare a place for you and if I go and prepare a place for you, I will come again, and receive you unto myself, that where I am, there ye may be also. **John 14:2-3**

What's Life About?

The vine is dried up, and the fig tree languisheth; the pomegranate tree, the palm tree also, and the apple tree, even all the trees of the field, are withered: because joy is withered away from the sons of men. **Joel 1:12**

When God's people don't understand their purpose or the power that rests within them, they flounder. That's why He gave us these H.E.L.P.s. They're increasing revelations of God's person and His power. Not understanding Who the Lord is and why He created us causes people to ask questions that can't be answered outside of the Word of God and the person of Jesus.

These are questions like, "What's the purpose of life?" "What am I doing here?" and "What's the point of it all?" All of these questions are answered with the realization that a loving, omnipotent and Holy God created us for His pleasure.

Thou art worthy, O Lord, to receive glory and honour and power: for thou hast created all things, and for thy pleasure they are and were created. **Rev 4:11**

The word "pleasure" from the KJV in the above verse isn't exactly right. Despite the translations of the above verses, we certainly were not created for God's entertainment or amusement. The way the sentence reads in Greek is: *dia*, (on account of, or because of), *theléma* (an act of will, or wished or desired). So God made us simply because He wanted to, or willed us to, come into existence. A verse that I've referred to several times throughout the book, Colossians 1:16, reiterates this point:

> *And He is before all things, and by Him all things consist.*

Neither of these verses tells us exactly why He created us, only that He did create us. The answer to the question of "why" is better gleaned by several scriptures. God is a creative Being, and He must have felt the inclination to create us. That inclination is not unlike the artist who paints a beautiful scene on canvas, or the sculptor who shapes a masterpiece out of clay. That said, this explanation for His motivation also falls short.

Genesis 1:27 says:

> *So God created man in His own image, in the image of God created He him; male and female created He them.*

God "created" us in His "own image" and He did this because He is a personal Being. Consider that we as homo sapiens are personal beings as well. We are socially and familially inclined and it makes sense that these are inherited traits from our Creator. This transference of traits is manifest from Genesis 1:27.

Have you ever heard someone say that a baby has his father's eyes? "His own image" gives us the impression that not only do we figuratively look like our Father, but we've also inherited His character trait of being a personal being. Mankind approaches all aspects of life from this inter-relationship mindset. Our creation relationship with our Father will forever tether us to His Person because we're given a choice on how we will live our lives, self-serving or God-serving.

In that relationship, we can personally know God and have a willful choice to love Him, worship Him, serve Him, and fellowship with Him. If God forced us to do these things, we wouldn't have free will. We would be mindless robots, which He certainly doesn't need or want. He was, and always has been, full, complete and content being Himself, with or without us.

God didn't create us because He needed us. After all, He's God and He needs nothing. He doesn't feel lonely, so He wasn't looking for a "friend." He does love us so very much, but that's not the same as needing us. If He didn't create us, God would still exist. He never changes (Malachi 3:6). Even though He didn't need to make us, He was pleased with His handiwork of our fashioning.

> *And God saw every thing that he had made, and, behold, it was very good. And the evening and the morning were the sixth day.* **Gen 1:31**

He dubbed mankind, and the rest of His earthly creation, as being "very good". This tells us that although He didn't need us, He approved of His handiwork and would later call us "friends".

> *Ye are my friends, if ye do whatsoever I command you. Henceforth I call you not servants; for the servant knoweth not what his lord doeth: but I have called you friends; for all things that I have heard of my Father I have made known unto you.* **John 15:14-15**

Friendship aside, we are more than simple acquaintances to Him, and by His own volition He loves us.

Only the LORD had a delight in thy fathers to love them, and he chose their seed after them, even you above all people, as it is this day. **Deut 10:15**

The God of Creation whose hand fashioned everything that you see, feel, or can imagine didn't need anyone or anything but He created you, He chose you, and He loves you just because He wants to. That makes you very special, indeed.

A Time for Strength

These things I have spoken unto you, that in me ye might have peace. In the world ye shall have tribulation: but be of good cheer; I have overcome the world. **John 16:33**

I've firmly stated several times that I believe that Christians will go through the tribulation. A large part of my understanding has come from the panoramic view of history that the Lord showed me when I first got saved. In everything that He showed me, I didn't see a rapture. But rather than getting sidetracked by some useless eschatological discussion about the rapture, let's focus on the premise of the above verse.

Regardless of what we see, persecution, famine, earthquakes, wars, economic collapse and more, if our eyes are truly on Him we're already equipped and destined to be overcomers. We're supposed to be, as I pointed out in Romans 8:37, more than conquerors through Jesus who loves us. That victorious attitude will not only help us survive, but thrive in those crazy days. The simple fact is that you can't be an overcomer unless you have something to overcome. Opposition like we've never seen is a certainty.

Finally, my brethren, be strong in the Lord, and in the power of his might. Put on the whole armour of God, that ye may be able to stand against the wiles of the devil. For we wrestle not against flesh and blood, but against principalities, against powers, against the rulers of the darkness of this world, against spiritual wickedness in high places. Wherefore take unto you the whole armour of God, that ye may be able to withstand in the evil day, and having done all, to stand. Stand therefore, having your loins girt about with truth, and having on the breastplate of righteousness and your feet shod with the preparation of the gospel of peace. Above all, taking the shield of faith, wherewith ye shall be able to quench all the fiery darts of the wicked and take the helmet of salvation, and the sword of the Spirit, which is the word of God. **Eph 6:10-17**

Overcomers stand, but not weakly as if our legs were barely under us. We are to stand firm in the evil day, ready to fight and to win. When we are strong and courageous, appropriating His strength and courage, we put ourselves in the place where God can, and will, do the miraculous around us.

Joshua and Caleb had to go into the Promised Land. The only way they would succeed was to overcome literal giants who happened to also be cannibals. In order to obtain God's promise, they had to defeat the biggest obstacles and the most powerful enemies on earth at that time.

Now after the death of Moses the servant of the LORD it came to pass, that the LORD spake unto Joshua the son of Nun, Moses' minister, saying, "Moses my servant is dead. Now therefore arise, go over this Jordan, thou, and all this people, unto the land which I do give to them, even to the children of Israel. Every place that the sole of your foot shall tread upon, that have I given unto you, as I said unto Moses. From the wilderness and this Lebanon even unto the great river, the river Euphrates, all the land of the Hittites, and unto the great sea toward the going down of the sun, shall be your coast. There shall not any man be able to stand before thee all the days of thy life. As I was with Moses, so I will be with thee. I will not fail thee, nor forsake thee. Be strong and of a good courage for unto this people shalt thou divide for an inheritance the land, which I sware unto their fathers to give them. Only be thou strong and very courageous, that thou mayest observe to do according to all the law, which Moses my servant commanded thee. Turn not from it to the right hand or to the left, that thou mayest prosper whithersoever thou goest. This book of the law shall not depart out of thy mouth; but thou shalt meditate therein day and night, that thou mayest observe to do according to all that is written therein: for then thou shalt make thy way prosperous, and then thou shalt have good success. Have not I commanded thee? Be strong and of a good courage; be not afraid, neither be thou dismayed: for the LORD thy God is with thee whithersoever thou goest." **Joshua 1:1-9**

There are so many comparisons within this story for us. The Hebrews at that time had just come out of forty years of wandering in the desert. For twenty-first century Christians, life may soon turn into a desert.

In the above passage, God said to Joshua three separate times to be "strong and courageous". He also told them three separate times that He would be with them. Why did He emphasize their need to be strong and to look to Him? They had seen God do the miraculous over those forty desert years and of course they had an understanding and anticipation of what their promise was, but the fact was that they were about to face off with giants! Sometimes, in spite of the promises that God has given us, the obstacles in front of that promise may seem too big to overcome. That's why God reminded them to be strong and courageous and to depend on Him in their battles. The same can be said of us.

Today, we're about to face off with the supernatural in the extreme and we will experience tribulation in ways we can't even imagine. If you lean on Him and don't lose heart, the same God who helped the Israelites will help you overcome your giants.

So I say to you on behalf of our King: Christian, be strong and very courageous and the Lord will fight for you.

Not About Religion

As you might have gathered from the things you've read here, I'm not really a religious kind of guy. In fact, I pointedly reject any semblance of religion and the vanity of earthly priesthoods, titles, religious attire or pious religious attitudes. After all, Jesus didn't come to be served, but to serve. Instead, the religious-minded of this earth all have someone to serve them.

But so shall it not be among you: but whosoever will be great among you, shall be your minister. And whosoever of you will be the chiefest, shall be servant of all. For even the Son of Man came not to be ministered unto, but to minister, and to give His life a ransom for many. **Mark 10:43-45**

Knowing and walking with Jesus isn't about religion. It's about relationship. I love the Lord and I love His Word, and the only 'trapping' I'm concerned about is being covered with the Blood of Lamb. The only color I'm interested in is the whiteness of the robe that He will one day give to me.

People may fail us and situations not of our own making may overwhelm us. But no matter who has forsaken you, no matter who has broken your heart, no matter who has hurt you, Jesus is everything that I've presented in this book and more and you can trust Him because He loves you. Our H.O.P.E. is based upon the Words of Jesus and entrusting that He is with us even unto the End of the Age. He will never leave you or forsake you. In the middle of whatever you're going through, you too have these ten H.E.L.P.s to lean on during your journey.

Don't get me wrong. Trust in Jesus needs to be grown naturally in our walk. Sometimes I still struggle. As an example of one of those lessons, one time I was furious at Him over something that I blamed Him for. And yes, He already knows your thoughts so you can be candid and honest with Him too.

In a moment of my candidness with Him, I was so angry that I kicked a chair. Kicking a chair wasn't the smartest thing to do because chairs are hard and they aren't forgiving and I ended up breaking my toe!

After a while I stopped grousing at Him, and the pain subsided enough for me to think. It was then that the Lord asked me a pointed question.

"Steve, have I ever let you down?"

I said, "No, Lord."

Then He asked, "Have I ever done anything to hurt you?"

"No, Lord."

"Have I ever lied to you?"

"No, Lord."

"Then why are you mad at me?"

What was I going to say? He was right. He didn't do anything but love me and put up with me. I knew my anger was misplaced.

I said, "I'm not, Lord. (Mad at Him) I'm mad at myself. Please forgive me, Lord. I repent."

God always wants the best for you even though, at times, in the midst of your anger or grief, it may not have seemed like it. We live in a messed-up world with messed-up people. He's truly the only One you can really count on.

> *I write unto you, little children, because your sins are forgiven you for His name's sake. I write unto you, fathers, because ye have known Him that is from the beginning. I write unto you, young men, because ye have overcome the wicked one. I write unto you, little children, because ye have known the Father. I have written unto you, fathers, because ye have known Him that is from the beginning. I have written unto you, young men, because ye are strong, and the word of God abideth in you, and ye have overcome the wicked one.* **1 John 2:12-14**

That word "abideth" is the very same word that we saw in Chapter 8 and comes from the Greek word *menó*, which means to "stay," "wait" or "remain". What this verse is telling us is that God's Word should remain imbedded in our hearts, captured and readily available to be retrieved whenever we need it.

Earlier I suggested that you memorize scriptures that deal with overcoming. This is a practice that I did long ago. But it wasn't just verses on overcoming. I immersed myself in His Word and read and studied it so much that I began to remember all kinds of verses. Between your intent to remember His Word, and the Holy Spirit bringing them to your remembrance, you develop a treasure chest of necessary "life" to help you through any circumstances, but you have to make the effort.

Notice I said necessary "life". Those scriptures, that Word, are more than just ink on paper. Jesus said His Word is alive and life.

> *For the word of God is quick, and powerful, and sharper than any twoedged sword, piercing even to the dividing asunder of soul and spirit, and of the joints and marrow, and is a discerner of the thoughts and intents of the heart.* **Heb 4:12**

That word "quick" is the word *zaó* in Greek and literally means to be alive. God's Word is alive and He wants that living Word to be held at all times "within our hearts".

> *It is the spirit that quickeneth; the flesh profiteth nothing. The words that I speak unto you, they are spirit, and they are life.* **John 6:63**

If you want H.O.P.E. in your life, your life has to be filled with His life, with His Word, and His Spirit. If we really believed what the Lord tells us about abiding in Him and having His Word and Spirit abide in us, we would act like thirsty men and women in the desert searching for water.

In this regard, our H.O.P.E. is based upon our intent to get close to Him.

He is Whatever You Need

Through our walk, our understanding of Who God is grows. As our relationship with Him grows, our perception of the power and person of Jesus grows and that perception leads to our revering Him.

> *For whatsoever is born of God overcometh the world: and this is the victory that overcometh the world, even our faith. Who is he that overcometh the world, but he that believeth that Jesus is the Son of God?* **1 John 5:4-5**

The word "believeth" from the above verse is another word that we looked at earlier in the book, but the concept is so important it bears repeating. This is the Greek word *pisteuó* from the root word *pístis*, which means "faith," but the verse is saying much more than we should simply have faith in Jesus. To "believe" in this context is to "entrust in," or to "trust in". As I said earlier, biblically believing is not just "believing". It's giving yourself over to something or someone fully. It means to entrust someone with your life, not for a moment, not for a season, but for the rest of your life and beyond. What John is telling us is that our entrusting of Jesus WILL give us the overcoming victory in the world.

"Entrusting" your life to Him leads to a transformational encounter with the Living God. When I think about H.O.P.E. in Jesus, I think about the abundant life that He gives us.

> *...I am come that they might have life, and that they might have it more abundantly.* **John 10:10b**

As an example, I don't gamble, but let's say I played the lottery and won $100 million after taxes.

With that money, I could do whatever I wanted. I could buy whatever I wanted and I could live however I wanted.

Yet, with all that money and even more, I would still be empty without Jesus.

I'm not advocating this, but let's say that we lived in a country where you could have as many wives as you wanted. And assume that I had a bunch, all with different personalities and talents, like King Solomon. Some of them would be great cooks, others would be great bakers, still others would be really good at cleaning and taking care of other domestic issues. And let's say that they waited on me hand and foot. (For the record my wife Loretta is all I need! I'm trying to make a point.)

Anyway, let's say that I also had tons of friends. Some of these friends would be very influential in government and business: bankers, lawyers, politicians, etc. Because they thought so much of me, let's say that my friends would do anything for me.

So let's say that between my money, wives and friends, I could have anything that I wanted and as much company from the people around me that I needed.

However, without Jesus, I would still be absolutely alone and destitute.

Lastly, for the sake of the discussion, what if I were smarter than Einstein and Hawking put together? What if I were the smartest man to have ever lived? What if I could solve any problem and knew more than even Google?

Nonetheless, without Jesus, I would still be totally and utterly lost.

It doesn't matter how good you have it, or how much goods you have, Jesus is still your H.O.P.E. He is "all in all". He is the only thing that really matters in life and He waits for us to abide in Him.

If you want God's Overcoming Power Everyday, H.O.P.E., you have to understand that everything you and I ever need is contained within Him . In fact, there are so many facets to Who God is, we only can scratch the surface of them in the Word. But as much as the human language can communicate Who God is, the Bible gives us some of His attributes and titles. Here are a few of them:

He is our Abba Father - *Rom 8:15,*

He is our Advocate - *I John 2:1,*

He is the Almighty - *Gen 17:1,*

He is our All in All - *Col 3:11,*

He is the Alpha & Omega - *Rev 22:13,*

He is the Ancient of Days - *Daniel 7:9,*

He is the Anointed One - *Psalm 2:2,*

He is the Author & Finisher of Our Faith - *Heb 12:2,*

He is the Beginning & the End - *Rev 21:6,*

He is the Bread of Life - *John 6:33,*

He is our Bridegroom - *Isa 62:5,*

He is the Bright Morning Star - *Rev 22:16,*

He is the Captain of the Lord's Host - *Jer 5:15,*

He is the Chosen One - Isa 42:1,

He is the Christ - Matt 22:42,

He is the Son of the Living God - Matt 16:16,

He is our Comforter - John 14:26,

He is an All Consuming Fire - Heb 12:29,

He is our Counselor - Isa 9:6,

He is our Creator - 1 Peter 4:19,

He is our Deliverer - Rom 11:26,

He is our Dwelling Place - Psalm 90:1,

He is Emmanuel - Matt 1:23,

He is the Eternal God - Deut 33:27,

He is the Everlasting God - Gen 21:33,

His Name is Faithful & True - Rev 19:11,

He is our Foundation - 1 Cor 3:11,

He is a Fountain of Living Water - Jer 2:13,

He is our Friend - Matt 11:19,

He is a Gift of God - John 4:10,

He is God Over All - Rom 9:5,

He is the Head of the Body - Col 1:18,

He is the Head of the Church - Eph 5:23,

He is the Holy One - Acts 2:27,

He is our Blessed Hope - Titus 2:13,

He is the Great I AM - Exodus 3:14,

He is Jehovah - Psalm 83:18,

He is Jesus - Matt 1:21,

He is the King of Kings & Lord of Lords - 1 Tim 6:15,

He is the Lamb of God - John 1:29,

He is Life - John 14:16,

He is the Light of the World - John 8:12,

He is the Lion of the Tribe of Judah - Rev 5:5,

He is the Living God - Daniel 6:20,

He is Living Water - John 4:10,

He is the Lord of All - Acts 10:36,

He is the Lord of Glory - 1 Cor 2:8,

He is Love - 1 John 4:8,

He is your Maker - Job 35:10 & Psalm 95:6,

He is our Merciful God - Jer 3:12,

He is Messiah - John 4:25,

He is the Mighty God - Isa 9:6,

He is the Only Begotten Son - John 1:18,

He is our Passover Lamb - 1 Cor 5:7,

He is our Peace - Eph 2:14,

He is the Great Physician - Luke 4:23,

He is the Prince of Peace - Isa 9:6,

He is our Redeemer - Job 19:25,

He is our Refuge & our Strength - Jer 16:19,

He is the Righteous One - 1 John 2:1,

He is the Rock of our Salvation - 1 Cor 10:4,

He is our Savior - Luke 2:11,

He is the Son of God - Matt 27:54,

He is the Son of Man - Matt 8:20,

He is the Son of the Most High - Luke 1:32,

He is our Source - Heb 5:9,

He is our Strength - Jer 16:19,

He is our Stronghold - Nahum 1:7,

He is our Strong Tower - Prov 18:10,

He is our Teacher - John 13:13,

He is True Light - John 1:9,

He is the Vine - John 15:15,

He is the Way, the Truth & the Life - John 14:16,

His name is Wonderful - Isaiah 9:6,

He is the Word of God - John 1:1.

He is all these things and more and He longs and waits for you to live for Him and only Him. This is Someone to Whom you can entrust your life and not be disappointed. This God will always love you and seek the best for your life.

He is truly, all in all.

Run the Race

When you strip away everything that we have, H.O.P.E. stands as a Person and His name is Jesus.

Our H.O.P.E. is fulfilled by wrapping our arms around the promises of God and believing that He is Who He says He is, that He loves us and that nothing can pluck us out of His hand. It's in that embrace that we fall more deeply in love with Jesus as our faith strengthens and our hope in Him is justified.

> *Thou wilt shew me the path of life: in thy presence is fullness of joy; at thy right hand there are pleasures for evermore.* **Psalm 16:11**

So, run the race. Do whatever it takes to develop your real, thriving, lasting relationship with Jesus Christ. I promise you - It's worth it. He is our H.O.P.E.

> *And, behold, I come quickly; and my reward is with me, to give every man according as his work shall be. I am Alpha and Omega, the beginning and the end, the first and the last.*
>
> **Revelation 22:12-13**

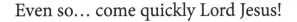

Even so… come quickly Lord Jesus!